Modernity and Ambivalence

Modernity and Ambivalence

ZYGMUNT BAUMAN

Polity Press

First published 1991 by Polity Press
in association with Blackwell Publishers Ltd.

First published in paperback 1993
Reprinted 1995

Editorial office:
Polity Press, 65 Bridge Street,
Cambridge CB2 1UR, UK

Marketing and production:
Blackwell Publishers Ltd,
108 Cowley Road, Oxford OX4 1JF, UK

ISBN 0 7456 0573 7
ISBN 0 7456 1242 3

A CIP catalogue record for this book is available from the British Library.

Typeset in 10 on 12 pt Garamond
by Acorn Bookwork
Printed in Great Britain by T.J. Press Ltd, Padstow

Contents

Acknowledgements

At various stages of my work I benefited from insightful critical comments on various chapters or fragments of chapters of this book, offered by David Beetham, Bryan Cheyette, Agnes Heller, Irving Horowitz, Richard Kilminster, Ralph Miliband, Stefan Morawski, Paul Piccone, Ritchie Robertson, Gillian Rose, Nico Stehr, Dennis Warwick, Włodzimierz Wesolowski, Jerzy J. Wiatr and many other colleagues and friends. I am deeply grateful for their help. Anthony Giddens's thorough and perceptive criticism had a decisive role in the final shaping of the project. Once again I am pleased to be able to thank David Roberts for his splendid editorial job.

In writing this book, I used some material contained in my various articles and reviews published in *Jewish Quarterly*, *Marxism Today*, *Sociological Review*, *Sociology*, *Telos* and *Theory, Culture and Society*.

One has to wait till the end of history
to grasp the material in its determined totality

Wilhelm Dilthey

The day that there will be a reading of the Oxford card,
the one and true reading,
will be the end of history

Jacques Derrida

Someone who writes nothing but postcards
will not have Hegel's problem
of how to end his book

Richard Rorty

Introduction: The Quest for Order

Ambivalence, the possibility of assigning an object or an event to more than one category, is a language-specific disorder: a failure of the naming (segregating) function that language is meant to perform. The main symptom of disorder is the acute discomfort we feel when we are unable to read the situation properly and to choose between alternative actions.

It is because of the anxiety that accompanies it and the indecision which follows that we experience ambivalence as a disorder – and either blame language for lack of precision or ourselves for linguistic misuse. And yet ambivalence is not the product of the pathology of language or speech. It is, rather, a normal aspect of linguistic practice. It arises from one of the main functions of language: that of naming and classifying. Its volume grows depending on the effectivity with which that function is performed. Ambivalence is therefore the *alter ego* of language, and its permanent companion – indeed, its normal condition.

To classify means to set apart, to segregate. It means first to postulate that the world consists of discrete and distinctive entities; then to postulate that each entity has a group of similar or adjacent entities with which it belongs, and with which – together – it is opposed to some other entities; and then to make the postulated real by linking differential patterns of action to different classes of entities (the evocation of a specific behavioural pattern becoming the operative definition of the class). To classify, in other words, is to give the world a *structure*: to manipulate its probabilities; to make some events more likely than some others; to behave as if events were not random, or to limit or eliminate randomness of events.

Through its naming/classifying function, language posits itself between a solidly founded, orderly world fit for human habitation, and a contingent world of randomness, in which human survival weapons – memory, the capacity for learning – would be useless, if not downright suicidal. Language strives to sustain the order and to deny or suppress randomness and contingency. An orderly world is a world in which 'one knows how to go on' (or, what amounts to the same, one knows how to find out – and find out *for sure* – how to go on), in which one knows how to calculate the probability of an event and how to increase or decrease that probability; a world in which links between certain situations and the effectivity of certain actions remain by and large constant, so that one can rely on past successes as guides for future ones. Because of our learning/memorizing ability we have vested interests in maintaining the orderliness of the world. For the same reason, we experience ambivalence as discomfort and a threat. Ambivalence confounds calculation of events and confuses the relevance of memorized action patterns.

The situation turns ambivalent if the linguistic tools of structuration prove inadequate; either the situation belongs to none of the linguistically distinguished classes, or it falls into several classes at the same time. None of the learned patterns could be proper in an ambivalent situation – or more than one of the learned patterns could be applied; whatever is the case, the outcome is the feeling of indecision, undecidability, and hence loss of control. The consequences of action become unpredictable, while randomness, allegedly done away with by the structuring effort, seems to make an unsolicited come-back.

Ostensibly, the naming/classifying function of language has the prevention of ambivalence as its purpose. Performance is measured by the neatness of the divisions between classes, the precision of their definitional boundaries, and the unambiguity with which objects may be allocated to classes. And yet the application of such criteria, and the very activity whose progress they are to monitor, are the ultimate sources of ambivalence and the reasons why ambivalence is unlikely ever to become truly extinct, whatever the amount and the ardour of the structuring/ordering effort.

The ideal that the naming/classifying function strives to achieve is a sort of commodious filing cabinet that contains all the files that contain all the items that the world contains – but confines each file and each item within a separate place of its own (with remaining doubts solved by a cross-reference index). It is the non-viability of such a filing cabinet that makes ambivalence unavoidable. And it is the perseverance with which construction of such a cabinet is pursued that brings forth ever new supplies of ambivalence.

Classifying consists in the acts of inclusion and exclusion. Each act of naming splits the world into two: entities that answer to the name; all the rest that do not. Certain entities may be included into a class – *made a class* – only in as far as other entities are *excluded*, left outside. Invariably, such operation of inclusion/exclusion is an act of violence perpetrated upon the world, and requires the support of a certain amount of coercion. It can hold as long as the volume of applied coercion remains adequate to the task of outbalancing the extent of created discrepancy. Insufficiency of coercion shows itself in the manifest reluctance of entities postulated by the act of classification to fit into assigned classes, and in the appearance of entities under- or over-defined, with insufficient or excessive meaning – sending no readable signals for action, or sending signals that confuse the recipients for being mutually contradictory.

Ambivalence is a side-product of the labour of classification; and it calls for yet more classifying effort. Though born of the naming/classifying urge, ambivalence may be fought only with a naming that is yet more exact, and classes that are yet more precisely defined: that is, with such operations as will set still tougher (counter-factual) demands on the discreteness and transparency of the world and thus give yet more occasion for ambiguity. The struggle against ambivalence is, therefore, both self-destructive and self-propelling. It goes on with unabating strength because it creates its own problems in the course of resolving them. Its intensity, however, varies over time, depending on the availability of force adequate to the task of controlling the extant volume of ambivalence, and also on the presence or absence of awareness that the reduction of ambivalence is a problem of the discovery and application of proper *technology*: a *managerial* problem. Both factors combined to make modern times an era of particularly bitter and relentless war against ambivalence.

How old is modernity? is a contentious question. There is no agreement on dating. There is no consensus on what is to be dated.[1] And once the

[1] Making one's own dating choice seems to be unavoidable if only to ward off an intrinsically barren discussion, diverting us from the substantive propositions (the current datings range as wide as the assumptions of the French historians – contributors to the *Culture et idéologie de l'état moderne* volume published in 1985 by the École Française de Rome – that the modern state was born at the end of the thirteenth century and fizzled out toward the end of the seventeenth, to some literary critics confinement of the term 'modernity' to cultural trends that begin with the twentieth century and end at its middle).

The definitional discord is made particularly difficult to disentangle by the fact of historical coexistence of what Matei Calinescu called 'two distinct and bitterly conflicting modernities'. More sharply than most other authors, Calinescu portrays the 'irreversible' split between 'modernity as a stage in the history of Western Civilization – a product of scientific and technological progress, of the industrial revolution, of the sweeping economic and social changes brought about by capitalism – and modernity as an aesthetic concept'. The latter (better to be called *modernism* to avoid the all too frequent confusion) militated against everything the first stood for: 'what defines cultural modernity is its outright rejection of bourgeois modernity, its consuming negative passion' (*Faces of Modernity: Avant-Garde, Decadence, Kitsch* (Bloomington: Indiana University Press, 1977), pp. 4, 42); this is in blatant opposition to the previous, mostly laudatory and enthusiastic

effort of dating starts in earnest, the object itself begins to disappear. Modernity, like all other quasi-totalities we want to prise off from the continuous flow of being, become elusive: we discover that the concept is fraught with ambiguity, while its referent is opaque at the core and frayed at the edges. Hence the contention is unlikely to be resolved. The defining feature of modernity underlying these essays is part of the contention.

Among the multitude of impossible tasks that modernity set itself and that made modernity into what it is, the task of order (more precisely and most importantly, of *order as a task*) stands out – as the least possible among the impossible and the least disposable among the indispensable; indeed, as the archetype for all other tasks, one that renders all other tasks mere metaphors of itself.

Order is what is not chaos; chaos is what is not orderly. Order and chaos are *modern* twins. They had been conceived amidst the disruption and collapse of the divinely ordained world, which knew of neither necessity nor accident; one that just *was* – without ever thinking how to make itself to be. That unthinking and careless world which preceded the bifurcation into order and chaos we find difficult to decribe in its own terms. We try to grasp it mostly with the help of negations: we tell ourselves what that world was not, what it did not contain, what it did not know, what it was unaware of. That world would hardly have recognized itself in our descriptions. It would not understand what are we talking about. It would not have survived such understanding. The moment of understanding would have been the sign of its approaching death. And it was. Historically,

---

portrayal of the attitude and achievement of modernity, as for instance in Baudelaire: 'Everything that is beautiful and noble is the result of reason and thought. Crime, for which the human animal acquires a taste in his mother's womb, is of natural origin. Virtue, on the contrary, is artificial and supernatural.' (*Baudelaire as a Literary Critic: Selected Essays*, trans. Lois Boe Hylsop and Francis E. Hylsop (Pittsburgh: Pennsylvania State University Press, 1964), p. 298.)

I wish to make it clear from the start that I call 'modernity' a historical period that began in Western Europe with a series of profound social-structural and intellectual transformations of the seventeenth century and achieved its maturity: (1) as a cultural project – with the growth of Enlightenment; (2) as a socially accomplished form of life – with the growth of industrial (capitalist, and later also communist) society. Hence *modernity*, as I use the term, is in no way identical with *modernism*. The latter is an intellectual (philosophical, literary, artistic) trend that – though traceable back to many individual intellectual events of the previous era – reached its full swing by the beginning of the current century, and which in retrospect can be seen (by analogy with the Enlightenment) as a 'project' of *postmodernity* or a prodromal stage of the postmodern condition. In modernism, modernity turned its gaze upon itself and attempted to attain the clear-sightedness and self-awareness which would eventually disclose its impossibility, thus paving the way to the postmodern reassessment.

this understanding was the last sigh of the passing world; and the first sound of new-born modernity.

We can think of modernity as of a time when order – of the world, of the human habitat, of the human self, and of the connection between all three – is *reflected upon*; a matter of thought, of concern, of a practice that is aware of itself, conscious of being a conscious practice and wary of the void it would leave were it to halt or merely relent. For the sake of convenience (the exact dating of birth, let us repeat, is bound to remain contentious: the project of dating is but one of the many *foci imaginarii* that, like butterflies, do not survive the moment when a pin is pushed through their body fo fix them in place) we can agree with Stephen L. Collins, who in his recent study took Hobbes's vision for the birthmark of the consciousness of order, that is – in our rendition – of modern consciousness, that is of modernity. ('Consciousness', says Collins, 'appears as the quality of perceiving order in things.')

> Hobbes understood that a world in flux was natural and that order must be created to restrain what was natural . . . Society is no longer a transcendentally articulated reflection of something predefined, external, and beyond itself which orders existence hierarchically. It is now a nominal entity ordered by the sovereign state which is its own articulated representative . . . [Forty years after Elisabeth's death] order was coming to be understood not as natural, but as artificial, created by man, and manifestly political and social . . . Order must be designed to restrain what appeared ubiquitous [that is, flux] . . . Order became a matter of power, and power a matter of will, force and calculation . . . Fundamental to the entire reconceptualization of the idea of society was the belief that the commonwealth, as was order, was a human creation.[2]

Collins is a scrupulous historian, wary of the dangers of projectionism and presentism, but he can hardly avoid imputing to the pre-Hobbesian world many a feature akin to our post-Hobbesian world – if only through indicating their absence; indeed, without such a strategy of description the pre-Hobbesian world would stay numb and meaningless to us. To make that world speak to us, we must, as it were, make its silences audible: to spell out what that world was unaware of. We must commit an act of violence: force that world to take a stance on issues to which it remained oblivious, and thus dismiss or bypass that oblivion that made it that world, a world so different and so incommunicado with our own. The attempt to communicate will defy its purpose. In this process of forced conversion,

---

[2] Stephen L. Collins, *From Divine Cosmos to Soverign State: An Intellectual History of Consciousness and the Idea of Order in Renaissance England* (Oxford: Oxford University Press, 1989), pp. 4, 6, 7, 28, 29, 32.

we shall render the hope of communication more remote still. In the end, instead of *reconstructing* that 'other world', we shall no more than *construe* 'the other' of the world of our own.

If it is true that we know that the order of things is not natural, this does not mean that the other, pre-Hobbesian, world thought of order as the work of nature: it did not think of order at all, not in a form we would think of as 'thinking of', not in the sense we think of it now. The discovery that order was *not natural* was discovery of *order as such*. The *concept* of order appeared in consciousness only simultaneously with the *problem* of order, of order as a matter of *design* and *action*, order as an obsession. To put it yet more bluntly, order as a problem emerged in the wake of the ordering flurry, as a reflection on ordering practices. Declaration of the 'non-naturalness of order' stood for an order already coming out of hiding, out of non-existence, out of silence. 'Nature' means, after all, nothing but the silence of man.

If it is true that we, the moderns, think of order as a matter of design, this does not mean that before modernity the world was complacent about designing, and expected the order to come and stay on its own and unassisted. That world lived without such alternative; it would not be that world at all, were it giving its thought to it. If it is true that our world is shaped by the suspicion of the brittleness and fragility of the artificial man-designed and man-built islands of order among the sea of chaos, it does not follow that before modernity the world believed that the order stretched over the sea and the human archipelago alike; it was, rather, unaware of the distinction between land and water.[3]

We can say that the existence is modern in as far as it forks into order and chaos. The existence is modern in as far as it contains the *alternative* of order and chaos.

Indeed: order and *chaos*, full stop. If it is aimed at at all (that is, in as far as it is thought of), order is not aimed at as a substitute for an alternative order. The struggle for order is not a fight of one definition against another, of one way of articulating reality against a competitive proposal. It

[3] An example: 'The individual experienced neither isolation nor alienation' (Collins, *From Divine Cosmos*, p. 21). This is, as a matter of fact, our – modern – construction of the pre-modern individual. It would be perhaps more prudent to say that the individual of the pre-modern world did not experience *the absence of the experience* of isolation or alienation. He did not experience belonging, membership, being-at-home, togetherness. Belonging entails the awareness of being together or 'being a part of'; thus belonging, inevitably, contains the awareness of its own uncertainty, of the *possibility* of isolation, of the need to stave off or overcome alienation. Experiencing oneself as 'unisolated' or 'unalienated' is as much modern as the experience of isolation and alienation.

is a fight of determination against ambiguity, of semantic precision against ambivalence, of transparency against obscurity, clarity against fuzziness. Order as a concept, as a vision, as a purpose could not be conceived but for the insight into the total ambivalence, the randomness of chaos. Order is continuously engaged in the war of survival. The other of order is not another order: chaos is its only alternative. The other of order is the miasma of the indeterminate and unpredictable. The other is the uncertainty, that source and archetype of all fear. The tropes of 'the other of order' are: undefinability, incoherence, incongruity, incompatibility, illogicality, irrationality, ambiguity, confusion, undecidability, ambivalence.

Chaos, 'the other of order', is pure negativity. It is a denial of all that the order strives to be. It is against that negativity that the positivity of order constitutes itself. But the negativity of chaos is a product of order's self-constitution: its side-effect, its waste, and yet the condition *sine qua non* of its (reflective) possibility. Without the negativity of chaos, there is no positivity of order; without chaos, no order.

We can say that the existence is modern in as far as it is saturated by the 'without us, a deluge' feeling. The existence is modern in as far as it is guided by the urge of designing what otherwise would not be there: designing *of itself*.

The raw existence, the existence free of intervention, the *unordered* existence, or the fringe of ordered existence, become now *nature*: something singularly unfit for human habitat – something not to be trusted and not to be left to its own devices, something to be *mastered*, *subordinated*, *remade* so as to be readjusted to human needs. Something to be held in check, restrained and contained, lifted from the state of shapelessness and given form – by effort and by force. Even if the form has been pre-ordained by nature itself, it will not come about unassisted and will not survive undefended. Living according to nature needs a lot of designing, organized effort and vigilant monitoring. Nothing is more artificial than naturalness; nothing less natural than throwing oneself at the mercy of the laws of nature. Power, repression and purposeful action stand between nature and that socially effected order in which artificiality is natural.

We can say that existence is modern in as far as it is effected and sustained by *design*, *manipulation*, *management*, *engineering*. The existence is modern in as far as it is administered by resourceful (that is, possessing knowledge, skill and technology), sovereign agencies. Agencies are sovereign in as far as they claim and successfully defend the right to manage and administer existence: the right to define order and, by implication, lay aside chaos, as that left-over that escapes the definition.

The typically modern practice, the substance of modern politics, of modern intellect, of modern life, is the effort to exterminate ambivalence:

an effort to define precisely – and to suppress or eliminate everything that could not or would not be precisely defined. Modern practice is not aimed at the conquest of foreign lands, but at the filling of the blank spots in the *compleat mappa mundi*. It is the modern practice, not nature, that truly suffers no void.

Intolerance is, therefore, the natural inclination of modern practice. Construction of order sets the limits to incorporation and admission. It calls for the denial of rights, and of the grounds, of everything that cannot be assimilated – for de-legitimation of the other. As long as the urge to put paid to ambivalence guides collective and individual action, intolerance will follow – even if, ashamedly, it hides under the mask of toleration (which often means: you are abominable, but I, being generous, shall let you live).[4]

The other of the modern state is the no-man's or contested land: the under- or over-definition, the demon of ambiguity. Since the sovereignty of the modern state is the power to define and to make the definitions stick – everything that self-defines or eludes the power-assisted definition is subversive. The other of this sovereignty is no-go areas, unrest and disobedience, collapse of law and order.

---

[4] In her insightful account of the role played by the concept of toleration in liberal theory, Susan Mendus comments: 'toleration implies that the thing tolerated is morally reprehensible. Another is the implication that it is alterable. To speak of tolerating another implies that it is to his discredit that he does not change that feature of himself which is the object of toleration.' (*Toleration and the Limits of Liberalism* (London: Macmillan, 1989), pp. 149–50) Toleration does not include the acceptance of the other's worth; on the contrary, it is one more, perhaps somewhat subtler and cunning, way of reaffirming the other's inferiority and serving an advance warning of the intention to terminate the Other's otherness – together with an invitation to the Other to co-operate in bringing to pass the inevitable. The famed humanity of the toleration policy does not step beyond the consent to delay the final showdown – on condition, however, that the very act of consent would further strengthen the existing order of superiority.

Paul Ricoeur (*History and Truth*, trans. Charles A. Kelbley (Evanston: Northwestern University Press, 1979)) suggested that – historically – 'the temptation to unify the true by violence has come from two quarters, the clerical and the political spheres' (p. 165). Yet 'the clerical' was nothing else but the intellectual put at the service of the political, or the intellectual with political ambitions. This said, Ricoeur's suggestion turns tautological: the marriage of truth and violence is the meaning of the 'political sphere'. The practice of science is in its innermost structure no different from that of state politics; both aim at a monopoly over a dominated territory, and both reach their aims through the device of inclusion/exclusion (of science Ricouer writes that it is 'constituted by the decision to suspend all affective, utilitarian, political, aesthetic, and religious considerations and to hold as true only that which answers to the criteria of the scientific method' (p. 169).

The other of modern intellect is polysemy, cognitive dissonance, polyvalent definitions, contingency; the overlapping meanings in the world of tidy classifications and filing cabinets. Since the sovereignty of the modern intellect is the power to define and to make the definitions stick – everything that eludes unequivocal allocation is an anomaly and a challenge. The other of this sovereignty is the violation of the law of the excluded middle.

In both cases, resistance to definition sets the limit to sovereignty, to power, to the transparency of the world, to its control, to order. That resistance is the stubborn and grim reminder of the flux which order wished to contain but in vain; of the limits to order; and of the necessity of ordering. Modern state and modern intellect alike need chaos – if only to go on creating order. They both thrive on the vanity of their effort.

Modern existence is both haunted and stirred into restless action by modern consciousness; and modern consciousness is the suspicion or awareness of the inconclusiveness of extant order; a consciousness prompted and moved by the premonition of inadequacy, nay non-viability, of the order-designing, ambivalence-eliminating project; of the randomness of the world and contingency of identities that constitute it. Consciousness is modern in as far as it reveals ever new layers of chaos underneath the lid of power-assisted order. Modern consciousness criticizes, warns and alerts. It makes the action unstoppable by ever anew unmasking its ineffectiveness. It perpetuates the ordering practice by disqualifying its achievements and laying bare its defeats.

Thus there is a *hate–love* relation between modern existence and modern culture (in the most advanced form of self-awareness), a symbiosis fraught with civil wars. In the modern era, culture is that obstreperous and vigilant Her Majesty's Opposition which makes the government feasible. There is no love lost, harmony, nor mirror-like similarity between the two: there is only mutual need and dependence – that *complementarity* which comes out of the opposition, which *is* opposition. However modernity resents its critique – it would not survive the armistice.

It would be futile to decide whether modern culture undermines or serves modern existence. It does both things. It can do each one only together with the other. Compulsive negation is the positivity of modern culture. Dysfunctionality of modern culture is its functionality. The modern powers' struggle for artificial order needs culture that explores the limits and the limitations of the power of artifice. The struggle for order informs that exploration and is in turn informed by its findings. In the process, the struggle sheds its initial hubris: the pugnacity born of naivety and ignorance. It learns, instead, to live with its own permanence, inconclusiveness – and prospectlessness. Hopefully, it would learn in the end the difficult skills of modesty and tolerance.

History of modernity is a history of tension between social existence and its culture. Modern existence forces its culture into opposition to itself. This disharmony is precisely the harmony modernity needs. The history of modernity draws its uncanny and unprecedented dynamism from the speed with which it discards successive versions of harmony having first discredited them as but pale and flawed reflections of its *foci imaginarii*. For the same reason, it can be seen as a history of *progress*, as the *natural history* of humanity.

As a form of life, modernity makes itself possible through setting itself an impossible task. It is precisely the endemic inconclusivity of effort that makes the life of continuous restlessness both feasible and inescapable, and effectively precludes the possibility that the effort may ever come to rest.

The impossible task is set by the *foci imaginarii*[5] of absolute truth, pure art, humanity as such, order, certainty, harmony, the end of history. Like all horizons, they can never be reached. Like all horizons, they make possible walking with a purpose. Like all horizons, they recede in the course of, and because of, walking. Like all horizons, the quicker is the walking the faster they recede. Like all horizons, they never allow the purpose of walking to relent or be compromised. Like all horizons, they move continuously in time and thus lend the walking the supportive illusion of destination, pointer and purpose.

Foci imaginarii – the horizons that foreclose and open up, circumvent and distend the space of modernity – conjure up the phantom of itinerary in the space by itself devoid of direction. In that space, roads are made of walking and wash out again as the walkers pass by. In front of the walkers (and the front is where the walkers look) the road is marked out by the walkers' determination to go on; behind them, the roads can be imagined from thin lines of footprints, framed on both sides by thicker lines of waste and litter. 'In a desert – said Edmond Jabès – there are no avenues, no boulevards, no blind alleys and no streets. Only – here and there – fragmentary imprints of steps, quickly effaced and denied.'[6]

Modernity is what it is – an obsessive march forward – not because it always wants more, but because it never gets enough; not because it grows more ambitious and adventurous, but because its adventures are bitter and its ambitions frustrated. The march must go on because any place of arrival

---

5 Cf. Richard Rorty, *Contingency, Irony and Solidarity* (Cambridge: Cambridge University Press, 1989), p. 195.

6 Edmond Jabès, *Un Étranger avec, sous le bras, un livre de petit format* (Paris: Gallimard, 1989), p. 34.

is but a temporary station. No place is privileged, no place better than another, as from no place the horizon is nearer than from any other. This is why the agitation and flurry are lived out as a forward march; this is, indeed, why the Brownian movement seems to acquire a front and a rear, and restlessness a direction: it is the detritus of burnt-out fuels and the soot of extinct flames that mark the trajectories of progress.

As Walter Benjamin observed, the storm irresistibly propels the walkers into the future to which their backs are turned, while the pile of debris before them grows skyward. 'This storm we call progress.'[7] On a closer scrutiny, the hope of arrival turns out to be the urge to escape. In the linear time of modernity, only the point of departure is fixed: and it is the unstoppable movement of that point which straightens up disaffected existence into a line of historical time. What affixes a pointer to this line is not the anticipation of new bliss, but the certainty of past horrors; yesterday's suffering, not the happiness of tomorrow. As for today – it turns into the past before the sun is down. The linear time of modernity is stretched between the past that cannot last and the future that cannot be. There is no room for the middle. As it flows, time flattens into the sea of misery so that the pointer can stay afloat.

To set an impossible task means not to endear the future, but to devalue the present. Not being what it ought to be is the present's original and irredeemable sin. The present is always wanting, which makes it ugly, abhorrent and unendurable. The present is *obsolete*. It is obsolete before it comes to be. The moment it lands in the present, the coveted future is poisoned by the toxic effluvia of the wasted past. Its enjoyment can last but a *fleeting* moment: beyond that (and the beyond begins at the starting point) the joy acquires a necrophilic tinge, achievement turns into sin and immobility into death.

In the first two quotations with which these essays begin, Dilthey and Derrida speak of the same: full clarity means the end of history. The first speaks from the inside of modernity still young and daring: history will come to an end, and we shall foreclose it by making it universal. Derrida looks back to the dashed hopes. He knows that history will not end and that therefore the state of ambivalence will not end either.

There is another reason for which modernity equals restlessness; the restlessness is Sisyphean, and the fight with the uneasiness of the present takes on the appearance of historical progress.

The war against chaos splits into a multitude of local battles for order.

---

[7] Walter Benjamin, *Illuminations*, trans. Harry Zahn (New York: Fontana, 1979), p. 260.

Such battles are fought by guerilla units. For most of modern history there were no headquarters to co-ordinate the battles – certainly not commanders-in-chief able to chart the whole vastness of the universe to be conquered and to mould local bloodshed into a territorial conquest. There were only the mobile propaganda squads, with their pep talk aimed at keeping up the fighting spirit. 'The governors and the scientists alike (not to mention the commercial world) see human affairs as patterned upon purpose . . .'[8] But the governors and the scientists are aplenty, and so are their purposes. All governors and scientists guard jealously their hunting grounds, and so their right to set purposes. Because the hunting grounds are cut down to the size of their coercive and/or intellectual powers, and the purposes are cut to the measure of their grounds, their battles are victorious. Purposes are reached, chaos is chased out of gates, orders are established within.

Modernity prides itself on the *fragmentation* of the world as its foremost achievement. Fragmentation is the prime source of its strength. The world that falls apart into plethora of problems is a manageable world. Or, rather, since the problems are manageable – the question of the manageability of the world may never appear on the agenda, or at least be indefinitely postponed. The territorial and functional autonomy which the fragmentation of powers brings in its wake consists first and foremost in the right not to look beyond the fence and not to be looked at from outside of the fence. Autonomy is the right to decide when to keep the eyes open and when close them down; the right to separate, to discriminate, to peel off and to trim.

> The entire thrust of science has been . . . to explain the whole as the *sum* of its parts and nothing more. In the past, it was assumed that if some holistic principle were found, it could merely be added to the parts already known, as an organizer. In other words, the holistic principle would be something like an administrator who runs a bureaucracy.[9]

The resemblance, let us add, is in no way accidental. Scientists and administrators share concerns with sovereignty and borderlines, and cannot conceive of the whole as anything but more administrators and more scientists with their sovereign and neatly fenced functions and fields of expertise (much as the way in which Mrs Thatcher visualized Europe). Urologists and laryngologists guard the autonomy of their clinical departments (and thus, by proxy, of kidneys and ears) as jealously as the

---

[8] Gregory Bateson, *Steps to an Ecology of Mind* (St Albans: Paladin, 1973), p. 134.

[9] John P. Briggs and F. David Peat, *Looking Glass Universe: The Emerging Science of Wholeness* (New York: Simon & Schuster, 1984), p. 147.

Whitehall bureaucrats who manage, respectively, industry and employment guard the independence of their departments and areas of human existence subject to their jurisdiction.

One way of putting it is that the grand vision of order has been small-changed into solvable little problems. More to the point, the grand vision of order arises (if at all) out of the problem-solving flurry – as the 'invisible hand' or similar 'metaphysical prop'. If it is given a thought, the harmonious totality is expected to arise, like Phoenix from the ashes, out of the zealous and astonishingly successful efforts to split it apart.

But the fragmentation turns the problem-solving into Sisyphean labour and incapacitates it as a tool of order-making. The autonomy of localities and functions is but a fiction made plausible by decrees and statute books. This is an autonomy of a river or an eddy or a hurricane (cut off the inflow and outflow of water, and there is no river left; cut off the inflow and outflow of air, and there is no tornado). Autarchy is the dream of all power. It flounders on the absence of autarky no autarchy can live without not secure. It is the powers that are fragmented; the world, stubbornly, is not. People stay multifunctional, words polysemic. Or, rather, people turn multifunctional because of the fragmentation of functions; words turn polysemic because of the fragmentation of meanings. Opacity emerges at the other end of the struggle for transparency. Confusion is born out of the fight for clarity. Contingency is discovered at the place where many fragmentary works of determination meet, clash and intertangle.

The more secure the fragmentation, the more desultory and less controllable the resulting chaos. Autarchy allows resources to be focused on the task in hand (there is a strong hand to hold the task firmly) and thus makes the task feasible and the problem resolvable. As problem-resolution is a function of the resourcefulness of power, the scale of problems resolvable and resolved rises with the scope of autarchy (with the degree to which practices of power that hold together the relatively autonomous enclave shift from the 'relative' to the 'autonomous'). Problems get bigger. So do their consequences. The less relative one autonomy, the more relative the other. The more thoroughly the initial problems have been solved, the less manageable are the problems that result. There was a task to increase agricultural crops – resolved thanks to the nitrates. And there was a task of steadying water supplies – resolved thanks to stemming the flow of water with dams. Then there was a task to purify water supplies poisoned by the seepage of unabsorbed nitrates – resolved thanks to the application of phosphates in specially built sewage-processing plants. Then there was a task to destroy toxic algae that thrive in reservoirs rich in phosphate compounds...

The drive to purpose-geared order drew its energy, as all drives to order do, from the abhorrence of ambivalence. But more ambivalence was the ultimate product of modern, fragmented, drives to order. Most problems today confronting the managers of local orders are outcomes of the problem-solving activity. Most of the ambivalence the practitioners and the theorists of social and intellectual orders face results from the efforts to suppress or declare non-existent the endemic relativity of autonomy. Problems are created by problem-solving, new areas of chaos are generated by ordering activity. Progress consists first and foremost in the obsolescence of yesterday's solutions.

The horror of mixing reflects the obsession with separating. Local, specialist excellence that modern ways of doing things made possible has the separating practices as its only – though commendably solid – foundation. The central frame of both modern intellect and modern practice is opposition – more precisely, dichotomy. Intellectual visions that turn out tree-like images of progressive bifurcation reflect and inform the administrative practice of splitting and separation: with each successive bifurcation, the distance between offshoots of the original stem grows, with no horizontal links to make up for the isolation.

Dichotomy is an exercise in power and at the same time its disguise. Though no dichotomy would hold without the power to set apart and cast aside, it creates an illusion of symmetry. The sham symmetry of results conceals the asymmetry of power that is its cause. Dichotomy represents its members as equal and interchangeable. Yet its very existence testifies to the presence of a differentiating power. It is the power-assisted differentiation that makes the difference. It is said that only the difference between units of the opposition, not the units themselves, is meaningful. Thus meaningfulness, it seems, is gestated in the practices of power capable of making difference – of separating and keeping apart.

In dichotomies crucial for the practice and the vision of social order the differentiating power hides as a rule behind one of the members of the opposition. The second member is but *the other* of the first, the opposite (degraded, suppressed, exiled) side of the first and its creation. Thus abnormality is the other of the norm, deviation the other of law-abiding, illness the other of health, barbarity the other of civilization, animal the other of the human, woman the other of man, stranger the other of the native, enemy the other of friend, 'them' the other of 'us', insanity the other of reason, foreigner the other of the state subject, lay public the other of the expert. Both sides depend on each other, but the dependence is not symmetrical. The second side depends on the first for its contrived and enforced isolation. The first depends on the second for its self-assertion.

Geometry is the archetype of modern mind. The grid is its ruling trope (and thus, so be it, Mondrian is the most *representative* among its visual artists). Taxonomy, classification, inventory, catalogue and statistics are paramount strategies of modern practice. Modern mastery is the power to divide, classify and allocate – in thought, in practice, in the practice of thought and in the thought of practice. Paradoxically, it is for this reason that ambivalence is the main affliction of modernity and the most worrying of its concerns. Geometry shows what the world would be like were it geometrical. But the world is not geometrical. It cannot be squeezed into geometrically inspired grids.

Thus the production of waste (and, consequently, concern with waste disposal) is as modern as classification and order-designing. Weeds are the waste of gardening, mean streets the waste of town-planning, dissidence the waste of ideological unity, heresy the waste of orthodoxy, strangerhood the waste of nation-state building. They are waste, as they defy classification and explode the tidiness of the grid. They are the disallowed mixture of categories that must not mix. They earned their death-sentence by resisting separation. The fact that they would not sit across the barricade had not the barricade been built in the first place would not be considered by the modern court as a valid defence. The court is there to preserve the neatness of the barricades that have been built.

If modernity is about the production of order then ambivalence is *the waste of modernity*. Both order and ambivalence are alike products of modern practice; and neither has anything except modern practice – continuous, vigilant practice – to sustain it. Both share in typically modern contingency, foundationlessness of being. Ambivalence is arguably the modern era's most genuine worry and concern, since unlike other enemies, defeated and enslaved, it grows in strength with every success of modern powers. It is its own failure that the tidying-up activity construes as ambivalence.

The following essays will focus first on various aspects of the modern struggle against ambivalence that in its course, and by force of its inner logic, turns into the main source of the phenomenon it meant to extinguish. Further essays will trace modernity's gradual coming to terms with difference and will consider what living at peace with ambivalence may look like.

The book starts with sketching the stage for the modern war against ambivalence, identified with chaos and lack of control, and hereby frightening and marked for extinction. Chapter 1 surveys the elements of the *modern project* – legislative ambitions of philosophical reason, gardening ambitions of the state, ordering ambitions of applied sciences – which construed under-determination/ambivalence/contingency as a threat and made its elimination into one of the main *foci imaginarii* of social order.

Chapters 2 and 3 consider the logical and practical aspects of the 'order-building' (classification and segregation) as productive of the notoriously ambivalent category of *strangers*. The question is asked – and answered – why the efforts to dissolve the ambivalent category result in yet more ambivalence and prove in the end to be counterproductive. Also, responses of those cast in the position of ambivalence are surveyed and evaluated. The question is asked – and answered – why none of the conceivable strategies stands a chance of success, and why the strangers' only realistic project is that of embracing their ambivalent standing, with all its pragmatic and philosophical consequences.

Chapters 4 and 5 present a case study of the modern fight against ambivalence and this fight's unanticipated, yet unavoidable cultural repercussions. Chapter 4 focuses on the assimilatory pressures exerted upon European, and particularly German, Jews, on the inner traps of the assimilatory offer, and the rational, yet doomed responses of its addressees. Chapter 5 follows some (and, as it transpired later, the most seminal) cultural consequences of the assimilation project – bent on exterminating ambivalence yet spawning ever more of it: particularly the discovery of under-determination/ambivalence/contingency as a *lasting human condition*; indeed, as this condition's most important feature. Propositions of Kafka, Simmel, Freud, Derrida (and some less known, yet crucial thinkers like Shestov or Jabès) are re-analysed in this context. And the road is traced leading from irreparably ambivalent social setting to the self-constitution of critical modern consciousness and, ultimately, the phenomenon called the 'postmodern culture'.

Chapter 6 explores the contemporary plight of ambivalence: its *privatization*. With the modern state retreating from its gardening ambitions, and philosophical reason opting for the interpretative rather than legislating mode – the network of expertise, aided and mediated by the consumer market, takes over as the setting in which individuals must face the problem of ambivalence alone, in the course of their private self-constructive efforts, search for certainty documented in social approval. The cultural and ethical consequences of the present setting are followed through – which leads into chapter 7, which attempts to draw conclusions from the historical defeat of the great modern campaign against ambivalence; in particular, this chapter considers the practical consequences of living 'without foundations', under conditions of *admitted* contingency; following the lead given by Agnes Heller, it ponders the chance of transforming contingency as the fate into a consciously embraced destiny;

and the related prospects of the postmodern condition generating tribal strife or human solidarity. The intention of the chapter is not to engage in the enterprise of social prognosis, doubtful as it must be inside a notoriously contingent habitat – but to set an agenda for the discussion of political and moral problematics of the postmodern age.

Any reader of the book will certainly note that its central problem is firmly rooted in the propositions first articulated by Adorno and Horkheimer in their critique of Enlightenment (and, through it, of modern civilization). They were first to spell out loudly and clearly that 'Enlightenment is mythic fear turned radical . . . Nothing at all may remain outside because the mere idea of outsidedness is the very source of fear'; that what modern men 'want to learn from nature is how to use it in order wholly to dominate it and other men. That is the only aim. Ruthlessly, in despite of itself, the Enlightenment has extinguished any trace of its own self-consciousness. The only kind of thinking that is sufficiently heard to shatter myths is ultimately self-destructive'.[10] This book attempts to wrap historical and sociological flesh around the 'dialectics of Enlightenment' skeleton. But it also goes beyond Adorno's and Horkheimer's propositions. It suggests that the Enlightenment, after all, has spectacularly failed in its drive to 'extinguish any trace of its own self-consciousness' (Adorno's and Horkheimer's own work is, to be sure, one of the many vivid proofs of that failure), and that myth-shattering thinking (which the Enlightenment could not but reinforce instead of marginalizing) proved to be not so much *self*-destructive, as destructive of the modern project's blind arrogance, high-handedness and legislative dreams.

[10] Max Horkheimer and Theodor Adorno, *Dialectics of Enlightenment*, New York: Herder & Herder 1972, pp. 16, 4.

1
The Scandal of Ambivalence

> The danger of disaster attending the Baconian ideal of power over nature through scientific technology arises not so much from the shortcomings of its performance as from the magnitude of its success.
>
> Hans Jonas

In the course of my study of the available interpretations of the Holocaust (much as other cases of modern genocide),[1] I was struck by the evidence that the theoretical consequences which would follow from the scrupulous investigation of the case are seldom followed to the end and hardly ever accepted without resistance: too drastic and far-reaching seems the revision which they force upon the self-consciousness of our civilization.

Resistance to accept the lesson the episode of the Holocaust contains manifests itself primarily in the manifold attempts to *exoticize* or *margi-*

---

[1] Zygmunt Bauman, *Modernity and the Holocaust* (Cambridge: Polity Press, 1989). Inability to come to terms with the evidence of modern genocidal tendencies is yet more striking in the case of genocidal acts committed by states that, unlike Nazi Germany, were not defeated in a war and hence never subjected to the victor's determination to prove the criminal nature of the enemy. Almost three years after the discovery of mass graves near the Belorussian township of Kuropaty, and the bringing to public awareness of the traces of summary executions of entire categories of the population marked for extinction, Vasil Bykov, a prominent Belorussian novelist, felt obliged to raise again questions which should have been answered long ago: 'After making public the gruesome discoveries made at the wasteland near Minsk, dozens of reports appeared in the press about similar mass graves uncovered in all regional centres of the Republic and many lesser towns. Who lies in these graves, who were the people shot in all those years, and – most importantly – who were the murderers? We have no answer yet to these questions, and one gets an impression that there are powerful forces not interested at all in such answers ever being given.' Quite recently, the Presidium of the Belorussian Supreme Soviet refused the accreditation to a correspondent of *Litaratura i Mastactva* – a journal that first published the Kuropaty story. (Cf. Vasil Bykov, 'Zhazhda peremen' ['Thirst for Change'], *Pravda*, 24 November 1989, p. 4.)

nalize the Holocaust as a *one-off historical episode*. The most common among such attempts is the interpretation of the Holocaust as a specifically *Jewish* affair: as the culmination of the long history of Judaeophobia reaching far into antiquity, and at best as the outcome of its modern form, antisemitism in its racist variety. This interpretation overlooks an essential disconuity between even the most violent outbursts of pre-modern Judaeophobia and the meticulously planned and executed operation called the Holocaust; it also glosses over the fact that – as Hannah Arendt pointed out long ago – only the choice of the victims, not the nature of the crime, can be derived (if at all) from the history of antisemitism; indeed, it collapses the crucial issues of the nature of crime into the question of unique features of Jews or Jewish–Gentile relations.

'Exoticization' is also achieved through deployment of another strategy: an attempt to interpret the Holocaust as a specifically *German* affair (at best, also an affair of some other nations, still more distant and bizarre, whose concealed yet innate murderous tendencies had been released and set loose by the German overlords). One hears of the unfinished business of civilization, of the liberalizing process that went awry, of a particularly morbid brand of national philosophy that poisoned the minds of citizens, of the frustrating vicissitudes of recent history, even of the peculiar perfidy and shrewdness of a bunch of conspirators; hardly ever, though, of what made the editors of *The Times*, *Le Figaro* and other most respected organs of enlightened opinion wax lyrical when they wistfully described the Germany of the 1930s as the paragon of the civilized state, of prosperity, of social peace, of obedient and co-operative workers' unions, of law and order. Indeed, as an example for the wan European democracies to follow for its rapidly falling rate of crime, almost total removal of violence from the street (barring the brief excesses of the Nazi honeymoon period and, of course, the *Kristallnacht* episode), industrial peace, safety and security of daily life.

The paramount strategy aimed at, simultaneously marginalizing the crime and exonerating modernity, is the interpretation of the Holocaust as a singular eruption of pre-modern (barbaric, irrational) forces, as yet insufficiently tamed or ineffectively supressed by (presumably weak or faulty) German modernization. One would expect this strategy to be modernity's favourite form of self-defence: after all, it obliquely reaffirms and reinforces the etiological myth of modern civilization as a triumph of reason over passions, as well as its corollary: the belief that this triumph has marked an unambiguously progressive step in the historical development of public morality. This strategy is also easy to pursue. It falls in with the well-established habit (forcefully supported by modern scientific culture, but rooted primarily in the protracted military, economic and political domination of the modern part of the globe over the rest) to define automatically all alternative modes of life, and particularly all critique of the modern virtues, as stemming from pre-modern, irrational, barbaric positions and hence unworthy of serious consideration: as a specimen of the selfsame class of phenomena which modern civilization swore to confine and exterminate. As Ernst Gellner put it twenty years ago with his usual brevity and straightforwardness, 'if a doctrine conflicts with the acceptance of the superiority of scientific-industrial societies over others, then it really is out'.[2]

The dream of legislative reason

Throughout the modern era, the legislative reason of philosophers chimed in well with the all-too-material practices of the states. The modern state has been born as a crusading, missionary, proselytizing force, bent on subjecting the dominated populations to a thorough once-over in order to transform them into an orderly society, akin to the precepts of reason. Rationally designed society was the declared *causa finalis* of the modern state. The modern state was a gardening state. Its stance was a gardening stance. It delegitimized the present (wild, uncultivated) condition of the population and dismantled the extant mechanisms of reproduction and self-balancing. It put in their place purposefully built mechanisms meant to point the change in the direction of the rational design. The design, presumed to be dictated by the supreme and unquestionable authority of Reason, supplied the criteria to evaluate present-day reality. These criteria split the population into useful plants to be encouraged and tenderly propagated, and weeds – to be removed or rooted out. They put a premium on the needs of the useful plants (as determined by the gardener's design) and disendowed the needs of those declared to be weeds. They cast both categories as *objects* of action and denied to both the rights of self-determining agents.

The philosopher, Kant[3] insisted in the *Critique of Pure Reason*, 'is not merely an artist – who occupies himself with conceptions, but a law-giver – legislating for human reason'. The task of reason for which the philosopher acts as the supreme spokesman is 'to establish a tribunal, which may secure it in its well-grounded claims, while it pronounces against all

---

[2] Ernest Gellner, 'The New Idealism', in *Problems in the Philosophy of Science*, ed. I. Lakatos and A. Musgrave (Amsterdam: Van Nostrand, 1968), p. 405.

[3] Quotations from Kant are taken from J.M.D. Meiklejohn's translation, *Critique of Pure Reason* (London: Dent, 1969).

baseless assumptions and pretensions, not in an arbitrary manner, but according to its own eternal and unchangeable laws'. The idea of philosopher's 'legislative power resides in the mind of every man, and it alone teaches us what kind of systematic unity philosophy demands in view of the ultimate aims of reason' (*teleologia rationis humanae*).

Philosophy cannot but be a legislative power; it is the task of good philosophy, of the right type of metaphysic to serve the men who require 'that knowledge which concerns all men should transcend the common understanding'. 'Reason cannot permit our knowledge to remain in an unconnected and rhapsodistic state, but requires that the sum of our cognitions should constitute a system.' The kind of knowledge that may indeed transcend the common understanding, composed of mere opinions and beliefs (*opinion*: judgement insufficient both subjectively and objectively; *belief*: the most perfidious sort of judgement, one 'recognized as being objectively insufficient', yet subjectively accepted as convincing), could and should only 'be revealed to you by philosophers'. In performing this task, metaphysics would be 'the completion of the *culture* of human reason'; it will raise that reason from the raw and disorderly state in which it is naturally given, to the level of orderly system. Metaphysics is called upon to *cultivate* harmonious perfection of thought.

> The supreme office of censor which it occupies, assures to it the highest authority and importance. This office it administers for the purpose of securing order, harmony, and well-being to science, and of directing its noble and fruitful labours to the highest possible aim – the happiness of all mankind.

Adjudicating on the matters of human happiness is the philosopher's prerogative, and his duty. Here Kant merely restates the centuries-long tradition of the sages, originating at least with Plato. In the seventh book of Plato's *Republic*,[4] Socrates advised Glaucon that once he had visited the realm of 'true philosophy', and thus ascended 'into real being' ('turning of a soul round from a day which is like night to a true day'), he must return to those who did not follow him on his expedition. (Sages who never return from their escapade to the world of eternal truths are as wrong as the ordinary men and women who never embarked on the journey; in addition, they are guilty of the crime of lost opportunity and unfulfilled duty.) Then he 'will see a thousand times better than those who live there' – and this advantage will give him the right and the obligation to pass

[4] Quotations from Plato are taken from W.H.D. Rouse's translation, *Great Dialogues of Plato* (London: New English Library, 1956).

judgements and enforce obedience to truth. One needs to proclaim the philosopher's duty – 'the care and guardianship of other people'.

> Then it is the task of us founders ... to compel the best natures to attain the learning which we said was the greatest, both to see the good, and to ascend that ascent; and when they have ascended and properly seen, we must never allow them what is allowed now.

'It is more likely that the truth would have been discovered by few than ny many' – declared Descartes[5] in the third rule of the *Rules for the Direction of the Mind*. Knowing the truth, knowing it with such certainty as can withstand the cross-currents of vulgar experience and stay immune to the temptations of narrow and partial interests, is exactly the quality that sets the few apart from the many – and stands them above the crowd. To legislate and to enforce the laws of reason is the *burden* of those few, the knowers of truth, the philosophers. They are called to perform the task without which the happiness of the many will never be attained. The task would require sometimes a benign and clement teacher; at some other time it would demand the firm hand of a stern and unyielding guardian. Whatever the acts the philosopher may be forced to perform, one element will remain – cannot but remain – constant: the philosopher's unchallenged prerogative to decide between true and false, good and evil, right and wrong; and thus his licence to judge and authority to enforce obedience to the judgement. Kant had little doubt as to the nature of the task; to explain it he drew his metaphors profusely from the vocabulary of power. Metaphysics was 'the queen', whose 'government' could 'under administration' of dogmatists turn into despotism, but still remain indispensable to hold in check 'nomadic tribes, who hate permanent habitation and settled mode of living' and hence attack 'from time to time those who had organized themselves into civil communities'. The specific service

[5] Quotations from Descartes are taken from Margaret D. Wilson's edition, *The Essential Descartes* (London: New English Library, 1969). Spinoza's 'On the Correction of the Understanding' is quoted from Andrew Boyle's translation, included in Dent's 1986 edition of Spinoza's *Ethics*. In his study *The Mind of God and the Works of Man* (Oxford: Clarendon Press, 1987), Edward Craig observes that the early modern era was 'an epoch which deified reason' – which also meant the philosophers' belief that 'man is like God'. Galileo proposed that though extensively human knowlege was negligible (as yet, at any rate), *intensively* it was equal to God's. Craig emphasizes the all-important correlation between the conviction that man is capable of objective certainty and that a total freedom from external determinants can be attained: the dream of cognitive and practical mastery went together, could not be separated and supplied legitimation to each other (pp. 13–37).

metaphysics is called upon to render is criticism of reason:

> To deny the positive advantage of the service which this criticism renders us, would be as absurd as to maintain that the system of police is productive of no positive benefit, since its main business is to prevent the violence which citizen has to apprehend from citizen, that so each may pursue his vocation in peace and security.

One may easily be tempted to play down these or similar tropes drawn from the rhetoric of power as a predictable part of all *protreptics* – the habitual laudatory preambula to philosophical treatises meant to ingratiate the subject with the prospective readers, and particularly with the powerful and resourceful among them. Yet the case for *legislative* reason was addressed to a special kind of reader, and thus the language in which the bid for attention and favours was couched was one familiar to such a reader and resonant with his concerns. This reader was first and foremost the government of the day, the despot approached with an offer of enlightenment – of a means to do more effectively the very thing he declared himself to be after. Like the earthly rulers, critical philosophy braced itself to 'strike a blow' 'at the root'. The enemies such philosophy was particularly apt to transfix and overpower were those of the 'dogmatic schools' of Materialism, Fatalism, Atheism, Free-thinking, Fanaticism and Superstition 'which are universally injurious'. It had to be shown then that these adversaries threaten mundane and intellectual orders alike; that their annihilation is attuned to the interest of the powers that be in the same measure as it conforms to those of critical philosophy; that therefore the task of royal legislators overlaps with the aim of legislative reason.

> If governments think proper to interfere with the affairs of the learned, it would be more consistent with a wise regard for the interest of science, as well as for those of society, to favour a criticism of this kind, by which alone the labours of reason can be established on a firm basis, than to support the ridiculous despotism of the schools, which raise a loud cry of danger to the public over the destruction of cobwebs, of which the public has never taken any notice, and the loss of which, therefore, it can never feel.

Yet there was more to Kant's choice of metaphors than consideration of expediency in the bid for royal sponsorship. There was a genuine affinity between legislating ambitions of critical philosophy and the designing intentions of the rising modern state; just as there was a genuine symmetry between the tangle of traditional parochialisms the modern state had to uproot to establish its own supreme and uncontested sovereignty, and the cacophony of 'dogmatic schools' that had to be silenced so that the voice of universal and eternal (and hence *one* and uncontested: 'nothing will be left to future generations except the task of illustrating and applying it *didactically*') reason could be heard and its '*apodeictic certitude*' could be appreciated. Modern rulers and modern philosophers were first and foremost *legislators*; they found chaos, and set out to tame it and replace it with order. The orders they wished to introduce were by definition artificial, and as such had to rest on designs appealing to the laws that claimed the sole endorsement of reason, and by the same token delegitimized all opposition to themselves. Designing ambitions of modern rulers and modern philosophers were meant for each other and, for better or worse, were doomed to stay together, whether in love or in war. As all marriages between similar rather than complementary spouses, this one was destined to sample delights of passionate mutual desire alongside the torments of all-stops-pulled rivalry.

Securing supremacy for a designed, artificial order is a two-pronged task. It demands unity and integrity of the realm and security of its borders. Both sides of the tasks converge on one effort – that of separating the 'inside' from the 'outside'. Nothing left inside may be irrelevant to the total design or preserve autonomy *vis-à-vis* the exceptionless rulings of the order ('valid for every rational being'). 'For pure speculative reason is an organic structure in which there is nothing isolated or independent, but every single part is essential to all the rest; and hence, the slightest imperfection, whether defect or positive error, could not fail to betray itself in use' – just as in the case of political reason of the state. In the intellectual and political realms alike, the order must be both exclusive and comprehensive. Hence the two-pronged task merges into one: that of making the boundary of the 'organic structure' sharp and clearly marked, which means 'excluding the middle', suppressing or exterminating everything ambiguous, everything that sits astride the barricade and thus compromises the vital distinction between *inside* and *outside*. Building and keeping order means making friends and fighting enemies. First and foremost, however, it means purging *ambivalence*.

In the political realm, purging ambivalence means segregating or deporting strangers, sanctioning some local powers and delegalizing the unsanctioned ones, filling the 'gaps in the law'. In the intellectual realm, purging ambivalence means above all delegitimizing all grounds of knowledge that are philosophically uncontrolled or uncontrollable. More than anything else, it means decrying and invalidating 'common sense' – be it 'mere beliefs', 'prejudices', 'superstitions' or sheer manifestations of 'ignorance'. It was Kant's crowning argument in his devastating case against extant dogmatical metaphysics that 'this so-called queen could not refer her descent to any higher source than that of common experience'. The duty of philosophy Kant set out to establish was, on the contrary, 'to destroy the illusions which had their origin in misconceptions, whatever darling hopes and valued expectations may be ruined by its explanations'. In such a philosophy, '*opinion* is perfectly inadmissible'. The judgements admitted into the philosophical tribunal of reasons are *necessary* and carry 'strict and absolute universality', that is they brook no competition and leave outside nothing that may claim any recognized authority. For Spinoza the only knowledge deserving of this name is one that is certain, absolute and *sub speciae aeternitatis*. Spinoza divided ideas into strictly separate categories (leaving no room for 'the middle case') of such as constitute knowledge and such as are false; the latter were flatly denied all value and reduced to pure negativity – to the absence of knowledge. ('False or fictitious ideas have nothing positive . . . through which they may be called false or fictitious; but only from the want of knowledge they are so called.') In Kant's view the speculative philosopher is 'the sole depositor of a science which benefits the public without its knowledge' (the public awareness of being benefited is irrelevant to the validity of the benefits; it is the warranty of the philosopher that counts). Kant repeats: 'In the judgments of pure reason, opinion has no place . . . For the subjective grounds of a judgment, such as produce beliefs, cannot be admitted in speculative inquiries.' Descartes would readily concur: 'A man who makes it his aim to raise his knowledge above the common should be ashamed to derive the occasion for doubting from the forms of speech invented by the vulgar' (*Second Meditation*); intuition and deduction, both systematically deployed by philosophers, 'are the most certain routes to knowledge, and the mind should admit no others. All the rest should be rejected as suspect of errors and dangerous . . . We reject all such merely probable knowledge and make it a rule to trust only what is completely known and incapable of being doubted' (*Rules for the Direction of the Mind*).

These are, in an outline, the main characteristics of what Richard Rorty was to dub *foundational philosophy* – having first charged Kant, Descartes and Locke with joint responsibility for imposing the model on the following two hundred years of philosophical history.[6] As I have implied above,

---

[6] 'Philosophy can be foundational in respect to the rest of culture because culture is an assemblage of claims to knowledge, and philosophy adjudicates such claims . . . We owe the notion of philosophy as the tribunal of pure reason, upholding or denying the claims of the rest of culture to the eighteenth century, and especially to Kant, but this Kantian notion presupposed general assent to Lockean notions of mental processes and Cartesian notions of mental substance.' (Richard Rorty, *Philosophy and the Mirror of Nature* (Oxford: Basil Blackwell, 1981), pp. 3–4)

Commenting on Kant's assertion that appearances must themselves have grounds which are not appearances, Hannah Arendt observed that 'the philosophers' "conceptual efforts" to find something beyond appearances have

such foundational philosophy had its correlate in what may be called the *foundational politics* of the rising modern State; there was a striking symmetry of declared ambitions and practised strategies, as well as similar obsession with the question of sovereignty of legislative power expressed as the principle of universality of legal or philosophical principles.

Kant, Descartes and Locke (like Francis Bacon before them) were all moved by the dream of a masterful (that is, *collectively* free from constraints) humanity – the only condition in which, they believed, human dignity may be respected and preserved. Sovereignty of the human person was their declared and subjectively genuine concern; it was in the name of this sovereignty that they wished to elevate Reason to the office of supreme legislator. And yet there was a certain *Wahlverwandschaft* – elective affinity – between the strategy of legislative reason and the practice of the state power bent on imposition of designed order upon obstreperous reality. Regardless of the conscious purposes of the thinkers, the legislative reason of modern philosophy and of the modern scientific mentality in general were resonant with the practical tasks posited by the modern state. The two activities beckoned to each other, invigorated each other, reinforced each other's credibility and confidence. Much as the would-be despot needed reassurance of the universal validity of his particular intentions, legislative reason could not easily reject the temptation to train – to enlighten the despot for the role of its executor.

The practice of the gardening state

At the threshold of the modern era Frederick the Great, admittedly the monarch most closely approximating *les philosophes*' ideal of the enlightened despot, and indeed a favourite address of their blueprints, set the

always ended with rather violent invectives against "mere appearances" ' (*The Life of the Mind*, Part One: 'Thinking' (London: Secker & Warburg, 1978), p. 24). Philosophers sought to prove the 'theoretical supremacy of Being and Truth over mere appearance, that is, the supremacy of the *ground* that does not appear over the surface that does' (p. 25). Let us add that the postulated 'ground' was by definition out of the reach of ordinary, lay and commonsensical sensual impressions, and thus its supremacy reflected symbolically and legitimized the supremacy of the mental over the physical, and of the practitioners of 'theoretical practice' over those engaged merely in the menial, manual operations. The search for grounds and denigration of appearances was an integral part of the assault against non-philosophical, autonomous truth-claims. To quote Arendt again, 'the fact is, that there is hardly any instances on record of the many . . . declaring war on philosophers. As far as the few and the many are concerned, it has been rather the other way round.' (p. 81)

tone for the social-engineering ambitions of the new state:

> It annoys me to see how much trouble is taken to cultivate pineapples, bananas and other exotic plants in this rough climate, when so little care is given to the human race. Whatever people say, a human being is more valuable than all the pineapples in the world. He is the plant we must breed, he deserves all our trouble and care, for he is the ornament and the glory of the Fatherland.

While Frederick the Great merely demonstrated how eagerly he wished to absorb the Enlightenment lesson, at least some of his successors did their best to 'make philosophy into a material force' and thus treat humans as one does bananas and pineapples, using for this purpose the unprecedented technological resources and managerial capacities offered by the modern State. And they understood literally the precept of breeding, which Frederick the Great could treat as no more than a wistful metaphor. In 1930 R.W. Darré, later to become the Nazi Minister of Agriculture, wrote:

> He who leaves the plants in a garden to themselves will soon find to his surprise that the garden is overgrown by weeds and that even the basic character of the plants has changed. If therefore the garden is to remain the breeding ground for the plants, if, in other words, it is to lift itself above the harsh rule of natural forces, then the forming will of a gardener is necessary, a gardener who, by providing suitable conditions for growing, or by keeping harmful influences away, or by both together, carefully tends what needs tending, and ruthlessly eliminates the weeds which would deprive the better plants of nutrition, air, light and sun .... Thus we are facing the realization that questions of breeding are not trivial for political thought, but that they have to be at the centre of all considerations ... We must even assert that a people can only reach spiritual and moral equilibrium if a well-conceived breeding plan stands at the very *centre* of its culture ...[7]

---

[7] R.W. Darré, 'Marriage Laws and the Principles of Breeding', in *Nazi Ideology before 1933*, ed. Barbara Miller Lane and Leila J. Rupp (Manchester: Manchester University Press, 1978), p. 115. In *L'homme régénéré* (Paris: Gallimard, 1989), Mona Ozouf proposed that the French Revolution, itself the high point in the history of Enlightenment, focused its intentions on the 'formation' of *un nouveau peuple*, by the same token positing the 'new breed of men' as *a task* (p. 119). The aimed at 'regenerated' society composed of 'new people' was to be, among other things, 'une société purgée de ces membres douteux' (p. 143). In this way, according to Ozouf, the French Revolution was in a sense a 'premonition' of times to come; it anticipated the course of later exercises at the 'society building'; temptingly, it left unfulfilled the 'projét de visibilité absolue où l'indétermination est insupportable' and just started on the way leading 'des Lumiéres au Goulag' (p. 120).

In 1934 the world-famous biologist Erwin Bauer, holder of many scholarly distinctions, then the director of the Kaiser Wilhelm Institute for Breeding Research, was more specific yet:

> Every farmer knows that should he slaughter the best specimens of his domestic animals without letting them procreate and should instead continue breeding inferior individuals, his breeds would degenerate hopelessly. This mistake, which no farmer would commit with his animals and cultivated plants, we permit to go on in our midst to a large extent. As a recompense for our humanness of today, we must see to it that these inferior people do not procreate. A simple operation to be executed in a few minutes makes this possible without farther delay ... No one approves of the new sterilization laws more than I do, but I must repeat over and over that they constitute only a beginning.

As was his learned colleague Martin Stämmler in 1935:

> Extinction and selection are the two poles around which the whole race cultivation rotates ... Extinction is the biological destruction of the hereditary inferior through sterilization, then quantitative repression of the unhealthy and undesirable ... The ... task consists of safeguarding the people from an overgrowth of the weeds.[8]

To underline the ambitions of the state now firmly set on substituting a designed and state-monitored plan for uncontrolled and spontaneous mechanisms of society, the medical metaphor soon joined forces with the traditional gardening one. Thus, one of the most prominent and acclaimed zoologists of world-wide fame and the 1973 Nobel Prize winner, Professor Konrad Lorenz declared in June 1940:

> There is a certain similarity between the measures which need to be taken when we draw a broad biological analogy between bodies and malignant tumors, on the one hand, and a nation and individuals within it who have become asocial because of their defective constitution, on the other hand ... Any attempt at reconstruction using elements which have lost their proper nature and characteristics is doomed to failure. Fortunately, the elimination of such elements is easier for the public health physician and less dangerous for the supra-individual organism, than such an operation by a surgeon would be for the individual organism.[9]

---

[8] Quoted after Max Weinreich, *Hitler's Professors* (New York: Yiddish Scientific Institute, 1946), pp. 30–4.

[9] Quoted after Benno Müller-Hill, *Murderous Science, Elimination by Scientific Selection of Jews, Gypsies and Others, Germany, 1933–1945*, trans. George R. Fraser (Oxford: Oxford University Press, 1988), p. 14.

Let us emphasize that none of the above statements was ideologically motivated; in particular, none of them was aimed specifically at the Jews, or stemmed predominantly from antisemitic sentiments. (As a matter of fact, there were quite a few Jews among the most vociferous scholarly preachers of gardening and medical techniques in social engineering. For instance, as late as in 1935, and shortly before his dismissal for reason of Jewish origin, the noted psychiatrist Dr F. Kallmann advised compulsory sterilization of even the healthy, yet heterozygous carriers of the 'abnormal gene of schizophrenia'. As Kallman's plan would require sterilizing of no less than 18 per cent of the total population, the author's zeal had to be held back by his Gentile colleagues.) The quoted scientists were guided solely by proper and uncontested understanding of the role and mission of science – and by the feeling of duty towards the vision of good society, a healthy society, an orderly society. In particular, they were guided by the hardly idiosyncratic, typically modern conviction that the road to such a society leads through the ultimate taming of the inherently chaotic natural forces and by systematic, and ruthless if need be, execution of a scientifically conceived, rational plan. As it transpired, the admittedly unruly and anarchistic Jewry was one of the many weeds which inhabited the plot marked for the carefully designed garden of the future. But there were other weeds as well – carriers of congenital diseases, the mentally inferior, the bodily deformed. And there were also plants which turned into weeds simply because a superior reason required that the land they occupied should be transformed into someone else's garden.

The most extreme and well documented cases of global 'social engineering' in modern history (those presided over by Hitler and Stalin), all their attendant atrocities notwithstanding, were neither outbursts of barbarism not yet fully extinguished by the new rational order of civilization, nor the price paid for utopias alien to the spirit of modernity. On the contrary, they were legitimate offspring of the modern spirit, of that urge to assist and speed up the progress of mankind toward perfection that was throughout the most prominent hallmark of the modern age – of that 'optimistic view, that scientific and industrial progress in principle removed all restrictions on the possible application of planning, education and social reform in everyday life', of that 'belief that social problems can be finally solved'. The Nazi vision of a harmonious, orderly, deviation-free society drew its legitimacy and attractiveness from such views and beliefs already firmly entrenched in the public mind through the century and a half of post-Enlightenment history, filled with scientistic propaganda and the visual display of the wondrous potency of modern technology. Neither the Nazi nor the communist vision jarred with the audacious self-confidence and the hubris of modernity; they merely offered to do better what other modern powers dreamed of, perhaps even tried, but failed to accomplish:

> What should not be forgotten is that fascist realism provided a model for a new order in society, a new internal alignment. Its basis was the racialist elimination of all elements that deviated from the norm: refractory youth, 'idlers', the 'asocial', prostitutes, homosexuals, the disabled, people who were incompetents or failures in their work. Nazi eugenics – that is, the classification and selection of people on the basis of supposed genetic 'value' – was not confined only to sterilization and euthanasia for the 'valueless' and the encouragement of fertility for the 'valuable'; it laid down criteria of assessment, categories of classification and norms of efficiency that were applicable to the population as a whole.

Indeed, one must agree with Detler Peukert that National Socialism merely 'pushed the utopian belief in all-embracing "scientific" final solutions of social problems to the ultimate logical extreme'.[10] The determination and the freedom to go 'all the way' and reach the ultimate was Hitler's, yet the logic was construed, legitimized and supplied by the modern spirit.

Gardening ambitions and the spirit of modernity

Once the issues of desirability of order and the duty of rulers to administer its introduction had been settled, the rest was the matter of cool calculation of costs and effects – the art in which the modern spirit also excelled.

---

[10] Detler J.K. Peukert, *Inside Nazi Germany: Conformity, Opposition and Racism in Everyday Life*, trans. Richard Deveson (New Haven: Yale University Press, 1987), pp. 223, 222, 208, 248. The modern dream of a uniform, harmonious order of society, and the equally modern conviction that the imposition of such an order upon recalcitrant reality is a progressive move, a promotion of the common interests and, by the same token, legitimate whatever the 'transitional costs' can be found behind every case of modern genocide. Thus the builders of the modern Turkish state murdered the bulk of the 'harmony-spoiling' Armenian population because 'they sought to convert the society from its heterogenous makeup into a homogenous unit. Here genocide became a means for the end of a radical structural change in the system.' The vision of state-administered progress removed all moral compunctions that the bestiality of the mass murder might have caused. The architect of the Armenian genocide, the Minister of Internal Affairs Taleat, explained: 'I have the conviction that as long as a nation does the best for its interest and succeeds, the world admires it and thinks it moral.' (Cf. Vahakn N. Dadrian, 'The Structural-Functional Components of Genocide: A Victimological Approach to the Armenian Case', in *Victimology*, ed. Israel Drapkin and Emilio Viano (Lexington, Mass.: Lexington Books, 1974), pp. 133, 131.) As the later turn of events abundantly demonstrated, Taleat, it must be admitted, was not wide of the mark.

Again, the Nazis cannot claim any credit for the invention and codification of that art. Every single rule of the art had been established well before the glimpse of a caftaned Jew in a Vienna street inspired the young Hitler's anxiety about the purity of the world order.

As David Gasman found out and demonstrated, 'one of the earliest if not the earliest comprehensive programme embodying National Socialist principles in Germany arose in the context of a movement which prided itself on its scientific ideology and modern view of the world'. The movement referred to was the famous 'Monist Society', led by one of the most influential scientists of the nineteenth century, Ernst Häckel, who boasted impeccable scientific credentials and universal acclaim in the academic world of his time, and to this day is highly respected for his exceptional contribution to the promotion and popularization of the authority of modern science. For many contemporaries, 'if there existed one organization which truly expressed the modern temper, it was the German Monist League of Häckel with its radically scientific and positivistic spirit and programme'. One of the foremost figures in the League, Dr Schallmayer, warned the Germans that any politics that treated lightly and neglected the nation's heredity resources was to be fought against as bad and dangerous politics. It was left to Häckel himself to spell out the logical conclusions: 'by the indiscriminate destruction of all incorrigible criminals, not only would the struggle for life among the better portions of mankind be made easier, but also an advantageous artificial process of selection would be set in practice, since the possibility of transmitting the injurious qualities would be taken from those degenerate outcasts'. As the stream of 'bad genes' thins down thanks to the combination of 'scientific' measures of physical destruction and reproductive manipulation, the nation will count its benefits – 'lessening of court costs, prison costs, and expenses on behalf of the poor'.[11]

---

[11] David Gasman, *The Scientific Origins of National Socialism* (London: Macdonald, 1971), pp. xiv–xv, xxvi, 91, 98. In his revealing study of the 'natural scientific' obsessions of the Nazi movement, Robert A. Pois (*National Socialism and the Religion of Nature*, (London: Croom Helm, 1986)) documents Hitler's 'absolute belief in the supremacy of science over any form of religious belief . . . Indeed, Hitler's apparent tendencies towards a sort of biologism have caused some analysers of National Socialism to suggest that Hitler had no ideology but rather was devoted to a crude nexus of naturalistic beliefs.' (p. 39) Hitler's language was replete with references to the 'laws of nature', and his praise of science as the guide of proper action was boundless and unqualified. He insisted that National Socialism was 'a doctrine that is nothing more than a homage to reason' and that 'science is bound to win'. (Cf. Adolf Hitler, *Secret Conversations: 1941–1944*, trans. Norman Cameron and R.H. Stevens (New York: Farrar, Straus & Young, 1953), pp. 33, 51.)

Half a century later Germany acquired a government determined to put the scientific advice in practice. Presumably to gasps of horror from the audience, the *Führer* of the National-Socialist League of Physicians informed the Party congress in 1935 that 'more than one billion reichsmarks is spent on the genetically disabled; contrast this with the 776 million spent on the police, or the 713 million spent on local administration, and one sees what a burden and unexcelled injustice this places on the normal, healthy members of the population'. The figures were backed by impeccable statistical methods any scientific institute would be proud of. Calculation was meticulous and scrupulous, and the results breathed the air of scientific respectability: in 1933 the Prussian State spent on every *Normalvolksschuler* 125 marks, but 573 marks on each *Hilfsschuler*, 950 marks on every *Bildungsfahige* and *Geisteskrank*, and 1500 marks on any one of the *blind- oder taub-geborenen Schüler*.[12] The data hardly called for comments. Modern reason bowed to the facts: the problem had been clearly spelled out, the rest was the matter of the right technological solution.

The gardening–breeding–surgical ambitions were in no way specifically German. Even the retrospectively most sinister among the expressions of grand social-engineering ambitions – eugenics, that 'science of human heredity and art of human breeding' – was born outside Germany. It basked in the international prestige and deference that an advanced and resourceful science would expect to achieve long before Hitler and his companions patched together their vision of the Thousand-Year Reich. It was no one else but the distinguished head of the Cold Spring Harbor Laboratory, Professor C.B. Davenport, who gave the public accolade and blessing to the top German expert-breeder of human animals, Professor E. Fischer, by nominating him his successor as President of the International Federation of Eugenic Organizations.[13] The grandiose German plan to place the reproduction of society on a scientific basis and eliminate the

---

[12] Cf. Robert Proctor, *Racial Hygiene: Medicine under Nazis* (Harvard University Press, 1988), p. 181.

[13] Müller-Hill, *Murderous Science*, pp. 28–9. The experimental station at Cold Spring Harbor, led by Charles Benedict Davenport from 1904 on, was founded by Carnegie Institution of Washington, with the brief to identify individuals who carried 'defective germ plasm'. (Cf. Stephan L. Chorover, *From Genesis to Genocide: The Meaning of Human Nature and the Power of Behaviour Control* (Cambridge, Mass.: MIT Press, 1979), p. 41). Indeed, in many respects eugenic and other demographic-regulatory practices recommended by American scientists and implemented by American politicians served as a source of inspiration for the German planners of genocide. German 'racial hygienists drew upon the examples of American immigration, sterilization and miscegenation laws to formulate their own politics in these areas (Robert Proctor, *Racial Hygiene*, p. 286).

heretofore unharnessed (and hence haphazard) forces of heredity and selection was simply a radical expression of the universal ambitions inherent in modern mentality; it was, indeed, a relatively small part of a much wider totality. It earned its terrifying fame not because of its uniqueness, but because unlike most similar sentiments elsewhere – it did actually achieve its purpose: it was put into practice with the help of technological and organizational resources available to a modern society fully mobilized by the unchallenged might of a centralized state.

Just how big the company was in which German dreamers of a custom-made and purposefully designed world found themselves may be demonstrated by cases drawn from distant, even opposite cultural traditions and political camps. Eugenics was pioneered simultaneously in several European countries; as in many other areas of modern intellectual activity, English scholars vied for pride of place with their German colleagues. The Eugenics Education Society was founded in Britain in the nineteenth century (Galton established the highly successful journal *Eugenics* in 1883) and given a tremendous boost by the panic caused by the discovery of the poor physical and mental quality of army recruits during the Boer War. British eugenists were not short of engineering ambitions. They posited in front of the educated public a truly breath-taking vista:

> Would it not be possible to 'breed out' certain grave hereditary ailments in the way that Mendelian geneticists had learned to breed 'rustiness' out of wheat, and perhaps also to develop mental or physical faculties in men that were generally regarded as desirable? . . . Eugenics would then stand to genetics in rather the same relationship that engineering does to mathematics.

The prospect of scientifically managing the presently defective human stock was seriously debated in the most enlightened and distinguished circles. Biologists and medical men were, of course, in the forefront of the debate; but they were joined by famous people from other areas, like the psychologists Cyril Burt and William McDougall, the politicians Arthur Balfour and Neville Chamberlain, the whole of the infant British sociology, and on various occasions by J.B.S. Haldane, J. M. Keynes and Harold Laski. Concepts like 'tabid and wilted stock' (coined by Whethams in 1911), 'degenerate stock', 'submen', 'low-grade types' and 'biologically unfit' became staple figures of intelligent debate, while the tremendously influential Karl Pearson sounded in 1909 the alarm that shook the reading and debating public: 'the survival of the unfit is a marked characteristic of modern town life'. (He merely expressed already widespread concerns; here as elsewhere, British scholars were well attuned to the intellectual climate of the day. Six years before Pearson, Wilhelm Schallmayer stated in his award-winning essay that civilized man was threatened by physical degeneration, and that natural selection could not be depended upon as the basis for social progress and perfectibility of man; it had to be guided by some form of *social* selection. In her diary entry for 16 January 1903 the gentle and humane Beatrice Webb noted that human breeding 'is the most important of all questions, this breeding of the right sort of man')[14]

H.G. Wells, the English liberal, socialist and gallant fighter against narrow nationalism, religion and everything which smacked of a pre-scientific age, pondered throughout his long life and relentlessly preached to his numerous avid readers ('I doubt whether anyone who was writing books between 1900 and 1920, at any rate in the English language, influenced the young so much' – testified George Orwell on Wells's impact on the minds of the English educated classes)[15] the urgency of 'replacing disorder by order' and of placing scientifically informed planning agencies at the control desk of social development. To Wells the crowning argument in favour of a planned, socialist society was its affinity (indeed, synonymity) with recognition of the fundamental idea on which all true science is founded: 'the denial that chance impulse and individual will and happenings constitute the only possible methods by which things may be done in the world'. Like the scientist, the socialist wants

> a complete organization for all these human affairs that are of collective importance . . . In place of disorderly individual effort, each man doing what he pleases, the socialist wants organized effort, and a plan.

And here, of course, the by now familiar garden metaphor is summoned to assist in making the case persuasive: the socialist, like the scientist,

> seeks to make a plan as one designs and lays out a garden, so that sweet and seemly things may grow, wide and beautiful vistas open, and weeds and foulness disappear . . . what makes all its graciousness and beauty possible, is the scheme and the persistent intention, the watching and the waiting, the digging and burning, the weeder clips and the hoe.[16]

It was his love of wide vistas and straight paths which made Wells dislike

---

14 Cf. J.R. Searle, *Eugenics and Politics in Britain, 1900–1914* (Leiden, Noordhoff, 1976), pp. 8, 13, 29, 75.

15 George Orwell, 'Wells, Hitler, and the World State', in *Collected Essays* (London: Secker & Warburg, 1961), p. 164.

16 H.G. Wells, 'Socialism and the New World Order', in *Journalism and Prophecy, 1893–1946* (London: Bodley Head, 1984), pp. 278–9.

the Jews: Jews were 'firmly on the side of reaction and disorder'[17] and as such spoiled the landscape and thwarted the efforts of the planner. There was but a short step from this verdict to the application of the weeder clips. As it happens, the step was never taken. But there was little in Wells's declaration, and in the scientific ambitions in the name of which he wrote it down (though arguably not in some other segments of his profuse legacy) to prevent it from being taken.

On the face of it, the conservative and romantic T.S. Eliot would occupy an opposite pole on many a continuum on which the liberal and progressive H.G. Wells could be also plotted. Indeed, Wells's brash, all-stops-pulled bravery fed by scientific hubris would jar stridently with T.S. Eliot's world-view; but the desire of a harmonious, aesthetically pleasing and 'clean' society was common to both thinkers, as was the conviction that society would not become clean or harmonious if guided solely by its natural inclinations.

> The population should be homogenous; where two or more cultures exist in the same place, they are likely either to be fiercely self-conscious or both to become adulterate. What is still more important is unity of religious background; and reasons of race and religion combine to make any large number of free-thinking Jews undesirable. There must be a proper balance between urban and rural, industrial and agricultural development. And a spirit of excessive tolerance is to be deprecated.

All too often Eliot's ugly and sinister sentence about undesirability of free-thinking Jews is cut out of its context, deemed to provide by itself the complete and sufficient insight into the structure of Eliot's antisemitic prejudice. This is a mistake, and a dangerous mistake at that, as Christopher Ricks convincingly argues in his recent profound study of Eliot's antisemitism. However repulsive the quoted sentence may sound, 'it is importantly less objectionable than the sequence of sentences within which it is deployed'. The sequence, Ricks points out, 'is a more insidious incitement to prejudice than any single sentence'. Prejudice is most powerfully itself when expressed in 'plausible processes of corrupted reasoning, by the disguising of a *non-sequitur*'.[18] Indeed, it is only when anti-Jewish sentiments are riveted in an enticing vision of a total, harmonious design which the Jews allegedly disturb and prevent from implementation, that old Judaeophobia turns – at least potentially – into modern

---

[17] Bryan Cheyette, 'H.G. Wells and the Jews: Antisemitism, Socialism, and English Culture', *Patterns of Prejudice*, vol. 22, no. 3 (1988), p. 23.

[18] Christopher Ricks, *T.S. Eliot and Prejudice* (London: Faber & Faber, 1988), p. 41.

genocide. It is only the admixing of resentment of 'the Other' to the gardener's self-confidence which is truly explosive.

The praise of weeder clips and trimming scissors was not sung solely by intellectual dreamers and self-appointed spokesmen of science. It permeated modern society and remained arguably the most salient feature of its collective spirit. Politicians and practitioners of economic progress joined in the chorus. Scientific studies in eugenics conducted by Terman, Yerkes and Goddard, and the fashionable Binet's IQ test were used in the US Johnson Immigration Act of 1924 to separate the 'dangerous classes' who were 'destroying American democracy'; while Calvin Coolidge argued in 1922 that 'the laws of biology had demonstrated that Nordic peoples deteriorate when mixing with other races'. According to the John R. Rockefeller's expression of faith, that preceded both events by about a generation, 'The American Beauty rose can be produced in the splendour and fragrance which bring cheer to its beholder only by sacrificing the early buds which grow up around it. This is not an evil tendency in business. It is merely the working-out of a law of nature and a law of God.'[19]

Genetical deficiency, manifested in crime and idiocy, became – following the scientists' lobbying or advice – the legitimate reason for compulsory sterilization in the states of Indiana, New Jersey and Iowa (where the state law covered 'criminals, rapists, idiots, feeble-minded, imbeciles, lunatics, drunkards, drug fiends, epileptics, syphilitics, moral and sexual perverts, and diseased and degenerate persons'). Altogether twenty-one states of the USA enacted between 1907 and 1928 eugenic sterilization laws.[20]

And yet few demonstrations of the genocidal potency that the grand vision of perfect and rationalized society reveals when conjoined with the awesome powers of the modern state could compete in sheer scale with the communist revolutions (by themselves encouraged, if not caused, by the late-nineteenth-century eruption of social-engineering hopes). Modern communism was a most receptive and faithful disciple of the Age of Reason and Enlightenment, and, arguably, most intellectually consistent among its heirs. It absorbed in full *les philosophes*' injunction concerning the need and urgency of the Kingdom of Reason. Its self-confidence (and its impatience) grew as the spectacular successes and burgeoning authority of modern science made the project seem ever more plausible. On its

---

[19] Quoted after William J. Ghent, *Our Benevolent Feudalism* (New York: Macmillan, 1902). p. 29.

[20] Cf. Chorover, *From Genesis to Genocide*, p. 42.

travel to the backward and depressed East, envious of the all-too-tangible occidental superiority, that injunction merged with the native (that is, the native intelligentsia in the first place) determination to do by human hand what nature failed to achieve; whereby its haste and self-assurance reached the boiling point.

One could almost say with the benefit of hindsight that the vision of the Enlightenment was made to respond to dreams and cravings of East-European political visionaries – intellectuals and, more generally, 'educated classes'. No other social location was more perfectly reflected in the imagery of the social ideal standing ahead of social reality and pulling it forward; in the vision of society as pliable raw material to be moulded and brought into proper shape by architects armed with a proper design; in the image of society incapable, if left to its own course, of either improving itself or even comprehending what the improvement would be like; in the concept of knowledge as power, reason as the judge of reality and an authority entitled to dictate and enforce the *ought* over the *is*.

The nineteenth-century East-European educated classes were the most avid students and most loyal heirs of the Enlightenment legacy. They were social engineers first, commentators and interpreters a distant second, managerial technicians not at all. They were intoxicated with politics, power and the state. They needed a mighty lever to lift society all the way up to the ideal: only a state wielding absolute power could serve as such a lever; and such a state, both able and willing to serve, was still to be created. The present one was either not potent enough, or goaded by its current rulers away from using its potency for the right purpose. Like the ideal they were after, the state of the educated classes lay in the future. This made it even more a seat of freedom, unencumbered by sobering experience of political practice; necessity, as it were, might be glimpsed only together with the irrevocable certainty of the past.

All this created that 'délire universaliste de la table rase', the 'promethean vision of the absolute beginning which justifies any atrocity' the origin of which Jean-Marie Benoist[21] traced to the Jacobin experiment with rationalization through the guillotine – which, however, came into full

---

[21] Jean-Marie Benoist, 'Au nom des Lumières . . .', *Le Monde*, 6 January 1989. Looking back at the logic of the 'new order' building during the Jacobin rule, Bronislaw Baczko wrote that 'pour être pure et verteuse, fidèle à ses propres représentations, la République devait nécessairement s'épurer, se débarrasser des "impurs", des traîtres, des intrigants, des carriéristes, des vils profiteurs, éléments indignes d'elle, voire de ses pires ennemis cachés et dissimulés. La Révolution progressait donc nécessairement par l'exclusion.' (*Comment sortir de la Terreur: Thermidor et la Révolution*, (Paris; Gallimard, 1989), p. 52.)

blossom when married to the feeling of historical retardation and cast upon an empty (or forcibly emptied) political stage. It was such a marriage which ultimately and irreversibly deprived humans of the rights of moral subjects, having transformed them first into bricks with which the new order was to be built, or the debris which had to be removed to clear the building site.

Two points can be made after this brief – indeed, perfunctory – survey of the otherwise widely diverse, often diametrically opposed visions, which on a few occasions triggered off, and on other occasions lend plausibility to modern genocide.

One, modern genocide is not an uncontrolled outburst of passions, and hardly ever a purposeless, totally irrational act. It is, on the contrary, an exercise in rational social engineering, in bringing about, by artificial means, that ambivalence-free homegeneity that messy and opaque social reality failed to produce. One must agree with Helen Fein that:

> To understand genocides as a class of calculated crimes, such crimes must be appreciated as goal-oriented acts from the point of view of the perpetrators: genocide is rationally instrumental to their ends, although psychopathic in terms of any universalistic ethic . . . modern premeditated genocide is a rational function of the choice by a ruling elite of a myth or 'political formula' (as Mosca put it) legitimizing the existence of the state as the vehicle for the destiny of the dominant group, a group whose members share an underlying likeness from which the victim is excluded by definition.[22]

Two, all visions of artificial order are by necessity (in their practical consequences, if not always in their aforehand design) inherently asymmetrical and thereby dichotomizing. They split the human world into a group for whom the ideal order is to be erected, and another which enters the picture and the strategy only as a resistance to be overcome – the unfitting, the uncontrollable, the incongruous and the ambivalent. This Other, born of the 'operation of order and harmony', the left-over of classificatory endeavour, is cast on the other side of that *universe of obligation* which binds the insiders of the group and recognizes their right to be treated as carriers of moral rights.

Ordering – planning the order and executing it – is essentially a rational activity, attuned to the principles of modern science and, more generally, to the spirit of modernity. Like a modern business enterprise that had to separate itself from households in order to block the eroding impact of economically unjustifiable, moral responsibilities, kinship networks and

[22] Helen Fein, *Accounting for Genocide* (New York: Free Press, 1979), p. 8.

any other kinds of figurations ruled by face-to-face encounters – so the rationalizing drive of political agencies must seek liberation from 'ethical constraints'. It would try to gain such emancipation and make it absolute if allowed, that is if not thwarted by the resistance of yet uncolonized social forces. Hence every vision of a total order tends to include a prospect of incapacitation of such forces. If consistent, it entails not just a strategy through which the order can be introduced, but also a strategy allowing it to be kept henceforth intact and immune to all and any 'disturbing factors'. The imagination of the rationalizers is tempted by the prospect of a state of ultimate and stable perfection: one from which the very possibility of challenge to the established order will have been eliminated. The implementation of such a vision requires, however, the suppression or neutralization of autonomous determinants of individual action. 'What would the success of the Baconian project mean, when carried through to the willed conquest of the will as limit to domination? It would mean the universal dominion of system and the absence of man. Thus only would 'Nature' be conquered at last.' So suggests Theodore Olson. Francis Bacon's dream of the *House of Solomon* oscillates between the utopia and the dystopia that filled the busy days and the haunted nights of the modern era. The dream has never stopped being dreamed, Olson reminds us – Skinner's *Walden Two* being just a somewhat more ambitious and outspoken example of its latest manifestations. The success of Skinner's plan would mean: 'elimination of determinacy and particularity in human beings. Once again the result is the absence of humans and their replacement by the experimental environment and by its subjective correlate, universal adaptability. No will remains to frustrate the conquest of – or is it by? – Nature.'[23]

Science, rational order, genocide

Modern science was born out of the overwhelming ambition to conquer Nature and subordinate it to human needs. The lauded scientific curiosity that reputedly pushed the scientists 'to go where no humans yet dared to go' was never free from the exhilarating vision of control, management, making things better than they are (that is, more pliable, obedient, wiling to serve). Indeed, Nature came to mean something to be subordinated to human will and reason – a passive object of purposeful action, an object itself devoid of purpose and hence waiting to absorb the purpose injected

[23] Theodore Olson, *Millenarianism, Utopianism, and Progress* (Toronto: University of Toronto Press, 1982), pp. 283–4.

by its human masters. The concept of Nature, in its modern rendition, opposes the concept of humanity by which it has been spawned. It stands for the other of humanity. It is the name of the *aimless* and the *meaningless*. Denied inherent integrity and meaning, Nature seems a pliant object for man's liberties.

The numbness of Nature and the loquacity of science are locked together in an unbreakable bond of reciprocal legitimation. Being the other of human, the natural is the opposition of the subject of will and moral capacity. It is the powerful will of humanity as 'the master of the universe' and the exercise of its sole right to legislate meanings and standards of goodness that make the objects of mastery and legislation into 'Nature'. The objects may be rivers senselessly flowing in the wrong direction 'where they are not needed'. Or plants that seed themselves in places 'where they spoil the harmony'. Or animals that do not lay as many eggs or do not develop udders as big 'as would make them useful'. Or criminals and drunkards and feeble-minded that are geared to no meaningful uses and are thereby 're-naturalized' into degenerate 'former humans'. Or creatures of bizarre skin colour, bodily shape or behaviour, engaged in practices that make 'no sense' – whose presence 'may serve no useful purpose'. Anything that spoils the order, the harmony, the design, and thus refuses purpose and meaning, is Nature. Once it is Nature, it is to be treated as such. And it is Nature *because* it is so treated.

The argument is circular, and hence unassailable. Vision and practice tightly embrace each other and jointly delegitimize that 'outside' from which their secret union could be sized up, dissembled and decried. As W. Ryan warned,

> It is important not to delude ourselves into thinking that ideological monstrosities were constructed by monsters. They were not; they are not. They are developed through a process that shows every sign of being valid scholarship, complete with tables of numbers, copious footnotes, and scientific terminology. Ideologies are quite often academically and socially respectable and in many instances hold positions of exclusive validity, so that disagreement is considered unrespectable and radical and risks being labelled as irresponsible, unenlightened, and trashy[24]

Ryan does not speak here of the dedicated Nazis, nor of the 'Soviet science' under Stalin, notorious by its unashamed subordination to a blatantly political ideology. If he did, he would be able to count on unqualified endorsement of his words by fellow scientists. His warning, however, concerns a phenomenon seldom vented in the open: the norma-

---

[24] William Ryan, *Blaming the Victim* (London: Orbach & Chambers, 1971), p. 22.

tive, engineering ambitions that are inherent in all scientific enterprise, in scientific activity as such, and that may lend themselves easily and joyously to political uses – *any time* and *everywhere*; ambitions that are, themselves, politics. Chorover makes this final point very clearly:

> The sociobiological framework, upon which the justifications for genocide were ultimately built, was plainly not a Nazi invention. It had been erected in the name of science long before National Socialism became a reality . . .
>
> The Nazi extermination programme was a logical extension of sociobiological ideas and eugenics doctrines which had nothing specifically to do with Jews and which flourished widely in Germany well before the era of the Third Reich . . .
>
> The path was direct, from an allegedly objective brand of scientific discourse about human inequality to a purportedly rational form of moral argument about 'lives devoid of value' and then to the final solution: 'the release and destruction of lives devoid of value'.[25]

The non-Nazi and pre-Nazi, 'scientific' roots of genocide are being uncovered by a growing number of historians who start their research unaware of merely *retrospective* nature and the poor historical foundations of the haughty disavowal of the theory and practice of 'racial hygiene' as a one-off aberration. Robert Proctor has discovered that the commonly prevailing version of events, which held that German scientists of the Nazi era were pushed against their will by the unscrupulous rulers to partake of their fiendish practices, would not survive confrontation with the facts: 'it was largely medical scientists who *invented* racial hygiene in the first place. Many of the leading institutes and courses on *Rassenhygiene* and *Rassenkunde* were established at German universities long before the Nazi rose to power. And by 1932 it is fair to say that racial hygiene had become a scientific orthodoxy in the German medical community'. And lest there should be any vestige left of the common (self-consoling) conviction that the drive to racial purity was an idiosyncratically German distortion of scientific pursuits, let us note that the infamous Baur–Fischer–Lenz book that served as the main reference source and supreme scientific authority for the Nazi genocidal projects and their execution was enthusiastically reviewed by the most distinguished and enlightened journals in the West. The *New Statesman and Nation* called it 'a magnificent

---

[25] Chorover, *From Genesis to Genocide*, pp. 109, 80–1, 9–10. The phrase 'release and destruction of lives devoid of value' was in use already in 1920 and employed in the title of the book written by the psychologist Alfred Hoche and the jurist Karl Binding. Academic institutes totally devoted to the biological study of races were in existence at least from the beginning of the century; they enjoyed high scholarly esteem and attracted most eminent scientists and researchers.

textbook' and 'masterpiece of objective research and cautious hypotheses'. *The Spectator*, *Sociological Education*, *American Sociological Review*, *Sociology and Social Research* and numerous other periodicals proud of their objectivity and pursuit of truth echoed the admiration and failed to find any serious fault in the scholarly reasoning of the spiritual fathers of genocide.[26]

Christopher Simpson has recently collected the shocking evidence of how easily German science in the form given to it under Nazi rule could after the defeat of Hitler be absorbed by the Western liberal-democratic establishment. 'The mystique of white coats and high technology', keenly championed by scientists of all political colourings, helped to exonerate German experts, now deployed in the service of the victors, from responsibility for their wartime deeds in all but the most horrific cases that had already caused political outcry. In 1945, when the extent of genocidal atrocities first came into full view, the US National Academy of Science lay the foundation for the subsequent retrospective exculpation of German scientists and with them, by proxy, of the science as such – despite its zealous co-operation with what had to be described by that time (due to the logic of military defeat) as a crime against humanity. A special committee of the Academy came up with a truly mind-boggling idea that the wartime faithful service for the Nazis was in fact a form of the scientists' resistance: that by stubbornly clinging to their 'traditional ivory tower' of non-partisan objectivity, German scientists preserved 'an island of nonconformity in the Nazified body politic'.[27]

And yet Proctor's conclusion is unambiguous and merciless: there is 'little evidence that physicians ever refused to participate in Nazi programmes'. No punishment threatened those who would. No one ordered the scientists to participate in the blood-curdling experiments performed on prisoners, mentally ill and other outcasts: 'those who participated did so because they were given the opportunity and volunteered'. The results of the experiments were normally greeted by the academic establishment as high-quality, worthy material: the experiments were not undertaken by quacks, sadists and madmen, but 'by trained professionals; the results were presented at prestigious conferences and scientific academies'. Indeed, the initial attempt of some overenthusiastic followers of the *Volk* mystique to institute 'natural medicine' and reject the academic orthodoxy foundered on its own lack of resonance with the thoroughly modern and scientific character of the genocidal project: the bodies of knowledge associated

---

[26] Proctor, *Racial Hygiene*, pp. 38, 58.

[27] Cf. Christopher Simpson, *Blowback: America's Recruitment of Nazis and its Effects on the Cold War* (London; Weidenfeld & Nicholson, 1988), p. 34.

with racial hygiene 'were generally the province of orthodox, not heterodox, medicine; the techniques required for sterilization, castration, and so on, were not something the organic medical traditions could offer' – but something that rational science and its modern equipment certainly could.[28]

The findings of Ravensbrück 'research' were discussed by most illustrious academics of international repute, including the most prominent German physician Ferdinand Sauerbruch. He and his colleagues of no less impressive scientific credentials did not see any contradiction between their scientific vocation and the practices which they supplied with a theoretical foundation and instrumental tools. More often than not they embraced with relish the genuine opportunity to advance scholarship that the sponsorship of the Party and the generous State patronage had offered. The list of famous names of expert and diligent co-operators (that in addition to the first-rank luminaries like Lenz, Verschuer or Fischer included those of Rudolf Ramm, Kurt Blome, Gerhard Wagner, Lehmann, Baurmeister and quite a few others of similar respectable standing – many of whom continued their brilliant scientific careers after the fall of Nazi Germany, as universally acclaimed reputable specialists in human genetics) would found its rightful place in any 'Who's Who in the World of Science'. The bearers of those names considered themselves the followers and disciples of Virchow, Semmelweiss, Koch, Lister, Pasteur and Ehrlich; the trouble is that this claim is hard to question. They indeed followed the impartial rules of scientific fact-finding and pursued the most rational means to given ends (and instrumental rationality is, as we all believe, politically and morally neutral); they indeed worked to improve on the condition of human race, not fully secure when left to the spontaneity of nature; they indeed wished to construct a better, cleaner, more orderly world, better fit for whatever was seen as the proper human life.

And so one has no choice but to accept Proctor's verdict: 'One could well argue that the Nazis were not, properly speaking, abusing the results of science but rather were merely putting into practice what doctors and scientists had themselves already initiated.'[29] There would have been no genocide without the Nazi project of a racially pure Germany. But equally there would have been no such project without the science and technology that made it both thinkable and – so be it – respectable.

Almost four decades after the Nazi defeat Amitai Etzioni attended a world-wide conference that attracted the best minds that the scientific

---

28 Proctor, *Racial Hygiene*, pp. 220–1.

29 Müller-Hill, *Racial Hygiene*, p. 296.

community had to offer, as well as the politicians of the nation-states eager to apply up-to-date scientific theories and techniques to improve the lot of the population they ruled. Etzioni found out that:

> Participants at the conference switched rapidly from explaining, say, amniocentesis followed by abortion from the view of the parents (who may or may not wish to have a deformed child), to that of society (which may or may not be willing to put up $1.75 billion a year to take care of mongoloid children), from therapeutic goals (the prevention of the birth of a deformed child) to the use of the *same* procedures for breeding purposes (e.g., choosing the sex of the child to be born), from individual rights to society's problems, from voluntary schemes to coercive interventions (e.g., laws prohibiting the marriage of feeble-minded individuals.

The remarkable thing is that the scientists and the politicians alike hardly noticed the switch. One may surmise that it was precisely that switch and the facility with which it could be made that secured the invitation for some participants and attracted the others to the conference in the first place. 'If there is anything foolish which can be done', Etzioni warns, 'sooner or later there will be a government that will do it . . . at this point we do not have, even on paper, the mechanisms for stopping a particular development once it is proven undesirable.'[30]

---

[30] Amitai Etzioni, *Genetic Fix: The Next Technological Revolution* (New York; Harper & Row, 1973), pp. 102, 20, 30. In the last two decades attitudes that make Etzioni's premonitions sound real seem to have strengthened. One hears of previously unthinkable attempts to rehabilitate Nazi experiments on concentration camp inmates as 'scientifically sound material'. But one also finds contemporary scientists having ever more difficulty in understanding why they should refrain from engineering human life, with or without the consent of those affected, if only they *knew* that the anticipated results of intervention will be better than *status quo* and if the necessary tools, skills and funds were available. And so, for instance, Norman Stone writes in *The Guardian* (14 December 1989), in a review of Paul Windling's *Health, Race and German Politics between National Unification and Nazism, 1870–1945* (Cambridge University Press): 'in his horrible way, Hitler was pointing to a problem that is constant and, in today's "underclass", very serious. How do you stop single teenage mothers from breeding up tomorrow's football hooligans?' A sentence dropped just 'by the way' pushes aside the sad knowledge that history forced upon reluctant scientists. In a few words (all the more horrifying for being seen as trivially obvious), Norman Stone restates the whole philosophy that virtually invited Nazi political practices: he *knows* that the 'underclass' (of course, who else?) is a 'problem' (whose problem?); he *knows* that hooligans are born of single mothers (of and into the underclass, of course); and so he *knows* that the would-be single underclass mothers should be stopped from fornication. How? Here, one would suppose, 'Hitler was pointing to a problem that is constant' . . .

In his recent review of Proctor's study, Geoffrey Cantor wrote of 'the dangers

Müller-Hill's chronicle of the 'identification, proscription, and extermination of those who were different', which includes the dates of Hitler's appointment as *Reichskanzler* and of the Wandsee conference, ends with an entry that records Watson and Crick's discovery of the structure of DNA and the explosion of subsequent genetical research and genetical engineering experiments. He asks: 'Has anything been learnt from the outbreak of barbarism in Germany or will it be repeated on a worldwide scale in a yet more dreadful form and to a yet more dreadful degree?'[31] After the DNA discovery, the knowledge boasted by genetics and eugenics at the time of Professors Fischer, Lenz or Verschuer seems laughably primitive. Modern geneticists aim at writing down the entire, final 'Book of Life' – the whole of the human genetic code with all its possible variations. It has been quickly recognized that DNA-originated medicine will need a new industry to run it. There are already private companies devoted to the human 'genome', like one called Biogen, which resourcefully hastened to secure copyrights in anticipation of the wondrous (and highly profitable) *applied* knowledge the new scientific research is bound to produce. The United States Congress, true to its traditional and widely approved function, is worried that funds must be found to sponsor the pioneering work lest America should lose its present lead in biotechnology, while the US Department of Energy invites the researchers of the DNA structure to use its ample and underemployed electronic resources for their experiments. When pressed by the conscientious individuals still haunted by the fresh memories of scientific management of the 'race material', the scientists, the businessmen eager to exploit their findings and the politicians keen (at least for the time being) to exploit their prestige, respond indignantly: 'We do not intend to define "bad" traits, only graft the good ones . . .'

There is no reason to doubt the noble intentions of the scientists. There is less cause still to charge them with malice aforethought. What the lesson

---

inherent in scientists pursuing the limited goals defined by science. For the power without responsibility can easily be directed towards the most inhumane ends. What was manifestly lacking among the German doctors and scientists was open and critical discussion of the social, political and *ethical* significance of their research. Even today such discussion is all too rare.' (Geoffrey Cantor, 'Biology and Destiny', *Jewish Quarterly*, Winter 1989.) Given the inextricable link between 'de-ethicalization' and the instrumentality of science that Cantor documents so well, the word 'even' in the last sentence comes as a surprise. All this finds its apt summary in Hans Jonas's verdict: 'Never was so much power coupled with so little guidance for its use. Yet there is a compulsion, once the power is there, to use it anyway.' (*Philosophical Essays: From Ancient Creed to Technological Man* (Englewood Cliffs; Prentice Hall, 1974), p. 176.

[31] Müller-Hill, *Murderous Science*, p. 21.

of the Holocaust has taught us, however, is to doubt the wisdom of the scientists' claim of their right to tell good from bad; the capacity of science as moral authority; indeed, the ability of scientists to locate moral issues and to pass moral judgement of the effects of their actions.

Narrating inhumanity

Dehumanizing definitions of the enemy are not new in human history and hardly a peculiar feature of the modern age. They accompanied most wars – perhaps any war. During the combat, they were probably indispensable. The soldier had to suppress his aversion to kill and maim if he was not to be killed or maimed himself. There is a grim symmetry in battlefield contests. On both sides, suspension of the 'Thou shalt not kill' commandment regarding the Other becomes the condition of upholding it toward oneself (or, more perversely still, of coercing the Other to obey it). Defence of one's own right to live needs a denial of such right to the Other. In such a figuration, the Other need not – or so it seems – be defined. The Other defines himself – as the enemy – as he casts one's respect for his moral identity into conflict with the protection of one's own. One can deny his being *an enemy* only at one's own peril.

While ostensibly surviving intact the advent of the modern age, the old tradition of dehumanizing the enemy in combat has been, like everything else, thoroughly revolutionized by modern organization and technology. The contest of individual combat skills – the duel in which chances of survival were evenly cast on both sides – was replaced with wholesale slaughter at a distance. Symmetry of intentions is no longer self-evident and self-corroborating – it has to be construed and demonstrated. More importantly, the symmetry of intentions always points to the symmetry of practices, and modern weapons of mass annihilation are rationalized to stave off such symmetry. Unlike the combatants in a man-to-man battle, the objects of wholesale slaughter cannot have their humanity, however impaired, admitted. Modern weapons require a complete obliteration of the moral identity of their victims before they obliterate their bodies.

Paul Fussell, Professor of English at Pennsylvania and a veteran of the Pacific War, remembers that: 'Among Americans it was widely held that the Japanese were really subhuman, little yellow beasts and popular imagery depicted them as lice, rats, bats, vipers, dogs and monkeys.' Army and Navy journals wrote of the 'gigantic task of extermination', and some of the marines landing on the islands held by the Japanese duly inscribed 'Rodent Exterminator' on their helmets. Dehumanization of the enemy was, of course, reciprocal. Its persistence on both sides, the shared forgetfulness of the humanity of the other side, made the massacres possible – as they allowed the participants to think of them as of sanitary operations rather than murder. '... let's pour gasoline into their bunkers and light it and then shoot those afire who try to get out. Why not? Why not blow them all up, with satchel charges or with something stronger? Why not, indeed, drop a new kind of bomb on them ...?'[32]

With all its modern innovations war remains a situation in which adversaries retain the right to self-definition (in its developed stage at least, even if not always at the point of original assault). The enemy appears to be *objectively* an enemy, while my denial of his right to be protected by moral commandments appears – again – as an exercise in *reciprocity*. Not so with genocide. Here, the object of extermination is defined *unilaterally*. No symmetry is applied or intimated in any form. By any stretch of imagination, the other side is not an enemy, but a victim. It has been marked for annihilation because the logic of the order that the stronger side wishes to establish has no room for its presence. Most of the little wars which combined into the great war waged by Nazi Germany against the world were of this blatantly asymmetrical character – removal of the aliens occupying German living space, or alien races burrowing into German life and corroding the German spirit. The object to be destroyed was defined fully by the vision of the future German Reich. And as Rubenstein and Roth point out, 'If the Holocaust has a single overriding lesson, it is that there is absolutely no limit to the obscenities a determined and powerful aggressor can freely visit upon stateless, powerless victims.'[33]

Declaring that a particular category of people has no room in the future order is to say that this category is beyond redemption – cannot be reformed, adapted or forced to adapt itself. The Other is not a sinner, who can still repent or mend his ways. He is a diseased organism, 'both ill and infectious, both damaged and damaging'.[34] He is fit only for a surgical operation; better still, for fumigation and poisoning. He must be destroyed so that the rest of the social body may retain its health. His destruction is a matter of medicine and sanitation.

Hitler set the tone for all later Nazi narrative, describing his service to humanity (killing the Jews) as 'exterminating the pest'. Streicher's *Der*

---

32 Paul Fussell, 'Thanks God for the Bomb', first published in *New Republic*, reprinted in *The Guardian*, 21–2 January 1989.

33 Richard L. Rubenstein and John K. Roth, *Approaches to Auschwitz* (New York: SCM Press, 1987), pp. 333–4.

34 Sender L. Gilman, *Difference and Pathology, Stereotypes of Sexuality, Race and Madness* (Ithaca: Cornell University Press, 1985), p. 130.

Stürmer hammered this definition home with relentless monotony: 'Bacteria, vermin and pests cannot be tolerated. For reasons of cleanliness and hygiene we must make them harmless by killing them off.'[35] The modern scientific discourse of race (of an immutable, ascribed quality – hopelessly 'nature-ordained', admittedly hereditary, culturally unmanipulable, resistant to all remedy) from which the Nazi manufacture of the Other drew so lavishly, was from the start replete with the images of pathological deformation, degeneration, madness, sexual perversion. Theoretical concepts were inextricably interwoven with medical practices, taxonomic operations with surgical ones, conceptual oppositions with segregatory actions, abstract evaluations with social discriminations. Defining the Other as vermin harnesses the deeply entrenched fears, revulsion and disgust in the service of extermination. But also, and more seminally, it places the Other at a enormous mental distance at which moral rights are no longer visible. Having been stripped of humanity and redefined as vermin, the Other is no more an object of moral evaluation.

Reputable German scientists of today who still remember the illustrious scholars who inspired the Nazi policies of racial selection, segregation and 'purification', and later presided over their execution, cannot recall that their older colleagues or teachers were antisemites – or, indeed, that they (with very few exceptions) were politically committed men, let alone devoted Nazis. Even if the healing work of time has most probably left its trace on witnesses' memory, the unanimity of their verdict is truly striking. Allowing that the verdict is not fully faithful to the facts of the past, its outspoken motivation certainly throws some light on the current climate of the scientific establishment; it is, after all, in terms of this present climate that the past is being interpreted. And thus we learn that Professor Fischer was a completely apolitical person, devoted only to science and the expansion of knowledge – a kindly, sensitive and unassuming man. We hear that Professor Lenz was equally devoted to his vocation. He was a mixture of the scientist guided by the hunger for knowledge and the unwordly utopian; no trace of malice – a man of good intentions throughout. We are told by a former assistant of Fischer that the latter insisted on writing accurate expert reports (about the degree of racial contamination of vetted persons) according to pure scientific criteria; leniency, in his view, was to be disdained as it was not a scientific concept. Irmgard Haase, Professor Verschuer's former helper, is quite determined: we didn't have – she remembers – any qualms; it was science, after all. Professor E.Z. Rüdin, the daughter of Ernst Rüdin, spoke of her late father's misgivings about the

---

35 Quoted after Norman Cohn, *Warrant for Genocide* (London: Eyre & Spottiswoode, 1967), pp. 87, 205.

uses to which his objective scientific findings had been put. But, she asks, 'What should he have done? He would have sold himself to the devil, in order to obtain money for his institute and his research.'[36] And to the devil did he sell himself, without misgivings. After all, he defended the cause of science, its *resources*, its freedom of *research*, its *progress* – and what he did as a scientist was like science itself objective and hence immune to ethical recrimination: not a moral problem at all. Except for a few racist fanatics, the other titled administrators and consultants of genocide thought, in all probability, along the same lines – and needed no other motivation for what they did.

'Objectivity opened the door to every conceivable form of barbaric practice.'[37] So Müller-Hill sums up his painstaking research. Scientists hail objectivity. They disdain and avoid value judgements. Once they have done this, the rest is the matter of instrumental rationality. If the killing of mental patients is economically sound and technically feasible, why on earth should it not be done? Or why should one damage the chances of advancement of science by refusing to use the 'Jewish and Gypsy material' as experimental animals?

It helps that modern scientists are themselves organized into a bureaucratic structure – with its vertical and horizontal division of labour that casts most of them most of the time in the position of 'intermediate men' (Lachs), keeping them in the 'agentic state' (Milgram). Seldom do the experts watch the ultimate consequences of their actions. Even less frequently do they see their decisions through to their logical end. (Their contributions represent but partial functions in a complex network of interwoven activities; as function-performers, as units in a totality much larger than any one of them, they feel eminently exchangeable: if they do not do this or that, someone else will. Thus the *personality* of their actions, complete with personal responsibility, is all but wiped out.) Above all, they hardly ever face up to the end-results. If they wish, they may even remain unaware of these results.

Müller-Hill suggests that it follows from the very essence of the practice called science (the same essence we hold responsible for the spectacular attainments of science we admire and are grateful for) that 'the other

---

[36] Cf. Müller-Hill, *Murderous Science*, pp. 107–56.

[37] Müller-Hill, *Murderous Science*, p. 89. Hans Jonas wrote of the present-day scientists' rush toward genetical engineering: 'The potentially infinite, "transcendent" image would shrink to charts of desired properties, selected by ideology . . ., turned into blueprints by computer-aided geneticists, authorized by political power – at last inserted with fateful finality into the future evaluation of the species by biological technology.' (*Philosophical Essays*, pp. 180–1.)

person' disappears from view, becomes ever more remote and hence less significant (certainly, less *ethically* significant). The advancement of specialization and expertise has the reduction of 'the individual' to a cipher as its indispensable factor. 'The inexorable encroachment of science, which began in the eighteenth century during the Age of Enlightenment, on activities more properly belonging to the human individual who speaks and gives signs, has had unforeseen and devastating effects.'[38] What matters in science is to get interesting and accurate results, and to get them fast and cheap. Other considerations are mere hurdles to be jumped over or kicked out of the way. They cannot be anything else but 'constraints', regressive factors, manifestations of obscurantism and forces of darkness.

Having emancipated purposeful action from moral constraints, modernity rendered genocide possible. Without being the sufficient cause of the genocide, modernity is its necessary condition. The ability to co-ordinate human actions on a massive scale, a technology that allows one to act effectively at a large distance from the object of action, minute division of labour which allows for spectacular progress in expertise on the one hand and floating of responsibility on the other, accumulation of knowledge incomprehensible to the layman and the authority of science which grows with it, the science-sponsored mental climate of instrumental rationality that allows social-engineering designs to be argued and justified solely in reference to their technical feasibility and availability of 'under-employed' resources (all these to be put in service of the relentless lust for order, transparency, unambiguity) are all integral attributes of modernity. But they also condition displacement of the moral by the instrumental action (or, rather, injecting instrumentality with moral significance of its own), and thus make genocide possible to accomplish – if only there are forces around determined to accomplish it. In other words, by radically weakening the hold of moral inhibitions, and making large-scale actions independent from moral judgement and exempt from the constraining impact of individual morality, modernity supplies the *means* for genocide. It also, however, supplies its purpose.

Stanley Milgram summed up the findings of his famous experiments in the following way: 'The act of shocking the victim [the act of ostentatious cruelty in which randomly selected, ordinary, middle-class and law-abiding Americans were invited to engage. Z.B.] does not stem from destructive urges but from the fact that subjects have been integrated into a social structure and are unable to get out of it.' Let us recall that the 'social structure' subjected to the experimental test was that of science. The

---

[38] Müller-Hill, *Murderous Science*, p. 102.

subjects of Milgram's experiments were told that the cruelty they were asked to commit was 'justified' by the cognitive benefits it would bring and by the contribution it would make to the development of scholarship. Anyway, this much the subjects had gathered on their own when they found themselves on the premises of a most prestigious university and received their orders from people in the awe-inspiring white coats. Such orders they were not inclined to contradict. They must have assumed that scientists ought to be trusted to pursue what is good and not to perpetrate *unnecessary* cruelty.

The most striking (though one of the least discussed) of Milgram's findings was, however, the effect of the weakening of such an 'integrated' (read: uncontested) structure of command by the display of disagreement between equally prestigious and resourceful authorities. 'It is clear that the disagreement between the authorities completely paralysed action'[39] – i.e., it paralysed the willingness of the subjects to implement commands ordering them to perpetrate cruelty. In the face of *pluralism* of authority, the moral drives of the subjects reasserted themselves and regained control over their conduct. Ethics returned, so to speak, from the enforced exile. Faceless objects of experiment have become faces again. The protective shield with which the well-structured, monolithic and single-purpose organization used to separate the subject from his responsibility now fell apart.

It seems that the sole factor truly capable of counterbalancing and eventually offsetting the genocidal potential dormant in the instrumental capacities of modernity and its instrumental-rational mentality is *pluralism of power*, and hence the pluralism of authoritative opinion. Only pluralism returns moral responsibility for action to its natural bearer: the acting individual. The dissipation of central management that pluralism inevitably entails means an absence of a managerial centre capable of dreaming about 'uniform and universal order', let alone able to implement it. Unity of definitions and meanings, of purposes, strategies, criteria of progress, images of perfection and the sense of direction the change is and ought to be taking – these most passionate of modern mentality's cravings – are then bound to remain unfulfilled or altogether wiped off the agenda. Instead, a lot of semiotic and axiological ambivalence emerges to remain a permanent feature of social existence, rather than its transient, as yet unrepaired, shortcoming. The ambiguity that modern mentality finds difficult to tolerate, and modern institutions set out to annihilate (both of

---

39 Stanley Milgram, *Obedience to Authority: An Experimental View* (London; Tavistock, 1974), pp. 166, 107.

them drawing from this intention their awesome creative energy), reappears as the only force able to contain and defuse modernity's destructive, genocidal potential. Hence the notorious duality of the modern tendency, oscillating between freedom and genocide, constantly able to stretch in either direction, spawning at the same time the most horrifying of contemporary dangers and the most effective means of preventing them – the poison and the antidote.

In his last book and testament, Primo Levi wrote of the countless perpetrators of big and small Holocaust crimes who tried to exonerate themselves by insisting that they 'merely followed the orders'. Levi accuses them of lying. What seems, however, most crucial, is that the murderers *could* say what they did, and still hope for the credibility of the lie. It was the bureaucratic-technological side of modernity that gave them this hope. It is the pluralism of modern democracy that alone may call the bluff of their excuses and dash the hope that the lie would not be exposed. Perhaps it may even do away with the actions that require a lie.

Having surveyed the course and the outcomes of the modern war against ambiguity, Hans Jonas found in the as yet undestroyed ambivalence the only force able to salvage modern technological civilization from its own, planned or unintended, consequences:

> The basic error of the ontology of 'not yet' and its eschatological hope is repudiated by the plain truth – ground for neither jubilation nor dejection – that genuine man is always already there and was there throughout known history: in his heights and his depths, his greatness and wretchedness, his bliss and torment, his justice and his guilt – in short, in all the *ambiguity* that is inseparable from his humanity. Wishing to abolish this constitutive ambiguity is wishing to abolish man in his unfathomable freedom.[40]

---

[40] Hans Jonas, *The Imperative of Responsibility: In Search of an Ethics for the Technological Age* (University of Chicago Press, 1984), pp. 200–1.

2

The Social Construction of Ambivalence

There are friends and enemies. And there are *strangers*.

Friends and enemies stand in an opposition to each other. The first are what the second are not, and vice versa. This does not, however, testify to their equal status. Like most other oppositions that order simultaneously the world in which we live and our life in the world, this one is a variation of the master-opposition between the *inside* and the *outside*. The outside is negativity to the inside's positivity. The outside is what the inside is not. The enemies are the negativity to the friends' positivity. The enemies are what the friends are not. The enemies are flawed friends; they are the *wilderness* that violates friends' *homeliness*, the *absence* which is a denial of friends' *presence*. The repugnant and frightening 'out there' of the enemies is, as Derrida would say, a *supplement* – both the addition to, and displacement of the cosy and comforting 'in here' of the friends. Only by crystallizing and solidifying what they are not (or what they do not wish to be, or what they would not say they are), into the counter-image of the enemies, may the friends assert what they are, what they want to be and what they want to be thought of as being.

Apparently, there is a symmetry: there would be no enemies were there no friends, and there would be no friends if not for the yawning abyss of enmity outside. Symmetry, however, is an illusion. It is the friends who *define* the enemies, and the appearance of symmetry is itself a testimony to their asymmetrical right to define. It is the friends who control the *classification* and the *assignment*. The opposition is an achievement and self-assertion of the friends. It is the product and the condition of the friends' narrative domination, of the friends' *narrative as the domination*. As far as they dominate the narration, set its vocabulary and fill it with meaning, friends are truly at home, among friends, at ease.

The rift between friends and enemies makes *vita contemplativa* and *vita activa* into mirror reflections of each other. More importantly, it guarantees their co-ordination. Subjected to the same principle of structuration, knowledge and action chime in, so that knowledge may inform the action and the action may confirm the truth of knowledge.

The friends/enemies opposition sets apart truth from falsity, good from evil, beauty from ugliness. It also differentiates between proper and improper, right and wrong, tasteful and unbecoming. It makes the world readable and thereby instructive. It dispels doubt. It enables the knowledgeable one to go on. It assures that one goes where one should. It makes the choice look like revealing the nature-made necessity – so that man-made necessity may be immune to the vagaries of choice.

Friends are called into being by the pragmatics of co-operation. Friends are moulded out of responsibility and moral duty. The friends are those for whose well-being I am responsible *before* they reciprocate and *regardless* their reciprocation; only on this condition the co-operation, ostensibly a contractual, two-directional bond, can come into effect. Responsibility must be a gift if it is ever to become an exchange.

Enemies, on the other hand, are called into being by the pragmatics of struggle. Enemies are construed out of renunciation of responsibility and moral duty. The enemies are those who refuse responsibility for my well-being *before* I relinquish my responsibility for theirs, and *regardless* my renunciation; only on this condition the struggle, ostensibly a two-sided enmity and reciprocated hostile action, may come into effect.

While the anticipation of friendliness is not necessary for the construction of friends, anticipation of enmity is indispensable in the construction of enemies. Thus the opposition between friends and enemies is one between *doing* and *suffering*, between being a *subject* and being an *object* of action. It is an opposition between reaching out and recoiling, between initiative and vigilance, ruling and being ruled, acting and responding.

With all the opposition between them, or – rather – *because* of that opposition, each of the two opposing modes stands for relationships. Following Simmel, we may say that friendship and enmity, and only they, are forms of *sociation*; indeed, they are the archetypal forms of all sociation, and together constitute its two-pronged matrix. They make the frame within which sociation is possible; they exhaust the *possibility* of 'being *with* others'. Being a friend, and being an enemy, are the two modalities in which the *Other* may be recognized as another *subject*, construed as a 'subject like the self', admitted into the self's life world, be counted, become and stay relevant. If not for the opposition between friend and enemy, none of this would be possible. Without the possibility of breaking the bond of responsibility, no responsibility would impress itself as a duty. If not for the enemies, there would be no friends. Without the possibility of difference, says Derrida, 'the desire of presence as such would not find its breathing space. That means by the same token that the desire carries in itself the destiny of its nonsatisfaction. Difference produces what it forbids, making possible the very thing that it makes impossible.'[1]

Against this cosy antagonism, this conflict-torn collusion of friends and enemies, the *stranger* rebels. The threat he carries is more horrifying than that which one can fear from the enemy. The stranger threatens the sociation itself – the very *possibility* of sociation. He calls the bluff of the opposition between friends and enemies as the *compleat mappa mundi*, as the difference which consumes all differences and hence leaves nothing *outside* itself. As that opposition is the foundation on which rest all social life and all differences which patch it up and hold together, the stranger saps social life itself. And all this because the stranger is neither friend nor enemy; and because he may be both. And because we do not know, and have no way of knowing, which is the case.

The stranger is one (perhaps the main one, the archetypal one) member of the family of *undecidables* – those baffling yet ubiquitous unities that, in Derrida's words again, 'can no longer be included within philosophical (binary) opposition, resisting and disorganizing it, *without ever* constituting a third term, without ever leaving room for a solution in the form of speculative dialectics'. Here are a few examples of 'undecidables' discussed by Derrida:

The *pharmakon*: the Greek generic term which includes both remedies and poisons (the term used in Plato's *Phaedrus* as a simile for writing, and for this reason – in Derrida's view – indirectly responsible, through translations that aimed at eschewing its inherent ambiguity, for the direction taken by the post-Platonian Western metaphysics). *Pharmakon*, as it were, is 'the regular, ordered polysemy that has, through skewing, indetermination, or overdetermination, but without mistranslation, permitted the rendering of the same word by "remedy", "recipe", "poison", "drug", "filter" etc.' Because of this capacity, *pharmakon* is, first and foremost, powerful because ambivalent and ambivalent because powerful: 'It partakes of both good and ill, of the agreeable and disagreeable.'[2] *Pharmakon*, after all, 'is neither remedy nor poison, neither good nor evil, neither the inside nor the outside'. *Pharmakon* consumes and overrides opposition – the very possibility of opposition.

The *hymen*: a Greek word again, standing for both membrane and marriage, which for this reason signifies at the same time virginity – the

---

[1] Jacques Derrida, *Of Grammatology*, trans. Gayatri Chakravorty Spivak (Baltimore: Johns Hopkins University Press, 1974), p. 143.

[2] Jacques Derrida, *Disseminations*, trans. Barbara Johnson (London: Athlone Press, 1981), pp. 71, 99.

uncompromised and uncompromising difference between the 'inside' and the 'outside' – and its violation by the fusion of the self and other. In the result, *hymen* is 'neither confusion nor distinction, neither identity nor difference, neither consummation nor virginity, neither the veil nor the unveiling, neither the inside nor the outside, etc.'

The *supplement*: in French this word stands for both an addition, and a replacement. It is, therefore, the other who 'joins in', the outside that enters the inside, the difference that turns into identity. In the result, the *supplement* 'is neither a plus nor a minus, neither an outside nor the complement of an inside, neither accident nor essence, etc.'[3]

Undecidables are all *neither/nor*; which is to say that they militate against the *either/or*. Their underdetermination is their potency: because they are nothing, they may be all. They put paid to the ordering power of the opposition, and so to the ordering power of the narrators of the opposition. Oppositions enable knowledge and action; undecidables paralyse them. Undecidables brutally expose the artifice, the fragility, the sham of the most vital of separations. They bring the outside into the inside, and poison the comfort of order with suspicion of chaos.

This is exactly what the strangers do.

The horror of indetermination

Cognitive (classificatory) clarity is a reflection, an intellectual equivalent of behavioural certainty. They arrive and depart together. How closely they are tied together, we learn in a flash when landing in a foreign country, listening to a foreign language, gazing at foreign conduct. The hermeneutic problems which we then confront offer a first glimpse of the awesome behavioural paralysis which follows the failure of classificatory ability. To understand, as Wittgenstein suggested, is to know how to go on. This is why hermeneutic problems (which arise when the meaning is not unreflectively evident, when we become aware that words and meaning are not the same thing, that there is a *problem* of meaning) are experienced as annoying. Unresolved hermeneutical problems mean uncertainty as to how the situation ought to be read and what response is likely to bring the desired results. At best, uncertainty is confusing and felt as discomforting. At worst, it carries a sense of danger.

Much of the social organization can be interpreted as sedimentation of the systematic effort to reduce the frequency with which hermeneutical

---

[3] Jacques Derrida, *Positions*, trans. Aln Bass (University of Chicago Press, 1981), pp. 42–3.

problems are encountered and to mitigate the vexation such problems cause once faced. Probably the most common method of achieving this is that of the territorial and functional separation. Were this method applied in full and with maximum effect, hermeneutic problems would diminish as the physical distance shrinks and the scope and frequency of interaction grow. The chance of misunderstanding would not materialize, or would cause but a marginal disturbance when it occurs, if the principle of separation, the consistent 'restriction of interaction to sectors of assumed common understanding and mutual interest',[4] were meticulously observed.

The method of territorial and functional separation is deployed both outwardly and inwardly. Persons who need to cross into a territory where they are bound to cause and to encounter hermeneutic problems, seek enclaves marked for the use of visitors and the services of functional mediators. Tourist countries, which expect a constant influx of large quantities of 'culturally undertrained' visitors, set aside such enclaves and train such mediators in anticipation.

Territorial and functional separation is a reflection of existing hermeneutic problems; it is, however, also a most powerful factor in their perpetuation and reproduction. As long as the segregation remains continuous and closely guarded, there is little chance that the probability of misunderstanding (or at least the anticipation of such misunderstanding) will ever diminish. Persistence and constant possibility of hermeneutic problems can be seen therefore as simultaneously the motive and the product of boundary-drawing efforts. As such, they have an in-built tendency to self-perpetuation. As boundary-drawing is never foolproof and some boundary-crossing is difficult to avoid, hermeneutic problems are likely to persist as a permanent 'grey area' surrounding the familiar world of daily life. That grey area is inhabited by *unfamiliars*; by the not-yet classified, or – rather – classified by criteria similar to ours, but as yet unknown to us.

The 'unfamiliars' come in a number of kinds, of unequal consequence. One pole of the range is occupied by those who reside in *practically* remote (that is, rarely visited) lands, and are thereby limited in their role to the setting of limits of familiar territory (the *ubi leones*, written down as danger warnings on the outer boundaries of the Roman maps). Exchange with such unfamiliars (if it takes place at all) is set aside from the daily routine and from the normal web of interaction – as a function of a *special*

---

[4] Frederick Barth, *Ethnic Groups and Boundaries; The Social Organization of Cultural Difference* (Bergen: Universitet Ferlaget, 1969), p. 15.

category of people (say, commercial travellers, diplomats or ethnographers), or a *special occasion* for the rest. Both (territorial and functional) means of institutional separation easily protect – indeed, reinforce – the unfamiliarity of the unfamiliars, together with their daily irrelevance. They also guard, though obliquely, the secure homeliness of own territory. Contrary to a widespread opinion, the advent of television, this huge and easily accessible peephole through which the unfamiliar ways may be routinely glimpsed, has neither eliminated the institutional separation nor diminished its effectivity. One may say that McLuhan's 'global village' has failed to materialize. The frame of a cinema or TV screen staves off the danger of spillage even more effectively than tourist hotels and fenced-off camping sites; the one-sidedness of communication firmly locks the unfamiliars on the screen as, essentially, incommunicado. The most recent invention of 'thematic' shopping malls, with Carribean villages, Indian reserves and Polynesian shrines closely packed together under one roof, has brought the old technique of institutional separation to the level of perfection reached in the past only by the zoo.

The phenomenon of *strangerhood* cannot, however, be reduced to the generation of – however vexing – hermeneutic problems. Insolvency of the learned classification is upsetting enough, yet perceived as something less than a disaster as long as it can be referred to a missing knowledge. If only I learned that language; if only I cracked the mystery of those strange customs . . . By themselves, hermeneutic problems do not undermine the trust in knowledge and attainability of behavioural certainty. If anything, they reinforce both. The way in which they define the remedy as learning another *method of classification*, another set of oppositions, the meanings of another set of symptoms, only corroborates the faith in essential orderliness of the world and particularly in the ordering capacity of knowledge. A moderate dose of puzzlement is pleasurable precisely because it resolves in the comfort of reassurance (this, as any tourist knows, is a major part of the attraction held by foreign trips, the more exotic the better). The difference is something one can live with, as long as one believes that the different world is, like ours, a 'world with a key', an orderly world like ours; just another orderly world inhabited by *either* friends *or* enemies with no hybrids to distort the picture and perplex the action, and with rules and divisions one may not know as yet, but may learn if needed.

Some strangers are not, however, the *as-yet-undecided*; they are, in principle, *undecidables*. They are the premonition of that 'third element' which should not be. These are the true hybrids, the monsters – not just *unclassified*, but *unclassifiable*. They do not question just this one opposition here and now: they question oppositions as such, the very principle of the opposition, the plausibility of dichotomy it suggests and feasibility of separation it demands. They unmask the brittle artificiality of division. They destroy the world. They stretch the temporary inconvenience of 'not knowing how to go on' into a terminal paralysis. They must be tabooed, disarmed, suppressed, exiled physically or mentally – or the world may perish.

Territorial and functional separation cease to suffice once the mere *unfamiliar* turns to be the true *stranger*, aptly described by Simmel as 'the man who comes today and stays tomorrow'.[5] The stranger is, indeed, someone who refuses to remain confined to the 'far away' land or go away from our own and hence *a priori* defies the easy expedient of spatial or temporal segregation. The stranger comes into the life-world and settles here, and so – unlike the case of mere 'unfamiliars' – it becomes *relevant* whether he is a friend or a foe. He made his way into the life-world *uninvited*, thereby casting me on the receiving side of his initiative, making me into the object of action of which he is the subject: all this, as we remember, is a notorious mark of the *enemy*. Yet, unlike other, 'straightforward' enemies, he is not kept at a secure distance, nor on the other side of the battleline. Worse still, he claims a right to be an object of *responsibility* – the well-known attribute of the *friend*. If we press upon him the friend/enemy opposition, he would come out simultaneously under- and over-determined. And thus, by proxy, he would expose the failing of the opposition itself. He is a constant threat to the world's order.

Not for this reason only, though. There are more. For instance, the unforgettable and hence unforgivable original sin of the late entry: the fact that he had entered the realm of the life-world at a point of time which can be exactly pinpointed. He did not belong into the life-world 'initially', 'originally', 'from the very start', 'since time immemorial', and so he questions the extemporality of the life-world, brings into relief the 'mere historicality' of existence. The memory of the *event* of his coming makes of his very presence an event in history, rather than a fact of nature. His passage from the first to the second would infringe an important boundary on the map of existence, and thus must be resolutely resisted; such a passage would amount, after all, to the admission that nature is itself an event in history and that, therefore, the appeals to natural order or natural rights deserve no preferential treatment. Being an event in history, having a beginning, the presence of the stranger always carries the potential of an

---

[5] Georg Simmel, 'The Stranger' (1908), in *On Individuality and Social Forms* (Chicago: University of Chicago Press, 1971), p. 143. 'Der Fremde', wrote Robert Michels, 'ist der Repräsentant des Unbekannten.' ('Materialen zu einer Soziologie des Fremden', in *Jahrbuch für Soziologie*, 1925, p. 303.)

end. The stranger has a freedom to go. He may be also forced to go – or, at least, forcing him to go may be contemplated without violating the order of things. However protracted, the stay of the stranger is temporary – another infringement on the division which ought to be kept intact and preserved in the name of secure, orderly existence.

Even here, however, the treacherous incongruity of the stranger does not end. The stranger undermines the spatial ordering of the world – the fought-after co-ordination between moral and topographical closeness, the staying-together of friends and the remoteness of enemies. The stranger disturbs the resonance between physical and psychical distance: he is *physically close* while remaining *spiritually remote*. He brings into the inner circle of proximity the kind of difference and otherness that are anticipated and tolerated only at a distance – where they can be either dismissed as irrelevant or repelled as hostile. The stranger represents an incongruous and hence resented 'synthesis of nearness and remoteness'.[6] His presence is a challenge to the reliability of orthodox landmarks and the universal tools of order-making. His proximity (as all proximity, according to Levinas)[7] suggests a moral relationship, while his remoteness (as all remoteness, according to Erasmus)[8] permits solely a contractual one: another important opposition compromised.

As always, the practical incongruity follows the conceptual one. The stranger who refuses to go away gradually transforms his temporary abode into a home territory – all the more so as his other, 'original' home recedes in the past and perhaps vanishes altogether. On the other hand, however, he retains (if only in theory), his freedom to go, and so is able to view local conditions with an equanimity the native residents can hardly afford. Hence another incongruous synthesis – this time between involvement and indifference, partisanship and neutrality, detachment and participation. The commitment the stranger declares, the loyalty he promises, the dedication he demonstrates cannot be trusted: they come complete with a safety valve of easy escape which most natives often envy but seldom possess.

The stranger's unredeemable sin is, therefore, the incompatibility between his presence and other presences, fundamental to the world order; his simultaneous assault on several crucial oppositions instrumental in the incessant effort of ordering. It is this sin which throughout modern history

---

6 Simmel, 'The Stranger', p. 145.

7 Cf. Emmanuel Levinas, *Ethics and Infinity, Conversations with Phillippe Nemo*, trans. Richard A. Cohen (Pittsburgh: Duquesne University Press, 1982), pp. 95–101.

8 Cf. Charles J. Erasmus, *In Search of the Common Good* (New York: Free Press, 1974), pp. 74, 87.

rebounds in the constitution of the stranger as the bearer and embodiment of *incongruity*; indeed, the stranger is a person afflicted with incurable sickness of *multiple incongruity*. The stranger is, for this reason, the bane of modernity. He may well serve as the archetypal example of Sartre's *le visquex* or Mary Douglas's *the slimy* – an entity ineradicably *ambivalent*, sitting astride an embattled barricade (or, rather, a substance spilled over the top of it so that it makes it slippery both ways), blurring a boundary line vital to the construction of a particular social order or a particular life-world.

No binary classification deployed in the construction of order can fully overlap with essentially non-discrete, continuous experience of reality. The opposition, born of the horror of ambiguity, becomes the main source of ambivalence. The enforcement of any classification inevitably means the production of anomalies (that is, phenomena which are perceived as 'anomalous' only as far as they span the categories whose staying apart is the meaning of order). Thus 'any given culture must confront events which seem to defy its assumptions. It cannot ignore the anomalies which its scheme produces, except at risk of forfeiting confidence.'[9] There is hardly an anomaly more anomalous than the stranger. He stands *between* friend and enemy, order and chaos, the inside and the outside. He stands *for* the treacherousness of friends, for the cunning disguise of the enemies, for fallibility of order, vulnerability of the inside.

Fighting indeterminacy

Of pre-modern, small-scale communities, which for most of their members were the universes in which the whole of the life-world was inscribed, it is often said that they had been marked by *dense sociability*. This shared verdict is however variously interpreted. Most commonly, 'dense sociability' is *mis*interpreted as a Tönnies-style intimacy, spiritual resonance and disinterested co-operation; in other words, as *friendship* with no enmity, or with enmity suppressed. As we have already seen, however, friendship is not the only form of sociation; enmity performs the function as well. Indeed, friendship and enmity constitute together that framework *inside which* the sociation becomes possible and comes about. The 'dense sociability' of the past strikes us, in retrospect, as distinct from our own condition not because it contained more friendship than we tend to experience in our own world, but because its world was tightly and almost

[9] Cf. Mary Douglas, *Purity and Danger* (London: Routledge, 1966), p. 39.

completely filled with friends and enemies – and friends and enemies *only*. Little room, a marginal room if at all, was left in the life-world for the poorly defined *strangers*. Thus the semantic and behavioural problems that the friends/enemies opposition cannot but generate arose but seldom, and could in principle be dealt with quickly and efficiently in the duality of ways the opposition legitimized. The community effectively defended its dense sociability by promptly reclassifying the few strangers coming on occasion into its orbit as *either* friends *or* enemies. Ostensibly a temporary station, strangerhood did not present a serious challenge to the neat and solid duality of the world.

All supra-individual groupings are first and foremost sediments (or, rather, on-going processes) of *collectivization* of friends and enemies – of that co-ordination of the lines dividing friends from enemies that enables many individuals to share their friends and their enemies. More to the point, individuals who shared a common group or category of enemies might thereby treat each other as friends. For communities characterized by dense sociability, this was the whole story, or almost a whole story. And this could remain the whole story as long as the allocation of strangers into one of the two opposite categories of either friends or enemies was easy and within the community's power.

The last requirement is not, however, met under modern conditions. Such conditions are marked by the *divorce* between physical density and dense sociability. *Aliens* appear inside the confines of the life-world and *refuse to go away* (though one never stops hoping that they will – in the end . . .). This new situation does not stem necessarily from the increased restlessness and mobility. As a matter of fact, it is the new intense and feverish mobility itself which arises from the state-enforced 'uniformization' of vast spaces; of spaces much too large for being assimilated and domesticated by old methods of mapping and ordering deployed communally. The new aliens are not visitors, those stains of obscurity on the transparent surface of daily reality, which one can bear with as long as one hopes that they will be washed off tomorrow (though one can still be tempted to do this right away). They do not wear swords; nor do they seem to hide daggers in their cloaks (though one cannot be sure). They are not like the enemies one knows of. Or at least that is what they pretend. However, they are not like the friends either.

One meets friends at the other end of one's responsibility. One meets enemies (if at all) at the point of the sword. There is no clear rule about meeting the strangers. Intercourse with the strangers is always an incongruity. It stands for the incompatibility of the rules the confused status of the stranger invokes. It is best not to meet strangers at all. Now, if one cannot really bypass the space they occupy or share, the next best solution is a meeting which is not really a meeting, a meeting pretending not be one, a *mismeeting* (to borrow Buber's term; '*Vergegnung*', as distinct from meeting, *Begegnung*). The art of mismeeting is first and foremost a set of techniques that serve to *de-ethicalize* the relationship with the Other. Its overall effect is a denial of the stranger as a moral object and a moral subject. Or, rather, exclusion of such situations as can accord the stranger moral significance. This, however, is a poor substitute for the ideal condition perhaps lost, but at any rate now unattainable: one in which the opposition between friends and enemies is not challenged at all, and thus the integrity of the life-world can be sustained with the simple semantic and behavioural dichotomies operated matter-of-factly by community members.

Like all other self-perpetuating social groupings, past and future, territorial or non-territorial, the modern national states collectivize friends and enemies. In addition to this common function, however, they also perform a new function specific to them alone: they eliminate the strangers, or at least they attempt to. Nationalist ideology, says John Breuilly, 'is neither an expression of national identity (at least, there is no rational way of showing that to be the case) nor the arbitrary invention of nationalists for political purposes. It arises out of the need to make sense of complex social and political arrangements.'[10] What has to be made sense of in the first place, and thus become 'livable with', is a situation in which the traditional, tested dichotomy of friends and enemies cannot be applied matter-of-factly and has been therefore compromised – as a poor guide to the art of living. *The national state is designed primarily to deal with the problem of strangers, not enemies*. It is precisely this feature that sets it apart from other supra-individual social arrangements.

Unlike a tribe, the nation-state extends its rule over a *territory* before it claims the obedience of *people*. If the tribes can assure the needed collectivization of friends and enemies through the twin processes of attraction and repulsion, self-selection and self-segregation, territorial national states must enforce the friendship where it does not come about by itself. National states must *artificially* rectify the failures of nature (to create by design what nature failed to achieve by default). In the case of the national state, collectivization of friendship requires indoctrination and force; the artifice of legally construed reality; and mobilization of solidarity with an *imagined community* (the apt term proposed by Benedict Anderson), in order to universalize the cognitive/behavioural patterns associated with friendship inside the boundaries of the realm. The national state

[10] John Breuilly, *Nationalism and the State* (Manchester: Manchester University Press, 1982), p. 343.

redefines *friends* as *natives*; it commands to extend the rights ascribed 'to friends only' to all – the familiar as much as the unfamiliar – residents of the ruled territory. And vice versa, it grants the residential rights only if such an extension of friendship rights is desirable (though desirability is often disguised as 'feasibility'). This is why nationalism seeks the state. This is why the state spawns nationalism. This is why for the duration of the modern era, now two centuries old, nationalism without the state has been as flawed and ultimately impotent as state without nationalism – to the point of one being inconceivable without the other.

It has been stressed repeatedly in all analyses of modern states that they 'attempted to reduce or eliminate all loyalties and divisions within the country which might stand in the way of national unity'.[11] National states promote 'nativism' and construe its subjects as 'natives'. They laud and enforce the ethnic, religious, linguistic, cultural *homogeneity*. They are engaged in incessant propaganda of *shared* attitudes. They construct *joint* historical memories and do their best to discredit or suppress such stubborn memories as cannot be squeezed into shared tradition – now redefined, in the state-appropriate quasi-legal terms, as 'our common heritage'. They preach the sense of *common* mission, *common* fate, *common* destiny. They breed, or at least legitimize and give tacit support to, animosity towards everyone standing outside the holy union.[12] In other words, national states promote *uniformity*. Nationalism is a religion of friendship; the national state is the church which forces the prospective flock to practice the cult. The state-enforced homogeneity is the *practice* of nationalist *ideology*.

In Boyd C. Shafer's witty comment, 'patriots had to be made. Nature was credited with much by the eighteenth century, but it could not be trusted to develop men unassisted.' Nationalism was a programme of social engineering, and the national state was to be its factory. The national state was cast from the start in the role of a collective gardener, set about the task of cultivating sentiments and skills otherwise unlikely to grow. 'The new education', wrote Fichte in his *Addresses* of 1806,

> must consist essentially in this, that it completely destroys freedom of will in the soil which it undertake to cultivate, and produces, on the contrary, strict necessity in the decision of will, the opposite being impossible ... If you want to influence [man] at all, you must do more than merely talk to him; you

---

[11] Boyd C. Schafer, *Nationalism, Myth and Reality* (London: Gollancz, 1955), pp. 119, 121.

[12] Cf. Peter Alter, *Nationalism*, trans. Stuart McKinnon-Evans (London: Edward Arnold, 1989), p. 7ff.

> must fashion him, and fashion him, and fashion him in such a way that he simply cannot will otherwise than you wish him to will.[13]

While Rousseau advised the Polish king on the way to manufacture Poles (at a distance, the 'man as such' was better seen in his true quality of the national patriot):

> It is education that must give souls a national formation, and direct their opinions and tastes in such a way that they will be patriotic by inclination, by passion, by necessity. When first he opens his eyes, an infant ought to see the fatherland, and up to the day of his death he ought never to see anything else . . . At twenty, a Pole ought not to be a man of any other sort; he ought to be a Pole . . . The law ought to regulate the content, the order and the form of their studies. They ought to have only Poles for teachers.[14]

Were the national state able to reach its objective, there would be no strangers left in the life-world of the residents-turned-natives-turned-patriots. There would be but natives, who are friends, and the foreigners, who are current or potential enemies. The point is, however, that no attempt to assimilate, transform, acculturate or absorb the ethnic, religious, linguistic, cultural and other heterogeneity and dissolve it in the homogeneous body of the nation was, or indeed could be, unconditionally successful. More often than not, melting pots were either myths of failed projects. The strangers refused to split neatly into 'us' and 'them', friends and foes. Stubbornly and infuriatingly, they remained indeterminate – their numbers and nuisance power seem to grow with the intensity of dichotomizing efforts. It was as if the strangers were an 'industrial waste' growing in bulk with every increase in the production of friends and foes; a phenomenon brought into being by the very assimilatory pressure meant to destroy it. The point-blank assault on the strangers had to be from the start aided, reinforced and supplemented by a vast array of techniques meant to make a long-term, perhaps permanent, cohabitation with strangers possible. And it was.

Living with indeterminacy

The inventory of reactions to the stubborn presence of strangers can be glimpsed from the standard catalogue of responses to 'sliminess' as such. Most items in such a catalogue refer to the attempts to defuse the 'slimy' by

---

[13] Quoted after Elie Kedouri, *Nationalism* (London: Hutchinson, 1960), p. 83.

[14] Jean Jacques Rousseau, *Considerations on the Present of Poland* (London: Nelson, 1953), pp. 176–7.

depriving it of its 'sliminess'. All such attempts follow the logical yet implausible strategy of separating again what the anomaly, pregnant with semantic ambiguity, blends; and that of removing the resistant residue out of sight – either physically or spiritually.

The prime choice is, of course, a radical cutting through the tangle of incongruencies by forcing the stranger to leave; to re-establish original order through bringing together, so to speak, personal and spatial estrangement. This most consistent of measures, however, is not always feasible – the absence of a 'natural abode' of the stranger in question being an extreme case. The stranger who is not just *out of place* but in addition *homeless* in the absolute sense, may become a tempting object of genocide. (In the pungent summary of Cynthia Ozick: 'The German Final Solution was an aesthetic solution; it was a job of editing, it was the artist's finger removing a smudge, it simply annihilated what was considered not harmonious.'[15]) Short of such a radical solution, one may dump the anomaly into one of the numerous variants of *Naartürmer* or *Naarshiffen*[16] – and thus achieve congruence between inherently incongruous 'exterritorial territory' and equally incongruous 'translocal locals'. Tribal reserves, native homelands and ethnic ghettos are most notorious among such variants.

If radical or nearly-radical solutions are either non-feasible or inconvenient, a cultural fence comes to the rescue as a second-best expedient. If the stranger cannot be made non-existent, he can at least be made untouchable. Social intercourse with the stranger may be severely reduced, and whatever communication remains is permitted be surrounded with a cumbersome ritual whose main function is to push the stranger outside the realm of the ordinary and to disarm him as the possible source of normative influence. (The 'the stranger has his own strange ways, let him keep them but remember that they fit only him and do not suit us, normal people' type of solution.) Strict prohibitions of *connubium*, *commercium* and *commensality* are the most common methods of cultural isolation and limitation of contact. Applied singly or in combination, they set the stranger as the Other and protect the ambiguity of his status from polluting the clarity of native identity. Cultural exclusion of the stranger, his construction as a *permanent* Other, outside the 'normal' divisions and categories, 'implies a recognition of limitations on shared understandings, differences in criteria for judgment of value and performance, and a restriction of interaction to sectors of assumed common understanding

---

[15] Cynthia Ozick, *Art and Ardour* (New York: Dutton, 1984), p. 165.

[16] Cf. Michel Foucault, *Madness and Civilization: A History of Insanity in the Age of Reason* (London: Tavistock, 1967), pp. 7–13.

and mutual interest'. Constraints are imposed 'on the kinds of roles an individual is allowed to play, and the partners he may choose for different kinds of transactions'.[17]

Keeping the stranger at a mental distance through 'locking him up' in a shell of exoticism does not, however, suffice to neutralize his inherent, and dangerous, incongruity. After all, he stays around. A moment of inattention, and the intercourse may well spill over the permitted limits. Thus the strangers remain the permanent 'slimy', always threatening to wash out the boundaries vital to native identity. The danger must be signalled, the natives must be warned and kept on the alert lest they should succumb to the temptation of compromising the separate ways that make them what they are. This can be attained by discrediting the stranger; by representing the outward, visible and easy to spot traits (*diacritica*, in Frederik Barth's terms) of the stranger as signs of concealed, yet for this reason even more abominable and dangerous, qualities. This is the social institution of *stigma*, brought two decades ago into the focus of social analysis by Erving Goffman.

In its original meaning 'stigma' stood for the bodily signs that signalled inferiority of character or moral wickedness. The concept can be applied more widely to all cases when an observable – documented and indisputable – feature of a certain category of persons is first made salient by being brought into public attention, and then interpreted as a visible sign of a hidden flaw, iniquity or moral turpitude. An otherwise innocuous trait becomes a blemish, a sign of affliction, a cause of shame. The person bearing this trait is easily recognizable as less desirable, inferior, bad and dangerous. Partners are put on the alert and forewarned of the possibly sinister consequences of carefree interaction. They are also armed with the information about the *virtual social identity* of the members of the stigmatized category; an identity difficult to be subsequently disproved, however hard the stigmatized try to assert the *actual identity* they defined.[18]

Stigma seems to be a convenient weapon in the defence against the unwelcome ambiguity of the stranger. The essence of stigma is to emphasize the difference; and a difference which is in principle beyond repair, and hence justifies a permanent exclusion. Indeed, such outward signs of an allegedly morbid interior are usually selected as do not give up easily to human cosmetic skills. In the modern world, with its belief in the omnipotence of culture and education (man is 'merely what education

---

[17] Barth, *Ethnic Groups and Boundaries*, pp. 15, 17.

[18] Erving Goffman, *Stigma: Notes on the Management of Spoiled Identity* (Harmondsworth: Penguin, 1968), p. 12.

makes of him' – Kant asserted confidently; 'l'éducation peut tout' – confirmed Helvétius), with its constant exhortations to self-improvement, and the axiom of the individual responsibility for self-construction – stigma remains one of those few residues of 'nature' which the redesigning and engineering zeal exempts from interference and leaves in their reputedly virgin state. Stigma draws the limit of the transforming capacity of culture. The outward signs may be masked, but cannot be eradicated. The bond between signs and inner truth may be denied, but cannot be broken.

Armed with such qualities, the institution of stigma is eminently fit for the task of immobilizing the stranger in his identity of the excluded Other. Were the stranger merely an 'uneducated' person, as yet untrained in local habits and not properly adapted to native conditions, the practical threat inherent in his 'multiple incongruity' would leave the native defenceless. More dangerously still, the inherent brittleness of *all* identity, including that of the native, will be blatantly exposed. An identity that anyone can *acquire* through diligence and effort is an identity which can also be *shed* at will. Such a 'put on, take off' identity is, however, much too weak a foundation to sustain the secure existence ('integrity') of the group. The acceptance of the 'merely cultural' (i.e., man-made, manipulable and rectifiable) roots of the stranger's idiosyncrasy means in practice the renunciation by the group of its passport- and visa-issuing authority and of its right to control the border traffic. And an unguarded border is, for all practical purposes, a contradiction in terms. Stigma staves off (or at least it promises to stave off) all such dangers. Stigma is a cultural product which proclaims a limit to the potency of culture. In stigma, culture draws a boundary to the territory which it considers as its task to cultivate, and circumscribes an area which *must* and *should* lie fallow.

Since the signs of the stigma are essentially irremovable, a category may cease to be stigmatized only if the signifier of stigma is reinterpreted as innocuous or neutral, or if it is completely denied semantic significance and thus made socially invisible. In modern society there is a constant pressure to do exactly this. The pressure cannot be easily neutralized. It comes from attributes quite central to, and constitutive of modern society, like the principle of equality of opportunity, freedom of self-constitution, responsibility of the individual for his own fate – and may not be effectively countermanded without contradiction and without generating new incongruities. After all, modernity is a rebellion against fate and ascription, in the name of the omnipotence of design and achievement. Stigma cannot but be a thorn in its flesh; it restores dignity to the fate and casts a shadow on the promise of limitless perfectibility. It is, therefore, at odds with everything modernity stands for and everything that modern society must believe in in order to reproduce its existence in the only shape it knows of and is trained to cultivate.

On the other hand, however, the principle of self-constitution, if pursued to its logical consequences, clashes with the authority of the national state to set apart legitimate from illegitimate responsibilities, legitimate from illegitimate hostilities; to draw the boundaries of the community of friends and chart the location of the enemies. These functions of the nation-state, known under the name of 'nation building' (that specifically modern variety of the task of constructing collective identity which every human grouping confronts), reach in modern conditions a gravity which few if any functions faced before. Collective identities, which once upon a time were 'given' unproblematically, 'naturally' and matter-of-factly, must now, so to speak, be artificially produced. This makes them more than ever precarious, an object of close attention of the designing–engineering–gardening modern powers.[19] There is, therefore, a genuine contradiction in the heart of modernity. There seems to be no possibility of satisfying both, equally pressing, needs at the same time. Beyond a certain point, the means deployed to meet one of the needs detract from the probability that the other need might ever be fulfilled.

In modern society, stigma is located in the very centre of the above contradiction. In an important sense, stigma is blatantly at odds with the outspoken principles instrumental in the reproduction of modern life; for this reason, the very institution of stigma is illegitimate and in many cases forced into underground existence and practised but surreptitiously and on the sly. At the same time it is practically indispensable. And so there is a paradoxical symmetry between the situation of the stigma and of the categories it stigmatizes. Both live under attack, both must hide their true identity and seek deceitful legitimations. Both work under conditions which make their actions self-defeating, or at least sharply limit their effectivity.

The liberal call to assimilate, arguably the most specifically, authentically modern of the nation-state policies, suffers from similar tensions reflecting one of the central contradictions of modernity. On the face of it, the liberal message of cultural assimilation sounds a death knell to stigma, as its saps the strongest of its foundations – the ascriptive nature of inferiority. The message amounts to a standing invitation to all and everybody to take their fate in their own hands and make it as good as they can. It proclaims the universal right to claim and attain the highest, worthiest and hence most

[19] More on this topic in Zygmunt Bauman, *Legislators and Interpreters* (Cambridge: Polity Press, 1987), chap. 4.

coveted values. It offers not just hope but a clear recipe of its realization: the best values, in the charmingly circular formulation of John Stuart Mill, are those recognized and practised by the best people. On a closer scrutiny, an inner contradiction is, however, revealed. The contradiction renders the offer as misleading (and in the end frustrating) as it is tempting. But it is a contradiction which the nation-state, set on the awesome task of 'homogenizing' the territory it rules and thereby legitimizing its claim to ascendancy, can ill afford to abandon – as the offer of assimilation (assimilation is always a one-directional process) obliquely reaffirms what was to be proved – the superiority and the benevolence of the native rulers.[20]

In no other field is the inner contradiction of the 'liberal solution' to the problem of heterogeneity more clearly visible than in the thrust to 'assimilate' the ethnic, religious or – more generally – *cultural* strangers. Determinants of 'strangeness' are in these cases eminently pliable; man-made, they can be in principle man-unmade. They can be also unmade (by definition of the 'merely cultural', as distinct from economic, political or, indeed, *social*) with the least expenditure of such resources which may be scarce or unavailable for reasons of someone else's monopoly: the unmaking calls only for a change in orientation, a shift in communal commitment, an honest effort of self-cultivation and self-refinement, or religious conversion – all things evidently within the individual's power. This is why the field under discussion provides the most obvious testing ground for

---

[20] To be effective as legitimation, the liberal programme in all its forms (and these include the idea of acculturation as a guarantee of membership rights) must insist that the values possessed by the superior people it calls to emulate are indeed universally available, and hence their possession is evidence of the superiority of those who possess them. In the unlikely case, however, of the offer having been taken up on a massive scale and successfully, the very superiority which it was meant to prove in the first place will have been washed away. One may say that liberalism can launch its offer without fear only because a great number of successful applicants is most unlikely (and thus the deception which the offer entails is unlikely to be exposed); or, to look at it from the other side, liberalism may preach this offer so confidently only because it believes that taking up the offer is much too tall an order for most of the 'less than best' people. The most important function of hope this offer nourishes is the possibility of 'blaming the victim': if you find yourself stuck to the bottom, you have no one but yourself to blame. And if you blame yourself, the odds are that you'll stay clear of mischief, while at the same time adding to the glory of the dominant values as elusive as they are, so you believe, omnipotent. And if you refuse to admit your guilt or ineptitude, reverting to stigma would be a most sensible, and hence most probable, response. It seems that, paradoxically, liberalism may use the declaration of war on stigma as a legitimizing device only if it expects the war not be fought of a total scale; and, if fought, never to be won.

the liberal programme, and the site where this programme (though not necessarily the intention which gave it birth) most commonly meets its defeat.

Ethnic-religious-cultural strangers are all too often tempted to embrace the liberal vision of group emancipation (erasing of a collective stigma) as a reward for individual efforts of self-improvement and self-transformation. Frequently they go out of their way to get rid of and to suppress everything which makes them distinct from the rightful members of the native community – and hope that a devoted emulation of native ways will render them indistinguishable from the hosts, and by the same token guarantee their reclassification as insiders, entitled to the treatment the friends routinely receive. The harder they try, however, the faster the finishing-line seems to be receding. When, at last, it seems to be within their grasp, a dagger of racism is flung from beneath the liberal cloak. The rules of the game are changed with little warning. Or, rather, only now the earnestly 'self-refining' strangers discover that what they mistook for a game of emancipation was in fact the game of domination.

Sander Gilman wrote of the 'conservative curse' which hangs over the liberal project: 'The more you are like me, the more I know the true value of my power, which you wish to share, and the more I am aware that you are but a shoddy conterfeit, an outsider.'[21] And Geoff Dench, the author of a most penetrating analysis of the strategies applied in the unequal struggle of emancipation, has the following advice to offer to the strangers about to fall into the trap of the liberal promise: 'By all means declare a belief in future justice and equality. This is part of the role. But do not expect it to materialize.'[22] The meaning of the liberal offer in general, and the 'cultural assimilation' programme in particular, is the affirmation of the dominance of that site in the society from which the offer has been made. To take the offer at its face value (and worse still, to act on it) means to expose that meaning.

Indeed, to define the problem of 'de-estrangement', of the *domestication* of the stranger, as the question of decency and industry of the stranger's effort at assimilation-through-acculturation, is to reaffirm the inferiority, undesirability and out-of-placeness of the strangers's form of life; to proclaim the stranger's original state is a stain that has to be washed off; to accept that the stranger is congenitally guilty and that it is up to him to expiate and prove his entitlement to absolution. His guilt is beyond

---

21 Sander L. Gilman, *Jewish Self-Hatred: Antisemitism and the Hidden Language of the Jews* (Baltimore: Johns Hopkins University Press, 1986), p. 2.

22 Geoff Dench, *Minorities in the Open Society: Prisoners of Ambivalence* (London: Routledge, 1986), p. 259.

dispute; it is the irreversibility of the removal of such attributes as constitute the guilt that he must now prove. The stranger must demonstrate the absence of old abomination. Worse still, to make his demonstration really convincing, he must, magically, force it in retrospect *never to exist in the past*. Displaying the presence of new rectitude will not suffice. The stranger cannot cease to be a stranger. ('I used to be a Jew,' said an assimilated hero of a Jewish joke. 'Oh, yes,' replied his partner, 'I know the feeling. I used to be a hunchback.') The best he can be is a *former stranger*, 'a friend on approval' and permanently on trial, a person vigilantly watched and constantly under pressure to be someone else than he is, told to be ashamed of his guilt of not being what he ought to be.

To prove an absence of a trait is an endemically inconclusive task (to unmake the past is downright impossible). The effort is unlikely ever to end. Even less likely is the attainment of a status in which no suspicion can be raised and no doubt voiced that the rehabilitation, however spectacular, is still incomplete, superficial or a sham. After all, what the 'cultural strangers' are called to attain through self-refinement is ultimately the elimination of their origin (even the origin of their distant ancestors).

This is the ultimate limit to the domestication-through-acculturation, but not its only difficulty. Acquisition of native culture is a thoroughly *individual* affair, while the production of 'cultural strangeness' is always *aimed at a collective*.[23] From the perspective of the native majority, 'all strangers are the same'. (As Simmel observed, in societies where taxes for the natives were differentiated according to wealth and status, the 'Jew tax' was the same for every member of the community.) The individuality of the stranger is dissolved in the category. It is the category, not its individual members, which is set and seen as the genuine, supra-personal carrier of that cultural difference which defies an unambiguous distinction between a friend and an enemy. The genuine *pars pro toto*, the individual stranger is cast metonymically as a microcosm of the category at large. He carries, so to speak, his category on his shoulders. He is unlikely to shed this burden as long as the category itself remains alive. Indeed, the person attempting to escape the stigma of the stranger alone, by individual effort, soon finds himself caught in a double bind. 'If the most able and successful members of the minority are morally tied to the least successful, participation in competitive areas of social life becomes for them something of a three-legged race.'[24] If they wash their hands and refuse all truck with

---

[23] Cf. Zygmunt Bauman, 'Exit Visas and Entry Tickets', *Telos*, No. 77 (Fall 1988), pp. 45–77.

[24] Dench, *Minorities in the Open Society*, p. 127.

'cultural inferiors' socially defined as their brethren, they invite accusations of the neglect of duty and, indeed, of complicity in the perpetuation of the collective guilt. If they devote their efforts to the arduous job of lifting the brethren from their misery and act as the agents of their collective elevation, this is immediately taken as a proof (if one was needed) of their continuous membership of the selfsame category of strangers from which they tried to escape. The continuing existence of the category of strangers is used as an argument against the authenticity of individual conversion. But so is any individual attempt to assist the emancipation of the category as a whole. If you do something, you lose. If you do nothing, they win.

Shifting the burden

As has been frequently observed, once caught in this quandary (offered the bait of social promotion and ultimately acceptance, yet at the price of admitting first one's own inferiority – the admission that the high-minded authors of the offer would never forget), the individual victims of the liberalist temptation tend to develop self-hatred – a powerful, creative–destructive sentiment, better captured by Norman Cohn's concept of *inner demons*. The torment caused by inner demons often turns into aggression against the category of origin – which serves as their prototype and is perceived as their embodiment. But it also leads to the queasy aversion to one's own self, as something incurably infested with a bacillus of an incapacitating and shameful disease.

The notorious restlessness of the stranger cast in the position of ambivalence which he has not chosen and over which he has no control (a restlessness that has been every so often construed by native opinion as evidence of an erratic, neurotic personality and promptly ascribed to the innate deficiency of the stranger's tribe), is thereby socially produced. It may serve as a textbook case of a self-fulfilling prophecy. It is not the outcome of cultural difference, but an affliction caused by an attempt to efface it: an endemic malady of the assimilatory pressure and of the unrealistic dreams of reclassification, admission and acceptance. One may conclude that defining the strangeness as a *cultural* phenomenon is the starting point of a process which leads relentlessly to the 'revelation' that ambivalence cannot be wished out of existence, that strangeness has foundations much more solid and much less manipulable than 'merely cultural', transitory and man-made differences in style of life and beliefs. The more successful the practice of cultural assimilation – the quicker this 'truth' will be 'discovered', as the increasingly stubborn incongruity of the culturally assimilating stranger is itself an artefact of his assimilation. The inherent *impossibility* of implementing the 'self-refinement' programme is then construed as the strangers' ineptitude or malevolence, *inability* or *unwillingness* to self-refine. In the wake of the eye-opening defeat of the programme of cultural assimilation, it is the idea of natural fate of the race that comes into favour.

3

The Self-construction of Ambivalence

The burden to resolve ambivalence falls, ultimately, on the person cast in the ambivalent condition. Even if the phenomenon of strangerhood is socially structured, the assumption of the status of stranger, with all its attendant ambiguity, with all its burdensome over- and under-definition, carries attributes which in the end are constructed, sustained and deployed with the active participation of their carriers: in the psychical process of self-constitution. Like all other roles (perhaps even slightly more than other roles), the role of the stranger needs learning, acquisition of knowledge and practical skills.

Being a stranger means, first and foremost, that nothing is *natural*; nothing is given of right, nothing comes free. The native's primeval union between the self and the world has been sundered. Each side of the union has been brought into focus of attention – as a *problem*, and a *task*. Both the self and the world are clearly visible. Both call for constant examination and both urgently need to be 'operated on', 'handled', *managed*. In all these respects the stranger's stance differs drastically from the native way of life, with far-reaching consequences.

The concept of a *clean slate*, of infinite pliability and self-pliability of humans, once favourite among educationalists and cultural missionaries, could well be patched together out of the strangers' experience. After all, it poorly reflects the condition of the 'native', born as he is 'into' the community and growing inside it without much challenge from the outside. His is the state of 'being situated' or 'tuned' (Heidegger), which can feed nothing but the *relativ-natürliche Weltanschauung* (Max Scheler): that is, a natural propensity to view the conditions otherwise circumscribed, confined to this place here and this time now, as 'natural' and thus beyond discussion. Being a native member of any community of meanings is tantamount to being supplied with guaranteed, 'objective' criteria of relevance, and a 'graduated knowledge' (Alfred Schütz) which ranges from shallow to deep, depending on the relevance of its objects – but is also fraught with deep holes of ignorance, often only thinly covered with a tapestry of 'taken for granteds'.[1] The fact that such knowledge may seem incoherent and inconsistent to a logician, or indeed to any *stranger* not 'tuned in', or tuned imperfectly – is neither here nor there. The only thing which truly counts is that it 'takes on for the members of the in-group the appearance of a *sufficient* coherence, clarity and consistency to give anybody a reasonable chance of understanding and of being understood'. (Note that this is a *stranger*, sociologist and refugee Alfred Schütz, who speaks here of *appearance*.) It is thanks to this limited yet crucial sufficiency that 'For those who have grown up within the cultural pattern, not only the recipes and their possible efficiency but also the typical and anonymous attitudes required by them are an unquestioned "matter of course" which gives them both security and assurance.'[2] Security and assurance is something one can ill afford to surrender lightly. To the extent in which they depend on the 'matter-of-fact' posture, one would expect the in-group members to defend jealously the non-negotiable, immutable, indeed absolute character of their world-view constructed of the shared graduated knowledge. As long as they do defend it with success, they remain effectively inoculated against the horrors of ambivalent existence.

The existential situation of the stranger is radically different. He is denied the luxury of smugness or self-oblivion. His is an opaque, not a transparent existence. The stranger is his own problem. His identity has been delegitimized; its determining, 'tuning' power has been declared as criminal at worst and demeaning at best. This is not, however, the end of the stranger's trouble. The peculiarity of the stranger's situation *vis-à-vis* the natives is not confined to the condition of *not* being 'tuned' the right way, and to the resulting absence of relevant knowledge and skills. It cannot be removed simply by the process of learning and self-training. Such a process is bound to be self-defeating. The same knowledge which serves so adequately the life functions of the natives may well prove useless to the strangers even if (and particularly if) conscientiously absorbed and assimilated. Despite the appearance to the contrary, it is not the failure to acquire native knowledge which constitutes the outsider as a stranger, but the *incongruent existential constitution* of the stranger, as being neither 'inside' nor 'outside', neither 'friend' nor 'enemy', neither *included* nor *excluded*, which makes the native knowledge

[1] Alfred Schütz, *Collected Papers*, vol. 1 (The Hague: Martinus Nijhof, 1967), pp. 9–12.

[2] Schütz, *Collected Papers*, vol. 2, pp. 95, 102.

unassimilable.[3] All the essential determinants of the stranger's plight lie beyond the reach of everything the stranger himself may do. The stranger's incongruence is born in the Procrustean bed of the binary opposition – the only hospitality the *relativ-natürliche Weltanschauung* of the natives can offer to the ambivalent world.

The first reason which renders the escape from strangerhood impossible is exactly the 'naturalness' of the native state. One is either 'situated' or not, either 'tuned' or not. The whole point of 'being tuned' is that it allows only one alternative state, or, rather, collapses all conceivable alternatives into one, and through that absolutizes its own condition. One stays 'being tuned' only as long as this one condition has no history – has not been brought into being or made up. One cannot 'situate oneself' or 'tune oneself in'. Or, rather, the very fact that 'situating' and 'tuning' are *performances* and not *fates*, deprives them of exactly this 'naturalness' which makes them what they are and effective as they are. The idea of 'self-tuning' is, for all practical intents and purposes, an oxymoron. The condition of 'being situated' or 'tuned' persists only as long as it is not brought into the focus of attention and does not become an object of manipulation (that is, remains fully under the spell of Heidegger's *das Man*, Sartre's *l'on*). Yet this – attending to and manipulating – is precisely what the stranger is forced to do, or – wilfully or obligingly – attempts to do. Either he is a newcomer to the group in a literal sense, and then what seems obvious to the natives looks hardly obvious to him, and what the natives do not give any thought to turns into a target of intense reflection for him; or the lifting of the 'graduated knowledge' from the grey area of 'evidencies' to the level of self-awareness is performed for the stranger by the native group itself, as they question his natural right to partake of what the in-group members are simply and with-no-questions-asked 'in'. Because of his ignorance, or because of the knowledge which has been forced upon him, the stranger cannot but call into question most of the things that the natives consider, or unthinkingly take as unquestionable. He has been defined *a priori* as a challenge to the clarity of the world and thus to the authority of reason. Now the *a priori* definition is confirmed by

---

[3] Let us observe that the very constitution of the host population as 'the natives' – one conceivable only in as far as there is a vantage point which is *not native* – already reveals the corroding, relativizing gaze of the stranger. Obliquely, it reinforces the strangerhood of the latter. The stranger confirms the dominant definition of himself by the sheer acceptance of the other model as 'native', and so a model wielding authority to define the rules of the behavioural game and the meaning of properly human existence.

his action. His gaze solidifies, renders tangible the mode of life which is effective only in as far as it stays transparent, invisible, uncodified.

Another reason reaches deeper still. The stranger cannot adopt the native culture as it stands without first attempting to revise some of its precepts; perhaps even such among the precepts as are crucial for the native state of security and self-assurance. The native culture defines him and sets him apart as a miscreant – 'neither friend nor foe'; as that ambivalent inside/outside which sets the limit of the life-world's order. The stranger is assigned no status inside the cultural realm he wants to make his own. His entry will therefore signify a violation of the culture he enters. By the act of his entry, real or merely intended, the life-world of the natives that used to be a secure shelter is turned into a contested ground, insecure and problematic. By the same token, the very good will of the stranger turns against him; his effort to assimilate sets him further apart, bringing his strangeness into fuller than ever relief and supplying the proof of the threat it contains.

Exclusion into objectivity

One cannot knock on a door unless one is outside; and it is the act of knocking on the door which alerts the residents to the fact that one who knocks is indeed outside. 'Being outside' casts the stranger in the position of *objectivity*: his is an outside, detached and autonomous vantage-point from which the insiders (complete with their world-view, including their map of friends and enemies) may be looked upon, scrutinized and censored. The very awareness of such an outside point of view (a point of view epitomized by the stranger's status) makes the natives feel uncomfortable, insecure in their home ways and truths. Besides, entry is always a passage, a changing of statuses – and this mysterious event of avatar more than anything else puts the 'yesterday's stranger – prospective native' in conflict with the world he wishes to enter, a world which draws its confidence (and its attraction for the stranger in the first place) from the assumption that no one is ever transformed, no one moves and no one ever finds himself outside. The episode of entry brands the 'former stranger' forever – as a *changeling*, a person who can pick and choose, who has the freedom which the 'just so natives' do not possess, whose status can never have the same degree of solidity, finality and irreversibility as that of the natives. The loyalty which is simply taken for granted in the case of the natives (and then understood not as decision to be loyal, but as commonality of fate), calls for suspicious and vigilant scrutiny in the case of yesterday's stranger; and forever so, as his commitment has been compromised from the start and beyond the hope of redemption by the original sin of being freely chosen. Whatever has been chosen may be renounced. The loyalty of the stranger will always remain doubtful. The very zeal with which he identifies with the new home sets him apart. His insistence on being at home is taken down as admission of guilt.

The *objectivistic* (rootless, cosmopolitan or downright alien) bias of the stranger is the most serious of charges the native community holds against him. Indeed, it is through this grievance that the native form of life may best sustain and reproduce its own *naturalness*, its inwardness, its self-centredness – all the most solid pillars of its identity. In the native world-view, the essence of the stranger is homelessness. Unlike an alien or a foreigner, the stranger is not simply a newcomer, a person temporarily out of place. He is an *eternal wanderer*, homeless always and everywhere, without hope of ever 'arriving'. The 'objectivity' (cosmopolitanism, antipatriotism, non-commitment, 'turncoatism') of his view consists precisely in his inability to make a distinction between the stations of his unstoppable pilgrimage: as far as he is concerned, all of them are just sites, confined in space, bound to become the past in the future. Passed by, and sooner or later left behind, they all look to him alike: they are all identical in their *negativity*, as none of them is a home. ('We have been good Germans in Germany and therefore we shall be good Frenchmen in France.' Hannah Arendt remembers this declaration of a refugee who just crossed the Rhine, escaping Hitler. He was earnestly applauded by his fellows in fate. No one laughed, Arendt comments.)

The natives may view the freedom they impute to the stranger with genuine horror, with a jaundiced eye, or (most commonly) with a mixture of both. To the stranger himself, however, freedom appears first of all as acute uncertainty. Unmitigated by at least a part-time availability of safe harbour, it tends to be experienced as a curse rather than a blessing. Freedom in the unalloyed state is lived as loneliness, and as a chronic condition is virtually unbearable. In the extreme case it verges on madness – but even in mild versions it tends to be medicalized as a mental problem. (Compare, for instance, Sander L. Gilman's penetrating study of the history of *neurasthenia* – a psychiatric concept which in the late nineteenth century integrated, as one disease-unit, the heightened restlessness, frantic self-criticism and obsession with success and social acceptance, observed or anticipated among various categories of people – all poorly defined in terms of the accepted social categories or weakly anchored in the existing social divisions.)[4] In each case, it is a state in which its occupier would not wish to remain permanently. Not of his own will, anyway.

---

[4] Sander L. Gilman, *Difference and Pathology: Stereotypes of Sexuality, Race and Madness* (Ithaca, Cornell University Press, 1985), pp. 129–30, 162, 214–5.

It is mainly for this reason that – despite all its inner incongruence – the offer of 'turning native' through the adoption of native culture, of assimilation, seems to the stranger such an alluring proposition. It promises what the stranger misses most – an unambiguous placement, safe harbour, home. The missing magnifies the attractions of what is missed. One would therefore expect from the stranger a degree of earnestness, commitment and emotional identification seldom to be found among the natives. One would also expect a tendency to proclaim the aspired-to identity loudly and publicly. One would anticipate the praise of the symbols and the articles of faith of the aspired-to community to be lavish and flowery. All this follows naturally from a need to convince the audience of having *acquired* a quality which other people – simultaneously viewers and actors – *possess* of right. But to those other people – the 'natives' – all this may seem excessive, 'in bad taste', ludicrous or duplicitous. In each case, what they see will tend to disprove the very point that the stranger zealously tried to prove.

The strategy that follows the assimilatory offer has therefore its intrinsic limits, like the offer itself. More often than not, it is self-defeating; if anything, it renders the strangeness of the stranger yet more obtrusive and vexing. Unfailingly, it reveals this strangeness as irredeemable – the quality which the promise of assimilation attempted to hide. The stranger had been promised that full 'domestication' would follow cultural reform; that refinement of manners, correct and etiquette-conscious public demeanour, careful avoidance of everything even remotely alien-sounding would suffice as the membership tickets to the exclusive club of native trend-setters. The bluff of this promise is called the moment it has been taken seriously and matched with a behaviour it ostensibly required. The real obstacles guarding the entry are now revealed. They prove to be economic, political and above all social – and none of them is likely to be as malleable, as amenable to subjective intention as the 'merely cultural' obstacles pretended to be. It becomes apparent that social divisions are neither caused, nor sustained by the differences in the degree of civility and cultural polish; that the deceit of the etiquette consists precisely in the tacit acceptance, by those who gain and those who lose alike, of the injunction to hide and the prohibition to reveal the true grounds of distinction and privilege. At the same time, when the grounds of inequality are exposed as tough and inflexible, their favourite defences are exposed as sham. No wonder that acting on the offer of acculturation tends to trigger the defensive reactions of the native community, ranging all the way from the reintroduction of ascriptive criteria of difference (albeit in a modern, 'rational', racist garb), through the medicalization of the otherness as such, and up to the annihilation of the obstreperous residue of difference by eviction or destruction of the stranger.

If recourse to racism seems to be the natural way of salvaging the *objective* of 'assimilation programme' in the wake of the bankruptcy of its ostensible *means*, so the retreat into 'strangerhood' as a substitute home of rootedness and confidence seems to be an equally natural way of salvaging the *purpose* of the cultural self-adaptation once the *vehicle* offered by the programme have proved ineffective.

Hardly ever was a programme of such a retreat so blatantly spelled out as in the work of Russian-Jewish philosopher Lev Shestov, in his later life a professor at the Sorbonne and one of the pillars of religious existentialism. Branded with the stigma of a despised and resented minority, yet excelling in the very activity which the despising and resenting majority brandished as the sign of its superiority and excellence, having passed with flying colours all the entrance examinations and yet been refused entry to the academic world that defined itself as the guardian of the absolute, universal values and hence alien to all parochial difference, Shestov[5] responded with a frontal assault against what was (as he set about to prove) an incurable *parochiality* of the very search for the *absolute* in general, and for the absolutely superior values in particular. The philosophers' search for the ultimate system, for complete order, for the extirpation of everything unknown and unruly – he declared – stems from the worship of firm soil and a secure home, and results in trimming down the infinite human potential. Such a search for the universal cannot but degenerate into a ruthless clamp-down on human possibilities. 'The solid ground sooner or later escapes from beneath man's feet, yet man continues to live without ground or with but a shaky ground under his feet, and then he stops counting the axioms as truths and instead calls them lies.' The bitter experience of a stranger chased away from the door at which he knocked comes out but thinly veiled from Shestov's own philosophical programme:

> The settled man says: 'How can one live without certainty about the day to come, how can one sleep without a roof over his head!' But an accident threw him out of his home forever, and he spends his nights in the woods. He cannot sleep: he is afraid of wild animals, of his own brother the vagabond. In the end, however, he entrusts his life to contingency, starts living the vagabond's life and even, perhaps, sleeps quietly at night.

---

[5] Lev Shestov, *Apofeosis bespochvennosti: Opyt adogmaticheskogo myshleniya* [Apotheosis of Rootlessness: An Essay in non-Dogmatic Thought] (Paris, YMCA Press, 1971), pp. 27, 32, 41, 49.

The task of philosophy, in sharp contrast to the entire philosophical tradition, is 'to teach men to live in uncertainty'; 'not to calm down, but to disturb'. 'Everywhere and with every step, on each or without any occasion, with or without reason, it is necessary to ridicule the most firmly accepted judgements and to state paradoxes. And then – one will see what happens.'

In an early display of the 'Black is beautiful' posture, Shestov does not deny the valour of all these things which the dominant thought made into the symbols of superiority. Philosophical orthodoxy stands accused of failing to deliver on its promise, of scoring miserably by its own standards. The promise and the standards are not questioned; on the contrary, Shestov insists that only his way of doing philosophy may do justice to both. Truth found inside a tightly sealed home is hardly of any use outside; judgements made inside a room which, for fear of draught, is never aired are blown away with the first gust of wind. The universality of truth and judgement born in confinement is but a cover for that constraint which feeds on the lust for domination and fear of the open space. A non-counterfeit universality may be born only of homelessness. 'As long as the truth is sought by the settled men – the apple of the Tree of Knowledge won't be eaten. The task can be performed only by homeless adventurers, by natural nomads . . .'

The table has been turned. It is now the stranger who can find the truth the natives are looking for in vain. Far from being a mark of shame, the incurable foreignness of the stranger is now the sign of distinction. The power of the homeowners is but a sham. The powerlessness of the homeless is but an illusion.

After Shestov few new ideas may be gleaned from Karl Mannheim's fulsome accolade of the *freischwebende Intelligenz*. As in Shestov the lack of social acceptance turns into a condition of undistorted communication: the outcast becomes a hero, the ambivalence of social position is revealed as objectivity of thought. In Maurice Natanson's apt commentary the advantage of Mannheim's intrepid truth-trapper is his 'nomadic existence': 'Bound by no formal commitments, he can move lightly through traditional formulations of social causation, control, and prediction.' It is thanks to his perpetual and irreparable homelessness that Mannheim's intellectual becomes an 'unmasker, penetrator of lies and ideologies, relativizer and devaluator of immanent thought, disintegrator of *Weltanschauungen*'.[6] Indeed, an awesome corrosive force; a creator who draws his strength from his power of destruction. If reality is so many fenced off and tightly

[6] Maurice Natanson, *Literature, Philosophy and the Social Sciences* (The Hague, Martinus Nijhof, 1962), p. 170.

guarded private plots, claims to truth remain but excuses for exclusion and eviction orders. One needs to break down the fences first.

Point by point, Mannheim disavows every single property of the 'settled' from which they have drawn their pride, contentment and sense of security. Thus any well-integrated group is self-centred and hence selectively blind: 'not every possible aspect of the world comes within the purview of the members of the group, but only those out of which difficulties and problems for the group arise.' Solidity of roots is a recipe for parochial narrow-mindedness: 'It is clearly impossible to obtain an inclusive insight into problems if the observer or thinker is confined to a given place in society.' The distrust with which the group treats the 'unfit' testifies to the group's own disabilities, rather than to the sins of the stranger. It is the ability of the outsiders 'to attach themselves to classes to which they originally did not belong', the fact that they 'could adapt themselves to any viewpoint . . . because they and they alone were in position to choose their affiliation' that the well-settled groups cannot stomach. 'Should the capacity to acquire a broader point of view be considered merely as a liability? Does it not rather present a mission?'[7]

The modern intellectual is a perpetual wanderer and a universal stranger. No one truly likes him for this very reason; in every place he is out of place. The continual rebuffs received everywhere and from everybody need not, however, result solely in fanaticism of desperation. The rejection may as well open the eyes of the rejected to the meaning and the value of the very position (or, rather, the 'un-position') which has been the source of their suffering. Rejection means, after all, freedom from obligations. Eviction means that group loyalties need not any more constrain vision, and thus 'the narrowness and the limitations which restrict one point of view' may be 'corrected by clashing with the opposite points of view'. The exile is a blessing: the outcasts have been banished to the only site 'from which a total perspective would be possible'. They are now ripe for the role of decision makers (or, more precisely, *good decisions* makers), as 'The formation of a decision is truly possible only under conditions of freedom based on the possibility of choice which continues to exist even after the decision has been made.'[8]

In other words, while making a bid for the unique and superior status of the modern intellectual, Mannheim draws on the popular fear of the

---

[7] Karl Mannheim, *Ideology and Utopia* (London: Routledge, 1968), pp. 26, 72, 141, 144. For the intellectual the peripheral perspective is not a matter of choice; paradoxically this is because – as Ortega y Gasset remarked – 'the world appears to the Intellectual to be where he questions it' (quoted after *Juden in der Soziologie*, ed. Erhard R. Wiehn (Konstanz, Hartung-Gorre, 1989), p. 29).

[8] Mannheim, *Ideology and Utopia*, pp. 72, 143.

awesome power residing in the non-man's land outside the safe and habitual family or community plots. He embraces the finality of the native verdict, the perpetuity of the exile. He also accepts the native conviction that the stranger will never become like the native and will never see the world through native eyes. Finally, he agrees with the worst of the native suspicions: that estrangement breeds enmity to all local values. But he reforges the stigma of shame and the legal justification of eviction order into a militant, defiant bid to superiority. To paraphrase Goffman, 'instead of leaning on his crutch, he gets to play golf with it'.

Only on universal (read: non-parochial) foundations, he proclaims on behalf of the intellectual stranger, may truth be built; and universality, as any native would accept, arises out of estrangement. The standpoint of the exile is the only cognitive determinant of universally binding truth. The well-entrenched and self-centred groups inflated their narrow opinions to ostensibly universal proportions with the help of thought-constraints and the banishment of dissenters. By so doing they prevented themselves from finding what they sought, and on the way discredited the very purpose of their search. Now the banished must protect the supreme value of universal truth from all further harm. They will do what those who send them into exile failed to achieve. They will prove that against all odds (and particularly against the dominant, native opinion) they are the staunchest, the most loyal and the most reliable defenders and promoters of the dominant values. And this they can do as long as they refuse to efface their difference, and insist on *remaining strangers*. It is through their estrangement that they serve the values which the group needs and wants to possess. The assimilatory programme may well have failed to secure unification, but it was a false unification that it offered in the first place. The real one will be attained precisely by those whom the promise of acceptance has failed.

The process of self-construction sets the stranger even further apart from the native group with which he still wants to ingratiate himself, now as much as at the initial period of assimilatory dream. The stranger offers a unique, helplessly ambivalent blend of universalist programme and relativist practice. In order to secure true universality of form of life – a purpose he shares with the native group (with *any native group*) – he must expose as false, and thus undermine, the security of values the native group (*any native group*) has grown to consider absolute. The stranger aims at the effacement of all divisions which stand in the way of uniform, essential humanity; this is the last hope he entertains to efface his own outsideness. To the native group, however, his thrust for *universality* means more than anything else a confrontation with the decomposing, corrosive power of *relativism*.

Excursus: Franz Kafka, or the rootlessness of universality

The Jews have been the prototypical strangers in Europe split in nation-states set on annihilation of everything 'intermediate', underdetermined, neither friendly nor inimical. In the continent of nations and nationalisms they were the only reminder of the relativity of nationhood and of the outer limits of nationalism, the last residue of wilderness in a world filled with local orders, self-propagating weeds in the world composed of carefully tended gardens, nomads among the settled (only Gypsies shared this feature of European Jews – and thus, for Hitler, they had to share their ultimate fate). They were the very danger against which nations had to constitute themselves. They were the ultimate incongruity – a *non-national nation*. Their strangeness was not confined to any particular place; they were *universal* strangers. They were not visitors from another country, as there was no such 'another country' – indeed, no country where they could claim not to be visitors or strangers. The Jews were 'strangerhood incarnated', the eternal wanderers, the epitomy of non-territoriality, the very essence of homelessness and absence of roots; an unexorcizable spectre of conventionality in the house of the absolute, of a nomadic past in the era of settlement.

As the universal and hence most radical of strangers, the Jews of Europe fathomed the full depth of the stranger's experience. For the most perceptive among them, universality of their strangerhood congealed as that universality of the human condition they thought they gleaned from the particularity of their experience; their particularity acquired a universal value. It is not that the Jews embraced universality more avidly and with more abandon than anyone else. It was, rather, that their experience, through its unique features, articulated the very pattern of universality. Strangers of all walks of life could look into this experience as in a mirror and see the details of their own likeness which other mirrors blurred and conveyed but vaguely. It was Franz Kafka's painfully lived, tormented Jewishness which permitted Camus or Sartre to glean in his work a parable of the universal predicament of modern man. It allowed Camus to read Kafka as an insight into the incurable absurdity of modern life, into 'l'étrangeté d'une vie d'homme';[9] it allowed Sartre to find in Kafka the very definition of the Stranger: 'L'étranger, c'est l'homme en face du monde . . .

[9] Pierre-George Castex, *Albert Camus et L'Étranger* (Paris: José Cortez, 1986), p. 56.

L'étranger, c'est aussi l'homme parmi les hommes ... C'est enfin moi-même par rapport à moi-même.'[10]

Like his nameless heroes, Kafka experienced guilt without crime, complete with its consequence: condemnation without judgement. He lived in a 'world in which it is a crime to be accused', in which the paramount skill for all those who did not want to be convicted of the crime was 'to avoid the accusation'.[11] This was the very skill, however, which it was impossible to obtain. From the world where the crime was to be accused, there was no escape. One would carry that world with oneself wherever one went. 'My imperfection is ... not congenital, not earned' – confides Kafka in his diary:[12] it is neither natural nor man-made. Neither fate nor deed. It is as incongruous as the position of the stranger among the natives, and as impossible to fight as the other incongruity. Indeed, where would one find the home of the imperfection? 'The reproaches lie around inside me.' 'I myself', as it were, 'am perhaps the best aid of my assailants. For I underestimate myself, and that in itself means an overestimation of others' – the outside is inside, the two intertwine, interpenetrate, merge.

One of Kafka's most quoted self-diagnoses is the verdict he pronounced in a letter to Max Brod on the generation of Germanized (or were they just Germanizing?) Jews to which he belonged: 'their hind legs were still mired in their fathers' Jewishness and their thrashing fore legs found no new ground. The ensuing despair became their inspiration.' Reality was an exact opposite of the liberalist utopia and proved utter irrelevance of the main strategic principle of assimilatory drive. ('Be a Jew at home, a man in the street.') In Martha Robert's pungent summary,

> at home the young Jews of Prague lived, thought, and wrote like Germans apparently resembling other Germans, but outside of their neighbourhoods no one was deceived, the 'others' recognized them instantly by their faces, their manners, their accent. Assimilated they were beyond a doubt, but only within the restricted area of their borrowed Germanism, or better still, they were 'assimilated' with their own uprootedness.'[13]

The most perceptive among the members of that generation, Kafka understood what the others barely, and only grudgingly, noticed: that he, like

---

[10] Brian T. Fitch, *L'Étranger d'Albert Camus* (Paris: Librairie Larousse, 1972), p. 94.

[11] Adrian Jaffe, *The Process of Kafka's Trial* (Ann Arbor: Michigan State University Press, 1967), p. 29.

[12] *The Diaries of Franz Kafka, 1910–23* ed. Max Brod (Harmondsworth: Penguin, 1964), pp. 18–9.

[13] Martha Roberts, *Franz Kafka's Loneliness*, trans. Ralph Mannheim (London: Faber & Faber, 1982), p. 35.

them, 'was Jewish even in the way of not being Jewish'.[14] Assimilation spawned the reality to which one strived to assimilate; the only one to which one could hope to assimilate. Assimilation fed on itself and came to be its own sole purpose. It led away from the world left behind but came no closer to the world ahead at which it apparently aimed.

By the dawn of the current century, when the self-defeating tendency of assimilation ('The value system they borrowed not only was never theirs in its entirety, but always contained elements inimical to them. The German always saw their adoption of it as merely a mask behind which glowered the unregenerate Jew. Sadly, for the German Jew the mask was the only reality.'),[15] became ever more strongly felt, the *Ostjuden* were gradually lifted from their recent unenviable role of the *inner demons of Western assimilation* (see chapter 4): that past, of which they kept reminding their civilized Western cousins, the latter had now little hope of ever consigning to oblivion. Somewhat less predictably, the *Ostjuden* were promoted to a new role of 'fulsome persons', who embodied everything the Western Jews most badly missed and belatedly regretted abandoning. 'Die Ostjuden sind ganze, lebensfrohe und lebenskräftige Menschen,' waxed wistfully Nathan Birnbaum in 1912. Martin Buber, who did more than anyone else to substitute the myth of the Eastern Jew as the symbol of cultural wholesomeness and health for the old myth of the *Ostjude* as the relic of the same precultural savagery the Protestant formalized ethics in alliance with the Enlightenment cult of civility set about to extirpate, inadvertently disclosed the sham of what had been trumpeted as a sudden reversal of the *Ostjude* fortune and the *Westjude* policy. As George L. Mosse convincingly argues, the discovery of a 'new and improved' version of the *Ostjude* was another link in a long chain of borrowings from the dominant culture, always prompted (overtly or subconsciously) by the urge 'not to differ', 'be like them', and thus 'be admitted'. Mosse found a truly striking similarity between Buber's sentimental account of the East-European ghetto and the ideology of Paul de Lagarde or other spokesmen for the budding German *Volksgemeinschaft*. Buber's favourite words were *Blut*, *Boden*, *Volkstum*, *Gemeinschaft*, *Wurzelhaftigkeit*; his favourite prefix – '*Ur*-'.[16] Hardly ever did the Jew borrow a majoritarian ideology which contained more 'elements inimical to them' . . .

---

14 Roberts, *Franz Kafka's Loneliness*, p. 13.

15 Gilman, *Difference and Pathology*, p. 174.

16 Cf. Ritchie Robertson, 'Antizionismus, Zionismus: Kafka's responses to Jewish nationalism', in *Paths and Labyrinths: Nine Papers from a Kafka Symposium*, ed. J.P. Stern and J.J. White (Institute of Germanic Studies of the University of London, 1985), pp. 29–31.

Kafka's own brief, yet intense and stormy encounter with the *Ostjuden* in the shape of a Mr Löwy, Mrs Tschissik and other actors of a Yiddish travelling theatre constituted arguably the most dramatic single event in his life. For the first time, Kafka saw 'people who are Jews in an especially pure form because they live only in the religion, but live in it without effort, understanding, or distress'.[17] These words in which love, admiration and envy are recorded, express also the sad wisdom of reality which contained no hope. Those pure Jews were pure only because they *did not understand* their purity. They did not know what Kafka did and what he *could not unlearn*. Not for him was their purity; not for him any of those traits which made them so alluring. There was no way back into the past. Or, rather, there was no past in Kafka to which he *could* return. In the course of his daily conversations with his new friends and mentors, it occurred to Kafka that for the Jews the word 'Mutter' is not just the name of Mother, but a *German* name for mother, which 'makes her a little comic'; for a Jew, 'Mutter' 'unconsciously contains, together with the Christian splendour Christian coldness also, the Jewish woman who is called "Mutter" therefore becomes not only comic but strange'. So perhaps 'Mama' would be a better name for a Jewish mother? It certainly would – 'if only one didn't imagine "Mutter" behind it' ...[18]

With insight added by malice, Richard Wagner wrote once of the homesick, irredeemable Jewish strangers that, having arrogantly destroyed their relationship with previous companions in sorrow, they always find it impossible to create a new connection with that society to which they pretend to belong. And so Kafka, in Robertson's words, felt that Western Jews like him 'were trapped uncomfortably between a sheltering Jewish community to which they could never return and Western society which would never completely accept them'.[19] Gruesome as it was, this suspension in an empty social space was still a lesser of evils. Much more macabre and grisly was the fact that the void was not 'out there', but *inside* the man who tried in vain to reach the two equally elusive supports. Lacking all socially recognized authority for self-definition, lacking even the language of which identities are made, the victim could exist only *through this emptiness*, in the undescribable, unnamed gap between a lost and an unfound realities. His friend Max Brod's story the *Jüdinnen* Kafka found curiously unsatisfying; seeking an explanation, he noted in his diary:

> The *Jüdinnen* lacks non-Jewish observers, the respectable contrasting persons who in other stories draw out the Jewishness so that it advances toward

---

[17] *The Diaries of Franz Kafka*, p. 64.

[18] *The Diaries of Franz Kafka*, p. 88.

[19] Robertson, 'Antizionismus, Zionismus', p. 28.

them in amazement, doubt, envy, fear, and finally, finally is transformed into self-confidence, but in any event can draw itself up to its full height only before them. That is just what we demand, not other principle for the organization of Jewish material seems justifiable to us.

The Jewishnes of the Western Jew could no more assert itself on its own. Even in his Jewishness – which, after all, he did his best to hide in the secure darkness of family closets – the Jew depended on the Gentile authority. It was they, the non-Jews, who were the 'respectable persons', who had the sole authority to define the meaning of being a Jew. It was they and they alone who decided on the principle which enabled the Jew to set the bits and pieces of his 'Jewish material' into a meaningful pattern. On their own, the Jews simply did not make sense. A story of the Jews on their own read as a lie; and as a hermetically impenetrable lie at that.

Perhaps more telling still is the unselfconscious ease with which the vantage point then shifts in Kafka's entry:

> In the same way, too, the convulsive starting up of a lizard under our feet on a footpath in Italy delights us greatly, again and again we are moved to bow down, but if we see them at a dealer's by hundreds crawling over one another in confusion in the large bottles in which otherwise pickles are usually packed, then we don't know what to do.[20]

Seeking the proof that his first impression of the *Jüdinnen*'s congenital fault was correct, Kafka must leave the perplexed mind of the insider and view the world through the discerning eye of the 'respectable person' himself. Authority of judgement is ultimately his, and in his mind alone all proofs may be begotten and made binding. And what Kafka saw through the eye of a rich tourist or a zoo-shop customer looking at the lizards, was that once heaped together and left to their own company, the Jews were ridiculously meaningless, incongruous and unappetizing. Like lizards in a pickle jar, Jews locked in their own company must be seen as out of their element, as thrown into an *unnatural* state. Like a lizard on a stony Italian gorge, the Jew 'makes sense' (to those whose sense counts; whose look endows things with sense) only *individually*, when constituted by the tourist's curiosity as a tourist attraction. The *natural* state of the Jew is to be singled out – in order to be looked upon, examined, assessed and evaluated by a non-Jewish eye. A verdict will then be passed, the only verdict which sustains the order and the meaning of Jewish existence. Other Jews do not matter, much as the other lizards in the jar. As one of Arthur Schnitzler's characters once observed, no Jew really respects another – no more than prisoners of war, especially when they have no

---

[20] *The Diaries of Franz Kafka*, p. 46.

hope. They may hate each other, or adore; sometimes even love. But never respect. All their emotional relations develop in that atmosphere of spiritual serfdom and ensuing duplicity in which respect is bound to stifle.

A universal stranger himself, and perhaps the most insightful among the universal strangers, Kafka unravelled and spelled out the universal traits of *strangerhood*, that true and only, though multi-faced, hero of all his literary work. To be a stranger, is to be refused and to surrender the right to self-constitution, self-definition, self-identity. It is to derive one's sense from the relationship with the native, and from the native's examining gaze. It is to forget the skill of making a meaningful pattern out of the inherited 'material'. It is to surrender one's autonomy, and with that the authority to make one's life meaningful. To be a stranger means to be able to live perpetual ambivalence, a vicarious life of *dissimulation*.

By himself, the stranger is devoid of all attributes, a true *man without qualities* (it was demanded that the Jews should be different from both non-Jews and Jews, Gilman observed). Whatever qualities may give him a body and thus draw him out of the void are graciously bestowed and may be withdrawn at a whim. In his absence of substance, the stranger is an archetype of universality; weightless, insubstantial, ineffable unless injected with other people's contents; nowhere at his 'natural' place; the very antithesis of the concrete, specific, definite. The stranger is universal because of having no home and no roots. Rootlessness relativizes everything concrete and thus begets universality. In rootlessness, both universality and relativism find their roots. Their hotly denied kinship is thus unmasked. They both, in their own ways, are products of ambivalent existence.

The intellectuals' neolithic revolution

The essence of the neolithic revolution was the passage from a nomadic to a settled life; or, what amounts to the same thing, from gathering the fruits of nature to growing such plants as nature itself failed to produce. If this was indeed the essence of the neolithic revolution, then we can say that its intellectual equivalent occurred in the years following Mannheim's depiction of the intelligentsia as the category of strangers who reforge the bane of their homelessness into the weapon of universal truth. Or, perhaps, this revolution took off well before that, only Mannheim failed to take note of it.

In America of the 1980s 'colleagues have replaced a public, and jargon has supplanted English', Russell Jacoby commented recently. 'American Marxists today have campus offices and assigned parking spaces.' Indeed, 'to be an intellectual requires a campus address'. Under such new conditions – both the opportunities and the constraints they augur – 'the Marxist theoretical "explosion" has the force of a seminar coffee break', while 'a critical vision is itself evidence of personal failings'.[21] But Régis Debray[22] has defined each successive period in the last hundred years of the French intellectuals' history by reference to the type of abode they occupied at the time (universities, publishing houses, mass media) – all different, but all equally homely, well furnished, safe, warm, accommodating and often even hospitable. Had they ever been nomads, the intellectuals are not any more. They have arrived. They have settled. They have their own plots to till.

Indeed, an enormous road has been passed since that *milieu artificiel* of aggrieved, militant and resolute draftsmen of the *Grand Design*, who – in Augustin Cochin's opinion – made a 'society' all of their own, in which 'les participants figurent comme libres, libérés de toute attache, de toute obligation, de toute fonction sociale'.[23] The juggernaut of the scientific-technological revolution promoted by panoptical state crushed that quasi-society glued together of discussion and opinion – and sucked in the debris. Free intellectuals of yore turned into university teachers, government consultants, experts and functionaries of warfare and welfare bureaucracies. The thought has emerged out of its estrangement. It has found the many homes it now inhabits cosy and comfortable. The knights of universality turned into the defenders of hospitals, colleges, opera houses and research institutes – of funds and jobs, of salaries and statute books. Long ago had they ceased to draw their ranks in a solidary opposition to the society which made them into strangers. Hardly ever do they draw their ranks together at all – unless the very right of the expert to rule within his own realm of expertise is at stake. Apart from this one issue on which they are all solidary, there is so much to divide them, so little to unite.

Mannheim's free-floating, estranged and inward-looking intellectual did not disappear altogether, though most certainly he is now an exception – at war not so much with parochial society, as with parochiality of his better established, sated and self-satisfied colleagues. It was that parochiality which Theodore Adorno (one of the most notorious among 'persons with no permanent address', a prototypical free-floater, never and nowhere

---

[21] Rusell Jacoby, *The Last Intellectuals* (New York: Basic Books, 1987), pp. 180, 220, 172, 203.

[22] Cf. Régis Debray, *Le Pouvoir intellectuel en France* (Paris: Ramsay, 1979).

[23] Augustin Cochin, *La Révolution et la libre pensée* (Paris: Plon, 1924), p. xxxvi.

accommodated to his own and his hosts' satisfaction) construed as the staunchest enemy of the 'attempt to change the world' which 'miscarried':

> What differs from the existent will strike the existent as witchcraft, while thought-figures such as proximity, home, security hold the faulty world under their spell. Men are afraid that in losing this magic they would lose everything, because the only happiness they know, even in thought, is to be able to hold on to something – the perpetuation of unfreedom.[24]

His companion, Max Horkheimer, agreed: 'Among the vast majority of the ruled there is the unconscious fear that theoretical thinking might show their painfully won adaptation to reality to be perverse and unnecessary.'[25]

Looking around at the rational world in which expertise and power merged and knowledge ceased to be the power of the powerless, Max Weber did not give much chance to people like Adorno and Horkheimer: 'The problem which besets us now is not: how can this evolution be changed? – for that is impossible, but ... what can we oppose to this machinery in order to keep a portion of mankind free from this parcelling-out of the soul, from this supreme mastery of the bureaucratic way of life.'[26] Long before Mannheim raised the spectre of the universal stranger as the Last Judge, Weber composed his funeral dirge for the free soul; keeping free a portion of mankind was the most he felt entitled to hope for. Adorno and Horkheimer represented such a portion; a very small portion, and to very small avail, to be sure. They were strangers many times over: unattached scholars in the world of well accommodated academics; Germans in a society which thought of them as Jews; exiles from a society which never fully became their home to a society which they never wished to make their home; European philosophers in a land of philistine anti-intellectualism.

They had other strangers like themselves for their only companions and reference. Theirs was the life of exile, with (in Robert Michels's memorable description) its 'brisk exchange of ideas on unoccupied evenings, the continued rubbing of shoulders between men of the most different tongues, the enforced isolation from the bourgeois world of their respective countries, and the utter impossibility of any "practical" action'.[27] Soon the impossible turned into the undesirable: what cannot be done is not

---

[24] Theodor W. Adorno, *Negative Dialectics*, trans. E.B. Ashton (London: Routledge, 1973), pp. 3, 33.

[25] Max Horkheimer, *Critical Theory*, trans. Matthew J. O'Connell *et al.* (New York: Herder & Herder, 1972), p. 232.

[26] Quoted after J.P. Mayer, *Max Weber and German Politics* (London: Faber & Faber, 1956), p. 128.

[27] Robert Michels, *Political Parties* (Glencoe: Free Press, 1919), p. 187.

worthy of doing. One can as well derive pride from one's impotence: deafness of the world testifies to the power of the message. With relish, Adorno and Horkheimer found in Paul Deussen's translation of *Upanishads* what they were groping for: a testimony of the irrevokable incompatibility between critical, uncompromising thought, and that effort aimed at the mobilization of popular consensus which practical action demands. To make such an effort, the idea needs to develop into a neat theoretical system. In the process, it cannot remain uncompromising for long; soon it stops to be critical either.[28] An active role in life is not compatible with the salvation of the soul; the search for logical cohesion that such an active role requires is not compatible with emancipatory critique. Upanishads (unlike Vedic religion), Cynics (unlike their Stoic successors), St John the Baptist (unlike St Paul) all refused to produce cohesive, harmonious, academically respectable systems, as they stoutly refused any track with politics in whose fetid atmosphere the unbound spirit cannot breathe.

The fewer and more exotic become the estranged, marginalized intellectuals in the world of well settled, practically engaged knowledge class, the more radical and otherwordly becomes their commitment to the universal and the absolute; the more jarring the contrast between the univocality of their loyalties and the ambivalence of their social location. They are strangers not just in relation to the 'natives' and their dominant values. First and foremost, most blatantly and most poignantly, they are strangers in relation to the *fellow members of the knowledge class*. They are traitors to their class loyalty, heretics to their church orthodoxy. The universality they seek is forged out of the opposition to that particularity for which their own knowledge class (the class they reject and by which they are rejected) serves them as the prototype. It is the 'academic science', the 'established wisdom', the 'bureaucratized knowledge' which now stands for the sin of surrender to selfish, parochial interests. It is against those tropes of fall that the wrath and the most poisonous arrows are now aimed.

Not that the arrows reach their intended targets. With knowledge effectively translated into institutionally entrenched expertise, Mannheim's vision of the homeless intelligentsia (an image which smacked of theoretical contrivance at the best of times) looks increasingly nebulous. The experts are anything but rootless. Nor can they be validly accused of *trahison des clercs*. They cannot betray commitments they have never

---

[28] Cf. the note attached to the American Edition of Theodor W. Adorno and Max Horkheimer, *Dialectic of Enlightenment* trans. John Cumming (New York: Herder & Herder, 1972).

undertaken. Theirs are specific tasks arising from specific problems. Set in a clear-cut, institutionalized section of an overall division of labour, they have no time for the ancient *querelle* between the nativists and the universalists, and no use for the battle between eternal truths and the scepticism of the modern Pyrrhonians. Their praxis as experts generates neither lust for certainty nor relativist inclinations. If anything, it invalidates both, and above all the conflict between them and the need to choose. Unlike in the huge, society-size gardens eyed greedily by the free-floating intellectuals, each of the little allotments which the experts cultivate can accommodate quite considerable (and absolute) designing authority, without making their own rather confining boundaries into a problem. With the shrinking urge to expand, fades out the lust for universality. With wilting interest in the neighbour behind the partition, peters out the horror of relativity.

It seems that the cognitive perspective of the knowledge class, split as it now is into a multitude of but loosely connected expert sections, favours neither universalism nor relativism, and considerably cools down the controversy between the two. No wonder the most popular philosophies of today are those which humbly admit localized, communally based boundaries of truth while at the same time striving to protect their prerogative of distinguishing between right and wrong inside the accepted borderlines. One can say that in such philosophies *communities* (or forms of life, or traditions, or languages) have become synonymical with the idea of truth: community is the area in which a truth may be agreed as objective and binding, while truth is objective and binding in as far as there is a community which accepts this and thus makes it into a reality inside its boundaries. Community and truth are two rhetorical figures which refer to each other, each one legitimizing itself through the other in the world of experts and compartmentalized truth.

The universality of rootlessness

The 'neolithic revolution' of the spiritual elite, the wondrous transformation of rootless intellectuals into the established knowledge class, is just a more spectacular (perhaps more deeply felt because of being 'closer home') case of a wider process which can be called *the privatization of strangerhood*. A paradoxical corollary of *privatization* is the *universality* of strangerhood: the mode of 'being a stranger' is experienced, to a varying degree, by all and every member of contemporary society with its extreme division of labour and separation of functionally separated spheres. If the members of the knowledge class live through such an experience, they do it as members of society at large, rather than as scientists, technologists, thinkers or artists. In these latter capacities, their specialized activities, firmly anchored with the help of productive and distributive companies, bureaucratic division of functions and hierarchy of command, institutionalized reward systems, 'networks', 'circles' and 'pegs' (like coffee-houses, clubs, journals) on which their group-identity is fastened[29] and which sustain, control and service them, are factors of integration and belonging, rather than estrangement. In their private capacities, however, – as individuals – the knowledge class members share in the universal existential mode, of which the experience of estrangement is a ubiquitous and important component. Strangerhood – more generally, the existential and mental ambivalence – has lost its particularity as human condition; with that loss, it has lost the once rebellious, potentially revolutionary, edge. Having become a *universal* human condition – a mode of 'existence as such' – it does not any more generate universality as dynamite about to explode the smug quotidianity of parochial life. Strangerhood is no more an insight into the other side of existence, a challenge to the here and now, a vantage point of utopia. It itself turned into quotidianity.

As Niklas Luhmann pointed out and convincingly argued, 'with the adoption of functional differentiation individual persons can no longer be firmly located in one single subsystem of society, but rather must be regarded a priori as socially displaced'.[30] That is, the individual is a 'displaced person' by definition: it is the very fact that he cannot be fully subsumed under any of the numerous functional subsystems which only in their combination constitute the fullness of his life process (the fact, in other words, that he does not belong fully to any of the subsystems and no subsystem can claim his sole allegiance) that makes him an individual. In relation to each of the subsystems, the individual is a unit of many meanings, an ambivalent compound – always a *partial stranger*. In relation to none of the subsystems is he completely a *native*. In terms of his biography, the contemporary individual passes a long string of widely divergent (uncoordinated at best, contradictory at worst) social worlds. At any single moment of his life, the individual inhabits simultaneously several such divergent worlds. The result is that he is 'uprooted' from each and not 'at home' in any. One may say that he is the *universal stranger*. One is tempted to say that he is 'fully at home' only with himself. (This

---

29 Cf. Warren O. Hagstrom's and Charles Kadushin's contributions to *The Production of Culture*, ed. Richard A. Petersen (London: Sage, 1976).

30 Niklas Luhmann, *Love as Passion: The Codification of Intimacy*, trans. Jeremy Gaines and Doris L.Jones (Cambridge, Mass.: Harvard University Press, 1986), p. 15.

circumstance, let us note, sends the last nail into the coffin of the *compleat mappa mundi*; yet at the same time it draws the revolutionary sting out of the resistance to parochiality of home-baked mini-orders.) Indeed, as Luhmann would express it, for the contemporary individual the ego becomes the seat and the focal point of all inner experience, while environment, split into fragments with little lateral connection, loses most of its contours, and much of its meaning-defining authority.

And yet such 'being at home with oneself' is highly problematic. It may come to be, if at all, only as an achievement of protracted and tortuous effort. The poor co-ordination between subsystems is reflected in the heterogeneity of the self. Partial estrangements are incorporated and experienced as the self's resilience to integration. The self is burdened with the impossible task of rebuilding the lost integrity of the world; or, more modestly, with the task of sustaining the production of self-identity; doing on its own what was once entrusted to the native community. In fact, it is now inside the self that such a 'native community', as the frame of reference for self-identity, must be construed. And it is only within the self's work of imagination that such community has its, necessarily precarious, existence.

During the *Sturm und Drang* phase of modernity's being in a state of homelessness, non-belongingness, ambivalence required an apology. The absence of an address to which such apology could be sent is one of the most conspicuous and consequential features of our own part of the modern era. Individuals mostly turn to their private lives as the only location where they may hope to build a home amidst the *universal homelessness*. Their hope is dashed, however.

> over and over again, the cold winds of 'homelessness' threaten these fragile constructions. It would be an overstatement to say that the 'solution' of the private sphere is a failure; there are too many individual successes. But it is always very precarious.[31]

And as far as the experience of estrangement is concerned, it is the fact that they are endemically *precarious*, even if they do not fail, which counts.

> A world in which everything is in constant motion is a world in which certainties of any kind are hard to come by . . . What is truth in one context of the individual's social life may be error in another. What was considered right at one stage of the individual's social career becomes wrong in the next.[32]

---

[31] Peter L. Berger, Brigitte Berger and Hansfried Kellner, *The Homeless Mind* (Harmondsworth: Penguin, 1973), p. 168.

[32] Berger *et al.*, *The Homeless Mind*, p. 145.

Today's world does not abolish strangerhood and the existential ambivalence with which it is infused. But it does not offer any hope that the stranger can be redeemed. And as the condition of ambivalence turns into an ever more universal experience, and thus the prospect of redemption grows increasingly dim, the emancipatory urge peters out.

There is a substantive difference between being a stranger in a well settled native world, and a stranger in a world on the move. In the first case, misery comes complete with the promise, hope and a programme of its termination. The apparently clear-cut hierarchy of native values and norms defines what is to be done, and defines it with uncontested authority. The natives embody the human *universal* which renders the stranger's form of humanity parochial and shameful. It is easy (perhaps natural) to confuse then the effort of assimilation to the dominant native standards with the promotion of universal truth; to define the malaise of a particular strangerhood as the deformation, or paucity, of universality; to identify the urge to efface a specific difference with the need of clearing the site for the uniform and absolute rule of universal standards. In the second case, however, though the strangers remain strangers, they do not live any more among the natives; indeed, there are no such natives in sight. In the absence of uncontested standards, of such standards as may sensibly claim, or aspire to, ascendancy – strangerhood does not feel like a temporary condition. Much less than before does it feel like an unbearable condition, one from which one has the duty to redeem oneself. Difference now bears no guilt; and the shame of being guilty of difference no longer prompts the culprit to escape from estrangement.

The vision of universality is born of rootlessness – but its supplies are being replenished only as long as the rootlessness remains a *particular* condition, a handicap, a disprivilege. Once rootlessness itself turns into a universal condition, particularity has been effaced, though not in the way once seen in the dreams of the rootless. Relativity becomes now the great equalizer; it is through peculiarity that one escapes the stigma of difference. It is only through setting oneself apart that one can share in the predicament of others, and participate on equal footing in the universal human condition. Strangerhood has become universal. Or, rather, it has been dissolved; which, after all, amounts to the same. If everyone is a stranger, no one is.

It remains to be seen to what extent the widespread aversion to grand social designs, the loss of interest in absolute truths, privatization of redemptive urges, reconciliation with the relative – merely heuristic – value of all life techniques, acceptance of irredeemable plurality of the world, in short all these worrying yet nevertheless exhilarating trends which are usually subsumed under the name of *postmodernity*, are a lasting consequence of that *abolition* of strangerhood which has been attained through raising it to the *status of a universal human condition*.

The threat and the chance

What the inherently polysemic and controversial idea of postmodernity most often refers to (even if only tacitly) is first and foremost an acceptance of ineradicable plurality of the world; plurality which is not a temporary station on the road to the not-yet attained perfection (imperfections are many and varied; perfection, by definition, is always one), a station sooner or later to be left behind – but the constitutive quality of existence. By the same token, postmodernity means a resolute emancipation from the characteristically modern urge to overcome ambivalence and promote the monosemic clarity of the sameness. Indeed, postmodernity reverses the signs of the values central to modernity, such as uniformity and universalism. And once it has been perceived as irreducible and unlikely to converge, neither to be dissolved in one life-form aiming at universality, nor degraded by one form aiming at universal domination, variety of life-forms is not merely grudgingly accepted, but lifted to the rank of a supreme positive value. Postmodernity is modernity that has admitted the non-feasibility of its original project. Postmodernity is modernity reconciled to its own impossibility – and determined, for better or worse, to live with it. Modern practice continues – now, however, devoid of the objective that once triggered it off.

In the absence of the intent to dominate, the presence of mutually exclusive standards neither offends the desire of logical congruity nor triggers off a remedial action. Ideally speaking, in the plural and pluralistic world of postmodernity, every form of life is permitted on principle, or, rather, no agreed principles are evident (or uncontestedly agreed) which may render any form of life impermissible. Once the difference ceases to be an oppression and is not construed as a problem calling for action and resolution, peaceful coexistence of distinct forms of life becomes *possible* in another sense than as a temporary equilibrium of hostile powers. The principle of coexistence may (just may) replace the principle of universalization, while the precept of tolerance may (just may) take place of those of conversion and subordination. Liberty, equality, brotherhood was the war-cry of modernity. *Liberty*, *diversity*, *tolerance* is the armistice formula of postmodernity. And with tolerance reforged into *solidarity* (see chapter 8), armistice may even turn into peace.

One can thus *hope* for the disappearance of one of the paramount grounds of the destructive urge as the self-assertion of different forms of life loses the character of a zero-sum game. Room for new forms can be found without vacating the space occupied by the extant ones, and thus the most important reason for the rhetoric and practice of destruction loses a good deal of its past cogency. (So does, we may add, the romantic heroism of revolutionary novelty. Revolutions retain their appeal only as long as the experience of difference remains intolerable. The acceptance of relativity and reconciliation to ambivalence defuses the attraction of radical and condensed change; indeed, it renders revolution meaningless. If there are no standards to be preserved at the expense of others, there are no standards which need to be moved out of the way to enable others to exist. The strategy of innovation entails a strategy of destruction only if the novelty is meant to displace.)

The acceptance of the permanence of differentiation (and of plurality of principally co-ordinated actions which support it) is intimately related to the demise of the grand designs of social engineering. The latter amounts to the erosion of the gardening or surgical stance which throughout the modern age characterized the attitudes and the policies of institutionalized powers – and above all the powers of the nation-state. Modernity proclaimed the essential artificiality of the social order and the inability of society to attain an orderly existence on its own. It also proclaimed that the establishment of the social order requires the asymmetrical distribution of agency – that is, dividing the society into actors and the objects of their actions. The exclusive claim of elected agency to define the state of order as distinct from chaos was articulated in the ideology of reason's superiority over passions, rational conduct over irrational drives, and knowledge over ignorance or superstition. Opposition between such abstract values both generated and reflected practical social divisions. Most importantly, it serviced the perpetual condensation of autonomy and choice on one pole of the social division and delegitimation of the autonomous will of the other side. By the same token, this opposition may lose most of its cutting power once the impulse of domination melts in the atmosphere of coexistence and (chosen or enforced) toleration. It may (just may) not survive for long the fading of the engineering ambition that was its meaning and reason. It derived its sense from missionary projects and crusades; it can hardly outlive them.

The memory of the opposition, however, prompts one to conceive of its fall from grace as being one of the rehabilitation of irrationality and the surrender of reason. What is perceived in such a way, however, is merely the sudden and not-yet-fully grasped meaninglessness of the distinction at a time when the planned and designed, man-made fate ceased to differentiate between forms of life anointed to govern and those marked for colonization or extinction. Irrationality is the waste of rationality industry.

Chaos is the waste accumulating in the production of order. The frightening incongruity of the stranger is the refuse left after the world has been cleanly cut into a slice called 'us' and another labelled 'them'. Ambivalence is a toxic side-product in the production of semiotic transparency. Irrationality, chaos, strangerhood, ambivalence are all names for that nameless 'beyond' for which the dominant powers that identified themselves as reason, as forces of order, as natives, as meaning have no use. They are by-products of designing ambitions, in the same way that weeds are the products of garden designs. They have no other meaning but someone's refusal to tolerate them. Or, rather, once the empirical solvents has been evaporated and only hard crystals of value are left, all their manifold meanings turn out to be that difference which someone, somewhere, refused to live with.

There are, as Dick Higgins suggested a decade ago, *cognitive* and *post-cognitive* questions. The first have lost much of their allure; the second are asked with growing frequency. Cognitive questions stemmed from the axiom of the current or prospective *oneness* of the world. In the one and only world, a world that suffers no alternative to itself, the task is to fathom what this world demands of those who wish to find their place in it. The questions are, therefore: 'How can I interpret this world of which I am a part? And what am I in it?' Post-cognitive questions do not enjoy the luxury that the old axiom offered. Indeed, they have hardly any axioms from which they may take off for a confident start. Nor do they have a clear address. Before they turn to exploring the world they must find out what world(s) is (are) there to be explored. Hence: 'Which world is it? What is to be done in it? Which of my selves is to do it?' – in this order.

Projecting back later discursive usages, Brian McHale renames Higgins's questions as, respectively, *modernist* and *postmodernist*.[33] He observes as well that according to orthodox philosophical divisions, cognitive questions belong to epistemology, while post-cognitive questions are primarily ontological; thus the 'post-cognitive' questions are not *cognitive* at all; at least not in the strict sense. They reach beyond the boundaries of epistemology. Or, rather, they return to the fundamental issue of being, which is to be settled *before* the epistemology may approach its task in earnest, and which most epistemological questions asked during the modern era assumed settled. And so the typically modern questions are, among others: 'What is there to be known? Who knows it? How do they know it, and with what degree of certainty?' The typically postmodern questions do not reach that far. Instead of locating the task for the knower, they attempt to locate the knower himself. 'What is a world? What kinds of

---

[33]Brian McHale, *Postmodernist Fiction* (London: Methuen, 1987), p. 10.

world are there, how are they constituted, and how do they differ?' Even when sharing concern about knowledge, the two types of inquiry articulate their problems differently: 'How is knowledge transmitted from one knower to another, and with what degree of reliability?'; as against: 'What happens when different worlds are placed in confrontation, or when boundaries between worlds are violated?' Note that postmodern questions have no use for 'certainty'; not even for 'reliability'. The oneupmanship of modernist epistemology looks hopelessly out of place in that pluralist reality to which the postmodern ontological inquiry is first reconciled, and then addressed. That overwhelming desire of power which animated the search for the ultimate (and which alone could animate it) raises here little passion. Only eyebrows are raised by the self-confidence which once made the pursuit of the absolute look like a plausible project.

It seems that in the world of universal ambivalence of strangerhood, the stranger is no more obsessed with the ambivalence of what is and the absoluteness of *what ought to be*. This is a new experience for the stranger. And since the stranger's experience is one most of us now share, this is also a new situation for the world. With such new experience, neither the stranger nor his world are likely to remain the same. But with what consequences?

Richard Rorty has recently summarized Proust's achievement in the following way:

> Like Nietzsche, he rid himself of the fear that there was an antecedent truth about himself, a real essence which others must have detected. But Proust was able to do so without claiming to know the truth which was hidden from the authority figures of his earlier years. He managed to debunk authority without setting himself up as authority, to debunk the amibitions of the powerful without sharing them.[34]

The great chance of postmodernity is to replicate on a massive scale Proust's personal achievement. The formidable danger of postmodernity is that – having failed the chance – it may resuscitate defunct (or merely hibernating?) ambitions of the adolescent modernity and feed into its own contemporaries desire to re-live them. History, Marx said, always occurs twice. First as a tragedy, later as a farce. But then, as in so many of his predictions, Marx could have erred as to the order in which the genres succeed each other.

---

[34] Richard Rorty, *Contingency, Irony, and Solidarity* (Cambridge: Cambridge University Press, 1989), p. 103.

4

A Case Study in the Sociology of Assimilation I: Trapped in Ambivalence

I would I were a Roman; for I cannot,
Being a Volsce, be that I am. Condition?
What good condition can a treaty find
I' th' part that is at mercy?

Shakespeare, *Coriolanus*, I, x, 4–7

In the title of this chapter, there is more than an incidental reference to the phrase *prisoners of ambivalence*, coined by Geoff Dench to subtitle his insightful and empathetic study of the plight of minorities in an open society. While acknowledging the truth of the master-image, I propose that the findings of this chapter are better conveyed by the metaphor of the *trap* than of *prison*. The story told in this chapter is of the modern offer of assimilation *luring* its victims into a state of chronic ambivalence with the bait of admission tickets to the world free from the stigma of otherness.

Literally, assimilation means making alike. Historical etymology shows that at some point during the seventeenth century the reference field of the term began to be stretched, gradually to embrace the uses most familiar and common today. Like other terms born of the novel experience of rising modernity and naming practices heretofore unnamed (or, rather, heretofore unexisting), it restructured the memory of the past, bringing out aspects unsuspected before. The processes the new term tried to capture were retrospectively postulated, sought, imputed or found and documented in past societies whose consciousness contained neither the concept nor the visions it awoke. A conscious, historically framed action has been, so to speak, 'dehistoricized', and envisaged as a perpetual and universal process; as a general characteristic of social life as such, rooted in the nature of human cohabitation (something like Tarde's all-too-human propensity to imitation) rather than tied to any historically specific body politic or political project. It suddenly seemed that everywhere and at all times differences between the ways human beings behave tend to wash out or at least blur; that whenever and wherever human beings of distinct habits lived close to each other, they would tend, with the passage of time, to become more like each other; sharply distinct habits would gradually give way and be replaced, so that more and more uniformity would result. This vision of the logic of human cohabitation stood in a stark contradiction to the quite recent and previously unquestioned, but now rapidly suppressed and forcibly forgotten, pre-modern practice which accepted the permanence of differentiation, considered 'sticking to one's kin' a virtue, penalized emulation and boundary-crossing – and on the whole viewed the differences with equanimity: as a fact of life calling for no more remedial action than spring storms or winter snows.

If the metaphorical origin of the term 'culture' has been by now amply documented, the same is not true of the concept of assimilation. This is regrettable, as the beginnings of modern uses of 'assimilation' provide a unique key to the *sociological hermeneutics* of the term, i.e. to the disclosure of the strategies of social action that originally sought expression in the borrowed trope, only to hide later behind its new 'naturalized' denomination, and of such aspects of those strategies as made the borrowed term 'fit' in the first place.

We learn from the *Oxford English Dictionary* that the earliest recorded use of the term 'assimilation', which preceded the later metaphorical applications by a century, was biological. In the biological narrative of the sixteenth century (*OED* records 1578 as the date of the first documented use) the term 'assimilation' referred to the acts of *absorption* and *incorporation* performed by living organisms. Unambiguously, 'assimilation' stood for *conversion*, not a self-administered change; an action performed by a living organism on its passive environment. It meant 'to convert into a substance of its own nature'; 'the conversion by an animal or plant of extraneous material into fluids and tissues identical with its own'. The first inchoate metaphorical uses of the term date from 1626, but it was not before the middle of the eighteenth century that the meaning was generalized into an unspecific '*making* alike'. The contemporary use, in which the onus is shifted towards the 'absorbed material' and away from the converting organism ('to *be*, or *become* like to . . .'), came last, and became common currency only about 1837 – exactly about the time when an invitation (or, more precisely, *the command*) to assimilate was first sent around by rising nationalisms.

We can surmise that what made such *biological* term attractive to those who sought a name for new *social* practices was above all the asymmetry it implied; the unambiguous unidirectionality of the process (the very opposition to the 'levelling up' implied by the 'getting more alike each other' image). As a part of biological narrative, 'assimilation' stood for the activity of the foraging organism, that *subordinated* parts of the environment to its own needs and did it by *transforming* them – so that they would become identical with its own 'fluids and tissues' (the organism as, simultaneously, the *causa finalis*, *causa formalis* and *causa efficiens* of the process and its outcome). The concept evoked the image of a living, active body, injecting its own contents and embossing its own form upon something different from itself, and doing this on its own initiative and for its own purpose (*having to do it* in order to remain alive); of a process, in the course of which the form and contents of the other entity went through a radical change, while the identity of the 'assimilating' body was maintained and, indeed, kept constant in the only way it could – by absorption. It was this imagery that made the *biological* concept eminently suitable for its new, *social*, semantic function. Once put to its new, metaphorical use, the concept captured the novel drive to uniformity, best expressed in the comprehensive cultural crusade on which the new, modern nation-states (or nations-in-search-of-a-state) had embarked. The drive reflected and augured the coming *intolerance to difference*.

The modern state meant the disempowerment of communal self-management and the dismantling of local or corporative mechanisms of self-perpetuation; by the same token, the modern state sapped the social foundations of communal and corporative traditions and forms of life. Self-reproduction of communally grounded forms of life either became impossible or at least met with formidable obstacles. This, in turn, broke the unthinking automaticism and the 'matter-of-factness' which marked the reproduction of patterns of human behaviour at its local and communal stage. Human conduct lost its previous appearance of naturalness; lost as well was the expectation that nature would take its course even if (or particularly if) unattended to and left to its own devices. With the backbone of communal self-reproduction crushed or fast disintegrating, the modern state was bound to engage in deliberate management of social processes on an unheard of scale. Indeed, it needed to generate *by design* what in the past could be relied upon to appear *on its own*. The modern nation-state did not 'take over' the function and the authority of local communities and corporations; it did not 'concentrate' the powers previously dispersed. It presided over the formation of an entirely new type of power, distinguished from all past powers by its unprecedented scope, depth of penetration, and ambition.[1]

---

[1] I have analysed this process at length in my *Legislators and Interpreters* (Cambridge: Polity Press, 1987), chaps. 3, 4.

The ambition was to create artificially what nature *could not* be *expected* to provide; or, rather, what it should not be *allowed* to provide. The modern state was a designing power, and designing meant to define the difference between order and chaos, to sift the proper from the improper, to legitimize one pattern at the expense of all the others. The modern state propagated some patterns and set to eliminate all others. All in all, it promoted similarity and uniformity. The principle of a uniform law for everybody residing on a given territory, of the identity of subjects as citizens, proclaimed that members of society, as objects of attention and vigilance of the state, were indistinguishable from each other, or at least were to be treated as such. By the same token, whatever group-distinctive qualities they might have possessed were declared illegitimate. As unauthorized and hence subversive, such qualities now generated anxiety: they testified to the non-completion of the task of order-building and the vulnerability of order.

In its essence, therefore, assimilation was a declaration of war on semantic ambiguity, on over- or under-determination of qualities. It was a manifesto of the 'either/or' dilemma: of the obligation to choose, and to choose unambiguously. More importantly still, it was a bid on the part of one section of society to exercise a monopolistic right to provide authoritative and binding meanings for all – and thus to classify sections of the state-administered body that 'did not fit' as *foreign* or *not sufficiently native*, out of tune and out of place, and thereby in need of radical reform. This prerogative was a single paragraph (though by no means a minor one) in the overall project to replace the *natural* state of things by an *artificially* designed order; in the bid on the part of the designers to exercise a monopolistic right to sort out the 'fitting' from the 'unfitting', the 'worthy' from the 'unworthy' categories, and to spell out the conditions under which transfer from the second to the first may (if at all) take place.

Above all, the vision of assimilation was a roundabout confirmation of social hierarchy of the extant forms of life. It assumed the superiority of one form of life and the inferiority of another; it made their inequality into an axiom, took it as a starting point of all argument, and hence made it secure against scrutiny and challenge. It effectively reinforced this inequality through making ambivalence (i.e., violation of politically and socially enforced categories) into a major crime, and punishing its carriers for its perpetration. By the same token, the discrimination of the 'unfitting' sectors of the social and political body was explained away by reference to their own flaws, imperfections and their very 'otherness'. The acceptance of assimilation as a vision and as a framework for a life strategy was tantamount to the recognition of the extant hierarchy, its legitimacy, and above all its immutability.

The vision and the programme of assimilation was also an important weapon in the effort of the modern nation-state to further sap the coherence and the power of resistance of competitive institutions of social control that limited or could limit its ambition of absolute sovereignty. Turned into an object of prospective assimilation, subjects of the state were expected to admit the inferiority of their present form of life. That inferiority was defined, upheld and enforced as a feature of the category as a whole, of a *collectively* maintained, communal form of life. The offer of escaping the stigmatizing classification through acceptance of a non-stigmatized form of life was, on the other hand, extended to the individuals *qua individuals*. Assimilation was an invitation to individual members of the stigmatized groups desist loyalty to the groups of origin (or the groups to which they had been designed by the classificatory decisions of state authorities), to challenge the right of those groups to set proper and binding standards of behaviour, to revolt against their power and renounce communal loyalty. Assimilation was, so to speak, an offer extended over the heads of, and in direct opposition to, communal and corporative powers. Assimilation was, therefore, an exercise in discrediting and disempowering the potentially competitive, communal or corporative, sources of social authority. It aimed at loosening the grip in which such competitive groups held their members. It aimed, in other words, at the elimination of such groups as forces of effective and viable competition.

Once this effect had been achieved – communal authorities robbed of their prestige and their legislative powers rendered ineffective – the threat of a serious challenge to the extant structure of domination was practically eliminated. The potential competitors were shorn of their power to resist and engage in a dialogue with even a remote chance of success. Collectively, they were powerless. It was left to the individual members to seek to wash off the collective stigma of foreignness by meeting the conditions set by the gatekeepers of the dominant group. The individuals were left at the mercy of the gatekeepers. They were objects of scrupulous examination and assessment by the dominant group, who held complete control over the meaning of their conduct. Whatever they did, and whatever meaning they intended to invest in their actions, would have *a priori* reaffirmed the controlling capacity of the dominant group. Their clamouring for admission automatically reinforced the latter's claim to dominance. The standing invitation to apply for entry, and the positive response to it, confirmed the dominant group in its status of the holder, the guardian and the plenipotentiary of superior values, by the same token giving material substance to the concept of 'value superiority'. The very fact of issuing the invitation established the dominant group in the position of the *arbitrating power*, a force entitled to set the exams and mark the performance. Individual members of the categories declared as substandard were now measured and evaluated by the extent of their conformity with the values of the dominant national elite. They were 'progressive' if they strove to imitate the dominant patterns and to erase all traces of the original ones. They were labelled 'backward' as long as they retained loyalty to the traditional patterns, or were not apt or fast enough in ridding themselves of their residual traces.

What made the standing invitation particularly alluring and morally disarming was the fact that it came in the disguise of benevolence and tolerance; indeed, the assimilatory project went down in history as a part of the *liberal* political programme, of the tolerant and enlightened stance that exemplified all the most endearing traits of a 'civilized state'. The disguise effectively concealed the fact that the assimilatory offer must have tacitly assumed, in order to make sense, the stiffness of discriminatory norms and the finality of the verdict of inferiority passed on nonconformist values. The tolerance, understood as the encouragement of 'progressive attitudes' expressed in the search of individual 'self-improvement', was meaningful only as long as the *measures* of progress were not negotiable. Under the policy of assimilation, tolerant treatment of *individuals* was inextricably linked to intolerance aimed at collectivities, their ways of life, their values and, above all, their value-legitimating powers. Indeed, the first was a major instrument in the successful promotion of the second.

The effective disfranchisement of alternative value-generating and value-legitimating authorities was represented as the universality of values supported by the extant hierarchy. In fact, however, the alleged universality of the authoritatively hailed and promoted values had no other material substratum than the expediently protected sovereignty of the value-adjudicating powers. The more effective was the suppression of possible sources of challenge, the less chance there was that the bluff of the claim of universality would be called, and that the pretence of the absolute validity of value-claims would be unmasked as a function of power monopoly. The degree to which the locally dominant values could credibly claim a supra-local validity was a function of their local supremacy.

The case of the German Jews

It so happens that a considerable part of the sociological theory of modern assimilation has been articulated in an explicit or implicit reference to the Jewish experience.[2] This has been hardly accidental, as both the assimila-

---

[2] Cf. for instance, the standard text, Milton Gordon, *Assimilation in American Life* (London: Oxford University Press, 1964).

tory programme of modern nation-states and the responses to it on the part of the targeted population had been most fully and explicitly developed in the context of Jewish assimilatory problems. As the Jews confronted the assimilatory pressure in virtually every modernizing society of Europe, their problems were at no time confined to one nation-state and from the start suggested a comparative perspective, implying a need and a possibility of generalization. The whole process could be scanned from a supra-local and a supra-national vantage point; a circumstance that revealed the universal spread of the limits and inner contradictions of the process, otherwise liable to have been overlooked.

In the academic and popular imagery of the Jewish assimilation, of the Jewish entry into the modern world (or Jewish emergence from the ghetto), the story of the German Jews occupies the central, and in many senses a prototypical, place. Quite a few circumstances have contributed to this prominence.

The most obvious is the fact that almost all Jewish, or Jewish-born founders and heroes of modern culture, from Marx to Freud, Kafka or Wittgenstein, wrote their seminal contributions to modern consciousness in German. Any investigation of the social and cultural context that gave them the courage and the determination to destroy and to create, and any search for a peculiar biographical experience that was to be later reprocessed and sublimated in their ideas, leads inevitably to the scrutiny of Jewish life in Germany (or, more correctly, in East-Central European countries under the influence of German language and culture).

Equally obvious is the pivotal position which German Jewry (and, more generally, German-speaking Jewish communities) occupied for more than a century among all other sections of European Jewry that fell within the orbit of modernizing processes. Up to the outbreak of the Great War and for a considerable part of the interwar intermezzo, German Jews boasted the richest, most comfortably settled, most culturally advanced and creative community in diaspora. Collectively, they were firmly established in the role of the main purveyor of Jewish ideologies, self-definitions and fashions. Through Moses Mendelsohn they served as a broker in the marriage between Judaism and Enlightenment. Through Theodor Herzl they rendered the same service to the marriage between Jewishness and modern nationalism. With equal power and authority, they set patterns for the reassessment and 'modernization' of the Jewish law, for the project of emanicipation-through-acculturation, or for the avenues of escape from Jewish identity. The *Allgemeine Zeitung des Judentums* had every right to advertise itself in 1890 as a 'spiritual gathering point for all cultivated Jews'.

Somewhat less obvious, yet a paramount factor in the prominence of German Jewry was its borderline position between the small, well-rooted and on the whole affluent Jewish communities of the West and the vast expanses of impoverished East-European Jewry. German Jews lived an insecure, challenging and adventurous frontier-style life in more than one sense. On the top of the evident geopolitical frontier there was a cultural one as well: while the Western Jews prided themselves in their growing cultural refinement, their Eastern relatives sank ever deeper in what by Western standards could be viewed only as pre-modern, retrograde, derisory and shameful mysticism, superstition and 'lack of culture'. Located nearer to Eastern Jewry than any other Western Jewish community (in fact, much too close for comfort – incorporation of Posen and Silesia into united Germany made topographical, political and social separation from the 'uncivilized' tribe unattainable), German Jews had to assume the frontier role of ethnographers, cultural interpreters and mediators. Secure in their authority of the collective narrator, they articulated the identity and the problematics of East-European Jewry for the use of all the other Jewish communities. One can venture a hypothesis that without German mediation, Eastern-European Jews would remain both voiceless and invisible to their Western brethren – at least until the start of their massive exodus to the West in the late nineteenth century. As it happened, their arrival was everywhere preceded by the German narration and the stereotype it forged and disseminated. The reception they received in the West and the policies they found applied to themselves were first tried and tested at the Jewish frontier-posts in Germany. Thus for the duration of 'high modernity' and through the heyday of Jewish assimilation, German Jewry remained the vital linchpin holding together the two branches of Jewish European diaspora. In the result, though not necessarily by their own design, they served as the testing ground for the viability of cultural assimilation as a vehicle of social integration in a modern (or, rather, modernizing) society. For the same reason, their history may offer the fullest inventory of the driving forces of assimilation, the dilemmas with which it confronts its pursuers, and the obstacles it is bound to encounter on the road to its target.

Last but not least, the exceptional fullness and paradigmatical potential of the picture offered by the history of German Jewry stems from the fact that it was in Germany and the German-speaking lands that modernization was first lived as a *conscious*, motivated process, informed from the start by the awareness of the ultimate destination and thus guided by publicly discussed and purposefully selected strategies. In line with the German modernizing experience in general, the Jewish-German modernizing experience has been therefore self-monitored, reflected upon and theorized to a degree unmatched in other, apparently similar, cases. It left in its wake an impressive volume of processed and pre-interpreted evidence which offers a truly unique insight into the life-world of people who had been drawn into the whirlwind of rapid social change, while remaining convinced of navigating the individual ships they sailed. What applied to Germany as a whole could not but be vividly and self-consciously reflected in the modernizing experience of its Jewry. As Jacob Katz commented in the book he recently edited, 'Jewish modernization in Germany turned articulated'.[3] No other Jewish community has documented its modernizing itinerary so thoroughly. If the modernization was discussed elsewhere at all, it was as a rule in the form of commenting on, or criticizing the ideas first given an articulate form by the Jewish thinkers and politicians in Germany, and drawing theoretical and pragmatic conclusions from them.

Because of these considerations, the history of the Jews inhabiting the German-dominated cultural area has been selected here as the focal case, and the principal factual source, in our exploration of the episode of Jewish assimilation, but also of the general sociological mechanisms of modern assimilatory processes.

The modernizing logic of Jewish assimilation

The universalizing ambitions of emerging nation-states, that later became a ubiquitous, and arguably the most salient, trait of all modernization, had been first proclaimed by the French Enlightenment, and made into a practical problem for most of Europe by the French Revolution – most vividly and poignantly by the Napoleonic conquest and the first modern attempt at pan-European unification that followed it. The dawn of universalistic ideals and strategies found the Jews still in virtually unscathed ghetto conditions. In Michael A. Meyer's opinion,

> As the eighteenth century wore on, it became more and more apparent that the concepts of a universal human nature, universal natural law, and universal rationality made the exclusion of the Jew a gross anomaly. But it was one thing to draw the conclusion abstractly and another to apply it. For most of the writers of the eighteenth century, particularly on the Continent, the flesh-and-blood Jew with his beard, strange garments, and wholly irrational ceremonial law seemed somewhat less than a human being.[4]

---

[3] *Towards Modernity: The European Jewish Model*, ed. Jacob Katz (New Brunswick: Transaction Books, 1987), p. 11.

[4] Michael A. Meyer, *The Origins of the Modern Jew: Jewish Identity and European Culture in Germany, 1749–1824* (Detroit: Wayne State University Press, 1979), p. 15.

The fact that the Jews differed from the rest of the population, or rather from every one of the many different parts of the population, was in no way unique. On the contrary, sharply distinct styles of life practised by, and ascribed or imputed to the mutually segregated ranks or estates, had remained a trivial and uncontested rule through the centuries which preceded the modern era. In this sense the distinctiveness of Jews made them just one case among many in a wide set of phenomena, collectively defined by the modernizing nation-state as its major, perhaps even the paramount, challenge and concern – as that diversity which must give way to the uniformity of the modern social order.

As in the rest of cases falling into this category, Jewish communal autonomy was an abomination from the point of view of the absolutist, all-penetrating and monopolistic tendencies of high-handed and valiantly nationalist state power. It had to be crushed, or reduced to the few traits viewed as irrelevant and innocuous thanks to the unconcern or indifference of the state. The peculiar legal status of the Jews – legal restrictions as well as privileges, residential and occupational exclusions as well as juridical autonomy – had to give way to new universal codes which recognized no group prerogatives, and thus could not recognize the legal form of discrimination.

If legal equality progressed but haltingly through the German lands, this was for reasons unconnected specifically with the Jews; the fate of German modernization was tied to the convoluted history of German unification. German Jews who viewed with a jaundiced eye the legal equality bestowed by the Napoleonic Code on their relatives across the Rhine, and ever more vociferously demanded their own *Gleichberechtigung*, strove, however, to speed up a process which (all the numerous and lengthy setbacks notwithstanding) was bound to come to completion anyway; all the more so for Germany's own modernizing impatience. Equality before the law meant, after all, the sapping of communal autonomy, discreditation of communal authority, undermining the centrifugal influences of communal and corporative elites; it was an indispensable part of the process which lead to the institution of modern state power with its monopoly of law-making and coercion.

Abolition of legal privileges and discriminations was but one aspect of the modern thrust toward uniformity. Modernization was also a *cultural* crusade; a powerful and relentless drive to extirpate differences in values and life-styles, customs and speech, beliefs and public demeanour. It was, first and foremost, a drive to redefine all cultural values and styles except those endorsed by the modernizing elite (and particularly the values and styles that resisted the *Gleichschaltung* process) as inferior: signs or stigmas of backwardness, retardation, mental impairment or, in extreme cases, of insanity. The cultural crusade had the establishment of strict cultural hierarchy as its ultimate purpose. Loyalty to discredited values and life-styles was tantamount to confinement to the lower rungs of the cultural ladder. When persevering in such loyalties, the individuals risked the exclusion from the universe selected for missionary activity, and a life-sentence of strangerhood. If, on the other hand, individuals attempted to shed the discredited values and acquire instead the endorsed ones this was interpreted as a further proof of the universal validity and desirability of the dominant values and the superiority of their social carriers.

Into this trap, the Jews – and particularly the richest and the most educated among them – fell with enthusiasm and abandon. It did stand to reason that once the cultural idiosyncrasies had been effaced and diversity dissolved in a uniform national culture, the indiscriminately *human* face would emerge and be recognized as such. Looking back at the era of high hopes and bitter frustration, Peter Pulzer commented on the

> uncritical acceptance of the pre-1848 orthodoxy that German national unification would bring Jewish salvation; there was a general unwillingness to recognize the dark side of all – not only German – nationalism, the intolerant, authoritarian, xenophobic and aggressive potential in the nationalist mentality. Nothing illustrated this better than the willingness of important sections of Jewish opinion to support the illiberalisms of the Liberal era, such as Kulturkampf and the anti-socialist laws.[5]

What did matter in the end was the fact that it was the native elite which usurped and jealously guarded the right to judge and decide whether the efforts to overcome cultural inferiority had been truly earnest and, above all, successful (indeed, it cannot be stressed too often that the whole idea of social improvement as the task of assimilation derived its sense from the presence of such a firmly entrenched and uncontested elite; to assimilate meant to acknowledge – even if obliquely – its unchallengeable superiority). For individuals aspiring to be admitted to the company of the elect, the world turned into a testing ground, and life into a permanent trial period. They had confined themselves to a life under scrutiny, to a lifelong and never conclusive examination. They soon learned, if they had not known it before, that they were under observation, that the observation would never lead to a final and irrevocable judgement, and that passing the successive trial with flying colours would not exempt them from further tests. They also learned that they would be allowed no influence on

[5] Peter Pulzer, 'Jewish Participation in Wilhelmine Politics', in *Jews and Germans from 1960 to 1933: The Problematic Symbiosis*, ed. David Bronsen (Heidelberg: Carl Winter, 1979), p. 82.

the content of the examination and on the standards by which the results were to be marked. These were set examinations, and the standing board of examiners had full freedom to change the papers and the rules of marking without notice.

Philip Roth encapsulated the consequences of this asymmetrical power structure with his usual wit and precision: 'Jews are people who are not what anti-Semites say they are.' The 'anti-Semites' – or, perhaps more correctly, the suspicious, watchful and vigilant housemasters – wrote the scenario for Jewish self-constructing and self-ennobling efforts by listing the traits for which the Jews stood condemned. They, the housemasters, had all the initiative, which extended over the whole length of the assimilation drama: from writing the scenario to the critique of the production and the ultimate sanction of firing the cast. What the Jews did, acquired its meaning from the evaluation by others. The Jews were called to prove that the charges raised against them were untrue (or *no more* true); but the same people who brought forth the charges would pronounce on the cogency of the proofs. Both the call to assimilation and the utter improbability of answering it properly (i.e., in a manner which the jury was likely to find satisfactory) stemmed from the same source: the power structure of cultural and social domination, which had been rendered all the more overwhelming and less challengeable by the abolition of legal differentiation and the declaration of political equality.

Summing up his life-long study of life and work of Heinrich Heine, S.S. Prawer found his hero having done everything he had been advised and goaded to do to 'rid himself' of his Jewishness. Heine tried to acquit himself of the task 'by ostentatiously showing himself unfit for the kind of mercantile or banking career in which so many Jews . . . had been signally successful . . .'; 'by seeking predominantly non-Jewish company at the universities of Bonn and Göttingen and subscribing to the duelling ethos of student fraternities'; by openly and publicly disavowing the Judaist lore as a fossil of bygone and shameful times, devoid of use or value for the modern man; by angrily objecting to being defined as a Jew by either enemies or friends; even by accepting that Jewishness was a 'disease' in need of a cure, and excelling in the derision and ridicule of all aspects of conduct or physique which had been stereotyped as specifically Jewish, like 'physical clumsiness and gracelessness, the "Jewish" nose, the insanitary appearance of Jews from Eastern Europe, Jewish pawnbroking and trade in cast-off clothing, the mercantile "genius" of the Jews, the parvenu behaviour of Jewish *nouveaux riches*, the *Fresser* or guzzlers who "despised the higher flights of the mind" ', or the traces of Yiddish in speech.[6]

---

[6] S.S. Prawer, *Heine's Jewish Comedy* (Oxford: Clarendon Press, 1983), pp. 760–1.

Indeed, Heine drew liberally from the catalogue of Jewish sins and faults which, by the resolution of the dominant cultural elite, had to be repented of or repaired as a condition of the 'all is forgiven' verdict. He used them with a passion which often dwarfed the fervour of the outsiders, thanks to his own supreme gift of wit and irony as much as to his singeing feeling of shame; having once accepted the superiority of the ideals which had not been his by birth, Heine must have been overwhelmed by the desire to cleanse himself of the birthmarks which the accepted ideals condemned. And yet Heine's efforts remained inconclusive and in the end unrewarded. The louder he protested his emancipation from Jewishness, the more his Jewishness seemed to be evident and protruding. (Martha Robert wrote of Freud, who unlike Heine never denied his Jewishness, but believed it to contribute to 'human science' as such, that 'his efforts to pass unnoticed only attracted atention'; Freud was 'identified as a Jew by the very effort which he hoped would make him unrecognizable'.)[7] The display of assimilatory passion was perceived as the most convincing proof of his Jewish identity. To the Frenchmen among whom Heine in the end settled as the self-appointed ambassador and champion of German culture, he might have been a German. To the Germans, he was unmistakably and unredeemably a Jew. Nothing Heine did and could do helped him.

It did not help Marx either to demonstrate his non-Jewish credentials by fighting out his political disagreements with such weapons as dismissing his ideological adversary Lassalle as a 'Jewish nigger', or announcing his disgust for Lassalle's 'constant babble with the falsely excited voice, the unaesthetic, demonstrative gestures, the didactic tone' as well as the 'uncultivated eating and the horny lust'. The resigned wisdom of Ludwig Börne (Heine's and Marx's contemporary) verbalized the experience of the whole generation, and anticipated that of several generations of German Jews to come: 'Some accuse me of being a Jew; some excuse me for being one; some even praise me for being a Jew. But all think about it.'[8]

Many decades after these words had been put on paper, another German Jew, Jacob Wassermann, was to find out that however German his touch, it would leave on everything the stamp of Jewishness. As his friend explained, sympathetically yet offering no hope of redemption, 'Jewishness is like a concentrated dye: a minute quantity suffices to give a specific character – or, at least, some traces of it – to an incomparably greater mass.' Wassermann found no evidence to prove his friend wrong. Everything he learned the hard way from his own life's experience pointed to

---

[7] Martha Robert, *From Oedipus to Moses: Freud's Jewish Identity*, trans. Ralph Mannheim (New York: Anchor Books, 1976), p. 17.

[8] Sander L. Gilman, *Jewish Self-Hatred: Anti-Semitism and the Hidden Language of the Jews* (Baltimore: Johns Hopkins University Press, 1986), pp. 206–7, 162.

the truth of his friend's opinion. No one among his German critics and companions 'would concede that I too bore a colour and stamp of German life' – even if the world viewed his novels as delectable specimens of high-quality German literature. Everything his German readers – admirers and detractors alike – found impeccably, unchallengeably 'German' in his work, free of a single hue or shade setting it apart from the accepted standards of the German novel, they ascribed to Jewish zeal, shrewdness or uncanny gift of imitation, rather than to Wassermann's Germanhood. His writing's 'unconscious and inherent characteristics seemed to them a product of deliberation, of Jewish ingenuity, of Jewish cleverness in adaptation and disguise, of the dangerous power of deluding and ensnaring'.[9]

After many years of incessant labour and a lot of widely acclaimed literary achievements, Wassermann lost faith in the final success of his efforts. He began to see that the lack of appreciation for his works as contributions to German literature, German art, German culture or German consciousness was not a temporary setback, an accidental outcome of

---

[9] Jacob Wassermann, *My Life as German and Jew* (London: Allen & Unwin, 1934), pp. 72, 116. Wassermann's experience of a Jew adopting the language and the culture of the host country and his homeland was by no means unique. It was replicated all around Europe. Of Polish cases similar to Wassermann's, for instance, Artur Sandauer wrote ('O sytuacji pisarza polskiego pochodzenia żydowskiego w XX wieku' [On the situation of the Polish writer of Jewish origin in the Twentieth Century], in *Pisma Zebrane*, vol. 3 (Warsaw, Czytelnik, 1985), p. 468): 'to assimilate' means to 'stay, defenceless, under the gaze of the others' and to accept without murmur the judgemental canons and the aesthetic criteria of others. By so doing, the 'assimilating individual' must also 'consent to his own ugliness'. Jewishness was declared ugly, and so were all the so-called 'Jewish traits'. One could do something (at least in theory) to escape the ugliness of Jewish religion – by conversion, or of Jewish habits or manners of speaking – by self-drill. There was nothing one could do about one's look – and this heinous gift of the genes tended to emerge unscathed from no matter how many bucketfuls of the baptismal water. Polish poet Antoni Slonimski, born Christian of an already Christian father, inherited from his ancestors a distinctly Jewish face together with their passionate adoration of Polish culture; the second did not help him against the first. Like the others – the unconverted, those who openly flaunted their Jewish roots and those who tried to hide or deny them – Slonimski had been disqualified as a Jew.

The emergent modern culture of Poland was full of converted and non-converted Jews. Coming from urban centres and boasting the best education Poland could offer, they easily assumed the role of cultural umpires toward whom the native poets and writers, more often than not of rural if not peasant extraction, looked for guidance and accolade. Expectedly, the growth of their importance in Polish culture went hand in hand with the increase in the intensity and spread of Polish antisemitism. Hence the 'unique phenomenon: the most beloved writers become, as persons, the most hated'.

neglect or misfortune. Bitterly, Wassermann bid farewell to the dreamers whose illusions he once shared and whose naivety he now understood: 'no accomplishment, no renunciation of self, no toil or passion, no figure or image, no melody or vision – will suffice to bring him [a German Jew], as a matter of course, the confidence and dignity and inviolability which the least of those who stand in the opposed camp enjoys in full'. Because he is not told, does not know or would not admit that non-negotiable truth, the German Jew is spared no humiliation. On the way to the ultimate defeat he turns into a figure of ridicule and derision. 'I had to employ the most fiery persuasion, the extremest effort where others needed only to beckon'; he is tempted to embark on conduct that the hostile and suspicious opinion had first demanded, only to brandish it later as a proof of Jewish arrogance and pushiness, and to deploy it as the clinching argument against granting the zealot a full citizenship of native culture. And the chase of the target whose remoteness grew with the diligence of the effort to reach it was prompted to go on forever, so that there would be no bottom to the humiliation of the runners and no shortage of excuses for their detractors: 'I was forced, with every fresh piece of work, to begin all over again a Sisyphean labour . . . Others enjoyed a credit account; they were permitted to draw upon it from time to time. I, however, had to present my credentials every time, to stake my whole fortune.'[10]

---

[10] Wassermann, *My Life as German and Jew*, pp. 120, 104. Again, Martha Robert offers a succinct and precise summary of the problem: 'Everyone knows that a native requires no special effort to conform to his country's customs and habits of thought, whereas a foreigner gives himself away by his need to explain and understand not only complicated matters, but the simplest trifles, the thousand nothings that are said and done in every moment of daily life' (*From Oedipus to Moses*, p. 17).

A younger contemporary of Wassermann, Walter Benjamin (justly described by George Steiner as the most important *German* aesthetician and literary critic of the twentieth century) pithily expressed what Wassermann and others like him learned about the tenuousness of the relation between what they did and how were they seen and dealt with: It is not really 'man who has a fate; rather, the subject of fate is indeterminable. The judge can perceive fate wherever he pleases; with every judgment he must blindly dictate fate. It is never man but only the life in him that it strikes – the part involved in natural guilt and misfortune by virtue of illusion' ('Fate and Character', in: *One Way Street and Other Writings*, trans. Edmund Jephcott and Kingsley Shorter (London: Verso, 1985), p. 128.) Elsewhere Benjamin would write empathetically of the plight of the courtier, whose proverbial and despised manipulativeness of a spineless changeling could be accounted for only partly by the lack of character; it also 'reflects an inconsolable, despondent surrender to an impenetrable conjunction of baleful constellations' that 'seem to have taken on a massive, almost thing-like cast' (quoted after *One Way Street and Other Writings*, 'Introduction' by Susan Sonntag).

The dimensions of loneliness

As the rejection acquired the awesome regularity of daily routine, loneliness turned from an episodic misfortune into the standard condition. Loneliness was now that world in which the business of life was to be conducted and to which the self had to adjust to endow life with meaning. Skilful dissector of human psyche as he was, Wassermann offered an uncompromising insight into this world of loneliness, suspended in the depopulated, ambivalent and meaningless space stretching between inaccessible worlds of togetherness and sharing:

> No individual claimed me as a being akin to him, nor did any group; neither the people of my blood, nor those whom I yearned to join; neither those of my own species nor these of my choice. For I had at last decided to make a choice; and I had made it. It was my inner destiny rather than a free decision that had brought about my secession from the old circle. The new, however, neither received nor accepted me.[11]

Looking back from his American exile on the drama of the Jewish unrequited and unconsummated love affair with Germanhood, Kurt Lewin could generalize the intensely personalized social tragedy of ambivalence

---

[11] Wassermann, *My Life as German and Jew*, pp. 46–7. And here is Martha Robert's rendition of a similar experience of Freud: 'If he was to become German, he had to destroy himself as a Jew in the name of something that he was not or not yet, or that he was only in his own eyes, and certainly not in the eyes of the community with which he aspired to merge.' (*From Oedipus to Moses*, p. 17.)

Of the interwar life of the Jews assimilated into Polish culture, Efraim Kaganowski, a Jewish writer from Warsaw, left a few shuddering sketches: 'Cafe *Ziemiańska*, where the avant-garde of the Polish–Jewish congregate. Writers, poets, artists come here – a curious family, that on every opportunity complains of the 'Jewish gathering'. They are not yet sure of their Polishness and suddenly notice that they are surrounded only by other Jews. This is why they feel here so well, at home.' 'It is hopeless in the narrow Jewish streets. But it is also gloomy in the affluent Jewish flats. And only late at night in a large Jewish bourgeois restaurant . . . you can meet creatures from another world, whom you have never seen so far in any Jewish place. They come with an expression of people who are lost on their way or of tourists in search of the exotic. One journalist whispers: "Do you see that man over there, with that woman? Do you know, who they are?" They found themselves for the first time in Jewish surroundings . . . After a while I saw that famous assimilator dancing with his companion among the Jewish crowd. But this Jewish night-life does not intoxicate. On their way back home the night guests do not feel drunk. The Jewish eyes are fearful and vigilant. These men want to be crushed in the crowd so that they can stop feeling how lonely they are.' (*Warszawskie Opowiadania* [Warsaw Stories] (Warsaw, Iskry, 1958), pp. 174–5.)

that Wassermann shared with so many others of his own and the preceding generations:

> It is characteristic of individuals crossing the margin between social groups that they are not only uncertain about their belonging to the group they are ready to enter, but also about their belonging to the group they are leaving . . . Not the *belonging to many groups* is the cause of the difficulty, but an *uncertainty* of belongingness.[12]

The educated elite among German Jews had ever less confidence, and mounting evidence to the contrary, that their bid for the full and unconditional membership of German society and culture had been accepted, or was likely to be granted in however distant a future. What made the uncertainty particularly unbearable was the lack of a rear line of trenches to which they could retreat in case of defeat. With the lines of retreat to the original Jewish community no longer passable, they were stuck in a no-man's land, exposed on all sides to enemy shells, with no place to hide in sight except the craters left by the past hits.

They had left the old trenches to advance, of course. But they left them also because the trenches did not seem any more a reliable defence, or did not look worth defending. However ineffective they might be found in other respects, the immediate, undeniable, tangible effect of the assimilatory pressures of the modern or modernizing, national or nationalizing state was the discreditation of private armies and collectively built fortifications. Attracted by the offers extended to individuals only, members left their communal hideouts if they could, and saw them as prisons rather than shelters if they could not. Communities which in the past learned to live and survive in a hostile or indifferent environment could not well retain their integrity for long when faced with the deceptively benign individual offers of homeliness and brotherhood, made all the more attractive by the alternative of an outspoken and unqualified condemnation in case of refusal. Not only were they not the only homes currently on the market, but their quality as accommodation had been questioned and was declared obsolete and inferior. The remaining residents resented their communal duties and tried hard to reduce them to bare, routine essentials, whose meaning they neither understood nor wished to fathom. Attracted by the glittering prizes on offer in other quarters, the residents grew up to consider their current addresses as liabilities – sometimes degrading, always constraining.

After a few decades of assimilatory adventure, little was left of the pre-modern coherence of the Jewish world. New generations continued to be

---

12 Kurt Lewin, *Resolving Social Conflicts*, ed. Gertrud Weiss Lewin (London: Souvenir Press, 1948), pp. 148, 179.

born into that world and be assigned to it by birth. But they poorly understood the meaning of the assignment. What they saw could hardly arouse enthusiasm, much less inspire devotion. 'Hardly any traces remained of either community or religion. Precisely speaking, we were Jews only in name', remembers Wassermann of his childhood, spent in the shadow of the 'Byzantine edifice' of a modern synagogue, whose 'upstart magnificence' was meant to hide the fact that 'faith is losing its power over the hearts of men'.[13] Once he had started on his long travel back to Judaism, it dawned upon Gershon (then Gerhard) Scholem that his father's Jewish identity was much too shallow to accommodate the roots he wished to strike. That identity was reduced to a ritual, and carefully stripped of all emotions. Jewish tradition, though accepted and even (perfunctorily) observed, was treated too lightly for Scholem's newly awakened Jewish sensitivity to stomach. He felt deeply offended when his father, a fairly representative member of the 'broad Jewish liberal middle class', 'numerically by far the strongest group' among German Jewry of the time, lit his cigar of the Sabbath candle, mumbling a mock blessing: 'boirei pri tobakko'.[14] Scholem came to believe that were he to identify himself as a Jew (and Scholem did not mean by that, either at that stage or any later period in his life, the Jewish orthodoxy in its rabbinical version), he would first have to discard the sham Jewishness in the form sustained and perpetuated by whatever remained of the Jewish community in Germany. In his famous though never dispatched letter to his father, Franz Kafka complained that he was offered no 'Jewish material' from which to mould his identity; one could hardly count the boring and lackadaisical synagogue services and farciful, tongue-in-cheek Passover feasts as a material that could be used to shape anything but spiritual homelessness. Kafka was condemned to live 'in the society where his birth placed him without entitling him to call himself at home';[15] one part of that society would always look upon him as an outsider and an intruder ('how wretched', complained Kafka in a letter to his sister Ottla, 'that one can never fully introduce oneself right away'), the other part offered him too few bricks and no mortar to build a house.

The very zeal with which the Jews tried to rid themselves of whatever the native elites declared to be the mark of an alien, was itself forged into

---

13 Wassermann, *My Life as German and Jew*, p. 16.

14 Gershom Scholem, 'On the Social Psychology of the Jews in Germany: 1900–1933', in *Jews and Germans from 1860 to 1933: The Problematic Symbiosis*, ed. David Bronsen (Heidelberg: Carl Winter, 1979), pp. 16–18.

15 Martha Robert, *Franz Kafka's Loneliness*, trans. Ralph Mannheim (London: Faber & Faber, 1982), p. 9.

the brand of Jewishness. With a twisted logic which to its victims looked more like a witch's spell, the Jewish *Entjudung*, the exercise in modesty and self-effacing, was perceived by the native opinion as *Verjudung*, that is as the Jewish invasion and conquest of vital areas of social and cultural life of the nation which should have been kept pure from corroding foreign influence. (Wagner accused Jewish artists, convinced of making a valuable contribution to German culture, of transforming the arts into *Kunstwaarenwechsel*.)[16] When Heine and Börne excelled as *journalists* – became proud masters of direct speech, light style, informed and ironic comment – journalism as such became a symbol of Jewishness – a Jewish invention for all, a Jewish retreat for some, a Jewish conspiracy for the most hostile among native opinion-makers. The acute and incurable tension between resilient Jewish particularity and the utopia of assimilation was destined to remain, in Jacob Katz's words, 'a central feature in the history of the Jewish community' in post-Enlightenment Germany.[17] Particularity remained resilient partly because legal emancipation arrived too late for the Jews to enter the old-established occupations previously prohibited; partly because they continued to practise the 'Jewish by definition' occupations to which they had been confined and in which they had been enclosed in the past; but also, and most remarkably, because as they entered new occupations and excelled in practising them, these new occupations showed a stunning tendency to be reclassified as Jewish. The professional pragmatics that these occupations framed and promoted was described as the emanation of Jewish spirit, and the skills they required were defined as inborn qualities of Jewish character.

The traditional, pre-modern Jewish *segregation* took on, therefore, a new and subtler form: that of *estrangement*. Territorial and functional separation was replaced (sometimes merely topped up) by social isolation and spiritual loneliness. Acculturation did not incorporate the Jews into German society, but transformed them into a separate, ambivalent and incongruous, non-category category of 'assimilated Jews', prised from the traditional Jewish community as much as from the native German elites. In the no-win game of assimilation, the German-educated Jews found themselves transferred from closely-knit territorial ghetto to the ghetto of social

---

[16] Cf. Steven E. Ascheim, '"The Jew Within"; The Myth of "Judaisation" in Germany', in *The Jewish Response to German Culture: From the Enlightenment to the Second World War*, ed. Jehuda Reinharz and Walter Schatzberg (Boston: University Press of New England, 1985), pp. 212, 228.

[17] Jacob Katz, *Out of the Ghetto: The Social Background of Jewish Emancipation, 1770–1870* Cambridge, Mass.: Harvard University Press, 1973), p. 190.

incongruity and cultural ambivalence. Unlike the old Jewish estate from which the assimilants wished to emancipate, the new class of assimilated Jews suffered a profound ambiguity of status, marked by the contradiction and continuous friction between the self-definition and socially binding classification.

The assimilating Jews acted under the pressure to prove their Germanhood, yet the very attempt to prove it was held against them as the evidence of their duplicity and, in all probability, also of subversive intentions. The circle was bound to remain vicious, for the simple reason that the values to which the Jews were told to surrender in order to earn acceptance were the very values which rendered acceptance impossible. *Germanhood*, like all nation-bound qualities, was singularly unfit for the purpose of assimilation driven by learning and self-improvement. Nation is not a product of learning, however protracted. Nation is a commonality of fate and blood – or not a nation at all. At the moment when the self-improvement of an individual starts, the question of national membership has been settled for a long time; no self-drilling zeal can re-make the past or declare it non-existent.[18] Anything one can acquire in the course of self-training must seem pitifully wan and unreal when confronted with the solidity of the sedimented and petrified past. There was, therefore, nothing accidental about the fact that the value system the assimilating Jews borrowed 'not only was never theirs in its entirety, but always contained elements inimical to them. The Germans always saw the adoption of it as merely a mask behind which glowered the unregenerate Jew. Sadly, for the German Jew the mask was the only reality.'[19]

The paradoxical outcome of the assimilatory effort was that the very activities and life-styles intended to obliterate the separation were seen as reasons for setting their bearers apart. Contrary to the popular adage 'Be a Jew at home, man in the street', the would-be Germans felt truly German *only at home*, where they could undisturbed play their game of illusions

---

[18] The Russian–Jewish philosopher Lev Shestov pursued in his writings the idea of omnipotence of faith. To believe in God, he asserted repeatedly, is to trust that *everything is possible*, and this includes as well the possibility of effacing the past (to make, for instance, the shameful act of poisoning Socrates 'never to have existed'). Shestov's audacious conception, much as his flight into religion understood mostly as the refusal to accept the finality of any wordly evidence, must have arisen from a very Jewish experience of the limits of freedom confined to the present and to the future, and of the consequences of the fact that Enlightenment, so to speak, *retro non agit*. Cf., for example, *Reason and Revelation* [in Russian] (Paris: YMCA Press, 1964).

[19] Bruno Bettelheim, *Autonomy in a Mass Age* (New York: Free Press, 1960), p. 173–4.

protected from the unsympathetic, scrutinizing gaze of the German street. They either consciously *sought* the company of people like them – of other Jews embarked on the perilous adventure of assimilation – or, much to their amazement and horror, *found* themselves in such a company through a process of negative selection. Wherever he moved – in Düsseldorf, in Hamburg, in Berlin, in Paris – Heine 'was surrounded by Jewish-born associates of various persuasions and various degrees of congeniality'.[20] Almost a century later Scholem found that the same was true of his highly assimilated, 'Germanized' family: they had practically no social intercourse with non-Jews. 'One day it dawned on me that for friendly intercourse our home was exclusively visited by Jews, and that my parents paid visits only to Jews.' Almost totally Jewish were the 'dancing classes' frequented by the adolescents of 'good German families'. On his jubilee, Scholem's father was paid courtesy visits by his Gentile associates, yet he felt that it would be 'unfair' to reciprocate.[21] (One of the ironic consequences of such social isolation was Jewish ignorance of the intensity of popular Judaeophobia; they neither met antisemites, nor stooped to read their press, and thus their 'hopes and readiness for integration grew as in a hothouse' – they were free to dream their dreams undisturbed by the counterevidence of harsh reality. They only had the opportunity to preach to the converted, and thus the Germany into which they wished to integrate existed mostly in their collective fantasy and remained immune to empirical test.)

---

[20] Prawer, *Heine's Jewish Comedy*, p. 762. Heine's fate repeated itself in the experience of another 'former Jew', Karl Marx – as Bakunin hastened to observe with malicious glee: 'Himself a Jew, he attracts, whether in London or in France, but especially in Germany, a whole heap of Yids, more or less intelligent, intriguers, busybodies and speculators, as the Jews are likely to be, commercial and bank agents, writers . . . correspondents . . . who stand one foot in the world of finance and the other in socialism.' (Quoted after Julius Carlebach, *Karl Marx and the Radical Critique of Judaism* (London: Routledge, 1978), p. 312.)

[21] Scholem, 'On the Social Psychology of the Jews in Germany', pp. 18–23. As Jacob Katz found out, 'Jews who aspired to social acceptance but had difficulty entering German circles may have found sitting in a mixed audience in the concert hall and theatre a convenient way of demonstrating their membership in society at large. Reading at home lacked, of course, this public dimension.' ('German Culture and the Jews', in *The Jewish Response to German Culture* ed. Reinharz and Schwarzberg, p. 90.) And yet the apparent escape route from loneliness proved blocked, as the avid Jewish theatre- and concert-goers and art-patrons discovered that they mixed mostly with each other. As Shulamit Volkov sharply observed, 'despite themselves, they were made into a partly segregated social element, though theirs was not a community of social exclusiveness but the social attraction among the likes' ('The Dynamics of Dissimilation: The *Ostjuden* and German Jews', in *The Jewish Response to German Culture*, p. 200.)

Powerful forces, of which Kafka said that they resided 'around inside me' – external and internal, external internalized and internal projected outside – all combined to draw German Jews, however fully 'assimilated', back upon themselves. It was that invisible, yet all-too-real (because tightly enclosed and in the end spiritually feeding on itself) community of part-refugees, part-outcasts whose experience was reforged into the 'Jewish Germany': the target of their assimilatory effort and the collateral against which the trust in the final success was borrowed.

Imagining the real Germany

The imagined 'real Germany' was the only Germany to which the Jews could reasonably hope to be admitted. The brightest among them understood this well, though they hardly ever gave up hoping that the empirically given 'Germany as it is, here and now' will in the end come close to the Jewish ideal. The courageous among them resolved to speed up the process of merger, preaching the glory of 'virtual' Germany, as Jews imagined it, against everything which distanced the 'empirically real' from the ideal – though they more often than not drew comfort from the belief that in their fight they had history on their side, and that in 'the long run' the ideal Germany would prove its truth against the resilient, yet temporary lie of reality. Of that 'virtual Germany', allegedly hidden inside the unprepossessing exterior of the practical one and struggling to get out, they were genuine, ardent and passionate patriots. Many Germans, however, failed to recognize in the object of Jewish loyalty and love the national home they themselves wished, depending on their political allegiances, either to preserve or to construct. 'In the struggle to piece together a unified German society out of a torn political fabric, the Jew became a symbol of all that frustrated the effort. He was the cosmopolitan, the remnant of the Enlightenment . . . feeding upon the German organism into which he could never be absorbed.'[22] And thus it had to be that 'emancipation meant not only a flight from the ghetto past but also from German history'.[23] The first made the second necessary; the first could not be accomplished without the second. The effort to assimilate cast the Jews into a head-on collision with the very society into which they aimed to assimilate.

---

[22] Meyer, The Origins of the Modern Jew, pp. 139–40.

[23] George L. Mosse, 'Jewish Emancipation: Between *Bildung* and Respectability', in *The Jewish Response to German Culture*, ed. Reinharz and Schwarzberg, p. 14.

What in practice expressed itself in an exchange of one – the orthodox Jewish – particularity for another, German, one – could only come to pass with the help of an ideology of annihilation of *all particularity* in the name of *universal* human values: of science, rationality, truth, which will embrace the whole of humanity. (The Jews, Immanuel Wolf wrote in 1822, 'must raise themselves and their principle to the level of science, for this is the attitude of the European world . . . And if one day a bond is to join the whole of humanity, then it is the bond of science, the bond of pure reason, the bond of truth.')[24] For the Germans, however, their own emancipation (i.e., the establishment of political, economic and cultural unity of the nation clamouring for a honourable place in the rapidly modernizing Europe) meant first and foremost a forceful promotion of German collective identity – with the usual accoutrements of joint and exclusive historical tradition and cultural lore. No wonder *Das Junge Deutschland*, a movement set up by the likes of Heine and Börne with the explicit intent to fight German political backwardness, cultural parochialism and ethical philistinism, was viewed by its German addressees with horror and revulsion and soon redubbed *Das Junge Palestine*. The Jewish efforts to render the Germany they loved more suitable for civilized human cohabitation (a transformation which, they believed, would add to the glory of Germany among the enlightened nations), were perceived as a subversive activity threatening to sap the integrity and strength of the rising national community. Friedrich Rühs ('The Jew does not truly belong to the country in which he lives.') and Heinrich Leo ('The Jewish nation stands out conspicuously among all other nations of this world in that it possesses a truly corroding and decomposing mind.') had set the pattern for what was to become a standard German response to the Jewish promotion of Enlightenment ideals.[25]

The Jewish enthusiasts of Enlightenment and Germany, and above all of enlightened Germany, did not accept the verdict; they refused to recognize its legitimacy and the credentials of those who reiterated it with monotonous and unflinching resolve. They saw themselves as authentic and lawful spokesmen for the true spirit of German culture, and could think of no reason why they should not do the job of preservation and resuscitation of everything noble in German tradition: the job that all-too-many non-Jewish Germans neglected or refused to perform. Already

---

[24] Immanuel Wolf. 'On the Concept of a Science of Judaism', in *Leo Baeck Institute Yearbook*, vol. 2 (London, 1957), p. 204.

[25] Cf. Jacob Katz, *From Prejudice to Destruction: Anti-Semitism, 1700–1933* (Cambridge, Mass.: Harvard University Press, 1980), pp. 87, 161.

Moses Mendelsohn (still barely tolerated in Berlin and granted the right of residence, normally denied to Jews, as a personal favour only) thought it fit and imperative to criticize his monarch Frederick the Great for writing poetry in French and neglecting the beauty of the German tongue. With the passage of years, the job was no closer to completion, but the zeal of its practitioners grew ever more intense. In 1912 Moritz Goldstein asked a worried question, whose validity and timeliness his Jewish intellectual readers stoutly refused to accept: What should one think of the fact that the German cultural heritage of that generation was to a very large extent in the custody of Jews, while the great majority of German people contested their authority for this?[26] Goldstein's query stirred a lot of commotion but evoked little practical reform. The most prominent among German-Jewish journalists of the time, like Maksimilian Harden or Theodor Wolff, excelled in the irreverent critique of the most cherished German institutions, and stood out from most of their non-Jewish colleagues by a total lack of constraint in profaning the sacred, including the army and the Kaiser himself; while the universally feared theatre critic Alfred Kerr exercised a truly dictatorial power over a wide spectrum of German artistic life.

The amazing self-confidence of the Jews turned into German educated classes could be sustained over generations of disappointments and defeats only by the belief in the distinction between the *essence* and the 'mere *appearance*' of Germanhood. According to this belief, the unpleasant reality of present-day German phobias was bound to be washed away by the pure waters of unsoiled humanity gushing from the fount of 'true Germanhood'; the truth of German spirit would eventually out, whatever the temporary setbacks. One needed to distinguish between German culture and the ways of the Germans (in a way strikingly similar to the distinction made later by Lukács between rational and authoritative 'class consciousness' and the short-lived and fraudulent 'consciousness of the class'). It was this belief that allowed Hermann Cohen to state in the preface to his *Ethik des reinen Willens*: 'While I must take a principled posture of opposition to this modern style of Germanism, I feel fortified by

[26] 'Suddenly, Jews are to be found in all the positions from which they are not deliberately excluded; they have made the task of the Germans their own; German cultural life seems to pass increasingly into Jewish hands . . . We Jews are administering the spiritual property of a nation which denies our right and our ability to do so.' Goldstein went on to define as 'our worse enemies' 'those Jews who are completely unaware, who continue to take part in German cultural activities regardless' (cf. Moritz Goldstein, 'German Jewry's Dilemma', in *Leo Baeck Institute Yearbook*, vol. 2, pp. 237, 239).

the knowledge that I am harking back to the original power of the essence of German spirit, contrary to its ephemeral distortions.'[27]

The 'original power' and the 'essence' of German spirit was woven of the memories of brief, 'classical' period of German Enlightenment, of the idealized images of Schiller, Lessing, Goethe, Kant, Herder, treated with reverence previously accorded only to the Old Testament patriarchs. The elevated place of Goethe in the pantheon of German culture was fought for, tooth and nail, in the intellectual salons run by Rahel Varnhagen, Dorothea Mendelssohn or Henriette Herz. There, as in the writings of countless Jewish biographers and analysts of the German classics, the prophets of German culture were praised for promotion of universal human values, and Germanhood itself was defined as an attitude of openness to the universally human, as an aptitude to articulate ideas valid for the whole of humanity. German Jews celebrated German spirit for its assumed (and most certainly avidly desired) emancipation from nationalistic parochialism. They painted the icon they worshipped with the brushes of extraterritorial Reason using the palette of species-wide morality. True, they also did their best to improve on the real face, so that it should resemble its idealized likeness. The most formidable German legal theorists of the rationalist school were almost all Jews (Georg Jellinek, Eduard Lasker, Eduard Gans, Hugo Preuss most prominent among them). And the call to German philosophers to return to their all-too-German and yet the most universalistic, Kantian roots, came from the Marburg Jew Hermann Cohen.

For most of his life, Cohen was a keen and unqualified believer in German–Jewish symbiosis. That there is an 'elective affinity' (*Wahlverwandschaft*) between Judaist and German essences was for Cohen 'not essentially a descriptive but a regulative' proposition. 'It said in effect: there are a number of social and intellectual forces at work in both the German and the Jewish historical cultures which can and should be used so as to advance as much and as quickly as possible whatever dynamic force they possess toward the goal of a cosmopolitan, humanistic, ethical

[27] Moritz Lazarus's attempt to develop a universally valid moral philosophy out of the Jewish ethical sources was ridiculed and bitterly attacked by Hermann Cohen as a 'ghetto concept', being as it was an attempt to consider a *Gesamtgeist des Judentums* independently of ancient Greek, Roman and modern civilizations. Cohen insisted that 'we German Jews' think and ought to think in 'the spirit of Lessing and Herder, Leibniz and Kant, Schiller and Goethe even in matters of our Jewish faith' (cf. David Baumgardt, 'The Ethics of Lazarus and Steinthal', in *Leo Baeck Institute Yearbook*, vol. 2, p. 213–4).

world society ...'[28] In other words, the essence of both Judaism and Germanhood resided in their shared tendency to obliterate their respective identities. Cohen's 'Germanness' was to be at its most German the moment it fulfils itself in the humanity which knows of neither German nor Jew.

It was for that reason that Hegel, by that time the dominant influence on German academic philosophy, was found by Cohen unacceptable. After all, Hegel obliged his followers to accept the real as the product of Reason, as the embodiment of rationality; something which Cohen could not do without surrendering his right to criticize Germany *as it was* in the name of Germany *as it should be* on Reason's behest and therefore could and would eventually become. The latter Germany had to be promoted as a morally imperative, rationally requisite entity – so that it could withstand well its present plight and remain intact even if remaining for a time an infinitely remote target for the empirically given political and social reality. It was for this reason that Cohen reached to Kant over Hegel's head in search of an adequate form and legitimation for philosophical disavowal of real Germany in the name of Germany as it ought to be. Kant entitled Cohen to aver bluntly and uncompromisingly in his *Begründung der Ethik* that the ultimate unity of mankind is simultaneously the criterion and the goal of ethics, and that ethics strives to re-create man in accordance with the *idea* of mankind.[29] Cohen's image of the true *Deutschtum* remained highly selective to the end. Young Nicolai Hartmann complained that he had to hide Nietzsche's books when Cohen's visit was expected.

At the same time, Cohen contributed heavily to the cult of the state as the superior authority entitled to brush aside and trample down if needed the entrenched interests of estates, classes, and their likes. The state was to perform the role of universalizing power; to this purpose it had the right and the duty to develop the law solely in accord with the idea of itself. This image of the state as universalizing and 'humanizing' power was born of the tender memory of the early-modern promises of the emancipating, liberating and enabling state. But it also easily lent itself to an entirely opposite interpretation, one which came to the fore when the other capacity of the German state (that to promote not the symbiosis, but the incompatibility of German and Jews) was revealed in all its homicidal splendour. The potential for such an interpretation was firmly and irre-

[28] Steven S. Schwarzschild, ' "Germanness and Judaism" – Hermann Cohen's Normative Paradigm of the German–Jewish Symbiosis', in *Jews and Germans from 1860 to 1933*, ed. Bronsen, p. 154.

[29] Schwarzschild, ' "Germanness and Judaism" ', p. 143.

movably set in the conception that defined emancipation as *homogeneity* rather than *pluralism*, as obliteration of differences rather than their equality, as an omnipotence of an engineering state rather than its containment by a freely self-asserting and self-managing, multi-cultural society. In the light of such a conception, one could hardly bear a grudge against those Germans who – rather than admit emancipation as a necessary condition for the blending of cultures – demanded self-effacement of Jewish identity as a precondition of the admission into German society. A generation or two later they would demand – and perpetrate – the effacement of the Jews themselves. And they would do it with the help of the selfsame omnipotent modern state, as always determined to universalize and thus make obligatory the only human condition it deems to accord with itself.

Rickert has reputedly suggested that Cohen's thought was not so much a matter of philosophy as of race. He was not wide of the mark. He would have come even closer to the mark had he added that it was a matter of a particular race in as far as it hoped to emancipate itself through assimilating itself to another one, which unlike itself was determined to preserve and cultivate its identity.

Shame and embarrassment

The assimilating pressure of native German society, which made the cultural conformity the condition of social and political emancipation, was reflected in the mind of the targeted minority as a challenge that the universality of human essence posited to communal parochialism and idiosyncrasy. Hence the typically *minoritarian* vision of the *majority* values, discussed above; but also a thorough and fully negative reassessment of own cultural tradition, typical of a minority smarting under severe assimilatory pressure. It was only with the help of both, closely related, mental operations, resulting in the *internalization of ambivalence* that the surrender of one particularity to another could be viewed, with a mixture of pride and self-recrimination, as a promotion from inferiority and backwardness of one's own communally circumscribed oddity to superior, progressive and universal human standards.

The traditional identity was dealt with in two mutually complementary fashions, practised by all 'self-universalizing' sections of the minority, though in varying proportions. In the case of the *Wissenschaft von Judentum* movement (that powerful intellectual current set to contest the charge of the basic incompatibility between the values inherent in Jewish history and those proclaimed and practised by 'human civilization' – or rather an image of such a civilization, conceived of from the perspective of the assimilatory task), the Judaist tradition was first *transfigured* and then *de-Judaized*. Transfiguration, in Scholem's estimate, consisted in 'one-sided concentration of interest on the matters which possessed apologetic value' – that is, on such constituents of the Judaist lore which could be represented as attuned to the rationalistic standards of the modern age. Correspondingly, such ingredients as could not easily pass muster were marginalized, declared alien, untypical or freakish, dismissed with a few words of ridicule, or simply passed over in silence. Above all, of course, this fate had befallen the mystical, messianic and gnostic strands of the Judaist tradition. 'From the point of view of the Enlightenment-minded, purified, rational Judaism of the nineteenth century they seemed not properly usable and hence were thrown out as un-Jewish or, at the least, half-pagan.' The contents of Jewish cultural lore were rearranged, so that some could be put on display to be examined and admired by the 'universalistically inclined' natives, while the rest was packed off into the tightly sealed and never visited, obscure cellars of the house. 'What went in the cellar was scrupulously avoided. These scholars considered only the intellectual relations of the salon: the Bible of Luther, Hermann Cohen and Kant, Steinthal and Wilhelm von Humboldt.' Once thoroughly cleansed of all the dissonant, 'uncivilized' items, and pared to the bones of 'pure universality', the Jewish tradition (or, rather, whatever remained of it) seemed indistinguishable from the dominant idiom (or whatever the latter was imagined to be), but for a few innocuous, indifferent and in the end amusing rituals and customs. There seemed to be no reason to insist on its separate identity and unique value. The only reasonable step which remained to be taken was to deliver a *coup de grace*. Indeed, as Moritz Steinschneider, one of the most prominent figures in the *Wissenschaft von Judentum* school, confided to Gotthold Weil, 'we have only one task left: to give the remains of Judaism a decent burial'.[30]

Rewriting the history and philosophy of Judaism was, for obvious reasons, a passion and a pastime of a select few. Once bent on reforging the assimilatory pressure into a vehicle of social advancement, the large majority of Jews was prepared to pay the full price of cultural adjustment for the promised entry into the native society. To such a majority, the task presented itself more humbly and mundanely as one of *Sittlichkeit* – of the acquisition of refined and respectable manners, new standards of cleanliness, sexual etiquette, proper public demeanour. With ambivalence internalized, the escape from the unenviable plight was now a personal task.

---

[30] Gershom Scholem, *The Messianic Idea in Judaism* (London: Allen & Unwin, 1971), pp. 306–9.

Whatever was 'distinctively Jewish' in all aspects of the art of life had to be repressed and suppressed, and the ways and means of the host nation unambiguously embraced as the only standards of universal human decency and propriety of behaviour. A resolution adopted in 1834 by the Conference of Jewish Schools in Baden may well serve as a pattern for what was to follow:

> It is a well known fact that in earlier times a degenerate so-called Jewish–German dialect established itself. It is characterized by, among other things, incorrect, often disgusting pronounciation and intonation ... The greater part of the Jewish community has, through acquiring education, abandoned this, and only a part of the lower classes has preserved it. Experience teaches us not only that such individuals are the object of mockery on the part of followers of other religions but also that they create a sense of disgust in their fellow co-religionists.[31]

Indeed, it was the emotion of disgust that triggered off and set in motion a genuine, wide-ranging self-centred cultural crusade. The feeling of disgust was seen as the price of joining the good society. This disgust was lived as the sign of refinement, and trusted to be such a sign: after all, the good society which set the rules of its own membership loudly proclaimed the formal etiquette of public demeanour to be both the necessary and the sufficient condition of humanity. The disgust aroused by the sight of difference was born of the promise of shared humanity about to reward the surrender to uniformity. The promise was fraudulent from the start; yet before its bluff was called, it could go on spawning ever new dreams and inspiring new actions. As it became increasingly apparent that the dreams were slow to materialize and the actions routinely refused to bring results, the memory of the promise filled the dreamers and the actors with *shame*, fed by the assumption of neglect. That shame, in its turn, gave the moribund promise a new lease of life and fortified it against the need to admit that the accumulated counter-evidence was final and irrefutable.

Shame was, indeed, the most effective protective shield of the civilizing myth, and – simultaneously – the most Jewish of emotions. ('What Jew has not cringed at what he regards as ostentatious behaviour . . .?' asked, purely rhetorically, Peter Gay.)[32] It diverted many a victim of the myth from

---

[31] Quoted after Gilman, *Jewish Self-Hatred*, p. 161. It was hardly coincidental that the role of shame as a major and most effective weapon deployed by the uniformity-promoting coercion called the 'civilizing process' has been discovered and analysed in depth by Freud and Elias.

[32] Amos Elon, *Herzl* (New York: Holt, Reinhart & Winston, 1975), p. 252; Peter Gay, *Freud, Jews and Other Germans: Masters and Victims in Modernist Culture* (New York: Oxford University Press, 1978), p. 110.

calling the bluff of the promise. Instead it prodded the victims to fix a critical eye on their own failings – by definition, all such genuine or imputed traits of private, and particularly their public, personae, as the native elites chose to single out as the excuse for rejecting the membership applications. The failing could be the dreaded *mauscheln*, of whom Herzl wrote in 1897 as of 'distortion of human character, unspeakably mean and repellent'. It could be worse still: *Yiddish*, by common agreement a degrading caricature of human, i.e. German, language. (Yiddish 'became a target of condescending fun for most German Jews, . . . [of] jokes and certain distancing derision, for Yiddish was, of course, the language of the *Ostjuden* . . . *Not* to speak Yiddish was one thing a German Jew, as a good German, did.')[33] It could be arrogant, noisy, and otherwise obtrusive behaviour in public places, or the Jewish habit 'to speak with one's hands'. (In a non-Jewish restaurant one sees people eating and hears them talking, in a Jewish restaurant one sees people talking and hears them eating – so went one of the typical self-deprecating jokes, that tribute which shame paid to the 'civilizing' prudery.)

In Shulamit Volkov's poignant words,

> Shame was experienced when one forgot or neglected, even for a moment, the strict rules of the civilization game. Embarrassment was aroused by the inappropriate behaviour of others. Because of the strict rules of behaviour that German Jews imposed upon themselves, shame was something they would always experience. Their peculiar sense of responsibility and solidarity kept them almost continuously in a state of embarrassment, too.[34]

As a matter of fact, the responsibility or solidarity to which Volkov refers can hardly be explained as signs of a peculiar familial piety of German Jews or of insufficient earnestness of their assimilatory attitude. Like the rest of the stern prerequisites of emancipation, the responsibility for the less fortunate members of the Jewish caste, who in the self-civilizing efforts lagged behind the elites, was imposed on the avant-garde of assimilation by the very logic of assimilatory process. Assimilatory success was to be assessed and marked individually, but the stigma from which the successful assimilation was meant to emancipate had been assigned collectively, to the community as a whole. As long as the Jewish masses persisted in their traditional ways, no amount of self-grooming on the part of their civilized elites would suffice to convince native opinion that Jewishness ceased to be a stigma, and to free the elites from their embarrassment –

---

33 Quoted from Theodore Reik, *Jewish Wit* (New York: Gamut Press, 1962).

34 Shulamit Volkov, 'The Dynamics of Dissimulation: *Ostjuden* and German Jews', in *The Jewish Response to German Culture*, ed. Reinharz and Schwarzberg, p. 210.

that 'shame by proxy'. Generation after generation, the advanced troops of assimilation had to confront the dilemma experienced already by David Friedlander, the immediate successor of Moses Mendelssohn. Friedlander, as Meyer found out, 'shared next to nothing with common Jews', moving most of his life in socially remote, rich and educated circles of Berlin industrialists and intellectuals. 'Yet for all his dissociation from lower class, orthodox, and East European Jews, Friedlander could not entirely turn his back on them. They and he both bore the name "Jew".'[35] Well before he *assumed* responsibility for the enlightenment of his retarded kinsmen and began to practice his solidarity, Friedlander (much as several generations of his successors) had been *burdened* with such responsibility and obliged to make solidarity his duty by the world around him.

It was because of the commonality of fate, not of the spirit, that responsibility and solidarity became as unavoidable as they were unwelcome and resented. And yet the action prompted by the desire to get rid from embarrassment only underlined the unity of fate and social standing which was the embarrassment's prime source. Hard as they tried to disavow their uncivilized kinsmen, the assimilants were judged by the overall performance of the community which the native society stubbornly considered as a single whole. Emphatic denial of responsibility only added evidence and cogency to the suspicion of duplicity and falsity of their pretentions. The resigned consent to responsibility, on the other hand, let to the grudging displays of solidarity that made 'self-evident' and thus reinforced the bond which made a mockery of the programme of individual emancipation. Once internalized, ambivalence proved to be a cage without an exit.

The inner demons of assimilation

In the folklore of assimilation, the *Ostjuden* (East-European Jews) were not allowed an identity of their own. Instead, their image was patched together out of the concerns and nightmares of the assimilating Western Jew. They served as a huge refuse bin of human characteristics into which all that nagged the conscience of the Western Jew and filled him with shame was dumped (and thus their stereotype offers a unique insight into the darkest corners of the tormented, shame-ridden soul of the victim and dupe of the assimilationist dream). According to Theodor Reik, in the German–Jewish jokes of the turn of the century, the Jews of Eastern Europe 'are depicted not in their own surroundings, but in contrast with the Western civilization and its demands'; for instance, the demands of

[35] Meyer, *The Origins of the Modern Jew*, pp. 60, 61.

'bodily cleanliness'. When forgetting to take his bath, the assimilating Jew shamefully revealed the not-yet-fully extirpated, still well-entrenched inside him, uncultured and uncultivated (Eastern) Jew who did not even know what the others meant when they spoke of bathing. ('A room with a bath?' Galician Jew Teitelbaum is asked in a Viennese hotel. 'What do you mean? Am I a trout?' replies Teitelbaum indignantly. 'Did you take a bath this morning?' another visitor from Galicia, Cohn, is asked. 'Why? Is there one missing?')

The embarrassment turned quite unbearable once the East-European Jews, heretofore more or less mythological figures safely enclosed in their distant ghettos and in the derogatory jokes of their Western neighbours, left their nature reserve in droves and began to settle in close proximity to the fortresses of assimilation. One could not leave home without looking in the face of the very source of one's shame: the same Jewish difference which the *Mensch*, on the way to turning into a *Kulturmensch*, had a duty to hide or, better still, to eradicate.

However much charity was reluctantly offered in the end, little love was lost between assimilated German Jewry and the poor or orthodox East-European neighbours. According to Wertheimer's evidence, only rarely did German Jews 'deign to mingle with refugees or immigrants [from Poland and Russia]; and on such occasions they acted out of duty rather than genuine concern for needy fellow Jews'. Their true feelings towards 'traditional' Jews were somewhat too blatantly for comfort, yet adequately expressed by Hugo Ganz:

> Their laziness, their filth, their perpetual readiness to cheat cannot help but fill the Western European with very painful feelings and unedifying thoughts, in spite of all the teachings of history and desire to be just. The evil wish arises that in some painless way the world might be rid of these disagreeable objects, or the equally inhuman thought that it would really be no great pity if this part of the Polish population did not exist at all. Either we must renounce our ideas of cleanliness and honesty or find a great part of Eastern Hebrews altogether unpleasant.[36]

---

[36] Jack Wertheimer, *Unwelcome Strangers: East European Jews in Imperial Germany* (Oxford: Oxford University Press, 1987), pp. 143, 148. Arnold Mostowicz – a perceptive Polish–Jewish writer, survivor of the Lódź ghetto and a person of wide European experience, notes that the German Jews he met in Germany, France and (during the war) in Poland 'not only considered the loyalty to chassidic mysticism and the self-separation of the Jewish community as the sign of backwardness and obscurantism, but displayed a truly racial distaste for any Jew coming from Eastern Europe'. They persisted in this attitude even when disowned by the Germans with whom they asserted their spiritual identity, and jumbled into the hovels of the Lódź ghetto. (Źólta Gwiazda i Czerwony Krzyz (Warsaw: PIW, 1988), p. 46).

The Slav and other neighbours inhabiting the lands to the east of the border were an easy target for the rampant all-German nationalism of the era of Bismarckian unification. As if anticipating Nazi rhetoric, they were described as disease- and epidemic-carriers, ordered to be deloused on crossing the German border, and often transported through the country in sealed trains allowed to stop only at properly equipped quarantine stations. In 1892 in Hamburg, and in 1894 in Marburg, new Jewish immigrants from Poland were blamed for the outbreak of cholera. Following the twisted logic of boundary building, the insalubrity of the orientals was related to their pre-human cultural standards, barbaric language (the Polish language was disdained as 'wretchedly degenerate', 'unviable', 'half-Asiatic' and generally inferior to the German), inborn restlessness and incapacity for national feelings and loyalty (German caricaturists' favourite subject was the wondrous transformation of the Polish rag-peddler Moische Pisch into the Berlin haberdasher Moritz Wasserstrahl into the Parisian couturier Maurice La Fontaine).[37] Jewish enlightened opinion followed the lead loyally, complete with the oxymoronic logic with which the substance of stigma was depicted. Thus, on one hand, oriental Jews were criticized for being 'fully alien to German Jews by virtue of their customs, outlook, and way of life'; on the other, in tune with the repetitive German charges about Jewish duplicity, it was held against them that they tried to shed the 'barbaric' garb with the same haste and thoroughness of which the assimilated German Jews were so proud. As the *Allgemeine Zeitung des Judentums* wrote on 28 May 1872, 'Those Jews may be registered with the police as Jews, but their way of living is thoroughly un-Jewish. Once these people cross the Polish border and take off their long coats, they no longer observe the Jewish law. The very people who lived so orthodox a life in Polish towns now have thrown overboard all Jewish laws.'[38]

Politically, socially and psychically the despisal of recent Jewish immigrants had its uses, particularly as it offered an occasion to share the deeply felt and publicly vented feelings of the Germans. In Wertheimer's apt summary,

> nothing, after all, unites one with others more than possession of a common enemy. Moreover, anti-Semitism had a special function in the German–Jewish psychic economy: hatred of outsiders diverted self-hatred to other targets. Finally, and most important: to construct this target for Jew-hatred would, many German Jews fondly believed, disarm German anti-Semitism altogether.

---

37 Wertheimer, *Unwelcome Strangers*, pp. 25–30.

38 Cf. Wertheimer, *Unwelcome Strangers*, pp. 144, 146.

Besides, 'the newcomers threatened to revive an image of the Jew that natives had worked so hard to obliterate'.[39]

In the psychological syndrome of assimilation, shame and embarrassment vied with each other for pride of place. Once the assimilatory pressure of native nationalism had been accepted as authoritative and legitimate those who accepted it as such internalized their ambivalent status and thus condemned themselves to a vigilance they would never be allowed to lapse or relax. They would forever remain on guard against those hidden aspects or their own selves which they now regarded as outmoded, disgraceful, and therefore shameful. And they would be eager to displace, project and exteriorize again the harrowing experience of ambivalence: they would forever obsessively scrutinize and censure other bearers of the hereditary stigma they wished to obliterate – but only to find to their dismay that the dreamt-of moment of disarmament and rest was no closer than before.[40]

---

39 Wertheimer, *Unwelcome Strangers*, pp. 158, 160.

40 John Murray Cuddihy (*The Ordeal of Civility: Freud, Marx, Levi-Strauss and the Jewish Struggle with Modernity* (New York: Basic Books, 1974)) repeatedly suggests that the torments of assimilation were the outcome of a 'culture shock' with which the successive generations of educated Jews, burdened with an 'uncanny pre-modern nexus', could not cope; they were unable to really embrace the 'Gentile culture' in which they felt 'ill at ease' because of its depersonalized courtesy replacing the truly Jewish warm and and utterly personal togetherness: 'The differentiations most foreign to the *shtetl* subculture of *Yiddishkeit* were those of public from private behaviour and of manners from morals.' The failure of the assimilation programme was therefore the result of Jewish incapacity to meet the modern standards alien to their inner nature. (Cuddihy identifies modernity with the rule of Protestant ethics, which he defines in turn as, first and foremost, the code of courtesy and detached, unemotional politeness.) The Jewish response to the incompatibility, according to Cuddihy, was a struggle *with* modernity, rather than a struggle for modernization. Indeed, the Jewish attitude to modernity was essentially subversive, as the Jewish thinkers fought to replace the impersonal etiquette of Protestantism with depersonalizing their own unwillingness or inability to modernize. Thus in Freud, who found that courtly love 'was so un-Jewish', 'social malaise becomes a medical symptom, *kwetches* become hysterical complaints, *tsuris* becomes basic anxiety, social shame becomes moral guilt, deviance becomes incapacity, strangeness becomes alienation; to be badly behaved is to be mentally ill'.

Cuddihy seems to accept that the refinement of public behaviour would indeed lead to social parity, as the assimilatory programmes promised, and that instead of the etiquette being a sham, it was the pretence to follow it by people incapable of doing it because of the 'particularistic inwardness of the ethnic nexus' which was the true cause of their misfortune. Thus engaging in another of the long series of 'blame the victim' exercises, Cuddihy has inadvertently supplied a faithful (only terminologically updated) restatement of all the essential arguments constantly

By the end of the nineteenth century (at least in continental Europe, and in Germany more than anywhere else), the universalist armour of the 'man as such' lost much of its original shine. It continued to glitter, if at all, solely in the collective memory of the more resilient and stubborn among the assimilators. The native elites were fast abandoning the universalist rhetoric, while seeking shelter for their nationalist ambitions in the urgently excavated or newly made-to-order 'shared heritage' of popular fate and culture. They now fortified themselves behind the ramparts of *Volksgeist* which no stranger was to be allowed to penetrate. The fast rising *Völker* prided themselves not so much of their refined *Geist* as of the healthy *Körper*. And thus, suddenly, one hears from Nathan Birnbaum that 'Die Ostjuden sind ganze, lebensfrohe und lebenskräftige Menschen', and reads essays of Martin Buber fraught with concepts like *Blut*, *Boden*, *Volkstum*, *Gemeinschaft* and *Wurzelhaftigkeit* drawn live from the nascent vocabulary of the German *Volk*.[41] Once more, the 'East-European Jews' turn into a myth construed according to the latest concerns of their more civilized Western kin. This time, however, the impact of shame is, so to speak, mediated. It does not feed fantasy directly, but through the prompting of a feverish search for the tradition one could glorify and take pride in. In the age of narcissistic, implosive *volkisch* nationalism one could reasonably bid for universal esteem only by reference to one's own pedigree of valour, masculinity, guts and stamina; to a tradition with roots set firmly in the beginnings of time, yet still alive, creative and forward-looking.

Or so, at least, some guilt-ridden Jews naively believed. The German Jews 'would not accept or believe that they were outsiders who were shunned by Germans – even by National Socialist Germans'.[42] As it was becoming ever more evident that to be a German meant to belong to a *Volk* rather than the Goethe- or Schiller-style, nebulous, *Eigenschaftenlos* humanity, many hoped that one could ingratiate oneself with the Germans by fashioning the Jewish equivalents of German *Volksgemeinschaft*, of

---

rehearsed by the rising nationalisms to justify the 'Catch 22' situation; one in which they placed their hapless ethnic minorities by simultaneously inviting them to join the majority through the expedient of cultural mimicry, and ridiculing them, or charging with duplicity and subversive intent, once the imitation turned to be too successful for the hosts' comfort.

[41] Cf. Robertson, 'Antizionismus, Zionismus'.

[42] Sidney M. Bolkosky, *The Distorted Image: German Jewish Perceptions of Germans and Germany, 1918–1935* (New York: Elsevier, 1975), p. 4.

Siegfried-type popular heroes, of the *Führer Prinzip*.[43] In all these respects, the *Ostjuden* came in handy. They stayed at a safe distance, they did not concern themselves with the worries of their assimilated brethren, and hence did not care about what the latter thought or said or had written.

The miraculous transmogrification of the ugly duckling into an admired swan was, therefore, the work of the same old magician who once conjured up the vision of the *Ostjude* as the filthy, ignorant and immoral savage left over from the pre-civilized times. Even while lavishing praise on his poorer Eastern kin, the Germanized Jewish intellectual retained – indeed, reasserted – his superiority: it was he, after all, who revealed and laid open the treasures which otherwise would remain dormant forever. It was he who gave shape to the virtues which the East-European Jews bore only unknowingly, incapable as they were of appreciating their own value. The laborious construction of the Jewish *Volk* out of the arbitrarily selected bits and pieces of ghetto life, much like the drawing of disparaging caricatures which preceded it, was prompted by Jewish assimilatory concerns and guided by the urge of redemption from shame, now as before prompted by the awareness of falling behind the dominant standards of the day. It definitely did not entail accepting East-European Jewry as equals; indeed, as subjects entitled to speak of and for themselves with an authority equal to that of their enlightened well-wishers.

It is worth noting that throughout the period of romantic dalliance with the image of a Chassid as a nearest Jewish equivalent of the *volkisch* hero and the *man of nature*, the newly found darlings were loved only at a distance (the larger the better). The earnestly claimed spiritual and religious affinity was not seen as a licence for physical proximity (the latter was, admittedly, a political, not an ideational matter). The influx of the *Ostjude* remained resented much as before. No one wished to seek the glittering splendours of the young swan in the ugly duckling of the 'neighbour next door'. The newly born East-European Jewish Siegfried bore travelling ill and was keenly advised to stay at home.

Unsettled accounts

In retrospect, the stormy, often tragic, occasionally ludicrous romance with assimilation seems to contain as much evidence of indignity as of the

[43] George L. Mosse, *Germans and Jews: The Right, the Left, and the Search for a 'Third Force' in Pre-Nazi Germany* (New York: Howard Fertig, 1970), pp. 89, 94, 101.

loftiness of spirit. Shortly before his death, Scholem wrote with bitterness and venom of the 'Godforsaken lack of dignity' of the 'servile, imploring and entreating' assimilators, who instead of concerning themselves with what they 'had to *give* as Jews', thought only of what they 'had to *give up* as Jews'; as self-styled and for that reason always over-zealous high priests of the native culture, they had to look comic to everybody but themselves.[44] And yet the acerbic and petulant Scholem's obituary to the German–Jewish dialogue that never was reads in places like a lament of a betrayed and offended lover, a victim of unrequited adoration. There was, perhaps, nothing *intrinsically* wrong with the idea of fusing the two cultures; it was rather the would-be German partners, who abandoned their own luminous heritage and could not bear the sight of the strangers picking it up and dangling it before their eyes, that visited a defeat upon a venture in no way moribund by itself.

The feelings which Scholem succeeds to control and on the whole suppress, only rarely allowing them to break up to the surface, have been given much freer rein by other writers. Posthumous spologias of the episode of assimilation abound, even though many of them masquerade as a self-righteous settling of accounts with the insensitive and ungrateful native partners of the dialogue. Often openly, but in most cases surreptitiously or even subconsciously, feverish attempts are made to absolve the dreamers of assimilation from the charge of stupidity or – worse still – of depraved character. For reasons that are easy to understand, the descendants of the German Jews must try harder than most: for it was in Germany that the vanity of the assimilation project was exposed with a brutality leaving nothing to the imagination and no room for controversy.

True, the outright and unashamed vindication of harshly rejected love advances is rare and by no means representative. (No one writes today like Jacob R. Marcus, who approved of Hitler's decision to close the border to 'an invasion by East-European Jews', both 'culturally alien' and 'intellectually inferior' and hence a threat to Germany; and who suggested that the amalgamation of German states was an idea pioneered by German Jewish patriots of 1848, of whom Hitler was a testamentary legatee.)[45] Most authors, with mixed success, are keen to make their scepticism manifest. No effort is spared to distance oneself from that joyful yet reckless abandon with which some of the ancestors dived headlong into the whirlpool of an alien and hostile element which they mistook for a cosy

---

44 Gershom Scholem, *On Jews and Judaism in Crisis* (New York: Schocken Books, 1982), pp. 62, 63, 80.

45 Jacob R. Marcus, *The Rise and Destiny of the German Jew* (Cincinnati: Union of American Hebrew Congregations, 1934), pp. 101, 93.

and inviting swimming pool. And yet no less an effort is made to disprove the graver charge of malice aforethought and to replace it with a lighter one of forgivable ignorance: after all, the hapless 'Germans of Mosaic persuasion' did not know, and could not know, what we do now. Their ignorance, so to speak, was their privilege. From all the knowledge they did possess, their strategy followed naturally, in an impeccably logical fashion. Almost everything they knew seemed to show that they were on the right track; hence their self-assurance and perseverance were well justified. It was not their fault that, in the end, things happened which they had no way of anticipating. Even the less endearing facets of their conduct and thought were expressions of their quite real (or apparently real) achievement on the road of their choice.

Thus George L. Mosse explains that the revulsion which acculturated German Jews felt for Jews across the border was not particularly Jewish. On the contrary, it testified to the well-nigh complete 'Germanness' of the German Jews. It reflected the 'clash between Germanic culture and the way of life of the Jewish settlements at its borders'. 'These men' – Mosse concludes, thereby obliquely dismissing suspicion of deeper, assimilation-born, specifically Jewish shame and fear – 'were patriots and their attitude toward the Slavonic and Jewish civilizations applied equally to all foreign civilizations ... The image of the Jew became a part of this general rejection of "foreigners".'[46] Another prominent historian, Peter Gay, could not agree more. He dismisses as unjust and condemnably revengeful the abuse heaped on the conduct of the German Jews of yore by 'East European Jews'. The truth is, says Gay, that

> Berlin's German Jews made fun of their brothers from beyond the borders not merely because they wanted to demonstrate that they were Germans, but precisely because they *were* Germans. Like the Gentile fellow citizens, they saw the new immigrants from the Ukraine and Galicia as uncouth, noisy, greedy, truly alien, and distinctly inferior. Thus, while the German Jew found *Ostjuden* embarrassing for fear that he might be identified with them, he found them so also because they were, to him, really embarrassing. The prejudice was just one more emblem of his Germanness.

Once more, this time posthumously, the victims of prejudice are invited to bear the guilt for their rejection. Once more, the guilt is shifted, at least an inch or two, away from those who did the rejecting. However clearly one sees now through the mist of self-deception, it is psychologically downright impossible to accept that there was nothing more than naivety and delusion in the enthusiastic and proud Jewish celebration of adopted

[46] Mosse, *Germans and Jews*, p. 73.

Germanhood. 'When they wrote monographs, painted portraits, or conducted orchestras' – Gay insists – the German Jews 'did so in ways which, I must repeat, were indistinguishable from the ways of the Germans.'[47]

In holding to this opinion, Gay is far from being alone. The most representative spokesmen of pre-Nazi German Jewry saw in the holy trinity of Geothe, Schiller and Lessing (supplemented on occasion by lesser yet equally revered saints like Kant, Fichte or Herder) not only the warrant for the alliance between German and Jewish cultures, but also vivid and clinching evidence that, in fact and by their own nature, the two cultures are immanently alike and guided by the same spirit. Long after the Germans transported the last residue of their Jewish admirers and self-appointed soul brothers to where the rejected East-European relatives once lived (and were murdered later), the cause of the 'elective affinity' of Jewishness and Germanhood has not been put to rest. One of the most perceptive (and, by self-definition, critical) among German–Jewish minds, Max Horkheimer, wrote profusely on the unbreakable kinship, nay identity, between Jewish and German versions of idealism, relentless and never compromised hope, and the philosophy of the endemic elusiveness of truth.[48]

The old argument seems to be going on unabated long after it had lost the last shred of pragmatic significance. The old battles are fought again, though this time solely in the tormented mind of one of the protagonists. (The other, German, protagonist – or was it rather an adversary? – has long ago granted the other side's theoretical victory, having first achieved a practical one.) Fought-again battles revive past shame of the 'uncouth aliens' and unwelcome strangers. This shame still hurts, now as suppressed memory, in the new and yet more painful form of guilt. It cries out to be exorcized or argued away. As the moment of redemption has been missed, the only way left is to prove that there was nothing to be redeemed in the first place. There must have been at least a rudimentary truth in Jewish Germanhood, and so there must have been some truth in the charges the German Jews proffered against their East-European neigh-

---

47 Gay, *Freud, Jews and other Germans*, pp. 187, 99.

48 Max Horkheimer, *Critique of Instrumental Reason* (New York: Seabury Press, 1974), pp. 107ff. Once he got down to a comprehensive evaluation of the Jewish romance with Germanhood, Gershon Scholem set to explode the myth of German–Jewish dialogue: 'I deny that there has ever been a . . . German–Jewish dialogue in any genuine sense as an historical phenomenon. To a dialogue belong two who listen to each other, who are ready to perceive who the other is and represents and respond to him.' (*The Messianic Idea in Judaism* (London: Allen & Unwin, 1971), p. 209.) The most Scholem would allow to have happened was a 'distant love' (Max Brod's term); and an unrequited one with that.

bours. If the latter were charged, they had only themselves to blame. Being accused, so it transpires, was their guilt. The guilt has outlasted the accusation.

The project of assimilation and strategies of response

The German–Jewish experience offers a useful standpoint from which some crucial, yet frequently underemphasized or overlooked facets of the mechanism of assimilation may be better seen.

1 Assimilation, as distinct from cross-cultural exchange or cultural diffusion in general, is a typically modern phenomenon. It derived its character and significance from the modern 'nationalization' of the state, i.e. from the bid of the modern state to legal, linguistic, cultural and ideological unification of the population which inhabits the territory under its jurisdiction. Such a state tended to legitimize its authority through reference to shared history, common spirit, and a unique and exclusive way of life, rather than to extraneous factors (like, for instance, dynastic rights or mere military superiority), which, on the whole, are indifferent to the diversified forms of life of the subjected population.

2 The gap between the project of homogeneity inherent in the idea of the nation and taken aboard by the nation-state, and the practical heterogeneity of cultural forms inside the realm under unified state administration, constituted therefore a challenge and a problem, to which national states responded with cultural crusades, aimed at the destruction of autonomous, communal mechanisms of reproduction of cultural unity. The era in which national states were formed was characterized by cultural *intolerance*; more generally, by nonendurance of, and impatience with all *difference*, and its unavoidable outcomes – diversity and ambivalence. Practices that departed from, or not fully conformed to, the power-assisted cultural pattern were construed as alien and potentially subversive for, simultaneously, the national and political integrity.

3 The *nationalization of the state* (or, rather, *etatization of the nation*) blended the issue of political loyalty and trustworthiness (seen as conditions for the granting of citizenship rights) with that of cultural conformity. On the one hand the postulated national model served as the ideal objective of cultural crusade, but on the other it was deployed in advance as the standard by which membership of the body politic was tested, and the practices of exclusion and discrimination, applied to

those that would be disqualified for failing the test, were explained and legitimized. In the result, citizenship and cultural conformity seemed to merge; the second was perceived as the condition, but also as a means to attain the first.

4 In this context, obliteration of cultural distinctiveness and acquisition of a different, power-assisted culture was construed and perceived as the prime vehicle of political emancipation. The consequence was the drive of politically ambitious, advanced sectors of 'alien' populations to seek excellence in practising the dominant cultural patterns and to disavow the cultural practices of their communities of origin. The prospect of full political citizenship was the main source of the seductive power of the acculturation programme.

5 The drive to acculturation put the ostensible identity of politics and culture to the test, and exposed the ambivalence with which the fusion was inescapably burdened and which in the long run proved responsible for the ultimate failure of the assimilatory programme.

(a) Cultural assimilation was an intrinsically individual task and activity, while both political discrimination and political emancipation applied to the 'alien' (or otherwise excluded) community as a whole. As the acculturation was bound to proceed unevenly and involve various sections of the community to a varying extent and at varying speed, the advanced sectors seemed to be held back by the relatively retarded ones. They had been trapped in the situation of ambivalence they found in practice impossible to escape. Cutting the ties with the community offered no way out of the impasse, as the collective maturity for acceptance, like the carrying capacity of a bridge, would be measured by the quality of its weakest section. On the other hand the decision to act as a cultural broker or a missionary on behalf of the dominant culture in order to accelerate the cultural transformation of native community as a whole was read out as the confirmation of the kinship that held the emancipating elite down. It reinforced the commonality of fate between the acculturated and the 'culturally alien' sections of the community and further tightened the already stiff conditions of political acceptance.

(b) The evidently *acquired* character of cultural traits gained in the process of acculturation jarred with the *inherited* and *ascribed* nature of national membership only thinly covered by the formula of common culture. The fact that their cultural similarity had been *achieved* made the acculturated aliens different from the rest, 'not really like us', guilty of duplicity and probably also of ill intentions. In this sense, cultural assimilation in the framework of a national state was self-defeating. As it were, the national community, though itself a product of culture, could sustain its modality as a nation only through emphatic denial of a 'merely cultural', i.e. artificial, foundation. Instead it derived its identity from the myth of common origin and *naturalness*. The individual was or was not its member; one could not choose to be one.

(c) Though it effectively alienated its agents from their community of origin, assimilation did not lead therefore to a full and unconditional acceptance by the dominant nation. Much to their despair, the assimilants found that they had in effect *assimilated themselves solely to the process of assimilation*. Other assimilants were the only people around who shared their problems, anxieties and preoccupations. Having left behind their original community and lost their former social and spiritual affinities, the assimilants landed in another community, the 'community of assimilants' – no less estranged and marginalized than the one from which they had escaped, but in addition also incurably ambivalent. Incurably – as the new alienation displayed a marked tendency to self-exacerbation. The *Weltanschauung* of the assimilants was now forged out of the shared experience of their sole (though neither chosen nor wanted) 'community', and given shape by a discourse conducted mostly inside its framework. In the event it showed a marked tendency to underline the 'universalistic' character of cultural values and militate against all and any 'parochiality'. This circumstance set their perceptions, their philosophy and their ideals on a collision course with the 'native' ones and effectively prevented the gap between them from ever being bridged.

Despite the growing evidence of inconclusiveness and prospectlessness of assimilatory efforts, the social configuration sedimented by the policy of assimilation remained a trap from which there were few, if any, exits. It was, presumably, the profound and continuous isolation of the victims of assimilatory dreams which prompted the astounding steadfastness with which the majority of German Jews stuck to their guns through thick and thin. Probably for the objective or subjective lack of other realistic options, they resolutely refused to admit the futility of their dream even when the rising tide of vicious, racist antisemitism with discernible exterminatory undertones swept through the wounded country after the collapse of the German Empire. Gradually the drama of assimilation turned into a grotesque before it ended in tragedy. When the Weimar Republic, from its birth burdened with incurable sickness, entered its final years of decline and decay, leaders of the 'Germans of Mosaic persuasion' (in whose name less than forty years earlier Löwenfeld asked, rhetorically, 'are we closer to French Jews than to German Catholics?'), felt it necessary to invoke the threat of World Jewry's retaliation as their last sanction against approaching doom; by the same token, 'they made themselves suspicious in the eyes of those whom they wanted to convince of their loyalty and to whom they turned for support and protection'.[49] A few years later the day of reckoning finally arrived, the 'Germans of Jewish origin' felt obliged to make an unambiguous choice, and choose they did: the official organ of German Jewry declared that, as always before, German Jews 'stand with Germany against all foreign attacks'. They 'are, always have been, and can only be true to Germany'.[50]

Till the end, it was only a relatively small, though sober and perceptive minority which saw through the self-delusion and declared the project of assimilation dead and buried. Those few – like the French Jew Bernard Lazare, the subject of Hannah Arendt's eulogy – turned their rage against the *parvenus* – the bribed dupes of assimilation who brandished their individual gains to take attention away from their lesser brethren's losses: 'whenever the enemy seeks control, he makes a point of using some appeased element of the population as his lackeys and henchmen, rewarding them with social privilege, as a kind of sop'.[51] A somewhat larger minority, yet still a minority, came to the conclusion that the old policy of assimilation was moribund and that the idea could not be kept alive without a major revision. Those who discovered the inner contradictions, and hence the ultimate futility, of assimilatory hopes in general, or at least of the original policy of assimilation, sought a remedy, or an alternative strategy. The remedy was a political action aimed at reforming or revolutionizing the rules which guided in practice (as distinct from declared theory) the granting of political and social rights. ('As soon as the *pariah* enters the arena of politics, and translates his status in political terms, he becomes perforce a rebel.')[52] This action intended, so to speak, to take the

---

[49] Leni Yahil, 'Jewish Assimilation vis-à-vis German Nationalism in the Weimar Republic', in *Jewish Assimilation in the Modern Times*, ed. Bela Vago (Boulder, Col., Westview Press, 1981), p. 47.

[50] Quoted after Bolkosky, *The Distorted Image*, p. 171.

[51] Hannah Arendt, *The Jew as a Pariah: Jewish Identity and Politics in the Modern Age*, ed. Ron H. Feldman (New York: Grove Press, 1978), p. 77.

[52] Arendt, *The Jew as a Pariah*, p. 77. The posture taken by the *parvenus*, the product and the instrument of the assimilation trap, and the ultimate fate determined by such posture, inspired Arendt to spell out 'the moral of history': 'Since that time it has become a mark of assimilated Jews to be unable to distinguish between friend and enemy, between compliment and insult, and to feel flattered when an antisemite assures them that he does not mean them, that they are exceptions – exceptional Jews.' 'The collapse of German Jewry began with its splitting up into innumerable factions, each of which believed that special privileges could protect human rights – e.g., the privilege of having been a veteran

nation-state at its word; to force it to abide by its own expressed intention to make the admission to the national community dependent solely on the demonstrated conformity with national values and culture, and thus to get rid of the ambivalence that assimilation went on gestating while having it delegitimized in the first place.

The essence of this response to the ever more apparent failure of the nationalist state to deliver on its promise has been succintly expressed by Milton Himmelfarb: 'Both honour and interest required that they should try to change the state of society in which it made a substantial political and social difference whether one was a Jew or a Christian. Temperament and circumstances determined whether they would work for that change in conventional or in revolutionary ways.'[53] Indeed, there was no shortage of German Jews who had chosen either of the two ways. Barred from active political participation in the overtly nationalist parties and movements (in spite of all the ultra-patriotic enthusiasm, and genuine German-nationalist dedication that many an assimilant profusely and sincerely demonstrated), the Jews entered in disproportionally large numbers the liberal camp and its many, mostly cultural and journalistic, extensions. They hoped to use the extant institutions of political power to enforce the assimilatory promise as a contract binding *both* sides; to remove, by political means, all social and cultural obstacles to the conclusiveness of assimilatory efforts. At the same time, a large number of Jews flocked into the nascent social-democratic movement for much the same reasons – though with less trust in the capacity of the 'really existing' liberal order to improve on its

---

of World War I, the child of a war veteran, or if such privileges were not recognized any more, a crippled war veteran or the son of a father killed at the front. Jews "*en masse*" seemed to have disappeared from earth, it was easy to dispose of Jews "*en détail*".' (pp. 107, 109)

That the *parvenu* phenomenon was not a 'German–Jewish disease', but a universal accompaniment of Jewish assimilation, and in all probability an inevitable product of assimilatory pressures as such, was suggested by Bernard Lazare in 1901, in the midst of the Dreyfus affair. Indeed, his pungent portrait of French Jewry of the time prefigures the conduct of German assimilated elite: 'It isn't enough for them [French assimilated Jews] to reject any solidarity with their foreign-born brethren; they have also to go charging them with all the evils which their own cowardice engenders. They are not content with being more jingoist than the native-born Frenchmen; like all emancipated Jews everywhere they have also, on their own volition, broken all ties of solidarity. Indeed, they go so far that for the three dozen or so men in France who are ready to defend one of their martyred brethren you can find some thousands ready to stand guard over Devil's Island, alongside the most rabid patriots of the country.' (p. 129)

[53] Milton Himmelfarb, *The Jews of Modernity* (New York: Basic Books, 1973), p. 9.

performance to date. In their assessment of the magnitude of change required to wipe out the stigma of Jewishness, they followed the perception of Karl Marx – whose father's accomplishment, in Murray Wolfson's opinion, was (much like the accomplishments of their own fathers) 'to establish a sense of shame in his son – both for his parents' Jewishness, and for the servile aspect of his father's [Heinrich] attempt to escape from it'. Rather than parental servility, Karl concluded, no less was needed than 'an organization of society which would abolish the preconditions for huckstering, and therefore the possibility of huckstering' – thus rendering impossible the very 'huckstering Jewishness' for which Heinrich Marx felt the compulsion to apologize. 'On the other hand, if the Jew recognizes that this *practical* nature of his is futile and works to abolish it, he extricates himself from his previous development and works for *human emancipation* as such and turns against the *supreme practical* expression of human self-estrangement.'[54]

By the end of the nineteenth century it had become evident that the advancement of Jews inside the existing German polity had its limits, and that economic and educational successes of individuals did not by themselves guarantee political equality, social acceptance, and freedom from prejudice and discrimination. Weak and submissive German liberalism stopped short of breaking the political monopoly of conservative and nationalist land-owning elites. According to Wistrich's calculation, after 1893 non-baptized Jews virtually disappeared from the Reichstag benches of German bourgeois and conservative parties. They entered, however, *en masse* the parliamentary representation of the rising socialist movement, where beginning from 1881 they regularly made up more than 10 per cent of the group (a proportion ten times higher than in the population as a whole).[55] Inside the SPD, however, the Jews constituted a very special category. Unlike most of the rank-and-file and the non-Jewish members of the leadership, they came mostly from well-off middle-class families;

[54] Murray Wolfson, *Marx: Economist, Philosopher, Jew; Steps in the Development of a Doctrine* (London: Macmillan, 1982), pp. 13, 88. The scattered and perhaps never fully articulated experience of assimilatory agony could well had served as the raw material from which Marx moulded his composite picture of the proletarian outcast/freedom-fighter: 'a class in civil society that is not a class of civil society'; 'a social group that is a dissolution of all social groups'; 'This class can no longer lay claim to a historical status, but only to a human one'; 'it is the complete loss of humanity and thus can only recover itself by a complete redemption of humanity'. (Cf. Karl Marx, *The Early Texts*, ed. David McLellan (London: Oxford University Press, 1971), p. 127.)

[55] Cf. Robert S. Wistrich, *Socialism and the Jews: The Dilemmas of Assimilation in Germany and Austro-Hungary* (London: Association of University Presses, 1982), pp. 80–1.

above all, they were on the whole highly educated (in the 1912 parliament, for instance, eleven out of twelve Jewish socialist deputies, as compared to twelve out of ninety-eight non-Jewish, were university graduates). Without any conscious design on their part and without any noticeable pressures from outside, the Jewish activists of the socialist movement found themselves heavily concentrated in selected areas of party activity. They constituted a majority among party journalists, theorists and teachers of party schools. These roles assured them of a central and highly prestigious role in party life, and through it in German politics as a whole. The same roles, however, made their position inside the party increasingly awkward and widely resented – the moment when the radical political movement of the early years ossified into a highly bureaucratized establishment interested more than in anything else in the preservation of secure (and thus increasingly comfortable) routines and serving as an outlet of upward social mobility for the trade-union and other 'grassroot' activists.

Once integration and preservation, rather than ideological mobilization, became the need and the call of the day, the theoretical schisms and hair-splitting in which the Jewish educated party elite excelled came to be viewed with suspicion and growing resentment by the increasingly pragmatic and instinctually utilitarian leadership. New leaders of the Party of the Noske generation, administrators and bureaucrats promoted mostly from the trade-union establishment, felt threatened and ill at ease when forced by sophisticated intellectuals and 'persons of principle' to debate issues of no visible immediate use or relevance to their practical worries and tasks at hand. They saw the party intellectuals as an alien body, as foreign invasion in affairs rightfully belonging to the German workers. Following the well established German pattern, the effort to elbow out the now vexing interference of ideological principles and theoretical precepts took the form of an attack against the *Ostjuden*. The committed and radical ideologists were best dismissed when called 'dirty Polish Jews', while their dedication to the theoretical purity of socialist ideas was explained away by reference to their incurably East-European mentality and inability to understand the spirit and the cravings of the German working class.

An alternative strategy, so to speak, was grounded in the conviction that the practice of the nation-state cannot be reformed, that the failure of assimilation is neither contingent nor rectifiable, and that the state may be a home only for a nation; that, in other words, a nation-without-a-state may gain emancipation only through constituting itself into a state, or at least gaining a state-like sovereignty. At the receiving end of assimilatory pressure, the nation-state found a fertile soil for self-propagation. It bred a counter-nationalism of sorts, that reflected mirror-like all the characteristic marks of the modern nation-state of whose rejection it had been born: its uniformizing ambitions, intolerance to difference and peculiarity, promotion of the ascribed character of communal membership, and blending the issue of political membership with cultural and ideational conformity. It meant a whole-hearted acceptance of the overall pattern, with only one's own role in its implementation put in question.

There is little doubt that the birth of political Zionism, most certainly in its most consequential, Herzl's version, was the product of the disintegration of assimilatory efforts, rather than a fruition of the Judaist tradition and the resurrection of love of Zion. As Carl E. Schorske put it, Herzl, known for the distaste with which he regarded the traditional Judaism which he blamed for a physically and mentally malforming impact on the Jews,

> generated his highly creative approach to the Jewish question not out of immersion in the Jewish tradition but out of his vain efforts to leave it behind ... Even Herzl's conception of Zion can be best understood by viewing it as an attempt to solve the liberal problem through a new Jewish state as well as to solve the Jewish problem through a new liberal state.[56]

Schorske's opinion is widely shared by all but the most politically committed scholars. In Egon Schwartz's view, 'The most apt formula to date for Herzl's life and work describes his Zionism as composed of the fragments of frustrated Austrian liberalism and his culture as a total fullfilment of the ideal of assimilation.'[57] (As Scholem's memorable verdict goes, from the vantage point of *German* Jews the Zionist programme was first and foremost a way to solve the *Ostjuden* problem. The suggestion that the Zionists should actually go to Palestine themselves, first made gingerly in 1914, came as a shock to many philanthropic Zionist sympathizers who saw themselves as Germans.) Herzl's Zionism can be seen as an attempt to achieve a double feat: to salvage the Jews from the collapse of European liberalism and to salvage liberalism from the consequences of its collapse in Europe.

---

[56] Carl E. Schorske, *Fin-de-siècle Vienna: Politics and Culture* (London: Weidenfeld & Nicholson, 1979), pp. 151, 147.

[57] Egon Schwartz, 'Melting Pot or Witch's Cauldron?', in *Jews and Germans from 1860 to 1933*, ed. Bronsen, p. 280. Hannah Arendt was most emphatic when insisting on Western Zionism's assimilatory roots: 'The hollow word-struggles between Zionism and assimilationism have completely distorted the simple fact that the Zionists, in a sense, were the only ones who sincerely wanted assimilation, namely, "normalization" of the people ("to be a people like all other peoples"), whereas the assimilationists wanted the Jewish people to retain their unique position.' (*The Jew as a Pariah*, pp. 145–6.)

Assimilation's ultimate frontiers

A most comprehensive list of conceivable and practically deployed strategies of response to the inner and ultimately destructive ambiguities of the assimilatory project would not, however, exhaust the socio-historical significance of the modern romance with uniformity, particularly as it begins to be seen now. In the long run, the consciously developed strategies, together with the hotly disputed ideologies that promoted and justified them, recede into the past where they can be viewed with a good share of detachment and (bitter, as it were) irony, and turn into matters of predominantly archival interest. What comes to the fore instead, as the genuinely lasting, perhaps irremovable, sediment of the assimilatory episode, is the historical role of the assimilatory context as a vantage point from which the deepest insight into the modern human condition could be made: as that social location inside which the predicament later to be experienced universally, through the whole of modern society, was first visited upon a selected minority, forcing it into intense self-reflection and analysis.

Assimilation was the front line of social engineering, the cutting edge of the advancing order. With spontaneity discredited and nature's self-monitoring capacity questioned, order became synonymical with monopoly of power, with control and repression of resistant 'otherness'. Ambivalence (an unwanted bridge cast over the postulated abyss between the orderly inside and the outside wilderness, or a leaky, osmotic membrane which reduces to naught all attempt at separation) was that denial of order which the production of order in general, and its assimilatory arm in particular, could not help turning out in an ever increasing volume. In the production of uniformity, ambivalence was the industrial waste. As with all refuse, it was shunned, viewed with disgust, and suspected of magic, poisoning powers.

If the assimilation was the front line of modern social engineering, the Jews found themselves throughout Europe in the forefront of assimilatory efforts. An admittedly unwieldy, scattered group spilling over any national border, they served everywhere as a symbol and a reminder of the assimilation's inner weaknesses, and, worse still, of the elusiveness of the dreamed-of order. Robert Casillo's thorough and revealing study of anti-semitism, fascism and mythology in the thought and work of Ezra Pound (a poet who took the modernist ambition most seriously and reforged it into a personal life-mission) offers a most penetrating analysis of a phenomenon which may well serve as an archetypal case of the demonology spawned by the modern project of man-made perfection:

> the Jews, whom Pound treats as intolerably other, are essential to his text . . . Without the Jews, without the arbitrary assignment of difference and confused otherness to this group, without the arbitrary repression of the parasite through violence, Pound would never be able to carry out, if only provisionally and questionably, his major project of calling things by their right names . . . The possibility of anti-Semitism is always present in Pound whenever his text either consciously or unconsciously transgresses its own categories, laws, and assumptions, at moments of confusion, contradiction, and undecidability. In short, anti-Semitism is inseparable from those instances in which Pound cannot command meaning, where unequivocal significance is undercut by the overdetermination or polysemousness of metaphor, where his essential and seemingly fixed and univocal concepts . . . prove to be inherently confused and finally undecidable.

'The contradictory and confused representation of Jews in Pound's writings' – Casillo concludes – testifies 'to his persistently undefined attitude towards Nature, History, the feminine, instinct, sexuality, the unconscious, production and many other concepts whose precise definition is demanded within Pound's project of cultural reconstruction.'[58] Through the medium of the Jews, the many unresolvable contradictions of the ordering project had been separated, 'objectified', set apart from the project itself, glued together into a coherent whole, soothingly construed as an alien contribution born of inimical motives, brought into the limelight, and condemned. They were thereby both located and intellectually disavowed, and thus made ready for the physical, albeit merely symbolic, extinction.

Pound's mind moved between two universes. One was bright, harmonious, beautiful, elevated – because transparent and orderly. The second was dark and impenetrable, populated by microbes, germs, bacilli, fungus. (Let us note that bacteria, viruses and other inhabitants of the microscopic universe have two attributes in common: because of their *corrosive*, disintegrating action they are by nature enemies of health and organic balance; and they are *invisible*, and thus difficult to spot and to keep at a safe distance. The same two traits define all ambiguity; in particular, they define the Jews – assimilated or eager to assimilate – as seen from the control desk of the ordering project.) Each of Pound's universes needed

---

[58] Robert Casillo, *The Genealogy of Demons: Anti-Semitism, Fascism, and the Myths of Ezra Pound* (Evanston: Northwestern University Press, 1988), pp. 18, 19.

the other. Obviously, the second needed the first to carry on its parasitic[59] existence. But the first needed the second as well: as an excuse for the infinite postponement of its own arrival, as an apology for its own impossibility. As there could be no ambivalence in the world of light, all ambivalence that there was had to be accommodated in the world of darkness. The deepest meaning of ambivalence is the impossibility of order. The meaning of Pound's darkness was the impossibility of light; and the impossibility of admitting that impossibility.

Pound hated the Jews (and he hated them with all his heart and all his mind, with that genuine, wholesome hatred which cannot any more distinguish between physical disgust and intellectual horror) because he strove for the perfect grid of words in which all things have their own rightful places, every thing has one place only, and no place is occupied by two things at a time. Such a perfect grid is a most potent metaphor of order – that order for which earthly powers strove since the very dawn of modernity. Like those powers, Pound woke up to the evasiveness of his ideal: construction of order seemed to result only in the piling up of ambiguities. Like the powers frustrated in their chase after the elusive national monosemy of land, Pound – in his own chase for elusive monosemy of language – needed to find the primeval source of stubborn ambivalence. Both found it in the Jews.

'Jew slime', 'morass of high kikery', 'sewers of Pal'stine', 'the vague and stinking pea-soup', 'crowling slime of a secret rule'[60] – these are a few of the garbs in which the Jews appear in Pound's version of the war of the worlds. All verbal garbs suggest formlessness, slipperiness and putrefaction; they also suggest the treachery of a slushy ground and a viscosity that augurs no escape. 'Slime', 'swamp', 'miasma', 'cesspool' are the favourite tropes of Pound's Jewish discourse. In the end, they all mean the same: chaos. For Pound, as for the modern, pushing, adventurous world which he represented at its most extreme and obsessive, the Jews stood for that confusion which confounded the dream of order. They had been chosen

---

[59] 'Parasite', as J. Hillis Miller brilliantly argued (cf. 'The Critic as Host', in *Deconstruction and Criticism* (New York: Seabury Press, 1979), p. 219), is a member of the family of words 'in para', which refer to 'something simultaneously this side of a boundary line, threshold, or margin, and also beyond it, equivalent in status and also secondary and subsidiary, submissive, as of guest to host, slave to master . . . Though a given word in "para" may seem to choose univocally one of these possibilities, the other meanings are always there as a shimmering in the word which makes it refuse to stay still in a sentence.'

[60] Cf. Casillo, *The Genealogy of Demons*, p. 84.

for this role – because, collectively, they offered the most conspicuous evidence of the dream's defeat.

Not that the Jews rejected incorporation into the new world that strove to be neatly split into nationally administered plots. It was, rather, the *topological incongruence* of the design that rendered the plan self-defeating, triggered off the search for a scapegoat and thus, obliquely, made the incorporation of Jews implausible. *Sliminess of Jews was itself a product of the drive to a world without slime*. Ambivalence of the Jews was as much the attribute of modernity as was the obsessive chase after a transparent – designed and monitored – social order.

For the great majority of Western Jews, assimilation meant little more than a change of habits – another language game, another game of daily intercourse, another sartorial or behavioural symbolic code. Be like thine neighour; do not stand off; in the crowd of like people, be inconspicuous; Judah Leib Gordon's injunction 'Be a Jew at home, man in the street' meant 'Be invisible in public places'; make your Jewishness indistinguishable. All this, in turn, meant accepting the hosts' right to define the code, studying that code earnestly and diligently, gaining flawless mastery in its application. It has been repeatedly noted that assimilating Jews became *en masse* acknowledged masters in the performing arts. They excelled in fathoming and absorbing the intent of someone else's score, line or routine. They also flocked in great numbers into professions with well-established, clear and tight rules which set apparently univocal standards of proper and improper. Were they allowed to, they would gladly enter civil service and governmental offices with their stiff and monotonous bureaucratic routine. They showed a lot of good will to turn into Riesman's 'other-directed' or Whyte's 'organization' men. They were avid learners, and they gladly acceded to the natives' right to teach. Their talent for mimicry was so uncanny as to become off-putting. This talent also proved to be their undoing – whenever and wherever the hosts were unsure of themselves, or set rules that promised more that they intended to deliver, rules that turned to be inclusive while designed to exclude. In such cases, the vigilance of the rule-setters was aroused. Not the otherness, but the skill of mimicry, the speed with which the outward trappings of otherness were shed, became then their main worry, the charge and the target.

Drumont, sensing an 'Oriental', unreformed and unreformable Jew inside the exquisitely French carapace, set the tone for what was to come. New conditions of acceptance were to be unashamedly self-cancelling: a Jew could *become* a Frenchman only if he *was* a Frenchman; that is, if he was not a Jew. The states of being a Jew and being a Frenchman were declared mutually exclusive – neither stages of a life-process, nor two faces of the same identity. For Drumont and other writers in Drumont's line, national identity was not a matter of learning, but fate. Or, rather, there were clear and impassable limits to what the learning could do to one's dentity.

Admittedly, racism was the most loud-mouthed and high-pitched voice in the new chorus: there are things that cannot and should not be assimilated. There are things which are alien and will never cease to be alien. What nature separated, man would not join. Above all, nature decreed purity of kinds. When pure kinds mix, monsters arise. Monsters of ambivalence. Ambivalence cannot be removed through good will and self-reform. It must be eradicated by forceful separation (extermination if needed), and prevented from returning by equally forceful segregation.

Racism was the shrillest voice of alarm in the face of ambiguity. But the alarm was, and still occasionally is, voiced in a less raucous, though no less anxious, form. Invariably, it conveys a fundamental disbelief in the Jew's capacity *truly* to become what he professes to be, and what he demonstrates to have become with such an apparent success. It aims at revealing 'the essence' behind 'appearances': the essence of the Jew behind the appearance of 'man as such'. More exactly, behind the outward, deceiving likeness of an American, Frenchman or Englishman.

Of this latter style (admittedly, a toned down, roundabout and hypocritical, yet a form of racism all the same), the widely read burlesque of John Murray Cuddihy offers a refined example. The central message of Cuddihy's lampoon is straightforward enough: Jewishness of the Jews is ineradicable and assimilation is phoney. The assimilated Jew is a contradiction in terms: an ambiguity – and incurably so. Cuddihy revels in unmasking the 'uncanny pre-modern nexus', the 'parochial ethnic tie', the 'stubborn, residual reality', hiding just beneath the skin of 'Harvard Professors' and other luminaries of American intellectual and cultural life. In conclusion, he announces the coming of 'novel Marranism'. Much, perhaps all, of the Jewish contribution to modern culture and science can be explained as the quest of Jewish intellectuals to cover up (before the others and before themselves) that 'social unease' which their duplicity could not but generate. Marx, Freud, Lévi-Strauss and their lesser (or perhaps better protected) companions were all, each in his own way, pursuing the same elusive goal; all the famous grand visions with which they enriched contemporary culture were but metaphors meant to ennoble their (otherwise embarrassing) private, tribal troubles. Thanks to Cuddihy's insight and vigilance we know now, for instance, what structuralism was all about:

> By means of the universal and ahistorical 'idealism' of the ideology of structural anthropology, the early involvement of Lévi-Strauss with the fact of his Jewishness, the ancient 'Jewish problem' has disappeared. The 'primal

antinomy', the primary 'donnée' of the socialization of Jews in the West in the post-Emancipation era, namely, the 'primitive classification' of the world into 'goyim' and 'ourselves' – has been swallowed up and assimilated, sublimed into the lofty binary oppositions of nature and culture, raw and cooked, night and day.[61]

No doubt Cuddihy puts his finger on a real problem: the indelible 'Jewish signature' on modern culture, the truly uncanny, unprecedented, massive participation of the assimilating and assimilated Jews in the cultural revolution of modernity; in that revolution which, at the same time, came 'from the very heart' of the 'modernity project', was the product of pressures and tension that the modern thrust for artificially designed order generated – and decisively influenced that project's discreditation. In line with a long tradition, Cuddihy attempts, however, to defend the objective against the disruptive tendencies its pursuit brought forth, by dismissing such tendencies as mere emanations of parochial and retrograde Jewish worries; while the truth of the matter was that the assimilatory pressure, that trade mark of modern politics, cast the Jews in social contexts from which contradictions of modernity were most poignantly experienced and hence easier to scan, to comprehend and to theorize. Jewish contributions to modern culture are better understood not as expressions of 'Jewish struggle with modernity', but as by-products of 'modernity's struggle with itself', side-effects which from that place into which modernity cast the Jews were better visible than from most other vantage points.

Indeed, the assimilatory pressures which – courtesy of the nationalist state and the state-sponsored *Kulturträger* – descended upon European Jews, did not simply result in torn souls, broken lives, despondency and despair. Neither did they present their victims solely with the choice between a war against a duplicitous society or emulating that duplicity and carrying it away from that society into distant and hopefully secure place where it could be turned from the sign of Jewish weakness into an instrument of Jewish strength. Certainly, the assimilatory episode did all these things. But it accomplished more than that. Without any prior intention, by default rather than by design, assimilatory pressures brought forth a social context of a unique and unprecedented creative potential. With an outcome virtually opposite to that which was intended, the pressures generated by the modern project heavily contributed to the birth and flourishing of modern culture – perhaps that project's most spectacular and precious, though largely unanticipated, side-product.

---

61 Cf. Cuddihy, *The Ordeal of Civility*, pp. 86–7, 8, 162.

The antinomies of assimilation and the birth of modern culture

The most perceptive among the victims of those assimilatory pressures that promised belongingness yet delivered desolation were painfully aware of a creative strength born of their sufferings. This was true of no one more than Franz Kafka, a man who shed all illusions and embraced his assignation of a 'Western Jew' in full – but as a writer's distinction rather than deprivation.

> Both of us [he wrote to Milena] are, after all, familiar with characteristic specimens of Western Jews; I am, as far as I can judge, the most Western Jew of them all – which means (if I may overstate the case) that I have not been granted a single second of tranquility, nothing has been granted to me, everything has to be acquired, not only the present and future, but also the past . . .[62]

It is the natives who are *granted* their existence, so that they can live it in tranquility – to *be* rather than to *become*. Ostensibly the strangers had been offered the same kind of happiness; but Kafka knew what so many among his companions in fate had been too slow to note or too stubborn or cravenly to admit: that the offer was a lie, as one cannot *acquire* what may come only as a *gift of fate*.

Unlike so many others sharing his plight, Kafka lived consciously his life of incertitude, unclarity, of striving for goals which always recede before they have been reached. Having been *granted* nothing, one does not *owe* anything. No prejudice blinkers the eyes, no loyalty binds the lips. This means no end to suffering. But this also means no limit to freedom. What remains is to live this freedom: a harrowing task, a breathtaking chance.

Kafka wrote – of someone like him, of himself:

> He has two antagonists; the first pushes him from behind, from his origin. The second blocks his road ahead. He struggles with both. Actually the first supports him in his struggle with the second, for the first wants to push him forward; and in the same way the second supports him in his struggle with

[62] Franz Kafka, *Letters to Milena*, trans. Tania and James Stern (New York: Schocken Books, 1953), p. 247. Walter Benjamin, a man of a life experience largely similar to Kafka's, a writer who one of the first among the creators of modern culture saw the self as 'a project', as 'something that needs to be built', something that is always being 'built too slow' so that 'one is always in arrears to oneself', wrote also of 'the purity and beauty of Kafka's failure'. (Cf. Susan Sonntag's introduction to *One Way Street and Other Writings*, p. 14.)

> the first; for the second of course forces him back. But it is only theoretically so. For it is not only the two protagonists who are there, but he himself as well, and who really knows his intentions? However that may be, he has a dream that sometime in an unguarded moment – it would require, though, a night as dark as no night has ever been – he will spring out of the fighting line and be promoted, on account of his experience of such warfare, as judge over his struggling antagonists.[63]

The assimilation episode, complete with its gruesome final act, was perhaps that 'dark night' from which the hapless victim of unwinnable war could emerge as the judge of the war's futility. The victims were given the chance of calling the bluff of the assimilatory offer; more than that, however, they could be among the first to see through the modern dream of uniformity, the first to shake free from the modern horror of difference, the first to assault point-blank the modern religion of intolerance; they could be among the first to glimpse the universal human condition in the status of the stranger as social outcast. As Hannah Arendt put it,

> out of their personal experience Jewish poets, writers and artists should have been able to evolve the concept of pariah as a human type – a concept of supreme importance for the evaluation of mankind in our day and one which has exerted upon the gentile world an influence in strange contrast to the spiritual and political ineffectiveness which has been the fate of these men among their own brethren.[64]

The assimilatory project of modernity gave birth to its own grave-diggers. Inadvertently it set a stage on which the drama of modern culture was to be played to full houses and to astounding and enduring acclaim. There was, one may say, an *elective affinity* between the experience of the objects of the assimilatory project (and, to put it more generally, of the modern thrust against ambivalence) and the emergence of the antinomial modern culture.

Elective affinity is not a causal relation. Neither is it a matter of 'similarity'. It is, rather, a relation of *isomorphism*, of 'commutation' between two autonomous sets of phenomena: the inner relations between phenomena of one set may be represented as replicas of those of the other. As each set may be 'structured' in more than one fashion, the structure called forth by the 'elective affinity' perspective is but one of many possibilities clustered in the presence of the sets. Like all structures, this one is a violation: it imposes its own priorities and its own irrelevancies; it coerces some phenomena into prominence while relegating others

---

63 Franz Kafka, *The Great Wall of China: Stories and Reflections*, trans. Willa and Edwin Muir (New York: Schocken Books, 1979), pp. 160–1.

64 Arendt, *The Jew as a Pariah*, p. 68.

into oblivion. This was the operation that Edmond Jabès (*Le Livre des questions*, 1963) had to carry out on *both* Jewishness *and* writing in order to be able to suggest that the 'difficulty of being a Jew' *coincides* 'with the difficulty of writing; for Judaism and writing are but the same waiting, the same hope, the same depletion' (or what Maria Tsvetayeva had to accomplish, when she insisted that 'all the poets are Jews').[65]

The antinomial motifs that combine into the phenomenon of modernity (the thrust toward universality dissolving in practice into the celebration of pluralism; the search for absolute foundation of truth that, uncoordinated, leads to the recognition of incurable relativism of knowledge; the dream of semiotic clarity that discloses the world as hopelessly equivocal; the cult of belonging that lays bare rootlessness; indeed, the very 'double location' of ambivalence – selected as the target of the modern project and yet lying at the heart of modern mentality), as well as the most notorious yet most self-destructive among the characteristically modern obsessions (naturalness through artificiality, spontaneity through management, freedom through design) did rebound in a social context in which, to quote *Finnegans Wake*, the main question was 'who is who when everybody was somebody else'. Destablization, 'until-further-noticeness', or the absence of clear-cut identities and of good reasons to prefer one to another were the paramount among life experiences, and yet life was lived under an incessant and overwhelming pressure to *construe* an identity both private and publicly approved, both agreeable and acceptable, for fear of banishment in case of failure or neglect. Being at war with each other (*because* they were at war with each other) modern culture and modern life conditions 'made sense' of each other. And it was the Jews, exposed to powerful assimilatory pressure, called and pressed to shed and to pick up identities, to build their own selves out of glimpses of somebody else's selves, to self-assert and self-deny, to become different from what they were and to become like what they were not, to simulate and dissimulate, – who were among the first to experience the full impact of the modern condition and to be made fully aware of the dire consequences of improper response.

In other words, the Jewish end of the modernizing thrust offered an optimal location for the formation and conscious articulation of such intellectual patterns as were to become distinctive marks of modern culture. And vice versa – such marks protrude more sharply and better

---

[65] Quoted after Jacques Derrida, *Writing and Difference*, trans. Alan Bras (London: Routledge, 1978), p. 132; Jacques Derrida, 'Shibboleth', in *Midrash and Literature*, ed. Geoffrey H. Hartmann and Sanford Budick (New Haven: Yale University Press, 1986), p. 338.

open themselves to scrutiny when seen in conjunction with the social situation with which they had become most conspicuously resonant. This does not mean to imply that modern culture is 'Jewish' in its character. Neither does it mean that Jews are 'modern' by nature. But this does mean that in its fight against ambivalence modernity cast the Jews (as it goes on casting other 'strangers') in a situation of ambivalence so profound and acute as to strip the human condition of its particularistic disguises; and to lay bare in the result that ambivalence that constitutes the universality of the modern human condition: the achievement and the bankruptcy of the modern project.

Harold Bloom wrote of the avidly modernizing, ostensibly all-absorbing yet practically all-segregating world: 'The psychic representative of the drive not in the individual consciousness but in human history, allegorically or ironically considered, is the image of a wandering exile, propelled onward in time by all the vicissitudes of injustice and outwardness . . .'[66] The exile, displacement, ambiguity and non-determination happened to be the lot of the Jews just before it turned into a universal human condition. It was, to be more precise, the lot of a few transitory Jewish generations, suspended in the empty space between a tradition which they already left and the mode of life which stubbornly denied them the right of entry. It was in that empty space that the ultimate contingency and ambivalence of the human existential predicament, and the ensuing curse and blessing of self-constitution and meaning-formation, had nowhere to hide, and thus forced their way into the vision of the human condition – nakedly, unashamedly and obtrusively. It so happened that the homeless Jewish intellectuals were the first to stagger (or, rather, to be pushed) into that space of no hiding.

Since then, homelessness, rootlessness and the necessity of self-construction ceased to be the trade mark of the Jews. The Jews have settled – while their non-Jewish neighbours have become less securely settled than they thought they were before. To put it in a different way: the Jews have been finally admitted to the world that in the meantime had lost much of its ability (or abandoned much of its pretence) to confer identity by granting or refusing admission. To give the matter still another wording: forced into the state of homelessness by assimilatory pressures of modernity (and thus discovering the contingency and ambivalence of being), the Jews were the first to sample the taste of postmodern existence. Later they found home, but not until the world itself turned postmodern. Then they lost their distinctiveness – but only because the state of 'being

---

[66] Harold Bloom, *Ruin the Sacred Truth: Poetry and Belief from the Bible to the Present* (Cambridge, Mass.: Harvard University Press, 1989), p. 161.

distinct' has turned into the only truly universal mark of the human condition.

With that, the assimilatory zeal of up-and-coming modernity has all but petered out. In the part of the world where it celebrated its greatest triumphs, modernity has learned (or – prudence calls for caution – *is learning*) to live with its own impossibility. Not just the black, but all colours are now beautiful, and they are allowed to boast their beauty together, though each sort of beauty is unlike the next. This may not yet be a rainbow *coalition*, but this certainly is a rainbow *coexistence*. And thus is a rainbow-like, polysemic and manifold culture, unashamedly ambiguous, reticent in passing judgements, perforce tolerant to others because, at long last, it becomes tolerant of itself, of its own ultimate contingency and the inexhaustibility of interpretative depths. Pound could not lose his Judaeophobia without abandoning the dream of undisturbed harmony, of a truly one-to-one correspondence between names and things; but he would not be able to retain his Judaeophobia for long (not in its vicious, paranoic and exterminatory form) were he to stop the dreaming.

By a hardly edifying, sinister paradox, the outburst of Jewish intellectual creativity which sedimented as modern culture was an outcome of the intolerance of modernity. Such a creative intensity is unlikely to survive (not, at any rate, in its original spectacular form) the entry into a world indifferent to difference and deaf to the blandishments of the preachers of ultimate perfection. Once the drama of assimilation is over (or, rather, *where* it is over), so is the story of uniquely creative and original Jewish cultural role.

5

A Case Study in the Sociology of Assimilation II: The Revenge of Ambivalence

> I don't know, I'll never know, in the silence you don't know, you must go on, I can't go on, I can't go on, I'll go on.
>
> Samuel Beckett

Not all assimilatory experience was tragic. Not all is culturally creative. As a matter of fact, the opposite seems to be the case – and ever more so, as throughout the Western world the crusading spirit of nationalism peters out in entertainment supplied by the factory-produced 'common heritage', while DIY, shop-promoted and personally assembled identities replace the etiological myths of common fate, blood, soil and collective missions. The daily life of assimilation is dull – uninspired and uninspiring. Hardly a source of agony; certainly not a stimulus to iconoclasm, intellectual dissent, cultural adventurism.

For the great majority of Western Jews, comfortably settled in the middle and upper-middle classes – national, local, yet not at all militantly parochial – assimilation means no more than keeping up with the Joneses. 'Thou shalt not step out of tune with thy neighbour' is its sole commandment – and this is a commandment easy to observe, unlikely to prompt worries more harrowing than, as Cynthia Ozick caustically commented, the urge of 'rushing out to buy a flag to even up the street'.[1] Assimilation has dissipated in a general conformity of public appearances peacefully cohabiting with variety of privatized contents. Overt uniformity is all the easier to maintain as the diversity (particularly as long as it remains unobtrusive) is being increasingly recognized as the foremost of personal virtues, a duty and a pride. Amidst the cornucopia of class, generational, occupational, regional, or just socially unattached, freely wandering lifestyles, it is difficult to set apart, as a special challenge, such forms of life as

[1] Cynthia Ozick, *Art and Ardour* (New York: Dutton, 1984), p. 159.

may be ethnically rooted and thus subject to other, more worrisome rules than the rest of the manifold dimensions of diversity. The memory of their past uniqueness survives, if at all, in the older and fast ageing generation's occasional hiccups of shame and embarrassment. On the whole, it seems, attention is focused, undramatically, on the efforts of the affluent Jewish residents of suburbia to 'be like' the rest of the affluent residents of suburbia, of the Jewish youth to absorb and replicate the up-to-date life style of the young, of the Jewish professionals to live and dress and deck the offices in the way right and proper for the professionals of equal standing, of the Jewish academics to act in accordance with the latest campus fashion.

The sting has been taken out of the assimilation pressure (or of that little that has been left of it) not because of anything the Jews have done but because what happened to the world into which the Jews have been assimilating. This is now a late-modern, or postmodern, world of universal particularity; a world integrated through its diversity, little worried by difference and resigned to ambiguity. The sharpness and profundity of differences which the assimilatory pressure is meant to efface have no objective measure but the intensity of a given nationalism's drive to ascendancy and domination.

Let us bring the latter point into sharper focus. In communist Eastern Europe, and particularly in the vast expanses of the Soviet Union, the Jews have in fact undergone a more thorough assimilation than anywhere in the West. In customs, language and cultural styles they are by and large indistinguishable from their neighbours to an extent unsurpassed even in the affluent American suburbia. They do not even have religious congregations and 'Jewish causes' to distinguish them, at least nominally, from other bureaucrats, medics, lawyers, craftsmen or tradesmen. And yet to say that the drama of assimilation is in their case finished would be in all probability fatuous and certainly premature. In the long years of communist rule the problems generated by national self-assertion have been refrigerated, not resolved. They only waited for a rise in political temperature to reactivate with a vigour which has only become more explosive for the longevity of hibernation. As this now happens, the totally acculturated Jews find themselves vulnerable and exposed no less – perhaps more – than any other ingredient of the witches' brew.

Among the suddenly awakened nationalisms confronting the unifying and uniformizing pressures of the Soviet state, the Jews, who unlike all other would-be sovereign nations have no territorial claims and not the slightest hope for economic or social self-sufficiency, are the only group naturally wedded, for better or worse, to that very state. The Jews are, in the full sense of the concept, a 'state-nation', dependent on state protection and owing to the central Soviet state their conditions of life and guarantees of collective safety. The resulting suspension in the void stretching between the state without a national base and the many aggrieved nations without states, the Jews seem to be custom-made for the role of a political football. On the whole period of modern Jewish history Hannah Arendt commented that 'During the 150 years when Jews truly lived amidst, and not just in the neighbourhood of, Western European peoples, they always had to pay with political misery for social glory and with social insult for political success.'[2] In the explosive mixture of unsatiated and insatiable nationalisms which is the present-day Soviet Union, the Jews are an obvious immediate target of venomous discharge against the state held guilty for the stifling of national ambitions. For the carriers of great-Russian ambitions (one can glean such ambitions from each issue of journals like *Nash Sovremennik*, *Moskva*, *Molodaya Gvardia*, *Literaturnaya Rossiya*), Jews symbolize the 'internationalist (Western-liberal) conspiracy' against the unique spirit and tradition of Mother Russia. If the great-Russian forces lose their battle and their grip over subordinated nations, the Jews may face for a change contradictory and incompatible assimilatory pressures coming from the new nationalist powers which will inherit the historic memory of the Jews as enemies of all and any national self-assertion.

In the experience of Western Jewry, however, one can speak of Jewish assimilation by and large in the past tense. The agony and the splendour of assimilation was there a relatively brief, and relatively localized, episode in modern history. It encompassed a few generations spanning the stormy yet short period needed for the modern states to entrench in their historically indispensable yet transitory nationalist form. It encompassed just a few generations thrown into the cauldron of seething nationalist passions; generations already cut off from their roots but yet unabsorbed by the new compound; generations forced to stretch themselves to the utmost, to build from scratch a domicile that others around them thought of as something one is normally born into and inherits. It is of such generations that Kafka spoke as of four-legged animals (truly, they would

---

[2] Hannah Arendt, *Origins of Totalitarianism* (London: Allen & Unwin, 1962), p. 56. The reborn outspoken Russian Judaeophobia shows every mark of the early-modern assimilatory project: it promises Soviet Jews tolerance on condition of the denial of their identity and their total subordination to the Russian cause. In a recent issue of *Pravda*, Stanislav Kuniayev, the editor of the journal *Nash sovremmennik* ['Our Contemporary'], famous for its preaching of essential incompatibility of the Jews and the Russian spirit, selected a few 'exemplary Jews' – like the collector of Russian folk songs Hilferding, the painter of Russian landscape Levitan, the Russian poets Antokolski, Pasternak, Mandelshtam and Gershenson (all emphatically 'non-Jewish' in their poetic personae) as the pattern he would wish the rest of the Jews to follow so that their acceptance in the Russian national home may be considered (cf. 'Za slovo – vesomoë!', *Pravda*, 20 October 1989, p. 3).

not pass muster as humans by the standards then in force), whose hind legs had already barely touched the ground, while the forelegs sought a foothold in vain. The empty, extraterritorial space in which these 'men without qualities' were suspended felt like an uncanny mixture of paradise and hell: the paradise of infinite chances, the hell of infinite inconclusiveness of success. For a few generations, the travellers – forced to take off, prohibited from landing – had no other abode but this empty space. The agony and splendour of assimilation was confined to that brief flight through the void of non-identity. Enticed, blandished or coerced to take into the air, the flyers – whether eager to soar or just forced to flutter against their will – made an easy prey for gamekeepers and poachers alike. But they also enjoyed the brief privilege of that vast and sharp vision called, with a touch of awe and jealousy, the 'bird's eye view'.

The outcome, of course, tends to colour the memory of the process. That the drama of Jewish assimilation was a tragedy rather than a cheerful and edifying moral tale has been brought home to the actors (that is, the actors lucky enough to survive the last curtain) mostly by the violent ending. Productions that have been spared such an ending are remembered with less horror, even with romantic nostalgia and pride. Where it did not lead to Auschwitz, assimilation is still recalled, in a Whig-history style, as the story of emancipation, liberation and the triumph of reason. The old core of American and British Jewry were never given the sobering chance of watching the faces of their kind, polite and civilized 'co-nationals' – neighbours and business partners – during the 'deportations'. But as we have seen before, with the passage of time even the survivors of German Jewry tended to tone down the disastrous aspects of the failed romance and tenderly remember its romantic pleasures. Such a tendency is more pronounced yet in the case of countries further away from the eye of the cyclone and thus only obliquely sharing in the responsibility for the final disaster. For instance, as David S. Landes recently observed, 'because those who write French history almost invariably love their subject . . . the story of French anti-Semitism is very problematical, hard to live with, and hard to reconcile with one's emotions. Jews and non-Jews have preferred not to talk about it, in the hope perhaps of avoiding thorny issues or of letting sleeping dogs lie.'[3]

---

[3] David S. Landes, 'Two Cheers for Emancipation', in *The Jews in Modern France*, ed. Frances Malino and Bernard Wasserstein (Hanover: University Press of New England, 1985), p. 302. Landes goes on to list the twelve expedients most widely used to play down the more sinister components of the chequered history of assimilation in France – like, for instance, implying that the Dreyfus Affair was just 'a storm in an urban teacup', or that French antisemitism was merely a part of a larger xenophobia (and just nothing to particularly worry about, nor related to assimilation's own logic . . .).

In all fairness, the assimilatory drama, in Germany or elsewhere, all its ups and downs notwithstanding, was never an unmitigated disaster. More importantly still, it could not be perceived as such by its actors before the final curtain fell on the *Vaterland* of the 'Germans of Mosaic persuasion' and went up again on Auschwitz and Treblinka. They did not know what their children do; their ignorance goes a long way towards explaining their dogged optimism in the face of adverse evidence. (That evidence we now see, with the wisdom of hindsight, as prodromal signs of the gathering storm; they, however, were entitled to explain it away as the last ramblings of the past, retreating under the pressure of the triumphant and unstoppable march of humane civilization.)

In Germany and the Austro-Hungarian Empire the emancipation of the Jews was a story of uninterrupted and astounding success by all standards accessible and deemed relevant at the time. In Sigmund Freud's paternal home the walls were pasted with portraits of famous Imperial statesmen and public figures, many of them Jews or of Jewish extraction. According to Robert S. Wistrich's splendid study, 'Jews were making their mark everywhere in banking, commerce, manufacturing, the liberal professions, the press, and politics. In the universities too, the expansion of the Jewish bourgeois elite was well under way by 1880.' Jewish students made 31 per cent of the total enrolment in Vienna classical *Gymnasien*, around 20 per cent in *Realschulen*, 48 per cent in the faculties of medicine, 22 per cent in law faculties and 15 per cent in philosophy.[4] In view of the apparently unstoppable, massive entry into the invitingly open, hospitable society, even the most extreme expressions of the assimilationist devotion to the nationalist dreams of the hosts[5] must have seemed less an aberration than

---

[4] Robert S. Wistrich, *The Jews of Vienna in the Age of Franz Joseph* (Oxford University Press, 1989), p. 173.

[5] Among many other penetrating portraits his study contains, Wistrich paints also one of the prominent Austrian historian and Pan-German ideologue Heinrich Friedjung, who believed that 'the highest duty of the political writer was to exert an influence on that obscure first cause of the history of all peoples, on the national character'. Friedjung lived to see the Pan-German movement, which he helped to create and whose cause he ardently promoted, expelling him from its ranks as a Jew. Unabashed, Friedjung went on offering his zeal and talent to the Germanization of the countless ethnic minorities that populated the Vienna-ruled empire (cf. Wistrich, *The Jews of Vienna in the Age of Franz Joseph*, pp. 160–1). As A.J.P. Taylor explained: 'Friedjung regarded himself as a German, but he was only a German by adoption: he had become a German, because he valued German culture, and the process was no less deliberate for being subconscious. He therefore tended to expect a similar subconscious recognition of German superiority from the other races and he could not understand the reluctance of the Czechs, the Slovaks, or the Croats to follow his example.' (See the Introduction to

they look today; it is difficult, and unfair, to laugh them off as merely products of political naivety or myopia.

We understand now better than the hapless participants of the drama ever could, that inside the sphere of German cultural influence (and political aspirations) the assimilatory dreams were doomed from the start – at least as a smooth and peaceful process. The amazing congestion of mutually contradictory and potentially inimical national claims was the main reason. The contradictions inevitably present in every assimilatory programme had been brought to the level of exceptional intensity by the sheer fact that no nationalism could be placated without antagonizing a few others, and thus no conformity was fully trusted, and each declaration of loyalty was constantly held, suspiciously, under a microscope.

> With which exactly among the myriad nationalities of old Austria were Jews expected to assimilate? Who in fact were the 'hosts' from the viewpoint of assimilating Jewry? How did one define who was 'Austrian' and 'un-Austrian' in an Empire divided into a multitude of regions, provinces, districts, political societies, warring ethnic groups, and linguistic entities?

Understandably, confronted with a wide range of choices, yet being by nature a 'state-nation', a group relying on the state and the state alone for the granting and the protection of their still precarious political and social rights, the Jews were inclined to opt for the state-culture and state-language, and these were German.

> But the Germanocentrism of Austrian Jewry was only one side of the problem. When in the second half of the nineteenth century Jews in Hungary and Galicia began to adopt a Magyar or Polish rather than a German orientation, the situation was scarcely improved. The Jewish realignment towards Magyars and Galician Poles almost immediately provoked the anti-Semitism of submerged, 'historyless' nationalities, oppressed by the Hungarian and Polish aristocracy.[6]

It was the hopeless incompatibility of the dreams of territorial ascendancy and power monopoly, entertained in equal measure by all the extant or potential nation-states of East-Central Europe in the late nineteenth and early twentieth centuries, that rebounded on the Jews with a vengeance. Out of all the ethnic, cultural and linguistical groups staggering under unbearable pressure of contradictory political claims, the Jews had been

---

Heinrich Friedjung, *The Struggle for Supremacy in Germany, 1859–1866* (New York, 1966), p. iv.) An enthusiastic *Kulturträger* on behalf of his adopted nation, Friedjung like so many other equally keen promoters of German cultural superiority put all his fingers in the doors which the rising 'lesser' nations tried hard to shut and keep closed.

[6] Wistrich, *The Jews of Vienna in the Age of Franz Joseph*, pp. 140, 206.

squeezed out as the very essence of failure and the frustration's main cause – as ambivalence *tout court*.

Even under 'ordinary' circumstances the exposure to assimilatory pressures has, at least potentially, a powerful eye-opening impact: it enables the most perceptive among its victims to see through secrets and mysteries of social existence which remain invisible to the placid and unperturbed 'natives'. With the circumstances reaching a complexity unmatched elsewhere, such an impact – such a chance – must have been unusually profound. I suggest that here, more than anywhere else, lies the cause of the spectacular 'Jewish breakthrough into modern culture'; of the astoundingly creative and original role which a few generations of freshly assimilated and assimilating Jews, in a certain phase of history of a selected area of the modernizing world, played in the shaping of what we now justly call the *culture of modernity*.

The counter-attack of ambivalence

Ionesco declared once: 'I feel that every message of despair is the statement of a situation from which everyone must freely try to find a way out.'[7] Let us note: it is the urge to get out that defines the state of despair; and in order to articulate itself as despair, this must be an urge with no obvious outlet, no marked exit. The way out has yet to be *found* or cut through the walls. And the search for the exit, or its construction, has to be conducted 'by everyone' – that is, individually. Presumably the community does not know of such a way, or would not say if it had, or it would not help if it said. This is why despair is what it is. It always points away from itself. Some would say: it points forward. But we call 'forward' that direction which the road that leads us out of the state of despair has taken. Progress, one may say, is a memory of past despair and a determination to escape from the present one.

The drama of assimilation turned out a lot of despair. And so it inspired an acute longing for the way out. As most tried ways proved to be blocked or circular or otherwise deceptive, a massive construction of new roads took off. As the search for the new roads grew in vigour, trust in the old ones continued to dissipate. It is not that the collapse of assimilatory dreams discredited a particular set of beliefs, previously embraced, now rejected; it rather disavowed the very habit of (to borrow Arnold's phrase) believing firmly, staunchly and dogmatically. As if the seekers of new ways

[7] Quoted after Martin Esslin, *The Theatre of the Absurd* (New York: Doubleday, 1961), p. 138.

anticipated the verdict to be passed later by George Orwell: 'Nothing is gained by teaching a parrot a new word.' 'The enemy is the gramophone mind, whether or not one agrees with the record that is being played at the moment.'[8] Deep suspicion and fear of the crowds gathered on the town square to celebrate their thoughtless togetherness, of the opinions which gave flesh to their unity, of the joyful abandon with which such opinions were stuck to – were most poignant among the feelings shared by people otherwise as different as Freud, Kraus, Schnitzler, Lukács, Adorno, Husserl, Tucholsky, Wittgenstein, Canetti or the elegant philosophers of the *Wienerkreis*. Any belief should arouse vigilance and trigger critical faculties for the mere reason of having been embraced by the intolerant multitude.

It was said of Freud that he profaned the past, poisoned the present, and killed the future. It was, undoubtedly, said by or for the crowd. For that crowd, the present was clean and tidy only if the past was sacred; and it was the neatness of the present which made the future alive (that is, made it like a perpetual, immortal present). Freud and others like him were seen as 'poisoning the present' because they refused to take anything on trust; because they declined to accept as truth what had been backed by general consent; because they refused to accept any truth as final and exempt any creed from critical testing. They were detractors of *common* sense – and because of that their act of treachery shook the very foundations of the present, which suddenly turned uncertain and unreliable. They did more, in fact: they implied that opinions have nothing else but their own feet to stand on, as the authorities behind which they hide have no right to issue truth certificates. They were destroyers of security, wreckers of order, ruiners of peace of mind.

Objecting in 1908 to Georg Simmel's university appointment, a certain Dietrich Schäfer took it for Simmel's 'most Jewish' trait 'his commitment to sociology: to see society as the principal formative agent of human community in place of state and church'.[9] In fairness to Schäfer, one must

---

[8] Quoted after Alok Rai, *Orwell and the Politics of Despair: A Critical Study of the Writings of George Orwell* (Cambridge: Cambridge University Press, 1988), pp. 152, 153.

[9] Quoted after Gay, *Freud, Jews and Other Germans*, p. 122. Playing down the role of the church as the foundation of human existence, or 'deconstructing' religion – Durkheim-style – as a mere 'social fact' and a coercion-supported 'integrative interest' of society must have shocked the contemporaries of Schäfer in a way difficult to imagine for our own contemporaries. To comprehend Schäfer's horror one needs to compare Simmel's crime with detraction, denigration or corrosion of those other, still sacred beliefs of which sociology stands accused today by the powers that be and other guardians of establishment: with the sins of

admit that he was not wide of the mark. When Simmel's profuse writings are compared with those of Weber, Sombart and the mass of lesser figures in the budding German *Sozialwissenschaften*, one is struck by the paucity of attention Simmel pays to the state, the church, and other 'foreground' powers that stamp social reality with the seal of sacred order; and by the marginal place Simmel allots such powers in his chart of things human. As a matter of fact, even the category of *society* plays but a subsidiary role in Simmel's sociology: society is just a fickle, fragile and perpetually changing form sedimented by the endless process of *sociality*. If the sociology of great religious systems was the life-long preoccupation of Weber, the philosophy of money was the *magnum opus* of Simmel. Where Weber spoke of the rationalizing impact of state bureaucracy, Simmel pondered the spontaneity of group formation. When Weber pursued the grounds of legitimate authority, Simmel explored the social conditions which stand behind the curiously sceptical and blasé cast of mind of modern man. While to Weber human intellect was first and foremost the source and the product of an increasingly rational ('principally co-ordinated', in the immortal Parsons rendering) order, to Simmel it was, alongside the money, that acid solution which dissolved all certainties and established hierarchies. If Weber searched for the secret of social order in that grip in which values hold human actions, Simmel wrote of that gray mass of impressions in which everything floats with the same specific gravity and nothing is unique, paramount or absolute. In Weber's eye, the imminent triumph of rational social order blended with the dominance of reason in the individual life of man; Simmel saw a yawning, unstoppably widening, oppressive and depressing gap between collectively sedimented civilization and the absorptive capacity of human spirit.

Belief is a belief is a belief; such seemed to be the message of that sociology of which 'Jewishness' Schäfer complained. Belief may be powerful and overwhelming; in fact it often is. However mighty, it always remains

---

similarly deconstructing the ideologies of patriotism or free market, depending on the legitimizing formula favoured by this or that power regime. Sociology's permanent accomplishment (even if not a purpose many of its practitioners deliberately choose) seems to be a critique and in the end sapping of what Theodor W. Adorno described as an 'attitude which at all costs defends order, even an order in which all those things are not in order' (*The Jargon of Authenticity*, trans. Kurt Tarnowski and Frederic Will (London: Routledge, 1973), p. 22). Of such an irreverent attitude to the most sacred value of all power Simmel stood accused as a Jew; being a Jew in an intensely nationalistic Germany, obsessed more than with anything else with its own 'national' unification, must have merely helped Simmel to pioneer a cognitive stance that later, in a rapidly 'postmodernizing' world, would be matter-of-factly taken by virtually all social philosophy.

nevertheless an *artefact* of society, of sociality, of human interaction. No recourse to eternal essence, primordial precepts, absolute grounds of truth – nothing, in fact, except the preference for one creed rather than another – which, as all preference, can be challenged, criticized and ultimately discredited and rejected.

Now one can hardly expect this sort of idea to be received by the servants of the modern nation-state as Good News and their harbingers to be rewarded. As so many times before, the anger focused on the messengers. Schäfer spoke for that majority who needed beliefs as truth – as the whole truth and nothing but the truth; beliefs as the sceptre of power, as legitimation of rule, as licence to uproot dissent and banish the dissenters. 'Society refuses to consent to the ventilation of the question because it has a bad conscience in more than one respect ... The society maintans a condition of cultural hypocrisy, which is bound to be accompanied by a sense of insecurity and a necessity for guarding what is an undeniably precarious situation by forbidding criticism and discussion,' sadly commented Freud on his singed fingers. And he knew what gave him the strength to stand up to that prohibition and go on piercing through the thick armour of hypocrisy: 'Nor is it perhaps entirely a matter of chance that the first advocate of psychoanalysis was a Jew. To profess belief in this new theory called for a certain degree of readiness to accept a position of a solitary opposition – a position with which no one is more familiar than a Jew.'[10] The 'Jew' to whom Freud refers, a person marked above all by solitude, by standing alone, is of course the Jew Freud knows from autopsy and introspection: the Jew of the era of nationalisms and assimilation, the Jew already cut from his origin but not yet admitted to any other home.

And yet there is more than a touch of paradox in the fact that the ultimate assault against social hypocrisy, against the false pretences of societally upheld truth, was in the case of Freud (like in the case of the *Wienerkreis* crusaders against metaphysics, of Husserl and other detractors of the 'natural attitude') launched from under the cover of another truth-bestowing authority – science. The war against indisputable truths took the form of a dispute about the right to make universally valid and binding statements, of an effort to wrench such an authority from the state, the church and other executive organs of the 'natives', and put it in the hands of such institutions as can reasonably hope to gain and to defend autonomy. As the roads to the seats of traditional – religious – authority remained solidly sealed, and those leading to the new – political – ones opened only to the holders of selected birth certificates, science stood

---

[10] Sigmund Freud, 'The Resistances to Psycho-Analysis' (1925), in *Collected Papers*, vol. 5 (London: Hogarth Press, 1950), pp. 170–1, 174.

alone as a game where skill, diligence, and talent, rather than the strength of hand, could be trusted to decide the outcome. Martha Robert wrote of Freud that 'in the society where he was fated to live and work, there were only two ways in which a Jew could escape humiliation: by making a great deal of money or by amassing enough knowledge to force general recogniton'. Of humiliation, Freud heard from his father, and there was enough of it around to prompt a frantic search for escape. Science seemed to offer one. Promising to distribute its prizes by talents and achievements only, and to respect solely the power of argument, it seemed to be the dreamed-of force able to free the present from its mortgage to the past. 'The two benefits' Freud expected of science: 'a great discovery that will make him famous and admittance to "good", enlightened society'.[11]

It was in science, therefore, that Freud sought the court of appeal against the humiliation administered by a society which was neither good nor enlightened. But he did not come to science as a litigant seeking the reversal of an unfavourable sentence or claiming damages. Wounded pride would not be healed simply by quashing the verdict. More was needed to restore honour. True, it had to be shown that the original sentence stemmed from false premises and that the lower court was guided by wrong advice; it had to be proved as well, however, that the court had overstepped its competence and was not entitled to pass the verdict in the first place. The original verdict had to be annulled, declared null and void; a pardon would not do. Freud came to science as a rebel – even if, politically, he was moderate, liberal, mildly conservative and devoid of any sympathy for red flags and barricades. He needed to use the authority of science to lay bare the bluff of another authority whose verdict he wished to invalidate. He needed a science whose authority could be so used. He had to build such a science, virtually from scratch. As in the case of Kafka, 'everything had to be acquired' as 'nothing was granted'.

Interpreting the astounding decision of Freud (in his last book – on Moses and monotheism) to announce Moses an Egyptian and to charge the Jews with his murder, Robert surmised that 'he wished to be the son not of any man or country, but like the murdered prophet only of his life work'.[12] But Freud's wishes, it seems, mattered little when, in his eighties, he finally got down to write his only historical novel about the glory and the tragedy of a man with whom he secretly identified himself most of his life. At that

---

[11] Robert, *From Oedipus to Moses*, pp. 51, 79. As Hannah Arendt commented, the children of the pioneers of assimilation 'discovered soon enough that there was only one way to be accepted into society – they must win fame' (*The Jew as Pariah*, p. 116).

[12] Robert, *From Oedipus to Moses*, p. 167.

stage, the treatment he accorded his hero could be no more a declaration of intent; it was, rather, an old man's last look back on the road now passed and left behind.

It is not that Freud did not wish to be the son of his father; he was not allowed to be one – not without being haunted by guilt and crippled by shame. As an incompletely assimilated newcomer to the capital, Sigmund's father set narrow limits to how far his prodigious son could go while still boasting filial piety and claiming the family heirloom. When Sigmund Freud, an avid traveller and greedy collector of antiquities, after many a delay and postponement finally reached the Acropolis, his first and most poignant and memorable feeling was one of guilt. It was that feeling which he remembered after the years:

> It must be that a sense of guilt was attached to the satisfaction in having got so far: there was something about it that was wrong, that was from earliest times forbidden. It was something to do with a child's criticism of his father ... It seems as though the essence of success were to have got further than one's father, and as though to excel one's father were still something forbidden ... The very theme of Athens and Acropolis in itself contained evidence of the son's superiority. Our father had been in business, he had had no secondary education, and Athens could not have meant much to him ...[13]

But – as Theodor Reik observed, 'being ashamed of one's Jewishness' and 'being ashamed of one's parents' are psychologically identical varieties of shame[14] (that is, if the parents happen to be Jews). In addition to being in business instead of going to a *Gymnasium* Sigmund Freud's father was a Jew as well, and – with or without secondary education – Jewish fathers in Vienna were unlikely to pave the road to the Acropolis for their sons. When the sons eventually ventured that far, they could hardly share with their fathers the joy of reaching the destination. Hence the guilt poisoning the bliss of arrival; the fly of betrayal in the ointment of pride.

Neither was being a son of one's country a matter of mere wish. Not the wish of the son, at any rate. The son was illegitimate, to start with. Applying for adoption was his only hope. The best he was allowed to expect was a *foster* homeland, perhaps a *step*-homeland, benevolent or stern, yet once removed at all times. Unlike the natural son, the stepchild could not claim love as of right. He had to prove his entitlement. He had to deserve it, to earn. His family membership was devoid of the security the membership is

---

13 Sigmund Freud, 'A Disturbance of Memory on the Acropolis', in *Collected Papers*, vol. 5, pp. 311–2.

14 Theodor Reik, *Listening with the Third Ear* (New York: Arena Books, 1964), p. 71.

all about. It could not but remain a flawed membership; a notice of exclusion could be served at any moment, while rejection could follow without notice. Even if neither exclusion nor rejection occurred, the fostered son would be told again and again that he owed his luck to the magnanimity of his foster parents. He would be asked to be grateful, lavish in his praise, doubly zealous and eager to oblige. If he did what he was asked to do, he would, however, be accused of insincerity or evil scheming, and his enthusiasm would be ridiculed, derided and ultimately quoted as evidence against the fullness of his belonging. Whatever he did to curry the favour of his adopted country it would be that country that would have the last word.

The step-homeland would decide the meaning of the stepson's intentions. One had truly to stretch oneself to the utmost to make sure that the meaning, when finally given, would correspond to the intention. It was not easy to match the country's freedom to vacillate and cavil. 'He had to conquer the world intellectually', wrote Erich Fromm of Freud, 'if he wanted to be relieved of doubt and the feeling of failure.[15] (As if to confirm Fromm's chastening wisdom, twenty-odd years after these words had been written, at the height of the government-sponsored antisemitic hue and cry, another Jew – Arthur Rubinstein – was fêted in Warsaw as 'the great son of the Polish nation'). And thus it was left to Freud 'to be the son of his life work'. Not because he wished to be, but because he resigned himself to be, and at the end of his life was left in no doubt that his own work was indeed the only place which he could justly and without fear of disappointment and denial call *his* country and – indeed – *his family*.

By all standards, Freud's life-work was a formidable homeland, the source of inexhaustible pride if one really must seek pride in the glory of one's country. To be sure, it was made to measure that country which refused to offer itself to Freud as a secure home, and in the end sent him into exile: it was as self-contained, complete, proselytizing, imbued with a missionary mission, intolerant to all dissent and bent on *assimilating*, absorbing its own alternatives before they matured into resistance and rebellion. 'Psychoanalysis itself is the culture of which it purports to be the description ...' The unconscious can only be structured as Freud's language, and ego and superego are Freud's texts: 'We have become Freud's texts, and the *Initiatio Freudi* is the necessary pattern for the spiritual life in our time.'[16]

---

[15] Erich Fromm, Sigmund Freud's Mission: An Analysis of His Personality and Influence (London: Allen & Unwin, 1959), p. 6.

[16] Harold Bloom, *The Breaking of the Vessels* (Chicago: University of Chicago Press, 1982), pp. 63, 64.

Freud, or ambivalence as power

'The word of God' – thus Scholem interprets the Judaist tradition – 'must be infinite, or, to put it in a different way, the absolute word is as such meaningless, but is *pregnant* with meaning. Under human eyes it enters into significant finite embodiments which mark innumerable layers of meaning . . . The key itself may be lost, but an immense desire to look for it remains alive.'[17] Quoting Rawidowicz, Susan A. Handelman reminds her readers that one (perhaps the only) thing God, through Moses, gave to the Jews, was a text *for interpretation*. Not a collection of definite propositions which merely await elucidation of their meaning (a meaning determined once for all and transparent for those who can and will read), but precisely a text *to be interpreted*, and reinterpreted, and interpreted again, as its meanings are many, inexhaustible and unpredictable, brought into being rather than revealed in and through the never ending process of interpretation. 'Interpretation is the great imperative of Israel, and the secret of its history.'

The gift of God was a text that 'continues to develop each time it is studied, with each new interpretation'. Each interpretation which strives to *replace* the expressed meaning of the text merely turns into its extension; metonymy is born of metaphor. The text is alive, yet dead if not galvanized by its constant denial. It exists through growth and perpetual self-regeneration. The process never ends, never can end, never will end. Interpretations feed back into the text, 'form part of the mesh and interweave with the text itself' – just like new cells and tissues produced by, and added to, a living organism. Each interpretation, having enriched the text, only adds urgency to its own work and calls for new study, new search for meaning; with every step toward the penetration of the text's latency, further and ever more complex latent meanings are added to that form of life which has been called the text. 'The concept of latent content that needs to be uncovered through hermeneutical procedure, which places both Freud and the Rabbis in direct opposition to the tradition of Protestant literalism, rejects any attempt to define meaning by a reduction

---

[17] Gershon Scholem, *On the Kabbalah and its Symbolism* (New York: Schocken, 1969), p. 12. Harold Bloom is blunter still: 'Kabbalah seems to be more of an interpretive and mythical tradition than a mystical one . . . Kabbalah differs finally from Christian and Eastern mysticism in being more of a mode of intellectual speculation than a way of union with God. Like the Gnostics, the Kabbalists sought Knowledge, but unlike the Gnostics, they sought knowledge in the Book.' (*Kabbalah and Criticism* (New York: Seabury Press, 1975), p. 47.)

of the manifest to any one single latent referent.'[18] The 'gift of the Jewish God', so to speak, was the overwhelming need to search for meaning, the knowledge that the thirst for meaning is as insatiable as the depth of divine wisdom is unfathomable, and the determination to continue the search – however partial and temporary the reward. The gift of God was, so to speak, the knowledge of *ambivalence* and the skill of living with this knowledge.

Drawing clear dividing lines between normal and abnormal, orderly and chaotic, sane and sick, reasonable and mad, are all accomplishments of power. To draw such lines is to dominate; it is the domination which wears the masks of norm or health, which appears now as reason, now as sanity, now as law and order. Domination is eager to represent the other side of the relation it conjures (already defined as insanity, disorder, anomaly, sickness) as an agent in its own right, as an equally potent and greedy partner, a carbon copy, a mirror image and a rival; but the putative opponent is merely a product of the defining power, a sediment of its monopolistic dream, a detritus of its uncompleted labour. Power turns out its enemies by denying them what it strives to secure for itself; and the enemy exists only of and through that denial. Through disgorging the enemy, power wishes to purify itself of ambivalence, to turn ambiguity into a neat division, polysemy into an opposition. When (if) it succeeds, the inseparable will have been separated, the indivisible divided, existence will no longer seem fragile nor the world mysterious. Classified without a residue, the world will prostrate awaiting command; it will be transparent – like the deeds and the intentions of the inmates in Bentham's Panopticon. Power is a fight against ambivalence. Fear of ambivalence is born of power: it is the power's horror (premonition?) of defeat.

It took a stranger like Freud – firmly kept on the receiving end of the war against ambivalence, yet rebelling against his casting – to see through reality's own ambivalent foundation. The splits proclaimed natural were but conventions promoted and revived by coercion; the so-called norm of social health was but an artefact of power-assisted repression. Except for the power's usurped right to narrate reality, there would be no obvious difference of status between 'normal' acts of 'normal' people and 'neurotic symptoms', between dreams and the 'real thing', between laudable reason and morbid passions, between luminous surface and benighted depth, between cosy inside and frightening outside. There would be no *id* without the *superego*.

---

[18] Susan A. Handelman, *The Slayers of Moses: The Emergence of Rabbinic Interpretation in Modern Literary Theory* (Albery: State University of New York Press, 1982), pp. 42. 49. 147.

'Certain common mental acts of normal people ... were to be regarded in the same light as the symptoms of neurotics: that is to say, they had a *meaning*, which was unknown to the subject but which could easily be discovered by analytic means.' 'Dreams are quite generally mental structures that are capable of interpretation.'[19] Everything – whether proclaimed meaningful or meaningless – has meanings; meanings which are to be rediscovered when surreptitiously suppressed, and tested and re-tested when ostensibly transparent. 'One way the psychoanalyst begins to interpret the seemingly meaningless is to imagine a context in which it would be meaningful. One way he begins to interpret an utterance with apparently only one obvious meaning is to imagine other contexts in which the same language would have other meanings.'[20] Psychoanalysis was to be *an art of interpretation*. It transformed the human world, *the whole of it* (not just the abnormal, the diseased, the unguarded, the uncontrolled part of it), into a text to be interpreted; it refused to accept the pinned-on labels as meanings, the filing-cabinet code-names as identities. By the same token, it had *deconstructed* that world. By asking questions, it sapped the *structure* whose substance was the prohibition of asking. It was the very essence of psychoanalytical challenge that no code of interpretation is privileged, no one meaning-giving context is obviously superior to others, no one meaning is to be chosen to the exclusion of others. Things are not what we are told they are or forced to believe they should be.

Only man is subject to neuroses, only human life has the structure of neurosis, as 'only man is doomed to be torn between two destinies, because in his ego there exists a faculty that incessantly watches, criticizes, and compares, and in this way is set against the other part of the ego'. This split into the watcher and the watched is the human condition incorporated and reforged into the drama of the psyche. In order to hide that they are not what they pretend to be, the powers of the world force man to

---

[19] Sigmund Freud, 'Two Encyclopedic Articles', in *Collected Papers*, vol. 5, p. 113. 'The Limits to the Possibility of Interpretation', *Collected Papers*, vol. 5, p. 153. As Jonathan Culler pointed out (in Jacques Derrida, *Writing and Difference* (London: Routledge, 1978), p. 207), Freud 'deconstructed' the common power-initiated oppositions as instruments of suppression of the 'undesirable'; hence the first, dominating, unit of each dichotomy can be fully understood only in the light that may be thrown upon it by the second, subordinate unit (i.e. experience in the light of the dream, sanity in the light of insanity, the 'normal' in the light of the 'abnormal'). 'Understanding of the marginal or deviant term becomes a condition of understanding the supposedly prior term.' '[D]econstructive reversals', in Culler's summary 'give pride of place to what had been thought marginal ...'

[20] Marshall Edelson, *Language and Interpretation in Psychoanalysis* (Chicago: University of Chicago Press, 1975), p. 24.

believe that he is not what he ought to be. Obsessed with self-scrutiny, man forgets to check the credentials of the world. Ambivalence of societal powers is transformed into the nagging fear of own inadequacy. Rebellion that was to be fizzles out in neurosis that is. This predicament, says Ernst Simon, 'is reflected in a particular way in the modern diaspora Jew'.[21] Freud, the modern diaspora Jew, experienced the full force of the blow. Picking the Jews as the prime target and the testing ground of assimilationist drive, modern powers made them into an unwilling avant-garde of the future world marked with polysemic ambiguity, relativism and chronic underdetermination. It was hardly a coincidence that the drive stumbled on those chosen as its principal victims.

The modern nationalist drive only added poignancy and acuteness to an experience in no way novel in diasporic history. Jews were used to be watched, criticized, compared: to be *judged*, without being allowed to pass their own judgement on the judges. They had learned fairly early (and stated that much in the Kabbalistic doctrine that developed at the threshold of modern time) that the evil which stands condemned by the judgement comes forth in the wake of the judging:

> the doctrine gradually developed which saw the source of evil in the superabundant growth of the power of judgment which was made possible by the substantification and separation of the quality of judgment from its customary union with the quality of loving kindness. Pure judgment, untempered by any mitigating admixture [and this is what the judgement by the other, a hostile, inimical judgement, usually is – Z.B.], produced from within itself the *sitra ahra* (the other side), just as a vessel which is filled to overflowing spills its superfluous liquid on the ground.[22]

The novelty brought about by modern times was the unique and remarkable feat of the assimilatory project: billeting of 'garrisons' inside the 'conquered cities', making the defendants into DIY magistrates, bullying the accused into perpetual self-condemnation and self-apology while ostensibly freeing them from external judgements and replacing trials with self-criticism. It was this novelty which more than anything else brought into relief the organic unity of good and evil, now appearing in the shape of the interpenetration and mutual determination of norm and anomaly, health and sickness, reason and madness.

'Madness usually occupies a position of *exclusion*; it is the *outside* of a culture. But madness that is a *common* place occupies a position of *inclusion* and becomes the *inside* of a culture . . . To say that madness has

---

[21] Ernst Simon, 'Sigmund Freud, the Jew', in *Leo Baeck Institute Year Book*, vol. 2, p. 297.

[22] Gershon Scholem, *Kabbalah* (New York: Quadrangle, 1974), p. 123.

indeed become our commonplace is ... to say that madness in the contemporary world points to the radical ambiguity of the inside and the outside.' This is the lesson Shoshana Felman drew from the discovery into which Freud was goaded by the modern invention of, so to speak, *interiorized surveillance*. Once that 'radical ambiguity' had been noted and recorded, however, another ambivalence – that innate to all interpretation and understanding – comes to the surface. Madness is a tribute paid to the superiority of reason; in its challenge to reason's verdicts, madness reaffirms that the domination of reason is unchallengeable. If, however, in order to perform this function madness must be construed as itself unreasonable (that is, *not* aware of being madness), while presenting itself as reason (i.e., acknowledging the sole authority of reason, the monopolistic right of reason to make points and take stands), how can we know where reason stops and madness begins?

> If madness as such is defined as an *act of faith* in reason, no reasonable conviction can indeed be exempt from the suspicion of madness. Reason and madness are thereby inextricably linked; madness is essentially a phenomenon of thought, or thought which claims to denounce, in another's thought, the Other of thought; that which thought is not. Madness can only occur within a world in conflict, within a conflict of thoughts.[23]

The modern world is a world of conflict; it is also the world of a conflict which has been *interiorized*, which has become an *inner* conflict, has turned into a state of personal ambivalence and contingency. This is a world which gives birth to madness in the same way a garden brings weeds into being. The gardener can tell garden plants from the weeds – because he has the power to define them as such; his verdict is binding as long as his authority to define lasts. What, however, if the authority has been challenged, as must be the case sooner or later if the 'plants' and 'weeds' are humans, and humans called upon to make themselves into garden plants and inoculate themselves against the cancerous growth of their 'weedy' underside? How can *they* tell the normal from the abnormal, the proper from the neurotic, reason from madness?

All paradigms which Harold Bloom found 'central to Freud' (creation through catastrophe, family romance and transference) he also found 'marked with ambivalence'.[24] They all mix *love* and *hate*, these birthmarks of friends and enemies. They all mix *attraction* and *repulsion*, these building bricks of friendship and enmity. Freud's paradigms seem to have

---

[23] Shoshana Felman, *Writing and Madness*, trans. Martha and Noel Evans and the author (Ithaca: Cornell University Press, 1985), pp. 13, 36.

[24] Bloom, *The Breaking of the Vessels*, pp. 57–8.

been moulded out of the experience of the *ambivalent third*, the stranger, brought into the world to carry the cross of the world's conflicts. At the end of Golgotha, looking down from the top of that cross, the stranger proclaims the sham of the world's order: that ambiguity which the oppositions sustaining the order can only cover up, but not heal.

No interpretation is complete and allowed to be satisfied of its truth, proclaims Freud – though it always strives to be such and while struggling may indeed 'get better'. 'Getting better' does not mean, however, coming closer to such truth as may legitimately *exclude* its alternatives. It means instead more tolerance for suspected and yet unknown counter-interpretations, more modesty and a perspective wide enough to *include* other, already guessed or yet unsuspected, possibilities. For reasons explained before, Freud claimed for his work the authority and prestige of science; but he wanted his work to be recognized as an enterprise every bit as serious and as effective as science may be at its best moments – while refusing to dissolve the identity of psychoanalysis in the currently dominant, high-handed practice of science as an exercise in monopoly and exclusion.

Above all, the question to which Freud stoutly refused to offer such an answer as would endear him to the scientistic establishment, was this: 'is there such a thing as a natural end to an analysis or is it really possible to conduct it to such an end?'[25] Of all interpretations of any of the analysed dreams, however cogent and plausible, Freud wrote that they 'remain possible, though unproven; one must become accustomed to a dream being thus capable of having many meanings. Moreover, the blame for this is not always to be laid upon incompleteness of the work of interpretation; it may first as well be inherent in the latent dream-thoughts themselves.[26] The analyst's work may bring satisfaction, may alleviate sufferings, even cure; but it may hardly ever end, and its effects may never be secure and final. The analyst's task 'is to make out what has been forgotten from the traces which it has left behind or, more correctly, to *construct* it'. Like an archaeologist, the analyst 'draws his inferences from the fragments of memories, from the associations and from the behaviour of the subject of analysis . . . But it is a "construction" when one lays before the subject of the analysis a piece of his early history that he has forgotten.' Is there any guarantee that the reconstruction is faithful to the actual events? Is it the truth, the one and only, that the analyst lays before the analysand? 'It may seem, that no general reply can in any event be given to this question . . . It

---

25 Freud, 'The Limits to the Possibility of Interpretation', p. 153.

26 Sigmund Freud, 'Analysis Terminable and Interminable', in *Collected Papers*, vol. 5, p. 319.

is true that we do not accept the "No" of a person under analysis at its face value; but neither do we allow his "Yes" to pass.' Every construction, as it were, 'is an incomplete one, since it covers only a small fragment of the forgotten events'. And thus Freud's scientists 'do not pretend that an individual construction is anything more than a conjecture which awaits examination, confirmation or rejection'.[27]

The world is ambivalent, though its colonizers and rulers do not like it to be such and by hook or by crook try to pass it off for one that is not. Certainties are no more than hypotheses, histories no more than constructions, truths no more than temporary stations on a road that always thrusts ahead but never ends. No more? Much cunning must have been deployed and much venom must have been poured upon ambivalence – that scourge of all intolerance and all monopolistic pretence – to speak of hypotheses, constructions or temporary stations as if they were 'no more than . . .' Ambivalence is not to be bewailed. It is to be celebrated. Ambivalence is the limit to the power of the powerful. For the same reason, it is the freedom of the powerless. It is thanks to ambivalence, to the polysemic richness of human reality, to the coexistence of many semiotic codes and interpretive settings, that the 'interpreter's associative knowledge is invested with remarkably broad powers, including even the hermeneutical privilege of allowing questions to stand as parts of answers'.[28]

Kafka, or the difficulty of naming

Of Kafka's well-nigh obsessive use of the conjunction *aber*, his insightful interpreter Herman Uytersprott has the following to say:

> Of all German authors, Kafka uses the adversative conjunction 'aber' by far the most. Indeed, he uses it on the average two or three times more often than all other authors . . . The cause of this lies in the remarkable complexity of a soul which cannot simply see and feel in a straight line, a soul which didn't doubt and hesitate out of cowardice and caution, but rather out of clear-sightedness. A soul which at every thought, every perception, every assertion, instantly heard a little devil whispering to him: *aber* . . . And then this soul had to write down this devilish 'aber' to our greater 'confusion inside of clarity'.[29]

---

[27] Sigmund Freud, 'Constructions in Analysis', in *Collected Papers*, vol. 5, pp. 360–5.

[28] 'Introduction', *Midrash and Literature*, ed. Hartmann and Budick, p. xi.

[29] Quoted after Jill Robins, 'Kafka's Parables', in *Midrash and Literature*, ed. Hartmann and Budick, pp. 267–8.

Kafka's *aber*, however, does not stand for mutual exclusion: it does not convey that certainty with which the *opposition* is normally stated, and the necessity of *choice* declared. Much like in Freud's vision of the endless, forever incomplete process of interpretation, it does not signal the determination of *ein Entweder-Oder*, but the resignation of *ein Nebeneinander* – of standing aside in an incongruous yet unbreakable union. Jill Robbins has recently pointed out again Kafka's constant use of *parataxic* juxtapositions: versions, explanations, interpretations of events and acts are piled upon each other, narrated *next to each other*; each on its own, in separation, apparently sensible, yet together making no sense because of logical contradictions – an incompatibility which renders them mutually exclusive. (*Parataxis* – another term 'in para' – means that 'clauses or phrases are arranged independently, a co-ordinate rather than a subordinate construction' – so that no hint is offered to the reader which version is to be preferred, which occupies the central place in the structure of interpretation; not even whether such a hierarchy exists, or whether the listed interpretations belong together or are drawn from separate worlds. Parataxis means, first and foremost, an absence of hierarchy. Like in Simmel's perception of the modern condition, all versions of description float, so to speak, with the same specific gravity, are equal to each other, and contain nothing which may suggest an easy choice.) Parataxically arranged inventories of explanations testify to the impossibility of an explanation; a parataxis of interpretations conveys a prospectless inconclusiveness of interpretation, the ultimate vacuity of understanding.

As they stand together, and because they stand together and cannot but remain in each other's company (as no one has the right to stand alone; on its own, each one is a lie), each interpretation cancels the rest. Between themselves, they provide what each one separately denies and hides: the impossibility of fathoming the full depth of the multilayered world of meanings. (One may recall the exercises in unravelling the hidden senses of apparently simple and self-explanatory conversational sequences, which Harold Garfinkel used to set for his students: those little practical demonstrations of the truth laid bare in Kafka's parataxes. As Garfinkel's students soon found out to their utter bafflement, no interpretation, however rich and elaborate, came anywhere near the complete inventory of all the silent assumptions which had to be made by the conversationalists to communicate, to sustain the fragile meanings of their utterances.) Each interpretation on its own promises understanding; together, they reveal the agony of the unrewarded and unrewardable dream of comprehension.

But they do more than that. Having listed two series of parataxic exchanges, Jill Robbins asks the crucial question: 'is there anything like an

"I" who can say this?'[30] The despair of hermeneutics bared by parataxis is not a despair which the interpreter can appropriate, make her own, assimilate, domesticate, inscribe in the rule-book of the game. The despair of hermeneutics precludes the possibility of an *understanding subject*. It has no subject. Being no one's despair, it calls the subject off. In the centre or underneath, a void is uncovered where the subject strove to be. This emptiness is the product of frustrated understanding; but this emptiness is also the beginning, the very possibility, of that effort to understand which is bound to come to nought in the end but which can never reach such a terminal point beyond which there is no beginning.

Void, ambivalence and unclarity might have resided there from the beginning of time. Rarely if at all glimpsed by the travellers, they did, however, remain fully unknown to the settled. To use Benjamin's distinction between two types of story-telling, there were few *sailors* to bring back home the stories of far-off, mysterious and frightening lands; while the *peasant* stories bore no hint of the abyss opening beyond the last fence of the village. The Jews were among the first to venture (or to be pushed) that far, and to go there in great numbers, and stay there long enough to have a good look at the surroundings. Those Jews were squeezed out into the void by contradictory assimilatory pressures; they travelled because they were not allowed to settle, and they knew that their condition was that of travel because they were told of the importance of staying put. They had

---

30 Robbins, 'Kafka's Parables', p. 269. Gershon Shaked ('Kafka, Jewish Heritage, and Hebrew Literature', in *The Shadows Within: Essays on Modern Jewish Writers* (Philadelphia: Jewish Publication Society, 1987)) wonders about the ostensible contradiction between 'intensely Jewish' Kafka's daily life, and the almost *judenrein* appearance of Kafka's work – but later he admits that the contradiction is illusory: there is a definite 'homology' between Kafka's 'man without history, man outside of time and space, who must be at home everywhere but who feels safe nowhere', and the 'extrahistorical, homeless dimension' of the 'collective consciousness of the assimilated Diaspora Jew' (p. 6). Shaked concludes: 'The conditions of space without definition and time without history correspond to the situation of the Jews of the Diaspora: expelled from the safety of Jewish ritual time and the space of the shtetl into a timeless, spaceless existence.' (p. 9) In a recent study, ('Franz Kafkas Judentum', in *Kafka und das Judentum*, ed. Karl Erich Grözinger, Stéphane Mosès and Hans Dieter Zimmermann (Frankfurt am Main: Athenäum, 1987)), Ernst Pawel proposes that it was the specifically Jewish predicament ('He was no Czech, he was no German. This fact, through substraction and the merciless syllogism of Prague politics, made him a Jew') which opened for Kafka the road to a universalism tied to no nationality or denomination, and transformed Kafka into a 'pioneer of a type', a paradigm for estrangement – which explains the 'astonishing popularity of Kafka's work in most remote and least expected lands, from inland Japan to the American grain belt' (p. 225).

been forced into the openness and ambivalence and they were fully aware how unmasterable and limitless that void and that unclarity were which they found in their unchosen abode. As Kafka confessed to Max Brod, his hind legs were still mired in his fathers' Jewishness while the thrashing forelegs found no new ground; the ensuing despair was his inspiration. No song is as pure – Kafka confided in a letter to Milena – as that sung by those in the depth of the inferno. It is their singing which we take for the angels' songs. 'In Prague', writes Martha Robert, 'Kafka could not be "assimilated": he was Germanized; that is, his language was his only substitute for anything of which destiny had deprived him: a native soil, a fatherland, a present and a past.' That language (it happened to be the German language in Kafka's case) was not a pass to any community and any shared present or any past any natives would accept (a fact all too visible for this being the *German* language, the language of a militantly nationalistic, self-centred and intolerant state). That language could be therefore embraced in its purity: unattached, self-enclosed and unbound; language as a void and openness, as ambivalence and a standing invitation to those seeking to understand.

He came in time to realize, says Martha Robert, 'that he was Jewish even in the way of not being Jewish'.[31] Robert writes: 'even'. Yet Kafka knew more than that; he did know that it was precisely in his not being Jewish in a communal, tribal, ritual sense – in his not being 'tribal' at all – that his existential predicament as a Jew expressed itself most fully. Having stripped Jews of their tribal rituals, modern assimilatory pressures – albeit inadvertently – opened the condition of Jewishness up to its own unfathomable possibility. The people who inherited the blank book and carried it with them for centuries without fully realizing the chance it entailed, now had their eyes forcibly opened to its blankness. To that blankness which was their chance. To the emptiness which was nothing else but an urge of fulfilment.

> I heard the sound of a trumpet, and I asked my servant what it meant. He knew nothing and had heard nothing. At the gate he stopped me and asked: 'Where is the master going?' 'I don't know', I said, 'just out of here, just out of here. Out of here, nothing else, it's the only way I can reach my goal.' 'So you know your goal?' he asked. 'Yes', I replied, 'I've just told you. Out of here – that's my goal.' (*The Departure*, trans. Tania and James Stern)

> . . . No one, no one at all, can blaze a trail to India. Even in his day the gates to India were beyond reach, yet the King's sword pointed the way to them.

---

[31] Martha Robert, *Franz Kafka's Loneliness*, tran. Ralph Mannheim (London: Faber & Faber, 1982), pp. 31, 13.

> Today the gates have receded to remoter and loftier places; no one points the way; many carry swords, but only to brandish them, and the eye that tries to follow them is confused. (*The New Advocate*, trans. Willa and Edwin Muir)

> I stand on the end platform of the tram and am completely unsure of my footing in this world, in this town, in my family. Not even casually could I indicate any claims that I might rightly advance in any direction. I have not even any defense to offer for standing on this platform, holding on to this strap, letting myself be carried along by this tram, nor for the people who give way to the tram or walk quietly along or stand gazing into shopwindows. Nobody asks me to put up a defense, indeed, but that is irrelevant. (*On the Tram*, trans. Willa and Edwin Muir)[32]

The goal is to be out of here. The King's sword had once pointed to gates that by now have receded, and the swords nowadays point in so many directions that the eyes following them are confused. One cannot explain why is he standing where he stands; why is he moving where he moves. But all this is irrelevant – as getting out *is the goal*. The only goal to be had. 'Yes', says Walter A. Strauss,

> Kafka is Ahaswerus the Wandering Jew, and he is also the embodiment of the special 20th century variation of the type: assimilated and yet not assimilated, attached to Judaism and yet detached from it, knight-errant and dragon; an emissary who is entrusted with a message he has not properly heard or clearly understood; liberator-hero whose strength is his weakness; a Parsifal – but this one is an '*impure* fool' – who asks too many questions and never the right one.[33]

Kafka is made of oppositions. Or, rather, of the denial of oppositions – of the *parataxis* of oppositions. Kafka's life, like modern life, is an in-between life: in between in space, in between in time, in between all fixed moments and settled places that, thanks to their fixity, boast an address, a date or a proper name.

If Martha Robert is right and in his novels and stories Kafka is speaking only of himself (which writer is not?), then it is his experience of the assimilated/unassimilated Jew, the knight-errant of modernity and the dragon the knight has been retained to kill, that has been reforged in those monstrous, hybrid, bastard, over- and under-defined, incongruous creatures that populate his writings. A man turned insect; an ape turned man; a dog turned philosopher; half-kitten, half-lamb; half-dead, half-alive; and

---

32 *The Collected Short Stories of Franz Kafka*, ed. Nahum N. Glatzer (Harmondsworth: Penguin, 1988), pp. 449, 415, 388.

33 Walter A. Strauss, *On the Threshold of a New Kabbalah* (New York: Peter Lang, 1988), p. 94.

that most incoherent of them all, incoherent to the point of coherence, *Odradek* – 'of German origin, only influenced by Slavonic', a thing that 'looks senseless enough, but in its own way perfectly finished. In any case, closer scrutiny is impossible, since Odradek is extraordinarily nimble and can never be laid hold of.' When you ask Odradek what his name is, or where he lives, he 'laughs; but it is only the kind of laughter that has no lungs behind it' (*The Cares of a Family Man*, trans. Willa and Edwin Muir).

When Kafka's heroes have names, these are laughable, inconsequential and – being of an unclear and contested origin – confuse instead of designating. It seems that the function of these names consists mostly in debunking the hubris of naming, in demonstrating the impossibility of designating. But the heroes of Kafka's major novels have no proper names at all. They are designated by signs without pretence to designate. They bear vanishing traces of names that perhaps have been forgotten (though this is of little importance as they certainly do not matter now); or inchoate, surreptitious beginnings of names still waiting to be named. The heroes are perhaps unnameable. Or their names are unpronouncable. 'I write my name into the openness' – Jabès was to put in words what Kafka said by his silence. In the openness of a society 'where his birth placed him without entitling him to call himself at home in it, the individual named Kafka was only half *presentable*, if at all'. His name must have been swallowed and dissolved by this openness which itself was an emphatic denial of the possibility of naming, of the eagerly sought yet ever elusive identity.

Once again, Jewish particularity turned into modern universality. Kafka's namelessness precedes, and ushers into, the *modern* world; one in which names are not received but made, and, while being made, fail to offer a fixed date and a settled place and abrogate the very hope of such an offer. At its threshold, modernity forced the Jews to visit that blankness, that 'land propitious to silence and infinite listening' (Jabès), which they till then half-knowingly occupied; and to chart it, and to bring the map on every return from their journey. That map the modern world could now use in its own journey into the blankness of its own future. Now, 'anyone or no one may be Jewish' (Derrida).

Simmel, or the other end of modernity

Simmel was perhaps the most prolific, most widely printed and most widely read sociologist of his time. And yet his life-long attempts to obtain a university appointment led him nowhere. He had been called to the chair at a provincial university at Strasbourg only one year before his death. Applications, supported by most authoritative recommendations and a most impressive publishing record, were regularly turned down. It could be that the appointment committees and the assessors they approached to opine on Simmel's work resented his Jewish origin – still a serious handicap, given the nationalist spirit and discriminatory practice of German universities. It is likely, however, that even more than Simmel's birth certificate the gatekeepers resented the substance of his sociology: so blatantly at odds with the standard sociological writings of the time, so different, so (they felt) *alien*, so *Jewish*.

Rejection of Simmel's sociology outlived its author. It took the academic sociologists many years to admit Simmel into the canon of their tradition. It took a few decades more to include Simmel among the 'founding fathers' of sociology. It is only now that Simmel is beginning to be recognized as a most (perhaps *the* most) powerful and perceptive analyst of modernity; as a writer who articulated, as heresy, what long after his death was to become the common sense of sociological wisdom; as a thinker more than any other in tune with contemporary experience; as the inventor of a sociological style that came to be appreciated as the most adequate, most in tune with the kind of social reality it was meant to narrate. Now, gradually, the same aspects of Simmel's sociology which at his own time confined him to the margins of the profession, are beginning to be seen as uncannily insightful anticipations of the shape of things to come. Simmel's past vices have turned into virtues, weaknesses into merits.

Simmel stood accused of a certain fragmentariness of his analyses. He approached social reality now from one perspective, then from another, each time focusing on just one social phenomenon, type or process. With such a practice, reality emerged from Simmel's writings as so many splinters of life and crumbs of information; a far cry from the complete, all-embracing, harmonious and systematic models of 'social order' or 'social structure' offered by other sociologists and considered *de rigeur* by the social sciences of the time. Reality dissipated, so to speak, in Simmel's hands; it fell apart and refused to be patched together again by the unifying impact of the church, the state or the *Volksgeist*. This upset many of Simmel's readers, and those resentful of the prospect of becoming his academic colleagues more than anybody else. Today we see that the 'bittiness' of Simmel's analysis was made to measure the human condition which Simmel, unlike his colleagues, sensed behind the façade of the totalizing ambitions of powers that be; of the self-same social reality that today has emerged from the debris of failed engineering dreams in all its splintered, fragmentary, episodic truth – and has been recognized as such. One may say that Simmel called the bluff of imagined totality at a time when most of his contemporaries still sang its praise. Having been squeezed out of the all-devouring order promoted by the 'supreme reality' of the state certainly sharpened Simmel's eye; it helped him to see early what the others were to find out much later. Glory has been conferred upon Simmel posthumously, thanks to the universal experience catching up with his once idiosyncratic insight. Now we all know what he had to fight his way through alone. One can read out the evidence of that fight from the sceptical, serene and dignified wisdom of Simmel's pioneering insights.

Take, for instance, Simmel's audacious de-sacralization (desecration?) of values. Celebrated as absolute and extemporal by the earthly powers wishing to bask in their reflected glory, values have been brutally brought by Simmel from their ideological pedestal down to where they belonged: the chase of a gratification that is never to be found where one hope to find it, and that paradoxically owes its attraction to the sacrifice it demands: all feelings of value 'are in general to be gained only by foregoing other values'; it is the 'detour to the attainment of certain things' which is 'the cause of regarding them as valuable'; things 'are worth just what they cost. This, then, appears secondarily to mean that they cost what they are worth'. It is the obstacles on the way, 'the anxiety lest the object may escape, the tension of struggle for it' which form the mystery of value.[34]

Simmel's observation point was not an office in state bureaucracy, nor any of its academic replicas. From his vantage point, no 'globalized', 'demographized' vision of 'society' (that is, of the territory claimed for state husbandry) was likely to emerge. Simmel scanned human condition from the perspective of a lonely wanderer, later to be dubbed *flâneur* by Walter Benjamin (when commenting on Baudelaire's famous essay on the way in which *modern* art may capture the elusive *modern* existence). The *flâneur* is a witness, not a participant; he is *in*, but not *of* the place he walks; a *spectator* of the never-ending spectacle of crowded urban life: a spectacle with constantly changing actors who do not know their lines in advance, a spectacle without a screenplay, or director, or producer – yet guaranteed to be billed forever thanks to the cunning and inventiveness of its characters. As seen by the *flâneur*, the spectacle has neither beginning nor end, no unity of time, place or action, no denouement nor a conclusion written *a priori*. Instead, it splits into episodes without cause and consequence. This spectacle has to construct itself as it goes; to build itself up, bit by bit, by its own resources. The interesting question, therefore (the only

---

34 Georg Simmel, 'A Chapter in the Philosophy of Value', in *The Conflict in Modern Culture and Other Essays*, trans. K. Peter Etzkorn (New York: Teachers College Press, 1968), pp. 52–4.

sensible question) is how come it could be done, and is being done over and over again, without a guide or a scenario. Simmel's sociology had no room for 'society'; Simmel was after the mystery of *sociality*. Simmel's sociology is about the art of building – rather than grand, harmony-conscious, architectural designs.

Unerringly Simmel diagnosed the demise, or perhaps the original lie, of that 'universal human nature' which at the early *Sturm und Drang Periode* of modernity served as a disguise for the assault against the difference and for the renewed attempts to stamp out the otherness. ('The perfected man', expected to emerge once all the constraints on 'universal condition' have been taken apart, 'could show no differences', 'since he was perfect'; 'all one need do' is to free the man 'individualized by empirical traits, social position, and accidental configuration' from 'all these historical influences and diversions that ravage his deepest essence, and then 'man as such' 'can emerge in him'.) Simmel noted also, well before others paid any notice, that the reality of modern life had defied the dreams of totalization; more to the point, the dreams were self-defeating. Under the impact of universalizing power, the human condition developed in a direction exactly opposite to the intention:

> throughout the modern era, the quest of the individual is for his self, for a fixed and unambiguous point of reference. He needs such a fixed point more and more urgently in view of the unprecedented expansion of theoretical and practical perspectives and the complication of life, and the related fact that he can no longer find it anywhere outside himself. All relations with others are thus ultimately mere stations along the road by which the ego arrives at its self. This is true whether the ego feels itself to be basically identical to these others because it still needs this supporting conviction as it stands alone upon itself and its own powers, or whether it is strong enough to bear the loneliness of its own quality, the multitude being there only so that each individual can use the others as a measure of his incompatibility and the individuality of his world.[35]

Those who have already understood and those who continue to cling convulsively to old illusions are in the same predicament. The 'settled', the native, the 'belonging' are no different from the estranged, rejected or homeless – only they do not know it yet. One needs strength to bear

---

[35] Georg Simmel, *On Individuality and Social Forms*, ed. Donald N. Levine (Chicago: University of Chicago Press, 1971), pp. 219–23. David Frisby's description of Simmel as the 'philosopher of the fragmented spirit' is extremely well pointed, as is his characterization of Simmel's aim as 'to experience in the individual phenomenon, with all its details, the fullness of its reality' (cf. David Frisby, *Fragments of Modernity: Theories of Modernity in the Work of Simmel, Kracauer and Benjamin* (Cambridge: Polity Press, 1985), pp. 39, 45.

loneliness. It is 'the belonging' ones that do not have such strength, and this is precisely while they run away from the fate of self-construction into the deceitful shelter of imagined membership.

As long as they stay in that shelter, they are unlikely to admit the truth of Simmel's discovery. How can one communicate one's experience? What is there to be transmitted in the course of such a communication? How can the knowledge that 'objectivizes' the contents of a subjective mind be apprehended by another mind in all its original subjectivity? These questions sound familiar to us; between themselves, we now readily admit, they constitute the agenda of the world we *all* live in, the 'late modern', or 'postmodern' world. But before it became the agenda of the world as such, it was the agenda of Simmel's sociological discourse. Simmel did what we all do now, only half a century before us: he placed the mystery of communication and understanding between *different* forms of life in the very focus of his investigation and in the centre of his reconstruction of sociality:

> In the socio-historical sciences ... the essential identity of knowledge and its object ... still leads us to the same mistaken conclusion: that form of naturalism which holds that knowledge is possible as a simple reproduction of its object and conceives the faithfulness of this reproduction as the criterion for knowledge itself. The task of enabling us to see the event 'as it really happened' is still naively imposed upon history. In opposition to this view, it is necessary to make clear that every form of knowledge represents a translation of immediately given data into a new language, a language with its own intrinsic forms, categories, and requirements ... [T]he sort of understanding that would be an immediate consequence of the homogenous nature of the two minds – would either be a form of mind reading or mental telepathy, or it would require a pre-established harmony of minds.[36]

Neither telepathy nor pre-ordained harmony being viable propositions, all communication between minds is bound to involve tortuous processes of coding and decoding, and above all of translation. Given the complexity of the process, communication will, most certainly, fail to reach its declared purpose: there will be left-overs of non-recovered meanings, and the thirst for further interpretation will never be quenched. 'Thus, the typical problematic situation of modern man comes into being: his sense of being surrounded by an immeasurable number of cultural elements which are neither meaningless to him nor, in the final analysis,

---

[36] Georg Simmel, *The Problems of the Philosophy of History*, trans. Guy Oakes (New York: Free Press, 1977), pp. 77, 66.

meaningful.'[37] This is, Simmel discovered, the ultimate destination of man cast into the modern condition. Simmel arrived there (or was he pushed?) before most of his contemporaries.

The other side of assimilation

Freud's revelation of ambivalence (his propensity to locate concepts on and between the boundaries, so that they defy the distinction between psychic and somatic, inside and outside, meaning and nonsense), Kafka's insight into the ultimate groundlessness of the human condition, Simmel's demotion of society to the play of sociality, Shestov's rehabilitation of suppressed human possibility – tie together in Jacques Derrida's philosophy of *undecidability*. In the words of two American editors of Derrida, 'the whole idea that logical consistency and the scientific method can lead us to the truths or truth governing human existence is the Platonian bias of Western thought that Derrida questions. He reads Freud as Freud read himself and others – with an eye toward the contingent, the haphazard, the chance event and lapse.'[38] The bias Derrida is up in arms against is the abhorrence of chance; the horror of the contingent which had started off and motivated the long march toward perfect and immutable order, toward the high-handed rule of necessity and the cognitive transparency of the world within reach (intellectual clarity and elimination of chance are, in fact, tautologically related – as one can have a truly clear and complete knowledge only of what is regular and repetitive, and thus carries no information), all of which have reached their culmination point in the designing/ordering/gardening ambitions of modernity.

Derrida restores the indeterminate to its rightful status of the ground of all being; or, rather, he exposes the sham of long attempts to chase it away from its position or belie its presence. Any effort to determine results in more indeterminacy; all attempt to code, to overcode, to fix must simultaneously increase the sum total (if one can speak here of sums) of randomness and indetermination. Each step in interpretation opens up new interpretative tasks. Interpretation ushers in more interpretation. Interpretation turns into a part of what it is interpreting and hence

[37] Georg Simmel, 'On the Concept and the Tragedy of Culture', in *The Conflict in Modern Culture*, p. 44.

[38] Cf. *Taking Chances: Derrida, Psychoanalysis and Literature*, ed. Joseph H. Smith and William Kenigen (Baltimore: Johns Hopkins University Press, 1984), pp. viiiff.

increases the totality to be interpreted; it is written in the world it is writing. It cannot but inscribe itself in the book the reading of which it is called to service. What sets Derrida's work apart is the full-hearted recognition of 'the methodological necessity of including itself in the issue and the problem, accepting responsibility for its own reflexivity and error'; the willingness 'to abandon the tradition of self-certainty, to stand aside from the conditions of sense defined in this tradition'. For Derrida, there is no ultimate outside point of view, the tough non-textual reality 'out there', to which the interpretation of the text could refer in hope of the last and final judgement. The text develops in the course of its interpretive penetration. Interpretation cannot but remain in that confusing, yet highly creative relationship with the text which is at the same time as metonymical as it is metaphorical; interpretation turns into an extension of the text as it tries to supplement it.

In her highly original study of contemporary literary criticism, Susan A. Handelman portrays Derrida's interpretive strategy as the re-emergence of the rabbinic interpretational mode in modern literary theory. The rabbinic hermeneutical rules, in sharp contrast to Greek thinking, 'arose not in a process of abstraction from the text, which could then be separated and manipulated independently of the text'. Rabbinical commentaries 'form part of the mesh and interweave' with the text itself. They clash sharply with what Handelman calls the 'Protestant literalism', characterized by the antithesis of literal and figurative and 'inability to exist within the tension of absence-in-presence characterizing the linguistic realm', by its fear of multiple meaning and an attempt to escape from it into 'a theology and hermeneutics of immanence, grace, and univocal meaning, and a finality to the free play of interpretation' – and viewing the 'entire past history of interpretation' as a *prefiguration* of 'the final and complete interpretation'[39] – a word destined to efface itself by turning into flesh.

Neither the juxtaposition nor the choice seem to be, as it were, simple or straightforward. Derrida's interpretive strategy is not a matter of rejection and return, of the repudiation of the hermeneutical tradition of the Christian world and resuscitation of that of the rabbis. Even less is it a matter of a simple substitution of the second for the first. It is, rather, the case of the Western hermeneutic having followed its own immanent logic of development and reached a critical point in that development where its inner antinomies could not be any more resolved by means it itself was capable of generating. One can say that if the rabbinical view of interpretation comes into its own it is so because the crisis of Western hermeneutics brought it to the point where this could happen.

---

[39] Handelman, *The Slayers of Moses*, pp. 49, 91, 131.

Jacques Derrida, obsessed as he is with the dialectics of signatures and dates (those most spectacular of human efforts to fix, to arrest, to solidify – and the most spectacular failures of such efforts; both the date and the signature efface themselves, as it were, by the sheer need to recur; they do their job of *individuation* thanks to their recurrence, but because of that recurrence their job cannot be done), suggests that: 'Formally, at least, the affirmation of Judaism has the same structure as that of the date.' That is, both are acts of self-effacement, inseparable from the act of self-assertion. 'I am Jewish in saying: the Jew is the other who has no essence, who has nothing of his own or whose own essence is not to have one. Thus, at one and the same time, both the alleged universality of Jewish witness . . . and the incommunicable secret of the Judaic idiom, the singularity of the "unpronouncable name".'[40] Having nothing of one's own, being a non-being, a void to be filled, a void stretched towards fulfilment, having no essence, having a no-essence to become the essence, a no-essence waiting for the essences of the world, is that 'Jewish signature', 'Jewish dating', which is the singularity of the Jew that makes Jewishness – at some point of history – universal.

Universality of absence and the void is the only universality there is; Jewish singularity is the only universality there is; all universality is Jewish. This was the meaning of Marina Tsvetayeva's 'All the poets are Jews.' Or Celan's 'The Jew, you know, what does he have, that really belongs to him, that isn't lent, borrowed, never given back.' Or Borges's 'My books are profoundly Judaic.' To define the Jew, is (as tempting and as impossible as) to define the writer, the poet, the spider-like creature suspended in the textual net which he goes on weaving; is to define the human.

Why do Jewishness and the universally human search each other out, define each other, blend? Why is it that Tsvetayeva, Borges, Celan, Joyce, trying to capture that void, that no-essence that is the first abode and the last retreat of universality, cannot but find the Jew in their net? ('First I thought I was a writer. Then I realized I was a Jew. Then I no longer distinguished the writer in me from the Jew because one and the other are only the torment of an ancient word', confessed Edmond Jabès. Elsewhere he admits that the Jew is 'the figure of exile, errancy, strangeness and separation, condition that is that of the writer as well'.[41] Why do they

---

[40] Derrida, 'Shibboleth', p. 337.

[41] Edmond Jabès, *Le Soupçon, le desert* (Paris; Gallimard, 1978), p. 85. As if to leave no doubt that more than temporary coincidence is involved, Jabès insists: 'never again will we escape exile' (*Elya*, trans. Rosemarie Waldrop (Bolinas, Cal.: Tree Books, 1973), p. 31). A most acute philosophical rendering of Jabès's cognitive plight as an epitome of the poetic mode in general came from Emmanuel Levinas's pen: 'Can one say with certainty that a true poet occupies a place? Is he not the one

discover that 'this difficulty in being wholly Jewish' is the same as 'everybody's difficulty in being altogether human'?[42] Reading cannot be fulfilled without writing. The reader is a writer while he reads; readers write their books into the books they are reading so that these books could be read. 'To discover', says Jabès, 'means, after all, to create.' Of the writer (and, let us repeat, every reader is a writer), Borges wrote:

> It is about a man who has an endless world before him and then he begins drawing of ships, of anchors, of towers or horses, of birds and so on. In the end he finds out that what he has designed is a picture of his own face. That, of course, is a metaphor of the writer; what the writer leaves behind him is not what he has written, but his image . . .

Once more, the issue of universality is at stake, but with a role reversal. 'Meaning', writes Robert Alter,[43] 'perhaps for the first time in narrative literature, was conceived as a process, requiring continual revision – both in the ordinary sense and in the etymological sense of seeing – again – continual suspension of judgment, weighing of multiple possibilities, brooding over gaps in the information provided.' And it was precisely that meaning as a never-ending process that had been discovered in the 'torments of the Ancient World', as seen anew by modern eyes:

---

who, in the profound sense of the term, *loses his place*, the one who, in fact, ceases to occupy a place, thus embodying the opening up of space itself, of which neither the transparence nor the emptiness – no more than the night and the mass of beings – yet show the bottomlessness or the excellence, the sky which becomes possible in him, his "cealumnity" or his "celestity", if such neologisms may be used? Bottomlessness or height – "the highest abyss", according to Jabès – where all interiority is swallowed up, cleaving air, more outer than outwardness, right to the nucleus; as if ordinary human breathing were already nothing but inhaling, as if the poetic utterance surmounted this want of breath to attain a breathing deep at last, to attain the inspiration which is the de-claustration of all things, the de-nucleation of being – or its transcendence – which lacks nothing more than a proximate. "I am only word", says Jabès, "I need a face".' (Trans. Susan Knight, in *European Judaism*, 1973, n. 1, p. 20.)

Of Elias Canetti, who, as 'exile writer', 'generalized relation to place: a place is a language', Susan Sontag wrote: 'That German became the language of his mind confirm's Canetti's placelessness.' Canetti is to Sontag a model *itinerant intellectual*, who, among other traits that sets him apart, is characterized by the fact that: 'His real task is not to exercise his talent for explanation but, by being witness to the age, to set the largest, most *edifying* standards of despair.' (Susan Sontag, 'Mind as Passion', in *Essays in Honour of Elias Canetti* (New York: Farrar, Straus & Giroux, 1987), pp. 90–1.

[42] Edmond Jabès, 'The Key', in *Midrash and Literature*, pp. 358–9.

[43] Robert Alter, *The Art of Biblical Narrative* (New York: Basic Books, 1981). p. 12.

> In a godless and secular century stunned by its glimpse of the void, Jabès uncovers the haunting ghosts of theology long thought to have been laid to rest. Nietzsche proclaimed the death of God over a century ago, but Jabès's work testifies that it was the death only of a certain God, a classical God – or perhaps it would be better to say a certain aspect of God, the luminous, assuring guarantor of meaning.[44]

Like the work of Freud, Kafka, Simmel, Shestov[45] or Jabès, the hermeneutics of Derrida stands *on the other side of assimilation*. The location

---

[44] Susan Handelman, 'Torments of an Ancient World', in *The Sin of the Book: Edmund Jabès*, ed. Eric Gould (Lincoln: University of Nebraska Press, 1985), p. 56.

[45] Born Lev Isaakovich Schwartzmann in 1866 in Kiev; died in 1938 in Paris. A brilliant student of law and mathematics in the universities of Kiev and Moscow, author of several widely read, discussed and acclaimed books in literary criticism and philosophy, he nevertheless, as a Jew, was barred access to Russian academic life and failed to secure a proper academic post. He left Russia in 1922 for France. There he acquired fame as one of the most original philosophers writing and publishing in the country and was offered a Sorbonne chair. Admired by many (notably Camus, D.H. Lawrence and W. Gombrowicz), highly esteemed even by those who found his acid, corrosive philosophy unpalatable (notably Edmund Husserl), he remained a solitary thinker, fitting none of the established philosophical schools (though sometimes, erroneously, identified with the existentialist movement, and claimed by the existentialists themselves, on the strength on his lifelong preoccupation with Kierkegaard). Nicolai Berdyavev noted the 'astounding independence' of Shestov's thought 'from surrounding currents of the time' (*Tipy religioznoj mysli v Rosii* [The types of religious thought in Russia] (Paris: YMCA Press, 1989), p. 407). He had only one true friend and acknowledged follower – a Frenchman of Rumanian–Jewish extraction, Benjamin Fondane, who was murdered in a German concentration camp in 1944.

The settled, the secure, the sheltered, the native – Shestov insisted – can keep their brittle order only when power-assisted. Their order is a fortress, heavily armed: with the principle of contradiction, with laws of logic proclaimed universally binding, with inquisitors, gaolers and executioners (Shestov did not live long enough to add: with Auschwitzes, with Gulags). Truths which need such a protection cannot be worthy of protection (conversely, real truths may do without consent of men); like Nietzsche's Apollonian harmony, they cannot be effectively protected either. The powers they muster to protect themselves testify to both the illegitimacy and the futility of their pretentions. It is, on the contrary, the feeble, the weak, the devoid of protection who are the bearers of the saving truth.

What the truths of the settled try in vain to hide is not, however, the pre-human perpetuity of the pagan forest, but the humanity of Jerusalem. Humanity means *limitlessness of possibilities*. It is the creative openness of human existence, its irrevocable non-finality, its capacity to break through any walls, however tough and heavily armed, which the coercive forces enlisted by Athens – the principle of contradiction, of the excluded middle, in union with absolutist states and religions – aim to contain in practice and pre-empt in theory. When Spinoza seeks knowledge *sub specie aeternitatis vel necessitatis*, when his successors declare such

certainly helped it to be what it was. The most spectacular, though totally unplanned and unanticipated achievement of the assimilatory drama was the setting of liminal, over- and under-determined spaces where modern experience could be lived and modern culture born. The would-be nations and the rising nation-states embarked on the assimilatory adventure brandishing the idea of a fundamental contradiction between Judaism and modern civilization. While pursuing the phantom of homogeneity, they spawned the conditions under which Jewishness had to undergo profound transformation. It did. And it did not emerge from the long and tortuous process of 'identity change' as an alien body, set awkwardly in the

---

knowledge the only one worth pursuing and possessing, when Leibniz declares that eternal truths entered the mind of God without asking His permission – the divine potency of man is mutilated and incarcerated. The forces of Athens are about harmony and clarity, but also about constraint and brutal force. They are set to extirpate everything they cannot absorb and hold in their power: the search for absolute knowledge means pursuit of absolute power.

From the depth of the abyss into which humanity was thrown by the most absolute of earthly states, Albert Camus wrote (*Le Mythe de Sisyphe*, 1942) of Shestov: 'il dépiste, éclaire et magnifie la révolte humaine contre l'irrémédiable. Il refuse ses raisons à la raison et ne commence à diriger ses pas avec quelque décision qu'au milieu de ce désert sans couleurs où toutes certitudes sont devenues pierres.' It is Shestov's rebellion against the pursuit of the irremediable which leads him away from Athens, to Jerusalem, to God. 'On ne se tourne vers Dieu que pour obtenir l'impossible. Quant au possible, les hommes y suffisent.' The greatness of God is His inconsistency. No absolute there, no constraint. Contrary to the God of the philosophers, nothing divine is *sub specie aeternitatis vel necessitatis*. God: this means that nothing is necessary. Because the meaning of God is that 'there is nothing that is impossible'. (Cf. Lev Shestov, *Athens and Jerusalem*, trans. Bernard Martin (Athens: Ohio University Press, 1966), pp. 424–5, 69.)

In the 'Introduction' to Shestov's *Umozrenië i otkrovenië* [Contemplation and Revelation] (Paris: YMCA Press, 1964 [posthumous]) Berdiayev summed up Shestov's thesis as 'God is above all the unlimited possibility'. This potency of God knows no bounds; much as it opens up the future, it is free to cancel the past. Shestov himself writes: 'The history of humanity – or, more precisely, all the horrors of the history of humanity – is, by one word of the Almighty, "annuled"; it ceases to exist, and becomes transformed into phantoms and mirages . . . The "fact", the "given", the "real" do not dominate us; they do not determine our fate either in the present, in the future or in the past. What has been becomes what has not been; man returns to the state of innocence.' (*Athens and Jerusalem*, p.68.) In his review of Shestov's study of Kierkegaard, Berdiayev noted, however, as a sign of weakness, the *hypothetical* status of God in Shestov's thought: God as the last hope, as the only chance, as the anchor of faith. 'If God exists, possibilities are unlimited . . . Then the victory over necessity that maims our life is feasible.' (*Tipy religioznoj mysli v Rossii*, p. 400) Athenian philosophy, declaring war on Jerusalem's revelation, cast doubt on that hypothesis, and thus reinforced the grip of necessity while banishing freedom from the realm of existence.

tissue of modern life; neither did it lose its identity in the indifferent flux of modern life where 'everything flows with the same specific gravity'. It emerged, instead, from the ordeal of assimilation as the seminal contribution to the obstreperous, critical and rebellious culture of modernity; modern consciousness that militates against the modern condition and thus calls the bluff of its pretences. It was the inner, perverse logic of coercive homogenization that rebounded in the *condition of the universal strangerhood* of its victims; a condition from which the precepts of modern culture were gleaned.

That this is what happened is shown by the fact that Jewish cultural activity, and particularly the Jewish activity in that culture which later came to be defined as modern, has been distributed (both spatially and temporally) unevenly. It reached the highest intensity in places and at times where the assimilatory obsessions were at their most fanatical and cruel, and the continuity of Jewish tradition freshest and least eroded. This place and time was East-Central Europe at the turn of the century. That seething cauldron of incomplete, uncertain, unsure-of-themselves nations; nations whose future was charged with the task of creating a new past; nations which could do justice to their own dreams only by doing injustice to others; nations which could secure their identity only through aggression; nations which had first to mould the reality which they would invoke to legitimize their presence. Insecurity breeds pugnacity. At no other place in Europe, and at no other time in European history, was the proselytizing zeal of would-be nations so venomous and the intolerance of budding nation-states so ruthless.

Cast among the conflicting territorial and cultural claims the Jews were denied the chance of successful assimilation before they – whether by design or by default – surrendered to its terms. As the most perceptive among them, like Gustav Mahler, were soon to discover, they were 'thrice homeless: as a Bohemian among Austrians; as an Austrian among Germans; and as a Jew: everywhere'. National claims were incompatible, and no one epitomized that incompatibility more blatantly than the Jews, these ubiquitously supra-national, universal strangers. True, the aspiring nations were quite eager to employ Jewish services in the pursuance of cultural conversion. The Jews were bearers of Magyarhood among the weaker, peasant Slavs, carriers of German culture among the Czechs of Prague, the prophets of German *Geist* in the multilingual capital of the Hapsburg Empire. One can suspect, however, that Jewish services were willingly resorted to mostly because the servants could be so easily dismissed once those services were no more needed. It all happened exactly as another perceptive East-Central European, Arthur Schnitzler, prophesized: 'Who created the German Nationalist Movement in Austria? The Jews. Who left the Jews in the lurch and indeed despised them as dogs? The German nationals. And just the same thing will happen with the socialists and the communists. Once the dinner is ready to be served, they will chase you from the table.'[46]

One can say perhaps that the more vicious was the assimilatory zeal, the more ham-fisted the agents of conversion – the more spatious and culturally vigorous tended to become 'the other side of assimilation'. (The latter did ultimately depend on the character and posture of native nationalism, and *definitely not* on the zeal with which the Jews responded to the invitation to assimilate and the success they made out of it.[47] The episode of the astonishing cultural creativity of the Jews was born of agony and suffering, much like the unversality of modern culture was born of the drama of modern parochialism. It was perhaps necessary first to agonize at the receiving end of the modern thrust to order, certainty and uniformity, to learn to live with polysemy, ambivalence and infinite possibilities of an undecidable world. In the event, the pole of the pillory went down in history as the crow's nest from which the land of modernity was first sighted.

---

[46] Quoted after Michael Ignatieff, 'The Rise and Fall of Vienna's Jews', in *New York Times Review of Books*, 29 June 1989, p. 22.

[47] The 'objectively measured' social and political success of Jews in many countries has by now left behind all the records of success in Central Europe which, according to a number of commentators, was the ultimate cause of their non-acceptance and in the long run led to their downfall. For instance, according to David Biale (*Power and Powerlessness in Jewish History* (New York: Schocken Books, 1986), p. 180), in the USA in the 1970s Jews constituted 20.9 per cent in top university faculties,11.4 per cent in government, business and labour unions and as much as 25.6 per cent in the media. Particularly the last figure is striking. The media, a relatively recent invention, made the Jews and their astounding 'success' more visible and accessible to public scrutiny than ever before (more, for example, than in the case of notorious *jüdische Presse* which put so much ammunition in the hands of German antisemites).

6

The Privatization of Ambivalence

With no earthly powers bent on eradicating it, ambivalence moved from the public to the private sphere. It is now, by and large, a personal affair. Like so many other global-societal problems, this one must now be grappled with individually and resolved, if at all, with private means. The attainment of clarity of purpose and meaning is an individual task and personal responsibility. The effort is personal. And so is the failure of the effort. And the blame for the failure. And the feeling of guilt that the blame brings in its wake.

The burden that the privatization of ambivalence has cast on individual shoulders calls for a bone structure few individuals can boast. A weaker backbone may collapse under pressure. To ward off the danger of collapse, artificial supports are needed. The private road to clarity requires a lot of socially provided services: detailed maps, reliable signposts, mileage counters.

Consider the following case.[1]

A decade or so ago Emily Cho offered to American women a computerized fashion-advice service. The questionnaire which prospective clients were asked to complete enquired what image the client wished to project, and how the client wanted that image to be modified to convey the individuality – indeed, the *uniqueness* – of her self and character. The rest was to be done by the computer, which would find out how the client should build up a wardrobe most likely to attain both purposes. Emily Cho's enterprise proved to be a huge success.

At the beginning, Emily Cho believed that her clients' attention should be drawn away as much as possible from the idea that 'their private hopes and dreams were being fed into a coldhearted computer'. Much to her surprise, she soon noticed that the opposite strategy is more effective: 'the idea of the computer was precisely what appealed to the women'. The clients seemed to be pleased with the involvement of high technology, which they apparently trusted with precision and accuracy of advice one can expect only from scientifically controlled practice. After all, 'what they demanded was a clear-cut formula of dressing well, rather than a capri-

[1] As reported by Kennedy Fraser in *The New Yorker*, 11 May 1981, pp. 126–35.

cious idea springing from another woman's brain'. Miss Cho believed, though, that the clients still needed to feel that the 'distant, possibly runaway machine' of the computer is not left on its own. The consciousness that another woman, Miss Cho herself, is present somewhere, to hold the computer in check, was reassuring. This is, at any rate, what Miss Cho came to believe.

There are a few observations, all relevant to our theme, that one can take note of while trying to make sense of the experience of Emily Cho and her clients.

First, it seems that what explains the fact that the clients took up Emily Cho's offer so keenly was that they found themselves facing an ambivalent task they could not easily tackle precisely because its two sides seemingly cancelled each other. The task was, no more and no less, one of establishing *autonomy* through *submission*: becoming an individual through belonging, and making a statement about one's own personality through impersonal means. The *uniqueness* they sought was to be *communally* (and thus unambiguously) determined. Individuality, one may say, would not do on its own, unless it was communicated and understood as such – and that means *shared* with others.

Second, the solution to the quandary. Emily Cho's customers saw the resolution of ambivalence as a *job* they had to carry out. Both the membership and the individual uniqueness were seen as attributes which are not given naturally, but need a conscious effort to be brought about and sustained; they have to be 'built up'. And building them up was seen as the task (perhaps a duty) of the person involved.

Third, the task of building-up entailed making *both* the membership *and* the individuality into visible *images*, that is objects perceptible to others; these must be *proper* images, that is such as are certain to be read out properly and interpreted according to the person's intention. Images, unlike the condition they are meant to deal with, should be free from ambivalence. It is for this reason that they must be expressed in a supra-individual, shared and *authorized* code.

Fourth, access to a shared code meant in practice the expression of membership and individuality in symbolic objects that have guaranteed socially accepted meanings, so that the probability of misreading is reduced. Such objects, it was assumed, exist. The task was to locate them, and eventually obtain them so that they could be used. In the case described, they could be obtained through a market transaction.

Fifth, contradictory claims being made by the market operators as to the hermeneutic value of competing objects, an authority (an impartial, 'objective opinion', more solid and reliable than the view of merely 'another person') was sought to reduce uncertainty and increase the chance of the right choice. Such an authority was willingly – and with relief – accredited to science, as an institution armed with in-built guarantees of non-partisanship and dispassion. (It was of such an institution that the computer served as tangible incarnation.)

Sixth, direct access to science being barred to the ordinary person, a mediator was needed to translate personal, subjective needs into questions which could be answered in the impartial and reliable, but hermetically sealed, highly technical language of science, and to translate back the scientific verdict into practical advice for the layperson. A private person could *understand* her needs, but only science *knew* the way of satisfying them. The sought mediator, one whom the client could truly *trust* (a concept developed, to great effect, by Anthony Giddens in his *Consequences of Modernity*, Cambridge: Polity Press, 1989) was one that combined the person's capacity to understand with the power of science to make right decisions.

Such a mediator is called an *expert*.

The expert is a person capable, simultaneously, of interrogating the fund of trustworthy and supra-personal knowledge and of understanding the innermost thoughts and cravings of a single person. As an interpreter and mediator, the expert spans the otherwise distant worlds of the objective and the subjective. He bridges the gap between guarantees of being in the right (which can be only social) and making the choices that one wants (which can be only personal). In the ambivalence of his skills, he is, so to speak, resonant with the ambivalent condition of his client.

In her own account of the experience, Emily Cho emphasized the importance of the 'humanity' of the mediator. Let us note, however, that for her clients Cho was an entity present, much like her computer, mostly as a 'belief'. We do not know whether the clients ever engaged in a personal intercourse with the head of the company; we do not know even if they ever met her in person. The clients believed that she existed, but for all they knew she was the 'being' on the receiving end of the questionnaire they filled and the source of the customized fashion-guidance they received. What seemed to make Emily Cho's existence important to the clients was not her 'humanity', but their own *trust* in the *function* of mediation and interpretation she performed. Emily Cho was the trust embodied; the fact that hers was a flesh-and-blood *human* body was secondary and contingent. In principle, a mechanical contraption capable of performing the same function could replace her – without noticeable damage to the satisfaction of the needs which made her services desirable in the first place. Joseph Weizenbaum found (much to his surprise, and soon to his dismay), that his computer program ELIZA, which simulated a psychoanalytical session, was enthusiastically welcomed not only by psychiatrists (who saw in it the chance of allowing people to 'talk about themselves, unburden themselves, gather insights into their troubled behaviour' in numbers much greater than the availability of trained analysts would permit),[2] but also by the prospective patients (indeed, the very presence of the computerized simulation of the psychiatrist 'released' a potential patient 'latent' in the exposed persons). Before his discovery, Weizenbaum (much like Madame Cho) believed that human intercourse was the crucial component of the psychotherapeutic process; that the process was effective in a morally acceptable way mainly thanks to the interaction of a human in need of help and another human ready and willing to help. As it transpired, however, the patients did not mind speaking to an 'inhuman artefact', as long as its openings looked adequate to what they felt was their problem, and its follow-ups were correct – that is logical – responses to the statements preceding them. In fact, Weizenbaum's secretary (who watched him working on the program for many months and hence could not possibly entertain any illusions as to its contrived nature) started one day 'conversing' with the computer; after exchanging just a few sentences she became so engrossed in the 'conversation' and experienced the exchange as so private and intimate an affair that she felt embarrassed by the presence of her boss and asked the professor to leave the room.

The expert, in other words, is defined not so much by the qualities and possessions which characterize her, but by the function she (he, or it) is perceived as performing by the recipients of the services. It is the problems that the recipients of expert services face in the course of their life-process that fully define the expert. The expert is, so to speak, a condensation of the diffuse need of trustworthy – because supra-individual – sanction of individuality.

The quest for love, or the existential foundations of expertise

According to Niklas Luhmann,[3] with the passage from a pre-modern, stratified society to the modern, functionally differentiated one (that is a

---

[2] Cf. Joseph Weizenbaum, *Computer Power and Human Reason: From Judgment to Calculation* (San Francisco: W.H. Freeman & Co., 1976). Theodore Roszak (*The Cult of Informtion: The Folklore of Computers and the True Art of Thinking* (Cambridge; Lutterworth Press, 1986), p. 36) lists other examples of computerized substitutes for psychotherapists, like Pamela McCorduck's 'geriatric robot' that will 'solve the problems of aging' by listening to old people's complaints.

[3] Niklas Luhmann, *Love as Passion: The Codification of Intimacy* (Cambridge, Mass.: Harvard University Press, 1986).

society in which divisions cut across the social locations of single individuals), 'individual persons can no longer be firmly located in one single subsystem of society, but rather must be regarded a priori as socially displaced'. All individuals are displaced, and displaced permanently, existentially – wherever they find themselves at the moment and whatever they may happen to do. They are *strangers* everywhere and, their efforts to the contrary notwithstanding, at all places. There is no single place in society in which they are truly at home and which can bestow upon them a natural identity. Individual identity becomes therefore something to be yet attained (and presumably to be created) by the individual involved and never securely and definitely possessed – as it is constantly challenged and must be ever anew negotiated. Following the path long before indicated by Georg Simmel (the individual doomed to a never-ending quest for a fixed point in himself, as he can no longer find it outside himself – all relations with others being ultimately mere stations along the road by which the ego arrives at himself), Luhmann seeks the causes of the individuals' tendency to interpret their situation 'in terms of their own person', that is, their preoccupation with self-definition, self-identity, self-assertion – in short, the causes of their ego-centrism and individualism – in the ever-increasing differentiation, complexity and hence opacity of interactive networks. General categories do not suffice now for self-identification, which may be reached only in the form of personal uniqueness.

At this moment, however, we encounter the paradox on which the existential condition of members of modern society rests. On the one hand, the individual needs to establish a stable and defensible difference between own person and the wider, impersonal and impenetrable social world outside. On the other hand, however, such a difference, precisely to be stable and reliable, needs social affirmation and must be obtained in a form which also enjoys *social* approval. Individuality depends on social conformity; the struggle for individuality demands that social bonds are strengthened and social dependence deepened. The subjective world which constitutes the identity of individual personality can only be sustained by means of intersubjective exchange. In such an exchange, one partner 'must be able to lend his support to the world of the other (although his inner experiences are highly individual)'.

Luhmann calls such an exchange love. It must be clear from the way in which the notion of 'love' has been introduced that in Luhmann's use it is semantically prised off from the traditional romantic associations of the term, and, indeed, does not refer at all to personal feelings or emotional states in general; Luhmann reaches, so to speak, to the coolly cognitive 'functional underlayer' of what is at the surface an emotionally charged relationship. In Luhmann's idiosyncratic use, 'love' stands for a particular *mode of communication*, in which persons may engage in principle *with or without* experiencing the affections which the term in its traditional and popular usage would impute or demand. There is, therefore, an inherent discrepancy between what is required for the function of the love-like intercourse to be fulfilled, and the criteria the persons are inclined to apply to find out whether the love relationship has taken place, and to evaluate it as proper or sham.

It is for this reason, Luhmann would say, that in social practice love relationships tend to be confused, ambiguous, tension-ridden; that they are likely to generate profound anxiety. Since it is assumed in the popular interpretation of love that the love-relationship may be effective only when prompted by 'sincerity'[4] and accompanied by 'true feelings', all practical instances of love intercourse must be contaminated by a gnawing suspicion that the partner may cheat by 'acting out' the feelings deemed necessary yet in this case missing. The search for love, determined by the modality of modern existence and hence bound to be resumed ever anew however bitter the experience has been thus far, carries therefore from the start an unhealthy admixture of the fear of guile. Consequently, it tends to be punctuated by attempts to overcome the uncertainty and find reliable methods to weed out fraud and tell the 'true love' from the mere pretence of a conperson.

Such attempts become all the more obsessive and feverish the more autonomous (i.e., unique), idiosyncratic (and hence bizarre from the point

---

[4] Luhmann's dispassionate, coolly functional analysis goes some way toward resolving the puzzle that so baffled Lionel Trilling: 'If sincerity is the avoidance of being false to any man through being true to one's own self, we can see that this state of personal existence is not to be attained without the most arduous effort. And yet at a certain point in history certain men and classes of men conceived that the making of this effort was of supreme importance . . . and the value they attached to the enterprise of sincerity became a salient, perhaps a definitive, characteristic of Western culture for some four hundred years.' (*Sincerity and Authenticity* (London: Oxford University Press, 1972), pp. 5–6.) Let us note that the apparently irrational phenomenon loses some of its mystery once we recall that the emergence of displacement as a universal condition of the 'free individual' coincided historically with the collapse of the authority of past institutional addresses of confession; the burden previously carried matter-of-factly by the church (burden created by its own construction of the 'insidedness of truth') was then shifted upon lay and unregulated agents and had to be managed with full consciousness of the problems involved. Hence Matthew Arnold's reflection ('Below the surface-stream, shallow and light, / of what we *say* we feel – below the stream / as light, of what we *think* we feel – there flows / with noiseless current strong, obscure and deep / the central stream of what we feel indeed') was not a sign of new social condition, but of new awareness.

of view of the 'norm') the individual personality becomes. Self-reliance makes the need for love yet more overwhelming than it is in the case of a self-effacing, heteronomous and submissive personality. More individuality needs more love to sustain it. Since, however, with the growth of personal autonomy and idiosyncracy the probability of social approval diminishes, the greater the need the less probable is its satisfaction.

In Luhmann's functional sense, love can be thought of as a mode of communication characterized by transforming an inner experience of one person into the action of another. 'The lover, who is expected to affirm idiosyncratic selections, is obliged to *act*, because he is confronted with a choice that has to be made' (that is, he has to choose between validating or dismissing the selections); 'the beloved, on the other hand, has only *experienced* something and expects him to identify with that experience. The one has to become involved, whereas the other (who is also forever tied to a projected world) only had to make the projection'. Luhmann's love is a highly egoistic, self-centred affair; no wonder that for the person on the receiving end of such love the emergent task is a tall order; the vigilance with which the performance will be watched and the demanding criteria by which it will be judged make it particularly burdensome. In ordinary love relationships, prospective lovers take up the task nevertheless, mostly in the (vain) hope that the initial asymmetry of the pattern will be in the end rectified by a reciprocating response, so that both partners will receive in exchange for their efforts services similar to those they themselves rendered. 'Ordinary' love relations postulate mutuality – that is, they demand that each partner agrees to assume simultaneously or successively both the 'projecting' and the 'affirming' roles, to 'project' and to 'act', to be a beloved and the lover at the same time. They postulate, therefore, that the interaction is not initiated (let alone sustained) merely by the needs of one of the partners, but by a *mutual* attraction of both sides, with both sides induced 'to stick together for better or worse'; in other words, by passion, not calculation.

Considering the enormity and the importance of the function that love is expected to perform for the 'universal stranger' (that '*a priori* displaced' inhabitant of the modern world), passion seems to be, however, a much too wan and fickle foundation for the hope that the function will be fulfilled on every occasion, continuously and in the required volume. The costs of maintaining the function-fulfilment at a sufficiently high level of intensity over long periods are enormous – while, as we have seen before, the primary needs which have made love a functional necessity do not by themselves generate and nourish affections. For the primary function of love to be performed, passion is superfluous; it is neither inevitable nor necessary. It is only the method of securing the implementation of function through imposing reciprocity on an essentially asymmetrical pattern which makes passion indispensable. But as this happens, the sustenance of reciprocity, and hence the implementation of function, begin to depend on the constant and continuous supply of emotion, which makes it fickle and vulnerable.

Some time ago Richard Sennett coined the name *destructive Gemeinschaft* for a relationship in which both partners obsessively pursue the right to *intimacy* – to 'open oneself up' to the partner, to share with the partner the whole, the most private truth about one's inner life, to be 'absolutely sincere', to hide nothing, however upsetting the information may be for the partner (a posture grounded in the belief that 'you interact with others according to how much you tell them about yourself'; in the 'fear that one has no self until one tells another person about it'; as well as in the fantasy that identity may indeed be freely construed by talking, that there is no 'tough reality', no society 'as something different from intimate transactions'[5]). In Sennett's view, stripping one's soul naked in front of the partner thrusts on the latter's shoulders an enormous burden; the partner is asked to give agreement to things which do not necessarily arouse his or her enthusiasm; moreover, he or she is asked to be 'sincere' and 'honest' in reply. Sennett avers that no lasting relationship, and particularly not a lasting *loving* relationship, can be erected on the wobbly ground of mutual intimacy. The odds against this happening are overwhelming: the partners set for each other demands that neither of them can meet (or would not wish to meet, considering the price); both suffer and feel tormented and frustrated in the result – and more often than not they decide to call it a day half way and stop trying. One or another partner chooses to opt out, and to seek self-assertion elsewhere.

Let us repeat: the destructiveness of the communion sought by the partners in love is caused first and foremost by the implication[6] of

---

[5] Richard Sennett, 'Destructive Gemeinschaft', in *Beyond the Crisis*, ed. Norman Birnbaum (Oxford University Press, 1977). Sennett goes on to trace the consequences that such a tendency to 'identity building through confession' have for the modern family: 'The fact of what the rules are objectively gets lost easily in a much subtler but stronger process of asserting the self, guilt over that assertion, and triumph over child in which the child is only a means to the parents' need for legitimation . . . These are precisely the means by which a confused sense of object relations is instilled into a growing human being; that is, the means by which a narcissistic character disorder is created.' (p. 196)

[6] The potentially destructive impact of the demand of mutuality with which the partners are surreptitiously burdened in each display of sincerity has been given its now classic rendition by David Riesman: 'One gifted boy of fifteen, whose interview I have analysed in detail elsewhere, stated that his best trait was sincerity, and proved the point by a gallant effort to be totally frank with the interviewer. It

reciprocity. To sustain the animus, to go on seeking genuine mutuality – one needs the courage to face the possibility of drawbacks and reversals. One must also learn to live with the shortcomings of the partner. Once aimed in both directions, intimacy makes negotiation and compromise necessary. And yet it is precisely negotiation and compromise which one or both partners may be too impatient, or too self-concerned, to bear lightly. After all, two *distinct*, often contradictory personal projections must be accepted and affirmed simultaneously – a task always difficult and often impossible.

No wonder a demand for the functional love-substitute arises out of the failed attempts to obtain the 'real thing' (and if there is demand, an offer will soon follow): a demand for something which would *perform the function* of love (i.e. supply confirmation of inner experience, having first patiently absorbed full confession), without demanding *reciprocity* in exchange: that is, something that would explicitly admit – and accept – the inherent asymmetry of the relationship. Here, we may postulate, lies the secret of the astounding success and popularity of psychoanalytic sessions, psychological counselling, group therapy, marriage guidance etc. In all such and similar cases, for the right to confess and be absolved, to 'open oneself up', make the innermost feelings known to another person, and in the end receive the longed-for approval of one's identity, one does not need to repay in kind; one needs only to pay money. By the same token (money being what it is: the means to *terminate* the exchange, to settle the account once for all and thus to ward off all future obligations) one obtains a service without assuming the duty to reciprocate. Monetary payment transforms the patient's or client's relation to the analyst into an impersonal one, and thus staves off the danger of a guilty conscience: it wipes off the stigma of selfishness from the patient's self-concern and lack of concern for the partner. The patient, so to speak, 'buys himself off' from the emotionally costly and onerous obligation of mutuality. And so one can, as it were, *be loved without loving*. One can be concerned with oneself, and have the concerns shared, without giving another thought to the person who has taken upon oneself the obligation of sharing merely as a part of a business transaction. In a straightforward monetary transaction, the patient purchases an illusion of being loved. (It has to be mentioned, though, that the one-sided love being as much 'against nature' as a one-

did not occur to him that such sincerity puts pressure on others in a social situation to be equally sincere; it is coercive, and tends to break down the etiquette which we use to protect our emotional life from strangers, from over-inquisitive relatives and friends, and at times from ourselves.' (*Individualism Reconsidered and Other Essays* (Glencoe: Free Press, 1954), p. 19.)

sided coin, or being, more precisely, in sharp disagreement with the socially accepted model of love – psychoanalytical exercise is notoriously plagued with the patients' tendency to mistake the 'as if' conduct of the analyst for an expression of 'true love', and to respond with a behaviour which steps beyond the strictly business-like, impersonal and admittedly asymmetrical terms of the agreement. This phenomonen of *transference* obliquely proves, if a proof was needed, the function of psychoanalysis as a paid-up substitute for love.)

Psychoanalytical techniques are just one specimen of a much wider category of goods and services which respond to the need of a love-substitute. In a market society, such goods and services come as commodities (though this does not seem to be their essential attribute; one may conceive of other ways in which such services could be distributed and obtained, and of other means than could achieve a similar reciprocity-quashing effect the monetary payment obtains with such success). The market puts on display a wide range of 'identities' from which one can select one's own. Commercial advertisements take pains to show the commodities they try to sell in their *social context*, which means as a part of a particular *life-style*, so that the prospective customer can consciously purchase symbols of such self-identity as he or she would wish to possess. The market also offers tools of 'identity making' which can be used differentially, i.e. produce results which differ somewhat from each other and are in this way 'customized' or 'personalized', better catering for the need of individuality. Through the market, one can put together various elements of the complete 'identikit' of a DIY self. One can learn how to express oneself as a modern, liberated, carefree woman; or as a thoughtful, reasonable, caring housewife; or as an up-and coming, ruthless and self-confident tycoon; or as an easy-going, likeable fellow; or as an outdoor, physically fit, macho man; or as a romantic, dreamy and love-hungry creature; or as any mixture of all or some of these.

The attractiveness of market-promoted identities is that the torments of self-construction, and of the subsequent search for social approval for the finished or half-baked product, is replaced by the less harrowing, often pleasurable, act of choice between ready-made patterns. The merchandised identities come complete with the label of social approval already stuck on in advance. The uncertainty as to the viability of self-constructed identity and the agony of seeking confirmation are thereby spared. Identikits and life-style symbols are endorsed by people with authority and by information that an impressively large number of people approve of them. Social acceptance does not need therefore to be negotiated – it has been, so to speak, 'built into' the marketed product from the start.

With such alternatives available and growing in popularity, the original method of solving the self-formation problem through reciprocal love stands ever smaller chance of success. As we have seen before, the negotiating of a *mutual* approval is a potentially traumatic experience for the partners in love. Success is not possible without dedicated and long-term effort, and a good deal of self-sacrifice on both sides. In all probability, the 'staying power' would be stronger, and the effort and the sacrifice would be made more frequently and with more zeal, were not the 'easy' substitutes available. With the substitutes widely promoted and easy to obtain (the only sacrifice needed is to part with a quantity of money) there is, arguably, less motivation for a more laborious and time-consuming effort. Often the first hurdle is enough for one or both partners to wish to slow down or opt out from the race altogether. More often still, the substitutes are first sought with the intention to 'complement' and hence to strengthen or resuscitate the failing love relationship; sooner or later, however, the substitutes unload that relationship from its original function and drain off the energy which prompted the partners to seek its resurrection in the first place. With love even less viable than before, the demand for expert service expands further – and so *ad infinitum*. Paradoxically (or is it a paradox?), the privatization of ambivalence incites and sustains the unstoppable growth of public expertise and a dense network of public specialists in resolution of private problems.

One of the manifestations of the devaluation of love has been extensively discussed by Richard Sennett; the tendency of *eroticism* to be ousted and supplanted by *sexuality*. Eroticism means the deployment of sexual desire, and ultimately sexual intercourse, as a building block of a lasting love relationship: of a *multifunctional* and thus stable social partnership – while sexuality means the reduction of sexual intercourse to one function only – that of the satisfaction of sexual desire. Such a reduction is often supplemented by precautions aimed at preventing the sexual relationship from giving rise to mutual sympathy and obligation, and thus from growing into a fully-fledged personal partnership. The 'emancipation' of sexuality from the context of eroticism (most fully expressed in *romantic* love) leaves all love relationships – sexual as well as asexual – considerably weakened. They now lack (or have to share with other users) a most powerful resource, and find their stability still more difficult to attain.

It is the failure of the 'ordinary', reciprocal model of passionate love to resolve acute problems generated by the '*a priori* displacement' of the modern person, that creates the need for marketed substitutes for love. With the growing availability of such substitutes, the weaknesses of traditional patterns are blatantly exposed, made salient, odious and above all intolerable. The comparative psychological cost of insisting on traditional solutions is perceived then as increasingly fanciful and unjustifiable, which in turn further boosts the demand for substitutes and – the market mechanism being what it is – leads in the long run to the quantitative and qualitative expansion of supply. The two factors are locked in a double bind of mutual reinforcement, with the traditional *solutions* (that is, romantic or passionate love) progressively devalued and stripped of attraction, and *expertise* as the substitute ever more in demand and available in growing volume and variety.

And so to return to the beginning: expertise being, so to speak, a *love without love* (love without the risks of reciprocity; love without the worrisome dependency on passion), it does not need to be offered by a *human* partner. On the user's side, nothing in principle bars the replacement of human experts by computer expert systems, or electronic conversationalists of Weizenbaum's ELIZA type (though such artificial intelligence replacements, filling the niche previously reserved for intimate interhuman bonds, cannot but be invested by their users with qualities appropriate to the place it now occupies; hence the cultic elements in the users' attitudes and widely noted tendency to *personalize* the electronic partners of intercourse). If anything, the added glamour value of high technology augments the authority of offered expertise, magnifies its perceived effectivity, heightens attached expectations and thus strengthens its allure and impact.

The paradox of such *individuality* as can be constructed only through *social* confirmation is the existential foundation of expertise. It offers the general pattern; the specific needs of functionally differentiated expertise may be seen as special cases. The case we have considered above in some detail may serve as a metaphor for virtually all manifold specialized branches of impersonal professional service aimed at personal use; a public industry serving the consequences of the privatization of ambivalence.

The redeployment of skills

From the point of view of the user, expertise offers socially approved solutions to individual discomforts and anxieties, having first equally authoritatively articulated them as *problems* that require solutions. Offered solutions are problem-specific. Before they may be offered, therefore, the problems themselves must already have been socially approved; they need a socially underwritten mapping of the life-world that constitutes them as 'problems' calling for 'solutions'. The expertise enters the life-world of the individual already at an early stage when diffuse and vague personal unease – uncertainty, ambivalence of experience – is articulated in the *interpersonal* language of *individual* problems demanding the application of *supra-individual* (i.e. 'objective' – authoritatively endorsed) solutions. In defiance of this ostensible logic, however, the availability of solutions more often than not precedes the articulation. Indeed, life experience is seen as ambivalent only if life without ambiguity is offered as a feasible option; personal discomfort is interpreted as a set of unresolved *problems* in as far as socially approved solutions are available and on offer. In the end it is exceedingly difficult to decide on the priority of expertise and existential problems; they cannot but be defined reciprocally, in each other's terms.

Social authority of expertise rests on four closely interrelated assumptions.

First, the individual is by and large a self-enclosed and self-contained agent, potentially in control of his or her own life-project. The individual is in possession of rational faculties that should in principle allow the selection (or, rather, the discovery) of the project best geared to the individual's own specific qualities. Persistently ambiguous identity and persevering uncertainty of choice are therefore symptoms of personal ignorance or neglect, and hence degrading and embarrassing. They are, for that reason, an uncomfortable condition, a justifiable cause for self-condemnation and unhappiness.

Second, personal discomfort (physical or spiritual) is an essentially remediable condition, and hence cannot and should not be tolerated. It is the duty of the individual to seek escape from the unhappy condition; persistence of discomfort is equivalent to the neglect of duty.

Third, each case of unhappiness has its specific cause, cut out in such a way that it can be singled out, set apart, 'targeted' and acted upon directly – in order to be neutralized or removed. Unhappiness is therefore explicable in terms which make remedial action feasible: to describe discomfort is to point out the method of its removal or relief. The duty of the individual is to seek such an explanation. Persistent non-specificity of suffering testifies to the lack of diagnostic knowledge.

Fourth, for each case of suffering (or, rather, for each *cause* of suffering) there is, or ought to be, an adequate remedy. Among the remedies on offer, one is the most adequate. It is again the duty of the individual to seek, find, select and apply that remedy. Persistence of suffering is an evidence of absence of practical knowledge and skills necessary to do it.

While starting from the axiom of the *privacy* of individual troubles, these assumptions construe individuals as inherently non-self-sufficient entities; autonomy of the individual, responsibility for self-definition translates in the end as the duty to find the right exit from the state of insufficiency, and above all as an obligation to seek actively such an exit. In other words, individuals are construed as agents who must rely on forces they do not control in order to gain satisfactory control of themselves.

Life in society is inconceivable without a set of skills which enable individuals to interact with others while preserving their own integrity (i.e., reproducing themselves as subjects capable of interaction). Such skills are available in any society, and they are always socially transmitted. Contrary to the suggestions of its numerous critics, the fact that modern society is composed of '*a priori* displaced' persons cast in a condition of 'universal strangerhood' does not make it an exception to the above rule; neither does it create a game with new rules. The notorious 'deskilling tendency', 'disappearance of social skills' etc. can hardly be viewed as unique characteristics of modern society. They can happen in this kind of society no more than in any other type. The history of societies has been, throughout, a history of learning as much as of *forgetting*. At all times some skills were devalued, fell into oblivion and disuse, only to be eventually replaced by new ones.

What seems to be a truly *modern* development is, however, a gradual yet relentless ascendance of such skills as must be mediated by extrapersonal, socially supplied tools that can be got hold of only through an act of exchange. These skills have systematically dislodged (and eventually ousted) older skills which enabled individuals to act without recourse to external help: the 'short-circuit' type of skills, which allowed individuals to act upon their motives with resources 'naturally' at their disposal. Modern men and women seem to share the fate of Tom and Jerry of the famous cartoon, who have totally forgotten the ancient art of the cat-and-mouse struggle conducted with the help of such reliable and constantly available weapons as paws and fangs and strategies of hide-and-seek, and so must use instead ever more sophisticated high-tech equipment and ever more elaborate and ingenious technologies of cunning ambush and high-speed escape.

To put it in a different way: modern society is a site of *mediated action*. Few, if any daily and mundane tasks may be accomplished without the assistance of supra-individual – specialized – knowledge, that may either come wrapped into a tool or a black-box type gadget, or be delivered in a verbalized form of spoken or printed briefing. The skills needed for effective performance of the task are enclosed in artefacts or in the commands of a step-by-step instruction. The skills individuals deploy on their own are thereby reduced to the service of one need alone: that of locating and getting access to artefacts or instructions adequate to the task they wish to perform. More often than not, only such tasks are contemplated and only such actions embarked on that have been made feasible by the available or known means.

This is not necessarily a novelty or a unique feature of modern society. In all social contexts the accessible know-how defines the range of actions likely to be considered and undertaken. What is indeed a modern novelty is the fact that the know-how in question is irretrievably split into two parts: one related to the actual performance of the task, another related to finding and using the reified or personal carriers of the former. Of the two parts, only the second is required of individuals engaged in activities within the scope of their life-world, and is likely to be possessed by them. The living cannot sustain their own life. The process of life is itself mediated.

Using popular metaphors, one can say that alongside other dimensions of the modern social system the life-world of modern individuals has been subjected to the processes of *Taylorization* and *Fordization*. The first process consists, as it were, in the simplification of choices with which individuals who are engaged in direct productive operations are confronted. Reduced to the bare essentials and cleansed as much as possible of all random and irrelevant factors, the situation in which such individuals are placed turns into an instrument with which the decision-makers higher up in the hierarchy manipulate, and in the end determine, the choices. Successful Taylorization spares the operators the torments of uncertainty and hesitation, as the decisions which remain to be taken by them personally are guided by single-factor criteria and hence lend themselves to an easy and reassuringly rational calculation. The process of Fordization, on the other hand, consists in removing the skills from the operator and investing them into the machinery he operates. It is now the *object* of labour, not the labour itself, that turns out to be skilful; skills become elements of the actor's *outer environment*. Fordization shifts responsibility for the results of action from the operator to the implements he operates, and in principle allows the individuals to engage in a well-nigh infinite range of skill-demanding activities, much in excess of the abilities they themselves might have mastered.

The combined effect of the two processes on the conduct of daily life is the elevation of a superstructure of expert decision-making above the level of the actual task-performance, coupled with the shifting of all skill-demanding decisions away from the performers. This double effect is achieved through the reduction of such tasks as the performers may confront to the most elementary and straightforward operations (like swallowing the right kind of expert-prepared and expert-prescribed pill in order to 'solve' – neutralize – a complex interpersonal problem); in its turn it further promotes such a reduction.

This reduction is experienced as liberation from the cumbersome necessities of life and feels like freedom. Since the assumed availability of solutions made living with unresolved problems uncomfortable, solutions are actively sought; finding them, choosing and appropriating is perceived as an act of emancipation and an increase in the scope of personal freedom. And yet – as the personal skills needed to deal directly with the problems are no longer available, and the solutions appear solely in the shape of marketable implements or expert advice, each successive step in the endless problem-solving, while experienced as another extension of freedom, further strengthens the network of dependency. Growing incompleteness and insufficiency of the individual and the ever more complex structure of dependency seem to be the ultimate effects of the privatization of ambivalence. Or at least they are under present conditions.

The hold of supra-individual expertise over the life-world of the individual is *self-reproducing*. Having effectively disposed of all viable alternatives, it displays virtually unencumbered capacity for growth. Since it is perceived as a condition of liberty rather than as oppression, its expansion is also unlikely to encounter serious resistance. Finally, the authority and social approval of expertise is no more dependent on the success of its results. Failure of a particular implement or recipe to deliver on its promise does not result in the client's disenchantment; more often than not it leads instead to self-recrimination and triggers off increased demand and a yet more frantic search for a better, more efficient expert service. If the individuals pause for a moment of reflection and try to spell out the canons of their life-strategy, they will most certainly identify the prospects of a happy, problem-free life with the unstoppable progress of expert knowledge and the technology it spawns.

The self-reproduction of expertise

Expertise creates and enhances the need of itself. The substitution of expert skills for personal ones does not mean solely the provision of more effective and foolproof, as well as less onerous, means to deal with the *extant problems*. It also means the creation and a principally unlimited multiplication of new problems which render expertise indispensable.

By separating knowing from doing and knowers from doers, the mediating expertise and the attendant technology make the life-world of *all* members of society (no one is an expert in the *totality* of life-world functions) into a territory of permanent and acute ambivalence and uncertainty. Indeed, a most prominent characteristic of modern society is 'a fundamental insecurity about activities that people have successfully engaged in for tens of thousands of years. One is not to rely on one's own experience but on expert knowers ...'[7] In a pithy summary of Harold Perkin, 'The twentieth century would become the century not of the plain man who knows where it hurts but of the professional expert who "knows best" what is good for him.'[8] Let us add that the state of 'being hurt' is itself expert-defined and perceived as such in the wake of the definition; the very fact that there is a 'better condition' brandished by the experts and declared to be within the reach of the individual moulds the experience of the present condition as hurtful and thus creates the very insecurity for which it offers remedy. It is the experts who set the standards of normality. However these standards are set, they leave outside a solid chunk of reality which, by the fact of being left outside, turns into an anomaly requiring treatment. Such an anomaly is not transient or contingent; it is an integral part of the norm-promoting process, and thus in essence uneliminable. Removal of a particular anomaly merely vacates room for another, brought forth by the further tightening of standards.

The general pattern has been vividly illustrated by the process of the 'medicalization' of social life, recently researched afresh by Ruth Harris: 'everywhere' – Harris found out – 'medical men saw danger' and their definitions of 'cases for medical treatment' grew consistently wider, so that they embraced conditions previously not considered to be of any medical interest. Medical men of the turn of the century made a consolidated bid for a redefinition of the state of society as a collection of medical problems. Thus the urban misfits – the homeless and beggars – were 'found' to be suffering of neurasthenia, strike-prone workers of hysteria, middle-class males of psychical stress, middle-class women of neurosis. '... psychiatric concepts were constructed around certain key dichotomies – normal and pathological, mind and body, higher and lower, right and

[7] Willem H. Vanderburg in *Democratic Theory and Technological Society*, ed. Richard B. Day, Ronald Beiner and Joseph Masciulli (New York: M.E. Sharpe, 1988), p. 10

[8] Harold Perkin, *The Rise of Professional Society: England since 1880* (London: Routledge, 1989), pp. 169–70. Vanderburg recognizes the ubiquitousness of technique as a *method of doing things*, and of expert technicians *as the doers* of things, as the decisive attribute of modern society: 'Modern societies are not so much characterized by the industrial and machine-related technologies as by the fact that almost every aspect of these societies is organized and reorganized on the basis of variety of techniques that together have helped to constitute a knowledge base that is drawn on to ensure that everything is done as effectively as possible.' (*Democratic Theory and Technological Society*, p. 7.) Many a crucial argument about the role of technology and export in framing and servicing daily life has been advanced in the writings of Ivan Illich.

left, equilibrium and destablization, economy and excess, control and disinhibition' – each one of them dichotomizing and each one producing a problem-ridden territory and a grey area of ambivalence of its own. 'Emphasis was placed on the success or failure of the women or men to live up to certain prescribed social roles'; the expert medical intervention was legitimized in advance by the original decision to prescribe roles (that is, to consider all idiosyncrasy as abnormality).[9]

On a closer scrutiny the self-declared servants turn into managers. Once the relationship of the individual to both nature and society has been effectively mediated by expert skills and their attendant technology, it is those who possess the skills and administer the technology that command the life-activities. The life-world itself is saturated by expertise – structured, articulated, monitored and reproduced. It is now the expert-produced and managed technique that constitutes the true environment of individual life. In this environment arises most of the ambivalence and insecurity, and thus most of the perceived dangers. Such dangers are produced in two essential ways.

First, the very precision, decisiveness and radicality with which the concentrated, focused, scientifically-based (and, above all, task-autonomous) expert knowledge, unlike the traditional and socially diffuse skills, is capable of dealing with the task at hand, tends to create acute imbalances in other areas of the life-world system. Unanticipated side-effects call for new expertise and create demands for its further division. Otherwise mutually isolated segments of the expertise network supply therefore ever new tasks for each other, and thus in their overall effect reinforce the standing of the network as a whole – even at moments of individual defeat and disgrace (or, rather, particularly at such moments).

Second, the more focused, specialized and autonomous a given field of

---

[9] Ruth Harris, *Murders and Madness: Medicine, Law and Society in the Fin de siècle* (Oxford: Clarendon Press, 1989), pp. 13, 19, 21. Once the process of restructuring daily life as a series of expert-assisted problems has taken off, it acquires a momentum of its own. Experts are needed to clear up the mess generated by the abundance of expertise and the sheer volume of problems no lay member of society can cope with without specialist help. The argument for new expertise then goes on according to the following pattern: 'many people often do not know fully what is happening to them through television. It follows that it is for the expert to detect and display such harm making processes. What is more, it follows that expert advice should be socially harnessed through suitable institutions to control and ameliorate such a potent medium.' (Malloy Weber and Barrie Gunter, *Television and Social Control* (Aldershot: Avebury, 1988), p. 231) The authors then leave no doubt that whatever the opinion about the latter proposal, the need of more expertise, and of the experts at the helm, is beyond dispute: the critics of control 'do not advocate less central control . . . Rather, they wish for more control but in a fashion of their particular choosing.'

expertise becomes, the chance grows that new skills (meaning new technical capabilities) will be invented, which at first will have no clear application. Their presence, however, will bring into relief areas of the life-world previously unnoticed; will redefine previously neutral or easily coped-with elements of life routine as vexing (made intolerable by the very fact of not having to be tolerated anymore); as factors not-adequately-defined, opaque, ambiguous, insufficiently controlled, and hence fear-generating; as problems that need to be 'dealt with', defused or removed. As information about new skills is disseminated, the urge is generated to purchase, hire and apply them. Instead of achieving the promised reduction in the number of problems which beset the management of the life-world, the progressive refinement of expert skills rebounds in the multiplication of problems. Skills seeking application masquerade as problems needing solution.

The first way in which expertise-demanding problems are multiplied in the course of their resolution has been perceptively and wittily analysed by Gregory Bateson.[10] Problem-oriented sciences and technologies are guided by perception of *purposes*: 'What happens is that doctors think it would be nice to get rid of polio, or typhoid, or cancer.' Once the purpose has been achieved, the doctors discover further problems and formulate further purposes; 'Medicine ends up, therefore, as a total science, whose structure is essentially that of a bag of tricks.' Some tricks are extremely valuable and their discovery brings freedom from quite real troubles. And yet 'Cannon wrote a book on *The Wisdom of the Body*, but nobody has written a book on the wisdom of medical science, because wisdom is precisely the thing which it lacks. Wisdom I take to be the knowledge of the larger interactive system – that system which, if disturbed, is likely to generate exponential curves of change.' To help visualize the overall results of the expert-type purpose-oriented thinking, Bateson offers a parable of Eden:

> On one of the trees there was a fruit, very high up, which the two apes were unable to reach. So they began to *think*. That was the mistake. They began to think purposively.
>
> By and by, the he ape, whose name was Adam, went and got an empty box and put it under the tree and stepped on it, but he found he still couldn't reach the fruit. So he got another box and put it on top of the first. Then he climbed on the two boxes and finally he got that apple.
>
> Adam and Eve then became almost drunk with excitement. *This* was the way to do things. Make a plan, ABC and you get D.
>
> They began to specialize in doing things the planned way. In effect, they

[10] Cf. Gregory Bateson, 'Conscious Purpose versus Nature', in *Steps to an Ecology of Mind*, pp. 402–14.

> cast out from the Garden the concept of their own total systemic nature and of its total systemic nature.
>
> After they had cast God out of the Garden, they really went to work on this purposive business, and pretty soon the topsoil disappeared. After that, several species of plants became 'weeds' and some of the animals became 'pests'; and Adam found that gardening was much harder work . . .
>
> Eve began to resent the business of sex and reproduction. Whenever these rather basic phenomena intruded upon her now purposive way of living, she was reminded of the larger life which had been kicked out of the Garden. So Eve began to resent sex and reproduction, and when it came to parturition she found this process very painful.

The moral of the parable is plain. Each problem-resolution begets new problems. (One is almost tempted to say: what passes for the resolution of a problem *A* is the articulation of problems *B*, *C*, . . . *n* that need to be resolved; knowledge increases in the course of problem-resolution, but so does the quantity of problems.) In fact it is the purpose-oriented action that bears the main responsibility for generating such aspects of the human condition as are experienced as uncomfortable, worrying and in need of rectifying. Chasing a specific remedy for a specific inconvenience, the expert-prompted action is bound to throw out of balance both the system-like environment of action, and the relations between the actors themselves. It is this artificially created imbalance which is later experienced as a 'problem' and thus seen as the warranty for the articulation of new purposes.

There is, however, one more message in the parable less immediately evident. It is hidden in Eve's redefinition of the 'larger life' necessities (which she presumably bore before with equanimity) as burdensome, annoying and unendurable – and, above all, unwarranted. With purposive thinking firmly in the saddle, no pain, suffering or just reality slightly short of promised and hence imaginable perfection seems to carry meaning and therefore needs to be lived with. Instead it is now perceived as contingency, as a discomfort which ought (with due determination and the right skills and resources) to be removed from life altogether. In this process, again, the capacity of purpose-thinking for self-propagation and expansion is revealed.

The second way in which the self-multiplication of expertise-demanding problems is assured has been analysed with striking poignancy by Jacques Ellul. Technology, says Ellul, develops because it develops;[11] technology

---

[11] Jacques Ellul, *Technological System*, trans. Joachim Neugroschel (New York: Continuum, 1980), p. 267.

proceeds in a causal, never in a goal-oriented fashion.[12] There seems to be a contradiction between Bateson's analysis of the dynamics of expertise in terms of purposes and Ellul's blunt verdict. The conflict is, however, merely apparent. The purpose-thinking supplies the general legitimation for the strategic role claimed by expertise and technology in the management of daily life. Once the authority has been obtained and entrenched, once the situation has been reached that 'man in our society has no intellectual, moral, or spiritual reference point for judging and criticizing technology', mostly because a closed circle has been created so that 'nothing can have an intrinsic sense; it is given meaning only by technological application'[13] – technology does not need any more a legitimation to keep it on course. Expertise and technology become their own legitimation. Indeed, technology becomes a set of 'solutions in search of problems'.[14] The sheer presence of technological know-how and spare resources takes over as the prime factor of further development that in turn justifies their need and their claims to an increasing share of social resources and growing social esteem.

> Technology never advances towards anything but *because* it is pushed from behind. The technician does not know why he is working, and generally he

---

[12] Jacques Ellul, 'The Power of Technique and the Ethics of Non-Power', in *The Myths of Information; Technology and Postindustrial Culture*, ed. Kathleen Woodward (London: Routledge, 1980), p. 243.

[13] Ellul, *Technological System*, pp. 318, 12.

[14] Margaret Blunden, Owen Greene and John Naughton, 'The Alchemists of Our Time', in *Science and Mythology in the Making of Defence Policy*, ed. Margaret Blunden and Owen Greene (London: Brassey, 1989), p. 84. The authors quote Lord Zuckerman to the effect that the weapon scientists generate ideas which only 'subsequently obtain *post hoc* strategic rationalization'. Ralph Lapp (*Arms Beyond Doubt: the Tyranny of Weapon Development* (London: Cowles, 1971)) alongside many other authors collected considerable evidence that the dynamics of armaments is guided by and large by the principle that 'if it can be done, it will be'. Inventions of new defensive methods only intensify the search for offensive weapons. New discoveries are mainly responses to the redefinition of problems that has been caused by other discoveries. The designers of offensive weapons and the designers of defensive weapons are racing against each other, supplying for each other 'problems' 'to be resolved'. Often the sheer reference to problems becomes redundant: new technology does not need anymore utilitarian justifications. Dietrich Schroer (*Science, Technology, and the Nuclear Arms Race* (New York: Wiley, 1984)) wrote of technologies that are difficult to resist simply because they are 'sweet and beautiful'. The more secure their funding, the more esoteric the specialist knowledge they boast, the fuller their institutional and intellectual autonomy, the more are technology and expertise guided by quasi-aesthetic criteria, turning into an 'art for the art's sake'.

> does not much care. He works *because* he has instruments allowing him to perform a certain task, to succeed in a new operation . . .
>
> There is no call towards a goal; there is constraint by an engine placed in the back and not tolerating any halt for the machine . . .
>
> The interdependence of technological elements makes possible a very large number of 'solutions' for which there are no problems . . .
>
> Given that we can fly to the moon, what can we do *on it* and *with it*? . . . When technicians came to a certain degree of technicity in radio, fuels, metals, electronics, cybernetics etc., all these things combined and made it obvious that we could fly into the cosmos, etc. It was done because it could be done. That is all.[15]

In other words, expertise becomes its own cause (rather than its own purpose). It is not, strictly speaking, the case of an 'expertise for its own sake' (or 'for' anything else, as it were). It is, rather, the case of an expertise that appears because the setting is there in which it can be generated, because that what has been already created 'cannot be wasted' and because it is wrong – unwise and shameful – not to do what one, in principle, is capable of doing. Major advances in the development of expertise and its technological implements are measured now by the discovery and targeting of the 'problems' to which it has become capable of providing 'solutions', rather than by finding solutions to already perceived and articulated problems. The already accumulated knowledge and know-how seek feverishly their application. They rechart the human condition as the object of their 'new and improved' practices.

Because of the causal, rather than teleogical, determination of the advances of expertise and its uses, it is in practice inconceivable that the development may ever grind to a halt. In particular, it is unthinkable that a facility already available, or thought to be within reach, may be laid aside and not be used deliberately because of some other, non-technical considerations, like for instance its moral questionability, or philosophical conceptions of the intrinsic value of human autonomy.

Whenever the latter clash with the application of technological potential, they are automatically classified as retrograde and by the same token dismissed and condemned. Alternatively, as the development of technological expertise is not subject to any specific purpose but the duty to deploy the deployable, all reasons for which a particular line of development might be abandoned are *a priori* delegitimized and dismissed as technologically meaningless and therefore irrelevant. All in all, the extrinsic, non-technological reasons are denied the right and authority to interfere with the direction the development of expertise and technical capability may

---

15 Ellul, *Technological System*, pp. 272, 273, 280.

take. The essence of the self-legitimation of expertise (and at the same time of its declaration of independence, self-sufficiency and moral immunity) is contained in the increasingly fashionable commercial slogan: 'Everything you can do, you can do better.' And in its obverse: 'It is a crime, or a sin, not to do better if you can.'

> [With the majority of products] supply comes before demand and the technical discussion on the characteristics of the products takes the place of any analysis of social demand. These technical arguments are twofold. On the one hand, since these new technical capabilities have appeared, it is necessary to utilize them so as not to be behind the times; on the other hand, their use allows one to do more, better and with less effort than before, and this can only lead to greater happiness.[16]

Let us cast another glance at the two factors which more than any other circumstances prevent expertise from slowing down its expansion, and its grip on the life-world from weakening.

First, as each act of expert problem-solving is focused on the task at hand, and as the perfection of expertise is measured by its ability to define the tasks at hand 'more precisely' (i.e. circumscribe them more narrowly), the more effective the applications of expert knowledge become the less likely the experts are to glean the effects of their actions on the areas left out of focus. The effects of individual, area-specific expert practices spill far beyond their ostensible (falsely assumed to be autonomous) sector of application and come into contact with other expert practices which, more often than not, are equally narrow-focused. If expert practices combine into a system, such system emerges *ex post facto* as an unanticipated consequence of many actions which can be effective only if they refuse to anticipate – indeed, acknowledge – the systemness of their consequences. No one overviews the process of system emergence, and no one may scan, much less control, the operation of the emergent system.

Yet this 'getting out of control' is not the result of complacency or an oversight. Neither can it be rectified or prevented. Were the systemic consequences of expert practice taken into account, effectivity of expertise would be undermined. Voluntary blindness to systemic consequences is the necessary *condition* of expert success. The spectacular results of expert intervention have not been achieved *despite* this blindness, but *because* of it. The choice is between blindness and impotence. Expertise thrives thanks to its skill of atomization, of splitting the natural system into

---

[16] Victor Scardigli, François Plessard and Pierre-Alain Mercier, 'Information Technology and Daily Life', in *Information Technology Impact on the Daily Life*, EEC Conference on the Information Society held in Dublin 18–20 November 1980, ed. Liam Bannon *et al.* (Dublin: Tywoly International Publishing, 1982), p. 41.

an ever growing multitude of ever smaller and hence more manageable tasks. Short of surrendering the very essence of its power, it cannot but gestate, therefore, a nature-like, unplanned and uncontrolled, yet man-made system out of the by-products of its own success. If this is the case, however, then the very progress of expert knowledge and practice adds to the unpredictability and uncontrollability of the system. As we have noted so many times before, the sheer effort 'to put things in order' spawns ever new areas of ambivalence running out of control. New problems continue to be produced, and with them new demand for expert action; no self-healing is conceivable if the disease is an outcome of external interference with natural self-equilibrating mechanism. Most new developments in expertise and expertly produced 'targeted' technology are aimed at the repairing of damage perpetrated by older technology and expertise. Damage done by expertise may be cured only by more expertise. More expertise means, in its turn, yet more damage and more demand for expert cure.

Second, access of expertise to the life-worlds of its clients (and vice versa) is mediated by the *market*. Expert services offered either directly or in the wrapping of consumer goods appear in the modern world primarily as commodities; while serving the needs of the consumer, they also bring profits to the merchandising agents. New expert offers promising to tap (or, rather, to generate) as yet non-satisfied demand are from the merchants' point of view particularly attractive for the extra gains expected to be creamed off because of the temporary scarcity of supply. The market thrives on novelty that makes the stale stocks obsolete and opens or conjures up new markets. Market forces encourage novelty.

Since the new offers are aimed at heretofore absent needs, the volume of demand cannot be measured in advance, and thus their promotion entails a financial risk. New needs must be sustained by the sheer power of persuasion. The propaganda campaign may misfire or its potential effects may be pre-empted by a competitive action. On the whole, only a small part of new products captures the imagination of the consumer in a degree needed to bring substantial profit. The few successful innovations must pay for the losses incurred by the bulk of abortive ones. Since it is virtually impossible to predict which of the products will succeed in their efforts to create their own consumers, market forces emulate the prodigal extravagance of piscine procreation: thousands of expert offers must be hatched for a few to stay alive long enough to become profitable. While inventiveness is virtually unlimited, the volume of market opportunities seems to be finite. Under the circumstances, no market agent can ever afford to suspend the search for novelty, lest it should be snatched by the competition.

Marketing expertise

The contemporary consumer market does not adjust the level of supply to the existing demand, but aims at the creation of new demand to match the supply potential. The scope of demand eventually created depends on the effective assignment of use value to the supplied products. Prospective consumers will be willing to pay for the product if (and only if) they agree that they have a need which the product promises to gratify. But the agreement is not a matter of discovery of a heretofore unknown or ignored truth. As Marshall Sahlins convincingly argues,

> the social meaning of an object that makes it useful to a certain category of persons is no more apparent from its physical properties than is the value it may be assigned in exchange. Use-value is not less symbolic or less arbitrary than commodity value. For 'utility' is not a quality of the object but a significance of the objective qualities.[17]

A product is unlikely to be sold unless a 'utility' is imputed – and accepted. The exchange value it can legitimately hope for will depend on the scope and attraction of such utility. (Let us note that the advent of information technology made this rule even truer than it ever was before. Information is, in Gordon B. Thompson's apt expression, an 'ethereal good' – very cheap to produce, even cheaper to reproduce, and not disappearing in the process of being consumed. Because of such unusual attributes, ethereal goods have 'to win' their 'consensus value'. 'The value of ethereal good is a function of attraction given to that good by the society.' 'Utility', or the social attraction, of ethereal goods grows with their use and hence the latter must be monitored for the exchange value to be established and possibly boosted, as in the case of pop 'Top Twenty' or book bestsellers lists).[18] To acquire utility, the product must be first given 'significance' – and that means that a connection must be successfully construed between the product and a need of which the consumer may, or may not be aware. It is through the creation of new needs that new potential utilities, and thus also new exchange-values, are brought into being. In as far as the expertise remains a commodity, it falls under the general market rule. The first problem which all experts must face is therefore the creation of a need for themselves and their services, strong

---

[17] Marshall Sahlins, *Culture and Practical Reason* (Chicago: Chicago University Press, 1976), p. 169.

[18] Cf. Gordon B. Thompson, 'Ethereal Goods: The Economic Atom of the Information Society', in *Information Technology Impact*, ed. Bannon *et al.*, pp. 88–9.

enough to generate a supply-clearing demand. As Harold Perkin put it, the professions

> live by persuasion and propaganda, by claiming that their particular service is indispensable to the client or employer and to society and the state. By this means they hope to raise their status and through it their income, authority and psychic rewards (deference and self-respect) . . . That on occasion the service is neither essential nor efficient is no obstacle to the principle. It only needs to be thought so by those providing and receiving it.[19]

We have discussed before the reasons for which a generalized demand for expertise can be considered as firmly and irrevokably established. Such reasons, let us recall, are related to the fact that the life-world cannot be any more sustained and reproduced without the assistance of the experts or their products, and to certain immanent features of expert practice responsible for the continuous reproduction of demand for new expertise on an ever growing scale. (In Vanderburg's summary, when 'faced with considerable problems, many of which are directly or indirectly related to the growth of technique, virtually the only response recognized as being viable is to resolve these problems by accelerating technical development'. It seems 'as if history has only one pathway left, namely that of technique').[20] If the discussed reasons assure that all needs, past or prospective, must be met with some kind of expert-managed solution and some kind of expertly designed technique, and that new solutions will be always offered to past or prospective needs – they do not by themselves guarantee success of any particular kind of expert commodity. 'Utility' of an already socially accepted expert product must be sustained against new competitive challenges, and new 'utilities' must be created to make room for novel, and previously not offered, expert products. The exchange value of expertise must legitimize itself in terms of its use value. Use value, in turn, must refer to the needs of the individual consumer. The invoked needs are, as a rule, of a general kind, and thus are able to claim 'objective' grounds for recognition. The merchandising of expertise consists then in the focusing of such general needs on a specific expert product.

There are several general needs to which appeals are most frequently, and successfully, made. In the case of some of them, new expert products promise to replace the absent or forgotten skills which once served their satisfaction. In the case of some others, new expert products promise to do

---

19 Perkin, *The Rise of Professional Society*, pp. 6, 360.
20 Vanderburg in *Democratic Theory*, p. 20.

better what their predecessors failed to do, thereby accomplishing a double feat: they sustain the popular trust in the capacity of expertise 'as such' to deliver on its promise, even if its individual offers are not up to the task; they also discredit and devalue past expert products which have reached the peak of their selling potential – so that space can be cleared for the continuing output of expertise. In both types of case, the expert backing for the merchandised products is the decisive selling point. Expert backing offers the consumer the craved-for certainty and balance of mind – a welcome change from the doubt and anxiety which would have remained (or would become) the lot of the individuals left to their own (now devalued and rendered obsolete) skills or insufficient resources. Expertise promises the individuals means and abilities to escape uncertainty and ambivalence and thus to control their own life-world. It presents the dependency on the experts as the liberation of the individual; heteronomy as autonomy.

We have already discussed at some length the mechanism which allows such dependency, disguised as freedom, to penetrate (or, depending on the point of view, to be admitted into) the life-world of the individual through activities aimed at the establishment of self-identity. Similar mechanisms operate in the case of other general needs. Closely related to the need for self-construction is the need for *distinction* – or, which amounts to the same, of the acquisition of an unambiguous location inside the social order. Marshall Sahlins has suggested that with the erosion of the old order, operated mostly by heredity and ascription (both resilient to individual manipulation), purchasable and consumable products took over as the essential building blocks of the new totemic system.[21] We may add that such products, imbued with totemic significance, offer individuals several things at once. They allocate specific patterns of life-style to specific rungs of the social ladder. They offer kits containing all the necessary symbols with which any life-style can be assembled. And they supply a social (though not necessarily 'money-back') guarantee that such assembly will indeed result in the genuine product. In other words, totemic products offer the overall framework within which all the future selection of life-projects must be located, define the acquisition of expert-produced skills and expert-produced objects as the prime vehicle of such selection, and inject the selection-process with certainty of social approval. In such a way, individual energy of self-assertion, through the DIY labour, is harnessed in the service of the reproduction of social order.

---

21 Cf. Sahlins, *Culture and Practical Reason*, pp. 176–7.

Hiding from ambivalence

Expert advice and expert-designed objects which allow their possessors to act in a way authorized by expert knowledge cater also for another crucial need of the individual: that of *rationality*. Characterized as it has been from its inception by a radical intolerance of any form of life different from itself, modern society can conceive of such difference only as ignorance, superstition or retardation. A form of life may be admitted into the realm of the tolerable and offered a citizenship status in the land of modernity only if first naturalized, trimmed of all oddity and in the end subjugated: only in a form, that is, in which it can be fully translated into the language of rational choice, which is modernity's own.

Assumption of a monopolistic right to invest meaning, and to judge all forms of life from the superior vantage-point of this monopoly, is the essence of modern social order. The assumption makes 'the error of one's ways' a constant possibility and a permanent source of fear for the modern man and woman. Certification of rationality of one's acts and beliefs becomes a residence permit which must be constantly renewed and can be renewed only on the ground of good behaviour. As Hans Peter Duerr points out, 'scientists constitute the force that does the categorizing, the intellectual "police force". They do not form one particular contingent, but are grouped into troops with different tasks. Some of these units could with a bit of malice be seen as virtual stormtroopers. In a blatant and rather transparent way, they mount the *defence* against what is strange.'[22] As in the case of any police force, the scientists' power to permit and to forbid is difficult to evade. Yet the ways through which the scientists arrive at their decisions are, for the lay member of sociey, even more difficult to fathom than in the case of the police invoking legal rules and statuses: expert knowledge is securely guarded against lay penetration by its esoteric and evanescent nature. The two circumstances together cast science as the uncontested manager of the paramount sources of uncertainty and thereby reproduce the classic pattern of power and dependency. Lay members of society must be rational, but they cannot be rational wihout being guided by the verdicts of science and without being offered algorithmic, or at least heuristic prescriptions for action that carry approval of the experts. Lay desire to be rational lubricates the fly-wheel of expertise.

Need to be rational is grounded, as it were, in the continuing (and, under the circumstances, irreparable) ambiguity and 'messiness' of the

---

[22] Hans Peter Duerr, *Dreamline: Concerning the Boundary between Wilderness and Civilization*, trans. Felicitas Goodwin (Oxford: Blackwell, 1985), p. 126.

life-world. Subjected to the intervention of uncoordinated, mutually autonomous, authorities, the life-world is fraught with contradictory messages, pressures pointing in opposite directions, needs which cannot be satisfied without sacrificing or endangering other needs. All this further exacerbates the real danger and the fear of error. One wrong turn may lead the individual into a blind alley or take him or her to a point of no return. The messy life-world might have had its rewards (thanks to the messiness, no option seems to be irrevocably foreclosed; in a messy life-world, there seem to be no points of no return), but no doubt it is replete with anxiety-arousing conflicts and so its blessings cannot but be mixed. A 'varied and unprogrammed exchange' with the human and natural environment is 'full of difficulties, temptations, hard choices, challenges, surprises'.[23]

The enshrinement of rationality of choice and conduct is itself a choice, a decision to give preference to order over muddiness, security over surprise, constancy of results over random succession of gains and losses. It denigrates contingency and glorifies unambiguity. Moreover, it presents full clarity of the life-world and a chance of gains free from the risk of losses as a *realistic possibility* and a sensible purpose to be strived for. It promises a world free of uncertainty, spiritual torments, intellectual hesitations. Not that such a sanitized world is to be uniform and dreary in its lack of alternatives and choices. But in such a world, however dazzling and full of temptation, variety will be tamed, and its sting will be pulled out. Variety will be retained only as a choice between actions which are all rational and safe, so that the *drama* of life will turn into pure and safe *entertainment*. In such a world, the very chance of wrong choice (i.e., irrationality) will be eliminated, and hence the very distinction between rationality and irrationality will cease to exist. The ultimate limit of rationality is its self-transcendence, when the battles from which it derived its martial glory in the past fizzle out and only windmills may be hired to play the role of the enemy.

In the Shannon-inspired 'informational' vision of the world and human practice that loomed tacitly as the intellectual background for most of the contemporary strategy of technological progress, the role of the 'evil empire' was played by *noise* or *randomness*. The random equals chaotic equals uncontrolled. The proclaimed target of information technology, like that of any other modern project and strategy, has been the elimination of noise. In practical terms, this means full control of the message by the sender (which includes the power to determine an unambiguous reception of the message by the recipient). With all random interference with the message and all choice of its interpretation subdued or elimin-

[23] Ellul, *Technological System*, p. 314.

ated 'it is precisely autonomous action which is repressed (or repressively tolerated) by the technological society'.[24] The ultimate limit of the war against noise is a fully controlled life-world and complete heteronomy of the individual – an individual located unambiguously on the receiving end of information flow and having his choices safely enclosed within a frame strictly defined by the expert authority.

The great American institution of the shopping mall offers a glimpse into such a world, coming closer than any other aspect of contemporary life to the ideal type of triumphant rationality. Malls are an escape from the messiness of the 'real world'. They offer a controlled, physically and spiritually secure environment for an alternative life-world, in which the joy of choosing is not polluted by the fear of error, as there are only 'rational choices' left – any choice has its propriety guaranteed in advance. Unlike the 'real' one, the world of malls is free from overlapping categories, mixed messages and semiotic unclarity rebounding in behavioural ambiguity. In the mall, the environment is carefully monitored (literally and metaphorically), neatly split into thematic sections, each reduced to clear-cut, stereotyped and easy-to-read symbols with virtually all danger of ambiguous interpretation removed. (Whatever ambivalence there is has been carefully planned, and the awareness of this makes it look safe and downright enjoyable.) Inside the mall the experts do not merely offer guidance through the mysteries of the world and safe passage around its traps. Experts have *created* this world, and created it according to their own thoroughly rationalized design, which for the reason of being rationally designed contains no mysteries or traps, and thus claims to be better – simpler, safer, more transparent – than the world left behind the thick walls and the electronically operated gates. In the expert-made world, the very irrationality has been colonized, everything including irrationality is subordinated to rational design, and thus rationality loses its militant edge. Even surprises are carefully programmed. The exhilarating experience of going on a binge, letting oneself go, being unreasonable – can be safely enjoyed. Even catastrophe is a concept in a game ingeniously designed by the experts and conducted according to rules which prevent it from running out of hand.

The malls do not sell commodities only. They sell an alternative life-world, one in which control and responsibility is ceded to the experts – and ceded willingly and joyously, as the surrender is rewarded with the comfort of always being in the right. In the malls it is the project of the expert-designed life-world that is merchandised and market-tested.

The malls are also a message – though this they are unknowingly. The

---

[24] Kathleen Woodward in *The Myths of Information*, ed. Woodward, p. xix.

message is one of the total collapse of the glorious dream of the perfect and global, reason-controlled order. Marx remarked that history occurs twice: once as a tragedy, the second time as a farce. The malls signify the grotesque restaging of the Enlightenment drama. They do offer a perfect, reason-controlled world with all extant (or deliberately designed) ambivalence carefully controlled: but the reason-ruled world they offer is a global order only thanks to the thick, impenetrable, heavily guarded walls inside which it is enclosed. The utopia of the sages has retired from the real world into a safe retreat where it need not fear any more the chaos its ordering zeal spawns. Electronic spies, anti-theft alarms and self-locking narrow entrances cut out this miniaturized utopia from the rest of the life-world abandoned to its apparently ineradicable messiness. Wonders of harmony and perfection are now offered as entertainment – for family Sunday outings and enjoyment. No one thinks they are real. Most agree, though, that they are better than real. And everybody knows that reality will never be like they are.

The tendencies and limits of the expert-designed world

According to Michel Benamon's witty classification, writers concerned with the prospects of the expert-led, technologized world may be divided into four groups, according to the classic 'four humours'. They range all the way from happy technophiles (guided by *Agape*: Marshall McLuhan and Buckminster Fuller being most prominent among them), through anxious technophiles (*Logos*: Lewis Mumford of the 1930s), hopeful technophobes (*Eros*: Goodman, Illich, Roszak, the late Marcuse), up to desperate technophobes (*Thanatos*: Ellul, the late Mumford, the earlier Marcuse);[25] from apostles of Good Tidings to the prophets of imminent doom. All the categories agree, however, that the change perpetrated in the life-world of modern man by the elevation of expertise and unstoppable technologization of the human environment has been radical and in all probability irreversible. The human world will never again be as it was before the ascendance of technology. Whether the change amounts to greater happiness or deeper misery is subject to dispute and bound to remain a moot issue. Depending on their own degree of optimism, anxiety or despair, observers and analysts have focused and will focus their descriptions and diagnoses on what they consider the more attractive, or

---

25 Michael Benamon, 'Notes on the Technological Imagination', in *The Technological Imagination: Theories and Fictions*, ed. Teresa de Lauretis, Andreas Huyssen and Kathleen Woodward (Madison: Coda Press, 1980), p. 67.

the less prepossessing traits of the expertly designed future. They would belittle, therefore, the significance of such attributes as detract from the unity of their vision. And yet they would hardly deny their presence. Though assigned widely varying importance for human well-being (and, sometimes, even varying value), certain features of the new world emerging at our end of the modern era are nevertheless almost universally acknowledged. In what follows, some of such features, which seem to be crucial for any assessment of the prospects of expert-led society, will be briefly discussed.

There is an aspect in the Shannon-initiated informatic revolution which seems to possess particularly far-reaching consequences for the new shape of the expert-guided world: namely the explicit bracketing away, and implicit denigration of the 'content' of the message, now fully replaced by the consideration of the measures of quantity. Information as a measurable value has been divorced – and emancipated – from the semantic 'content' of statements.[26] The historical act of divorce had two closely related results. First, the quality of both the sender and the receiver of a message have been made irrelevant to the evaluation of information, now focused exclusively on what is happening 'in the wire' between speaker and listener – on the task of delivering the message (whatever its content, and whoever has sent it) undistorted. This means not so much the neutrality or vaunted non-partisanship of information technology, as its unambiguous slant in favour of control (more precisely, in favour of the determining force of the sender over the recipient, secured through the hired services of the information-processing expert; a bias in favour of information as an object and a means of management). Second, information can be evaluated solely by its volume, without regard to its content. Information theory allows one to diagnose information and set preferences for its improvement without referring to the matters of significance or importance. (Or, rather, it leaves the right to pronounce on the value of transmission entirely in the communicator's hands.) Indeed, the theory and the technology which it spawns and legitimizes have no means of distinguishing between distinct sets of information in any other terms but their respective volumes. Two sets of information equal in quantity (as defined by an accepted method of measurement) are equivalent in all other respects (or, rather, 'other respects' can not be sensibly spoken about at all). This new position is well captured in the highly popular game of 'Trivial Pursuit' – a vivid, emotionally reassuring rehearsal of the irrelevance of the semantic aspect of information and an entertaining method of self-training in the use of quantity as the sole measure of quality of both knowledge and its owners.

---

[26] Cf. Roszak, *The Cult of Information*, pp. 10–12.

In its resolute drive towards more technical efficiency, expertise must dissolve all 'totalities' – as it focuses instead on their accessible and manageable segments. This perpetual tendency of expertise has recently received a formidable extension (and a potentially sinister twist) with the advent of information technology, and particularly of the new totalities of large interconnected computer networks. To the development of such totalities, the awesome expertise ingrained in software production, like all technically smart expertise, can contribute in a piecemeal fashion only. It can be effective in their construction only in as far as it remains oblivious of their emergent qualities, or consciously disregards their presence. Continuously, new fragments are added to the total system with little, if any, knowledge of their impact on the set of programs which had been fed in before. Despite (or is it because?) being an utterly artificial, man-made product, the computer system develops nevertheless in a nature-like, spontaneous and uncontrolled mode, so that no one is capable of overviewing the total effect. Geoff Simons has suggested that

> the largest software systems grow in an uncontrolled, increasingly incomprehensible, fashion. If a problem arises, a new piece of programme is written on an immediate technological 'fix': it may solve the problem in a short term, but its long-term effects on the established programmes are unknown and totally unpredictable. Hence the largest computer software systems evolve in a disorganized fashion, particular programmers understanding bits here and bits there, but no one understanding the system as a whole.[27]

One of the most remarkable consequences of the loosening connection and growing incommensurability between the operations of any single programmer and the capacity of the software system as a whole is the *flotation of responsibility* for the ultimate outcome of computer-mediated action. Such flotation is not, of course, a novelty introduced by the computer age. The advent of computer systems only added new momentum to an old and permanent tendency of technically oriented expertise – and enabled it to develop on an unprecedented, heretofore inconceivable scale. As we have seen before, expertise can perform adequately only if the systemic consequences of the problem-oriented performance are lost from sight or deliberately put aside. And yet before the advent of the computer age it was other experts who dealt with side-effects of expert practices; there was always an identifiable person standing behind every action. One could engage in an interminable argument as to the actual degree of each person's responsibility, and as to which one of the many

[27] Geoff Simons, *Silicon Shock: The Menace of Computer Invasion* (Oxford: Basil Blackwell, 1985), p. 161.

interconnected actions bore the decisive causal relation to the given effect. The argument could, however, be conducted (however counterfactually and inconclusively) in personal terms. It is this *possibility* which the advent of computer systems has all but excluded.

Our analysis has shown that the institutions socially gestated to fight individual (privatized) ambivalence have turned into the main mechanisms of keeping alive, reviving and reinforcing the very phenomenon they defined as the most sinister of life banes, the very phenomenon whose once-for-all elimination was declared as such institutions' *raison d'être*. They generate more ambivalence than they vanquish, and from this new ambivalent side-effect of their struggle against ambivalence they draw the energy they need to generate yet more ambivalence and the legitimation for the continuation of their action ... The sum total of ambivalence on both the personal and societal plane seems to grow unstoppably. Ambivalence seems to thrive on the very efforts to destroy it, making the original prospect of an orderly, rationally structured life-world inscribed into an orderly, rationally structured social system increasingly distant and nebulous. The trained urge to escape from the 'messiness' of the life-world has exacerbated the very condition from which escape was sought.

Creation of a world free of ambiguity, the transparent world of rational choices, failed to emerge from the ordering efforts of modern authorities – political and scientific alike. By almost universal admission it is not likely to result either from such efforts in the future, however impressive the advances of science and of its technical applications. Growing wiser and wary of too many hopes turned into nightmares, modern society seems now slowly to reconcile itself to the ineluctable partiality of orders it is capable of constructing – and thus to the non-finality of any ordering project and of the permanence and omnipresence of ambivalence. It might as well – just might – make the best of the condition it is no longer at war with; to do so, however, it would have to recant its crusade against 'irrational' ethics and values in general.

The drive towards the rule of reason, as long as it was hoped that it might end in victory, could serve as a temporary substitute for morally guided orientation.[28] In a world in which plurality of orders and ambivalence have been – enthusiastically or grudgingly – granted the right of permanent residence, such a substitute is no more available, and pluralism rebounds as a loss of orientation and helplessness – a bitter irony for an era that proclaimed the omnipotence of man.

---

[28] I have discussed this topic at length in *Modernity and the Holocaust*, chap. 8. See also my study 'Effacing the Face', in *Theory, Culture and Society*, vol. 7/1 (Spring 1990).

7

Postmodernity, or Living with Ambivalence

We could try to transform our contingency into our destiny.

Agnes Heller

In one respect the social sciences born in the age of Enlightenment have not failed – writes Agnes Heller: 'they have indeed provided self-knowledge, and they never ceased providing self-knowledge of *modern* society, of a *contingent* society, of one society among many, *our society*'.[1] And yet, let us observe, this partial success was itself a failure, if judged by the standards of the social sciences' ambition. Whatever modern social sciences did, they did not deliver *on their promise*; instead, with no knowing and even less intending, they delivered something they did not promise; to put it bluntly, they were delivering a reasonable product all along under the false pretences of supplying something else altogether . . . Awareness of contingency – of the contingency of the modern self, of the contingency of modern society – was not what they, their prophets, their apostles, their intended converts and aspiring beneficiaries bargained for. If one agrees with Heller that the social sciences, all their self-deception notwithstanding, did supply precious knowledge later to be appreciated as an insight into contingency, one must still insist that they did it while misconceiving the true nature of their business, or that they did it while trying to pass their products for something other than it was (thus remaining – knowingly or unknowingly – in breach of the official trading act . . .): that they informed of *contingency* while believing themselves to narrate *necessity*, of particular *locality* while believing themselves to narrate *universality*, of tradition-bound interpretation while believing

[1] Agnes Heller, 'From Hermeneutics in Social Science toward a Hermeneutics of Social Science', in *Theory and Society*, vol. 18 (1989), pp. 291–322. Other quotations from Heller that follow come from the same source.

themselves to narrate the extraterritorial and extratemporal truth, of undecidability while believing themselves to narrate transparency, of the provisionality of the human condition while believing themselves to narrate the certainty of the world, of the *ambivalence* of man-made design while believing themselves to narrate the *order* of nature.

It was all these beliefs (false beliefs), and not their deliveries (useful deliveries) that made the social sciences, and the mentality from which they arose, and the power structure that contemplated itself in that mentality, *modern*. For most of its history, modernity lived in and through self-deception. Concealment of its own parochiality, conviction that whatever is not universal in its particularity is but not-yet-universal, that the project of universality may be incomplete, but remains most definitely on, was the core of that self-deception. It was perhaps thanks to that self-deception that modernity could deliver both the wondrous and the gruesome things that it did; in this, as in so many other cases, ignorance, so to speak, turned out to be a privilege. The question is: is the fading of self-deception a final fulfilment, emancipation, or the end of modernity?

The distinctive feature of the belief in the truth of one's knowledge is not the conviction that the knowledge in question is satisfying, pleasing, useful, or otherwise worth holding to. Such a conviction does not require the belief in truth for support. More often than not, this conviction can be and is held without worry about authoritative confirmation that the belief in truth is sound. Where one cannot do without the 'well grounded concept of truth' is when it comes to tell others that they are in error and hence (1) ought or must change their minds, thus (2) confirming the superiority (read: right to command) of the holder of truth (read: the giver of command). The bid for truth as a claimed quality of knowledge arises therefore solely in the context of hegemony and proselytism; in the context of coexistence of autonomously sustained bodies of knowledge of which at least one refuses to coexist peacefully and respect the existing borders; in the context of plurality that is treated by at least one member as a vexing state to be rectified; in the context of a balance of forces under pressure to turn into asymmetry of power.

Truth is, in other words, a *social relation* (like *power*, *ownership* or *freedom*): an aspect of a hierarchy built of superiority–inferiority units; more precisely, an aspect of the hegemonic form of domination or of a bid for domination-through-hegemony. Modernity was, from its inception, such a form and such a bid. The part of the world that adopted modern civilization as its structural principle and constitutional value was bent on dominating the rest of the world by dissolving its alterity and assimilating the product of dissolution. The persevering alterity could not but be treated as a temporary nuisance; as an error, sooner or later bound to be supplanted by truth. The battle of order against chaos in wordly affairs was replicated by the war of truth against error on the plane of consciousness. The order bound to be installed and made universal was a *rational* order; the truth bound to be made triumphant was the *universal* (hence apodictic and obligatory) truth. Together, political order and true knowledge blended into a design for *certainty*. The rational-universal world of order and truth would know of no contingency and no ambivalence. The target of certainty and of absolute truth was indistinguishable from the crusading spirit and the project of domination.

While setting itself apart, making itself distinct so that it would be possible to reserve a position of command toward the rest of the *oikoumene*, modernity thought of itself as of the seed of future universality, as of an entity destined to replace all other entities and thus to abolish the very difference between them. It thought of the *differentiation* it perpetrated as of *universalization*. This was modernity's self-deception. This was, however, a self-deception bound to disclose itself even without outside help (there was, anyway, no 'outside' left, allowed the legitimacy to disclose anything); a self-deception that could last only as long as it worked toward that disclosure. The self-deception supplied the courage and the confidence to pursue that lonely work of universality that spawned ever more difference; to persevere in such a chase of uniformity as was bound to result in more ambivalence. The self-deception of modernity was pregnant with its self-disclosure.

It is perhaps the fruit of that pregnancy that Agnes Heller dubbed the 'death wish' that was to be found at the other end of the long march toward 'wish-fulfillment'; that was to be, as we tried to argue here, the latter's inescapable heir and successor. Awareness of contingency, though a prodigal child, was a fully legitimate offspring of blind self-confidence; it could not but be born of it and it could not be born of any other parent. The residents of the house of modernity had been continuously trained to feel at home under conditions of necessity and to feel unhappy at the face of contingency; contingency, they had been told, was that state of discomfort and anxiety from which one needed to escape by making oneself into a binding norm and thus doing away with difference. Present unhappiness is the realization that this is not to be, that the hope will not come true and hence one needs to learn to live without the hope that supplied the meaning – the only meaning – to life. As Richard Rorty observed: 'The vocabularies are, typically, parasitic on the hopes – in the sense that the principal function of the vocabularies is to tell stories about future outcomes which compensate for present sacrifices'[2] – and, let us add, give

2 Rorty, *Contingency, Irony and Solidarity*, p. 86.

name to present sufferings; they narrate the present as *specific* suffering that needs a *concrete* sacrifice to cease be a suffering *as such*. We are unhappy today, as we have been left with the old vocabulary but without the hope that fed it with life juices. The rustle of desiccated, sapless words reminds us ceaselessly, obtrusively of the void that is where hope once was.

Having been trained to live in necessity, we have found ourselves living in contingency. And yet, being bound to live in contingency, we can, as Heller suggests, make 'an attempt to transform it into our destiny'. One makes something a destiny by embracing the fate: by an act of choice and the will to remain loyal to the choice made. Abandoning the vocabulary parasitic on the hope of (or determination for) universality, certainty and transparency is the first choice to be made; the first step on the road to emancipation. We cannot forget contingency any more; were it able to speak, contingency would repeat what Nietzsche wrote to his discoverer, friend and prophet Georg Brandes on 4 January 1889 (the day he finally withdrew from the concerns of mundane life): 'After you had discovered me, it was no trick to find me; the difficulty now is to lose me . . .'[3] But we can transfer contingency from the vocabulary of dashed hopes into that of the opportunity, from the language of domination into that of emancipation. Heller writes:

> An individual has transformed his or her contingency into his or her destiny if this person has arrived at the consciousness of having made the *best* out of his or her practically infinite possibilities. A society has transformed its contingency into its destiny if the members of this society arrive at the awareness that they would prefer to live at no other place and at no other time than the here and now.

From tolerance to solidarity

But, let us comment, that awareness that ushers into emancipation is not the only thing that happens on the road to contingency as destiny. The emancipation which contingency as destiny makes possible (one of those 'practically infinite possibilities') entails the *acceptance* that there are other places and other times that may be with equal justification (or equal absence of good reason) preferred by members of other societies, and that

[3] Quoted after Martin Heidegger, *What is Called Thinking*, trans. F.D. Wieck and J.G. Gray (New York: Harper & Row, 1968), p. 53. Cf. also Shoshana Felman, *Writing and Madness*, trans. Martha Noel Evans and author (Ithaca: Cornell University Press, 1985), p. 62.

however different they are, the choices cannot be disputed by reference to anything more solid and binding than preference and the determination to stick to the preferred. The preference for one's own, communally shared form of life must therefore be immune to the temptation of cultural crusade. Emancipation means such acceptance of one's own contingency as is grounded in recognition of contingency as the sufficient reason to live and to be allowed to live. It signals the end to the horror of alterity and to the abhorrence of ambivalence. Like truth, emancipation is not a quality of objects, but of the *relation* between them. The relation opened up by the act of emancipation is marked by the end of fear and the beginning of *tolerance*. It is on tolerance that the vocabulary of contingency-as-destiny is bound to be parasitic to allow emancipation to articulate.

As Rorty convincingly explains, the language of necessity, certainty and absolute truth cannot but articulate humiliation – humiliation of the other, of the different, of the not-up-to-the-standard. The language of contingency, on the contrary, creates a chance 'of being kind, by avoiding humiliation of others'.[4] Let us observe, however, that 'being kind' is not the end of the story either – not the final station on the road to emancipation. 'Being kind' and the tolerance for which it stands as a locutionary and behavioural symbol may well mean mere indifference and unconcern deriving from resignation (that is, from *fate*, not *destiny*): the Other will not go away and would not become like me, but then I have no means (at the moment, at least, or in the foreseeable future) to force him to go or to change. As we are doomed to share space and time, let us make our coexistence bearable and somewhat less dangerous. By being kind I invite kindness. I hope that my offer of reciprocity will be taken up; such a hope is my sole weapon. Being kind is but a way to keep the danger at a distance; like the proselytizing urge of yore, it arises out of fear.

To unravel the emancipatory potential of contingency-as-destiny, it would not suffice to avoid humiliating the others. One needs also to *respect* them – and respect them precisely in their otherness, in the preferences they have made, in their right to make preferences. One needs to honour the otherness in the other, the strangeness in the stranger, remembering – with Edmond Jabès – that 'the unique is universal', that it is being different that makes us resemble each other and that I cannot respect my own difference but by respecting the difference of the

---

[4] Rorty, *Contingency, Irony and Solidarity*, p. 91. But remember the inherent dangers of toleration discussed in the introduction. The kindness of the tolerant attitude does not by itself exclude the worst there is in humiliation: the assumption of inherent inferiority of the tolerated object. By itself, toleration may well be just another form in which virtues of the tolerant are re-asserted.

other. 'The case of the stranger concerns me not just because I myself am a stranger, but because it raises, for itself, the problems that we confront in principle and in daily applications of liberty, power, duty and fraternity: in the first place, the problem of equality of men; secondly, of our responsibility towards them and towards ourselves.'[5] My link with the stranger is revealed as *responsibility*, not just indifferent neutrality or even cognitive acceptance of the similarity of condition (and certainly not through the disdainful version of tolerance: 'It serves him well to be like that, and let him be, though I cannot imagine to be such myself'). It is revealed, in other words, as commonality of destiny, not mere resemblance of fate. Shared fate would do with mutual *tolerance*; joint destiny requires *solidarity*.

The right of the Other to his strangerhood is the only way in which my own right may express, establish and defend itself. It is from the right of the Other that my right is put together. The 'I am responsible for the Other', and 'I am responsible for myself', come to mean the same thing. Having chosen them both, and having them chosen as one thing, one indivisible attitude, not as two correlated, yet separate stances, is the meaning of the reforging contingency from fate into destiny. Call this as you like: fellow-feeling, imaginative identification, empathy; one thing you cannot say about such a choice is that it follows a rule or a command – be it an injunction of reason, a rule empirically demonstrated by truth-seeking knowledge, a command of God or a legal precept.

As a matter of fact, there is not much you can say about the cause of it at all. The new solidarity of the contingent is grounded in silence. Its hopes lie in refraining from asking certain questions and seeking certain answers; it is satisfied with its own contingency and does not wish to be elevated to the status of truth, necessity or certainty, knowing too well (or, rather, feeling intuitively) that it would not survive the promotion. Solidarity comes into its own when the language of necessity – the language of estrangement, discrimination and humiliation, falls out of use. Trying to pinpoint the most decisive mark of the ideal society – in his rendition, the ideal *liberal* society – Richard Rorty settled for people who 'would feel no more need to answer the question "Why are you a liberal?" '. In such a society a person 'would not need a justification for her sense of human solidarity, for she was not raised to play the language game in which one asks and gets justifications for that sort of belief'.[6]

Contingent existence means existence devoid of certainty, and one certainty that is missing at this desolate site of ours, or difficult to be

[5] Cf. Jabès, *Un Étranger avec, sous le bras, un livre de petit format*, pp. 112–15.
[6] Rorty, *Contingency, Irony and Solidarity*, p. 87.

excavated from beneath the debris of modern truths, is the certainty of solidarity. The road from tolerance to solidarity, like any other road, is undetermined; it is itself contingent. And so is the other road, one leading from tolerance to indifference and estrangement; it is equally contingent, and thus equally plausible. The state of tolerance is intrinsically and incurably ambivalent. It lends itself with equal ease, or equal difficulty, to celebratory praise and scornful condemnation; it may give occasion to joy as much as to despair. Living in contingency means living without a guarantee, with just a provisional, pragmatic, Pyrrhonic, until-further-notice certainty, and this includes the emancipatory effect of solidarity.

Modernity could dismiss its own uncertainty as a temporary affliction. Each uncertainty came complete with the recipe for curing it: just one more problem, and problems were defined by their solutions. (Societies, Marx insisted, never put before themselves tasks until means for their execution are available.) The passage from uncertainty to certainty, from ambivalence to transparency seemed to be a matter of time, of resolve, of resources, of *knowledge*. It is an entirely different matter to live with the postmodern awareness of no certain exit from uncertainty; of the escape from contingency being as contingent as the condition from which escape is sought. The discomfort such awareness brings about is the source of specifically postmodern discontents: discontent against the condition fraught with ambivalence, against the contingency that refuses to go away, and against the messengers of the news – those who attempt to spell out and articulate what is new and what is unlikely ever to return to the old: those who, to use again Agnes Heller's terms, call to turn the fate into destiny. What the recipients of the news find difficult to accept is that whatever they resolve to do would lack the comfort of having the truth, or the laws of history, or the unambiguous verdict of reason on its side.

Indeed, anyone seeking practical success would gain little from an insight into the postmodern condition. It cannot be denied that knowledge of this condition fails abominably by the standards set by modern knowledge (or, rather, by the promise that knowledge made and turned into the foundation of its elevated social standing). Awareness of contingency does not 'empower': its acquisition does not give the owner advantage over the protagonists in the struggle of wills and purposes, or in the game of cunning and luck. It does not lead to, or sustains, domination. As if to make the score even, it does not aid the struggle against domination either. It is, to put it bluntly, indifferent to the current or prospective structures of domination. Whoever is after domination – current or prospective (or whoever is just prompted to evaluate the quality of knowledge by the power to do things it promises to supply or make respectable) must be infuriated by the blandness of the refusal of that knowledge to validate all claims to superiority. Equally furious must be he who wishes to explode the domination that is.

And yet it is just a matter of perspective whether a trait is seen as an affliction or sign of soundness, a vice or a virtue. Dashing the hope of empowerment-through-knowledge amounts to the emphatic disavowal and rebuttal of the power struggle aimed at ultimate domination. It also amounts to the promotion of coexistence: the only condition whose stability, nay permanence, it allows. The awareness of the postmodern condition discloses tolerance as fate. It also makes possible – just possible – the long road from fate to destiny, from tolerance to solidarity.

The Exorcist and *The Omen*, or modern and postmodern limits to knowledge

Pretences of knowledge can be doubted in two ways. One can point out that there are events for which the kind of knowledge there is (knowledge that has received endorsement from the sites that men of knowledge admit to be sound and credible) does not have a convincing, agreed narrative; events that cannot be made into a story that men of knowlege would recognize as their own. Or one can say that the narrative that knowledge does offer is not the only story that may be told of the events; not even the best story, or at least not the only one able to claim the right to be considered 'better tested'. The first kind of doubt is modern; the second is postmodern. To say this is not to speak of chronological succession. Both modes of doubt have been around as long as science itself. Their co-presence was one of the constitutive features of that modern culture which prodded modernity on its road to postmodernity.

The two doubts have been given widely popular (populist?) literary form in the two works of fantasy – both huge box-office successes in their novelistic as well as their cinematic renditions.[7] They may well serve us as parables for the two doubts that silently yet unflaggingly sapped, and in the end toppled modern self-confidence.

Father Damien Karras of William Peter Blatty's novel *The Exorcist* turned exorcist only *after* all his and his professional colleagues' psychiatric routines, based on the most formidable, impeccably scholarly and up-to-date therapeutic skills and scientific knowledge, came to nought. Karras was, one may say, a psychiatrist's psychiatrist. Bearer of the most enviable

---

[7] Cf. William Peter Blatty, *The Exorcist* – first published by Blond & Briggs in 1972 – here quoted from the London Corgi edition of 1974; David Seltzer, *The Omen* (London: Futura Books, 1976).

scientific credentials, an alumnus of the most prestigious professional schools, a universally respected practitioner with a long record of spectacular therapeutic successes, a theorist armed with a truly encyclopaedic knowledge of the best scientific psychiatry could offer, a recipient of the most prestigious distinctions the profession could bestow – he was the scientific authority incarnate. Calling him to act on Regan's case was the ultimate resort and last hope of psychiatric science and practice: all his illustrious co-professionals, one by one and all together, tried, did their best and failed; the most up-to-date therapeutic technology proved insufficient. Karras's own actions – much as his accounts of the actions – were kept strictly within the frame of the collectively guarded scientific idiom; they were carefully calculated to restate, reaffirm and reinforce everything the profession believed and wanted its public to believe. Karras was not a witch-doctor or natural healer, that agent of dark and barbaric forces resisting the modern science set to annihilate them; like his learned colleagues who turned to him for help, Karras was a bearer of modern intellect sworn to extinguish the last vestige of superstition.

Up to the last moment – with the ultimate mystery staring in his face – Karras doggedly asserts scientific reason's uncontested right to narrate the evidence, to compose the sole acceptable version of the story – and rebuffs the layperson's temptation to succumb to interpretations that science refused to tolerate. When hapless Regan's mother turns to Karras in utter despair (her 'freckled, clasped fingers twitched in her lap') – 'I just don't know . . . What do *you* think, Father?' – Karras's answer is professionalism itself: 'Compulsive behaviour produced by guilt, perhaps, put together with split personality.'

> 'Father, I have *had* all that garbage! Now how can you say that after all you've just seen!'
>
> 'If you've seen as many patients in psychiatric wards as I have, you can say it very easily,' he assured her . . .
>
> 'Then explain all those rappings and things.' . . .
>
> 'Psychokinesis.'
>
> 'What?' . . .
>
> 'It's not that uncommon, and usually happens around an emotionally disturbed adolescent. Apparently, extreme inner tension of the mind can sometimes trigger some unknown energy that seems to move objects around at a distance. There's nothing supernatural about it. Like Regan's abnormal strength. Again, in pathology it's common. Call it mind over matter, if you will.'
>
> 'I call it weird.' . . .
>
> 'The best explanation for any phenomenon,' Karras overrode her, 'is always the simplest one available that accommodates all the facts.' . . .

And so on. Karras would not concede an inch: phenomena are explicable, explanations are available, an energy's being unknown (as yet, of course) is not for that reason inexplicable. One that spent much time in wards where things are seen that a layperson would never set her eyes on, knows that. (You should trust the expert; he *saw* things you would never see.) And – as the final argument, the ultimate reassurance – this is *common* (statistically frequent; it happens to others). And it has its name: a respectable scientific name, like 'emotionally disturbed adolescent' or 'psychokinesis'.

The layperson, particularly one who like Regan's mother has been repeatedly disappointed by learned advice and driven into despair by its practical impotence, may refuse to draw comfort from what now seem empty promises of reason. Indeed, Regan's mother 'was staring in unblinking incredulity. "Father, that's so far out of sight that I think it's almost easier to believe in the *devil*!" ... For long, troubled seconds, the priest was still. Then he answered softly, "Well, there's little in this world that I know for a fact."' Regan's mother suggests another doctrine, another orthodoxy, another explanatory key; Karras responds with *humility*. Prudent modesty, sagacious self-limitation of the scientist, scepticism in the face of the-yet-unknown is his last line of defence against the only real danger: an alternative to science, a legitimate knowledge that does not draw its legitimation from scientific authority. When he finally decides to step into the Unknown (a step made perhaps easier by the fact that, unlike his fellow scientists, but like his patient Regan, he has himself a split personality – he is, after all, a devoted priest much as he is a learned psychiatrist), Karras makes sure that the prerogatives of science are not infringed: 'If I go to the Chancery Office, or wherever it is I have to go, to get their permission to perform an exorcism, the first thing I'd have to have is a pretty substantial indication that your daughter's condition isn't a purely psychiatric problem.'

David Seltzer's *The Omen* conveys a different message altogether. It speaks out the unspeakable: perhaps science's prerogatives are themselves a sham – nothing but a convenient hideout for the *devil*? Is 'the common', by the very fact of being common, reassuringly explicable? Are the explanations that science together with scientifically censored and endorsed common sense have to offer, really the 'simplest ones available'? Does not the lauded 'simplicity' stand merely for the satisfaction of scientific authority? Do not things, uncommon and common alike, lend themselves to other, alternative, heteronomous descriptions? And if they do, how to choose between the stories? And how are the choices made in practice by those who make them for us?

The Omen contains one series of events, but two narratives. One is the common and the ordinary, and therefore raising no brow: the kind of story told over and over again by the experts and their journalist popularizers, and thus becoming indistinguishable from the world it tells about. The other is a kind of story which the luckless hero of the book, the brilliant and erudite intellectual Thorn, could only suppose – *fear* – to be 'his imagination', and (as any other well-informed and civilized person certainly would) see as a good reason 'to see a psychiatrist'. One is the well-known story, repeated *ad nauseam* by the chorus of politicians, journalists and social scientists, of human and state interests, political platforms, not-wholly-eradicated irrational sentiments. The other?

> The coven was made up mostly of working class people, but a few were professional, highly placed men. On the outside they all led respectable lives – this their most valuable weapon against those who worshipped God. It was their mission to create fear and turmoil, to turn men against each other until the time of the Unholy One had come; a small group called Task Forces would forage out to create chaos wherever possible. The coven in Rome took credit for much of the turmoil in Ireland, using random sabotage to polarize Catholic from Protestant and fan the fires of religious war . . .
>
> [In 1968] Tassone was dispatched by Spiletto to South-East Asia, there organizing a small band of mercenaries in Communist-held Cambodia, to cross into, and disrupt the cease-fire, in South Vietnam. The North blamed it on the South, the South on the North, and within days of Tassone's entrance, the hard-won peace of this land was shattered . . .
>
> Knowing of his knowledge of the country, Spiletto sent Tassone to assist the revolution that eventually brought Idi Amin, the insane African Despot, to power . . .

And so on. Of the second story, 'only *they* knew'. 'No one else had ever had a clue.' Once told, their story would make as much sense – no more and no less – of terrorism, senseless killings, hostilities without a cause, civil wars, mass murders, crazy despots, as all the stories that officially guaranteed their rationality. The problem, however, was that this other, apocryphal story has been never told; not in public, that is. Those who saw things told by this story as they happened, all perished; the only surviving witness, Thorn himself, was – naturally – confined to a lunatic asylum. The world found it easier (and more reassuring) to assume that Thorn's unshared beliefs were symptoms of mental disturbance, than to accept the possibility that the world's own truth might have been just one of the many, that to every interpretation, however massively hailed, there might be an alternative. Murder, imprisonment, the verdict of insanity were the worldly truths' last lines of defence. Perhaps the only lines of *effective* defence.

Most of us would easily agree that the explanations Seltzer puts in the mind and on the lips of Thorn are ridiculous or outrageously insane. All the more striking is the point he tries to hammer home – that without recourse to force and suppression, the dominant truth cannot protect itself by the weapons of logic, canons of induction, rules of fact-collecting and all the other devices that, as it claims, suffice to guarantee its superior quality and hence its privileged standing. (Note that it is only Thorn's *story* that sounds unquestionably insane; the supposition that we would not be so sure of its insanity were not the supporting evidence suppressed, does not.) For every sequence of events, there is more than one interpretation that would pass muster. The choice, ultimately, is a political matter . . .

And so there are two doubts. The first kind of doubt does not undermine the authority of science. On the contrary, transforming the ideal of truth into the 'imaginary target' of knowledge-producing pursuits, into the horizon of the territory now being travelled through (a horizon always receding and forever elusive, and hence always beyond the reach of practical test) – this doubt effectively *protects* the authority of science from discreditation. In fact, it renders knowledge as such (at the cost of virtually each and any of its specimens) immune to questioning. It sees to it that no hostages are ever given to fate, and that in the game of knowledge the worthiness of the game is never at stake. It guarantees the immortality of knowledge as a truth-gaining enterprise by rendering it independent of the vicissitudes of each specific truth it spawns. It allows the enterprise to go on unabated while being demonstratively abortive: it transforms its very abortiveness into the mainspring – the motive and the legitimation – of its continuing vigour.

Ostensibly, this doubt puts in question the finality of any successive incarnation of the truth ideal. More surreptitiously, yet more importantly, it belittles the significance of any specific case of ignorance. It temporalizes ignorance – and so it disarms the uncertainty and ambiguity that ignorance brings in its wake. Instead of paralysing action, ignorance prompts more effort and boosts the zeal and determination of actors. Ignorance is a not-yet conquered territory; its very presence is a challenge, and the clinching argument of any pep talk summoning support for the next attack in the interminable, yet always confident of the ultimate victory, offensive of reason. It allows science to declare credibly its determination to work itself out of a job, while constantly staving off the moment when it could be asked to act on its promise: there is always a job to be done, and fighting ignorance is such a job. The first kind of doubt, therefore, harnesses ignorance to the chariot of science. In advance, ignorance is defined as another feather in science's cap. Its resistance is significant solely for the fact that it is about to be broken. Its danger is somewhat less terrifying as it is bound to be chased away – soon. The uncertainty and ambivalence ignorance nurtures is but an occasion to another display of the potency of reason, and so it breeds, ultimately, reassurance.

The second kind of doubt, is anything but innocuous. It hits where it hurts most: it undermines the trust that whatever is being said by science at a given time is the best one can say at that time. It questions the holy of holies – the creed of the superiority of scientific knowledge over any other knowledge. By the same token, it challenges science's right to validate and invalidate, legitimize and delegitimize – to draw the line between knowledge and ignorance, transparency and obscurity, logic and incongruity. Obliquely, it makes thinkable the most heretical of heresies: that instead of being a gallant knight bent on cutting off, one by one, the many heads of the dragon of superstition, science is one story among many, invoking one frail pre-judgement among many.

The second kind of doubt never for a single moment ceased to haunt modern mentality. From the start it was firmly entrenched in the inner recesses of modernity; fear of the 'unfoundedness' of certainty was, arguably, the most formidable among modernity's many inner demons. Many times over it put the modern project on the defensive. Even when, for a time, forced into the limbo of the subconscious, it went on poisoning the joy of victorious offensives. Unlike the first kind of doubt, found resonant and useful and therefore rapturously displayed in public, the second kind was treated with unqualified and unremitting hostility: it was marked for total and irrevocable destruction. It stood for everything the transparent and harmonious world that science was to build had to be purified of: unreason, madness, obscurity, undecidability.

Like all doubts, this one was creative as well: it strained human imaginative power to the utmost, giving birth to contraptions so varied as, for instance, Descartes's *cogito*, Husserl's *transcendental reduction*, Popper's principle of *refutation*, Weber's *rational constructs*, or the ever more ingenious research methods that – like the Swiftian wheel at the Academy of Lagado – were hoped to allow any able-bodied man to thresh out the healthy grain of truth from the chaff of error. From Descartes's *malin génie* and up to Husserl's heroic act of *epoché*, the war against uncertainty and ambiguity of evidence went on unabated – the most vivid testimony, if one was needed, to the ubiquitous and perseverant presence of the doubt.

It was the presence of the second kind of doubt – and its presence *as a doubt*, as a belief able to weaken the resolve needed for the success of the project – that was the distinctive mark of modern mentality. It is the disappearance of that doubt *as a doubt* (that is, the retention of the belief, yet the defusion of its past corrosive impact) that marks most vividly the passage of modernity into its postmodern stage. Modernity reaches that new stage (so sharply distinct that one is ever so often tempted to allocate it to an entirely separate era, to describe it in a typically modern style as a negation, pure and simple, of modernity) when it is able to face up to the fact that science, for all one knows and can know, is one story among many. 'To face up' means to accept that certainty is not to be, and yet persevere in the pursuit of knowledge born of the determination to smother and weed out contingency.

It was the treatment of the first kind of doubt as a temporary nuisance, as an irritant with a limited life-expectancy, sooner or later to be dead and buried, that was another distinctive mark of modern mentality. It was an axiom of that mentality that if there were one thousand potential items of knowledge as yet undisclosed, discovering one of them would leave but nine hundred and ninety-nine in the pool. The abandoning of that axiom marks the passage of modernity into its postmodern stage. Modernity reaches that new stage when it is able to face up to the fact that the growth of knowledge expands the field of ignorance, that with each step towards the horizon new unknown lands appear, and that, to put it most generally, acquisition of knowledge cannot express itself in any other form but awareness of more ignorance. 'To face up' to this fact means to know that the journey has no clear destination – and yet persevere in the travel.

There is one more mark of the passage of modernity to its postmodern stage: the two previously separate doubts losing their distinctiveness, becoming semantically indistinguishable, blending into one. The two limits of knowledge appear to be artefacts of modern diffractive vision; their alleged separateness, a projection of the now abandoned design. In place of two limits and two doubts, there is an unworried awareness that there are many stories that need to be told over and over again, each time losing something and adding something to the past versions. There is also a new determination: to guard the conditions in which all stories can be told, and retold, and again told differently. It is in their plurality, and not in the 'survival of the fittest' (that is, the extinction of the less fit) that the hope now resides. Richard Rorty gave this new – postmodern – project an epigrammatic precision: 'if we take care of political freedom, truth and goodness will take care of themselves'.[8] All too often taking care of truth and goodness resulted in the loss of political freedom. Not much truth and goodness has been gained either.

Unlike science and political ideology, freedom promises no certainty and no guarantee of anything. It causes therefore a lot of mental pain. In practice, it means constant exposure to ambivalence: that is, to a situation with no decidable solution, with no foolproof choice, no unreflective

[8] Rorty, *Contingency, Irony and Solidarity*, p. 80.

knowledge of 'how to go on'. As Hans Magnus Enzensberger recently remarked, 'you can't have a nice democracy ... Democracy is something which can get very much on your nerves – you are constantly battered by the most obnoxious things. It is like Freudian analysis. All the dirt comes out in democracy.'[9] The real problem of the postmodern stage is not to allow things to 'get on one's nerves' while hoping that they will not get on one's back. Lacking modernity's iron fist, postmodernity needs nerves of steel.

Neotribalism, or the search for shelter

Nerves of steel are the feature that a contingent being, conscious of its own contingency, needs most. Entertaining an unshared idea is an audacity that is flattering and exhilarating, but comes too close to madness for complete spiritual comfort. A shared idea, on the contrary, promises a shelter: a community, an ideological brotherhood, fraternity of fate or mission. The temptation to share is overwhelming. In the long run it is difficult to resist. It can express itself in surrender; or it can express itself in aggression. One may, following Hobbes's and Freud's advice, merrily or regretfully surrender part of one's freedom in exchange for a partial security (though this would not necessarily be the kind of security Hobbes or Freud implied). Or one may proceed to create a community *ab nihilo*, or rather to weave it out of the tenuous threads of one's own choice – by embarking on a proselytizing escapade. The two expressions are not as opposite to each other as it may seem: this is exactly what Adorno and Horkheimer pointed out. While examining the roads leading from Upanishads to Veda, from cynics to sophists, from St John the Baptist to St Paul – they find out in each case that the dash to domination always demands the surrender of purity of purpose and the loss of the very idea for which the domination was sought.

'A person who has chosen herself under the category of difference alone', writes Agnes Heller,[10] 'may not even notice that her choice did not come off. While cutting a comic figure in the eyes of others, she will not even be unhappy, but will instead live and die in the conviction that she had been good at the thing she had chosen (cause, calling, or a particular person) while the others were just fools.' As we know well, believing that

---

[9] Hans Magnus Enzensberger, 'Back in the USSR', *New Statesman and Society*, 10 November 1989, p. 29.

[10] Agnes Heller, 'The Contingent Person and the Existential Choice', *The Philosophical Forum*, Fall-Winter 1989–90, pp. 53–69.

'the others' (*all* the others) are fools, is – by popular acclaim – the least mistakable symptom of madness. For the collectivity conscious of its collectiveness, a solitary rejection of social rules (unlike a shared one, which is dubbed dissent or revolution) is an act grounded solely in aberration, an act testifying to the incapacity for acting (that is, falling outside the frame of the socially endorsed definition of action). Now awareness that this may be the case once and for all cuts out the possibility of happiness for the person wishing to make good use of her contingency (to transform fate into destiny). This is why one can find so few happy people among thinking men and women – caught as they are between the lust for authenticity and the fear of insanity that always lurks at the bottom of lonely self-affirmation. The bliss of the thoughtless, contingency easily turns into the nightmare of the thoughtful. Aware of the danger (it is this awareness that shows up in the admission of the authority of supra-individual standards), the contingent person *knows* that she 'walks a tightrope over an abyss, and is therefore in need of a good sense of balance, good reflexes, tremendous luck, and the greatest among them: a network of friends who can hold her hand'.

Contingency needs friendship as an alternative to the lunatic asylum. It needs it as the possessed needs an authoritatively administered exorcism and a neurotic needs a scientifically approved psychotherapy. (They need their respective remedies as a *shelter* from their inner demons; not an escape, but a *modus vivendi*; not to get rid of them, but to approve of them and thus to tame and domesticate them so that one can coexist with them in peace.) This is something like the present trend to release mental patients from the institutionally sealed pseudo-worlds back 'into the community'. Has not the community come to be seen – and is hoped to function – as a group therapy for us all? For us, burdened as we are with contingency that can be only detoxicated, never eradicated, and that would never allow us to step off that tightrope stretching over the abyss of lonely despair?

No wonder that postmodernity, the age of contingency *für sich*, of self-conscious contingency, is also the age of community: of the lust for community, search for community, invention of community, imagining community. The nightmare of our contemporary, writes Manning Nash,[11] 'is to be deracinated, to be without papers, stateless, alone, alienated, and adrift in a world of organized others'; to be, in other words, *denied* identity by those who, being others (that is, different from ourselves), always seem at a distance to be 'organized' and sure of the identity of their own. Nash is

[11] Manning Nash, *The Cauldron of Ethnicity in the Modern World* (Chicago: University of Chicago Press, 1989), pp. 128–9.

concerned with only one, ethnicity-type, response to this fear, but this response can stand as a pattern for all the others: 'The identity dimension of ethnicity (whatever its deep psychological roots) rests on the fact that fellow members of the ethnic groups are thought to be "human" and trustworthy in ways that outsiders are not. The ethnic group provides a refuge against a hostile, uncaring world.' Community – ethnic, religious, political or otherwise – is thought of as the uncanny mixture of difference and company, as uniqueness that is not paid for with loneliness, as contingency with roots, as freedom with certainty; its image, its allurement are as incongruous as that world of universal ambivalence from which – one hopes – it would provide a shelter.

The real reason for the universal (though by and large unrequited) love for community is seldom spelled out. It is sometimes given away unintentionally, as in a recent phrase of Chantal Mouffe:[12] 'it is always possible to distinguish between just and unjust, the legitimate and the illegitimate, but this can only be done from within a given tradition . . . In fact, there is no point of view external to all tradition from which one can offer a universal judgment.' Ostensibly this is a polemic against the false pretences of the impersonal, supra-human objectivism that guided modern strategies aimed at the suppression of contingency; another salvo in the unrewarding but on the whole pleasurable hostilities against 'positivistic science',[13] against the pious hope that one can be 'in the right' for all times, places and *for everybody*. In fact, Mouffe's message is that, even with absolute truth defunct and universality dead and buried, one can still have what the late, deceitful benefactors promised to give: the joy of being 'in the right' – though perhaps not at all times, not in all places at the same time, and only for some people.

'Tradition' (it could be in other texts 'community' or a 'form of life') is the answer to Richard Bernstein's anxiety expressed in his rejoinder to

---

[12] Chantal Mouffe, 'Radical Democracy: Modern or Postmodern?', in *Universal Abandon?: The Politics of Postmodernism* (Edinburgh: Edinburgh University Press, 1988), p. 37.

[13] As Peters and Rothenbuler wittily commented: 'Just as the street criminal is too productive a worker in our society to be utterly stamped out (he sustains the law, prisons, police, burglar alarm installers, crime beat reporters, and prime-time TV writers), so the positivist, with his adoring attachment to a reality apart from everything human, has sustained a major part of the academic criticism for the past decade (supporting Marxist, hermeneutic, and deconstructive criticisms, for instance, since he takes the political as the neutral, the made as the given, and the exercise of will as apparent truth).' (John Durham Peters and Eric W. Rothenbuler, 'The Reality of Construction', in *Rhetoric in the Human Sciences*, ed. Herbert W. Simons (London: Sage Publications, 1989), pp. 16–7.)

Rorty's response to contingency – perhaps too radical to elicit popular enthusiasm, and certainly calling for too much heroism to hope for a massive following. Having conceded to Rorty the lack of universal foundations for any belief or value locally upheld, Bernstein[14] could not deny himself the question: 'How are we to decide who are the rational discussants and in what sense they are "rational"? ... there are plenty of questions concerning justification, objectivity, the scope of disciplines, the proper way of distinguishing rational from irrational discussants, and *praxis* that are answerable and demand our attention.' All right, Bernstein seemed to be saying, one cannot establish authoritative rules stretching beyond the confines of a given community of meaning or tradition; but surely this need not mean that the game of rules is over? Surely it only means that the number of players is somewhat smaller than hoped for? Surely the referees and their decisions, which the players are not allowed to appeal against, are still in place and needed? The 'distinguishing between just and unjust' that is 'always possible' is the purpose for which Mouffe postulates 'tradition'.[15] The need of 'demand for our attention' is Bernstein's motive to do the same. The anguish of the contingent person seeking affirmation of her personal truth is aided and abetted by the anxiety of an intellectual seeking reaffirmation of her legislative rights and leadership role.

Michel Maffesoli[16] has recently suggested a highly felicitous concept of *neo-tribalism* to describe a world like ours – a world that contains, as its conspicuous feature, the obsessive search for community. (The term, it seems, tries to capture a phenomenon similar to that discussed by Eric Hobsbawm under the heading of *inventing of tradition*, and by Benedict

---

[14] Cf. Richard Bernstein, *Philosophical Profiles: Essays in a Pragmatic Mode* (Cambridge: Polity Press, 1985).

[15] Thirty-five years have passed since Dwight Macdonald articulated the myth of 'community' as a cure for present-day atomization and loneliness, yet his lyric poetry (replicated in this country to great effect by F.R. Leavis) is still distinctly audible in the confident, no-doubts-allowed convictions that the 'community' will do what the discredited 'society' spectacularly fails to achieve. Community, in Macdonald's immortal words, is 'a group of individuals linked to each other by common interest, work, traditions, values, and sentiments; something like a family, each of whose members has a special place and function as an individual while at the same time sharing the group's interests (family budget), sentiments (family quarrels), and culture (family jokes). The scale is small enough so that it "makes a difference" what the individual does, a first condition for human – as against mass [Macdonald would have probably written today 'contingent' – Z.B.] – existence. (Dwight Macdonald, 'A Theory of Mass Culture', *Diogenes*, 3/1953, pp. 1–17.)

[16] Cf. Michel Maffesoli, 'Jeux de masques', in *Design Issues*, vol. 4 (1988), nos 1&2, pp. 141ff. Maffesoli draws on earlier ideas of Gilbert Durand and Edgar Morin.

Anderson under the heading of *imagined community*.) Ours, Maffesoli suggests, is a *tribal* world, one that admits of but tribal truths and tribal decisions about right and wrong or beauty and ugliness. Yet this is also a *neo*-tribal world, a world different in most vital aspects from the original tribal antiquity.

Tribes, as we know them from ethnographic reports and ancient accounts, were tightly structured bodies with controlled membership. Gerontocratic, hereditary, military or democratic agencies, invariably armed with effective powers of inclusion and exclusion, monitored the traffic, limited as it was, over the boundary of the group. Remaining inside or outside the tribe was seldom a matter of individual choice; indeed, this kind of fate was singularly unfit to be reforged into destiny. The tribes of the contemporary world, on the contrary, are formed – as concepts rather than integrated social bodies – by the multitude of individual acts of self-identification. Such agencies as might from time to time emerge to hold the faithful together have limited executive power and little control over co-optation or banishment. More often than not, 'tribes' are oblivious of their following, and the following itself is fickle. It dissipates as fast as it appears. 'Membership' is relatively easily revocable, and is divorced from long-term obligations; this is a kind of 'membership' that does not require an admission procedure or authoritative ruling, and that can be dissolved without permission or warning. Tribes 'exist' solely by individual decisions to sport the symbolic traits of tribal allegiance. They vanish once the decisions are revoked or their determination fades out. They persevere thanks only to their continuing seductive capacity. They cannot outlive their power of attraction.

Neo-tribes are, in other words, the vehicles (and imaginary sediments) of individual self-definition. The self-construction efforts generate them; the inevitable inconclusiveness and frustration of such efforts leads to their dismantling and replacement. Their existence is transient and always in flux. They inflame imagination most and attract the most ardent loyalty when they still reside in the realm of hope. They are formations that are much too loose to survive the movement from hope to practice. They seem to illustrate Jean-François Lyotard's description of being as 'escaping determination and arriving both too soon and too late'.[17] They seem also to fit very closely the Kantian concept of *aesthetic community*.

For Kant, the aesthetic community is and is bound to remain an *idea*; a promise, an expectation, a hope of unanimity that is not to be. Hope of unanimity brings the aesthetic community into being; unfulfilment of that

[17] Jean-François Lyotard, *Peregrinations: Law, Form, Event* (New York: Columbia University Press, 1988), p. 32.

hope keeps it alive. The aesthetic community owes its existence, so to speak, to a false promise. But individual choice cannot be committed without such a promise. 'Kant uses the word "promise" in order to point out the non-existent status of such a republic of taste (of the United Tastes?). The unanimity concerning what is beautiful has no chance of being actualized. But every actual judgment of taste carries with it the promise of universalization as a constitutive feature of its singularity':

> The community required as a support for the validity of such judgment must always be in the process of doing and undoing itself. The kind of consensus implied by such a process, if there is any consensus at all, is in no way argumentative but is rather allusive and elusive, endowed with a spiral way of being alive, combining both life and death, always remaining *in statu nascendi* or *moriendi*, always keeping open the issue of whether or not it actually exists. This kind of consensus is definitely nothing but a cloud of community.[18]

Those among us who – prompted by the memories of the legislative era – wish a situation in which 'it is always possible to distinguish legitimate and illegitimate' to hold, are bound to be disappointed. The best they can obtain to support such a possibility under present postmodern conditions are but such aesthetic communities – *clouds of communities*. Such communities will never be anything like Tönnies's cosy and natural (cosy because natural) homes of unanimity. Tönnies-style communities evaporate the moment they know of themselves as communities. They vanish (if they have not evaporated before) once we say 'how nice it is to be in a community'. From that moment on, community is not a site of secure settlement; it is all hard work and uphill struggle, a constantly receding horizon of the never-ending road; anything but natural and cosy. We consol ourselves and summon our wilting determination by invoking the magic formula of 'tradition' – trying hard to forget that tradition lives only by being recapitulated, by being construed as a *heritage*; that it appears, if at all, only at the end, never at the beginning, of agreement; that its retrospective unity is but a function of the density of today's communal cloud . . .

Given our knowledge of contingency – now spilling over from the idea of the beautiful to that of being itself, to its truth and its *reason* – we cannot abandon our search for consensus: we know after all that agreement is not predetermined and is not guaranteed in advance, that it has nothing but our argument to stand on. Ours is the courage of despair. We cannot but redouble our efforts while going from defeat to defeat. The Kantian

---

[18] Lyotard, *Peregrinations*, p. 38.

antinomy of the judgement of taste showed that disputation was as much unavoidable as it was in the end inconclusive and irrelevant. This is a demonstration that both Habermas and his detractors lose from sight: Habermas, in as far as he presents the model of undistorted communication as a realistic prospect of truth-consensus, and his critics, when they try to disavow the effectivity of such a model for not offering a firm enough ground for agreement, and so tacitly imply that some other, presumably firmer grounds, ought to be sought and can be found.

Under these circumstances, the foremost paradox of the frantic search for communal grounds of consensus is that it results in more dissipation and fragmentation, more heterogeneity. The drive to synthesis is the major factor of endless bifurcations. Each attempt at convergence and synthesis leads to new splits and divisions. What purported to be the formula for agreement to end all disagreement proves to be, the moment it has been formulated, an occasion for new disagreement and new pressures for negotiation. All effort to solidify loose life-world structures prompt more fragility and fissiparousness. The search for community turns into a major obstacle to its formation. The only consensus likely to stand a chance of success is the acceptance of the heterogeneity of dissensions.

Such a prospect is hard to live with. To the injury of known contingency it adds an insult of human impotence to conjure up what nature failed to provide. Not only is one conscious of one's lack of foundation, but in addition one is not allowed to hope that the foundations will ever be built. Crusading truths lost their power to humiliate, but they also forfeited much of their past ability to offer the succour – the 'born-again', the 'my eyes have opened' feeling – that truths used to lavish on the converted. No wonder the postmodern condition is fraught with antinomies – torn between the chances it opens and the threats that hide behind every chance.

The antinomies of postmodernity

The collapse of 'grand narratives' (as Lyotard put it) – the dissipation of trust in supra-individual and supra-communal courts of appeal – has been eyed by many observers with fear, as an invitation to the 'everything goes' situation, to universal permissiveness and hence, in the end, to the demise of all moral, and thus social, order. Mindful of Dostoyevsky's dictum 'If there is no God, everything is permitted', and of Durkheim's identification of asocial behaviour with the weakening of collective consensus, we have grown to believe that unless an awesome and incontestable authority – sacred or secular, political or philosophical – hangs over each and every human individual, then anarchy and universal carnage are likely to follow. This belief supported well the modern determination to install an artificial order: a project that made all spontaneity suspect until proven innocent, that proscribed everything not explicitly prescribed and identified ambivalence with chaos, with 'the end of civilization' as we know it and as it could be imagined. Perhaps the fear emanated from the suppressed knowledge that the project was doomed from the start; perhaps it was cultivated deliberately, since it served a useful role as an emotional bulwark against dissention; perhaps it was just a side-effect, an intellectual afterthought born of the socio-political practice of cultural crusade and enforced assimilation. One way or the other, modernity bent on the bulldozing of all unauthorized difference and all wayward life-patterns could not but gestate the horror of deviation and render deviation synonymous with diversity. As Adorno and Horkheimer commented, the lasting intellectual and emotional scar left by the philosophical project and political practice of modernity was the fear of the void; and the void was the absence of a universally binding, unambiguous and enforceable standard.

Of the popular fear of the void, of the anxiety born of the absence of clear instruction that leaves nothing to the harrowing necessity of choice, we know from the worried accounts narrated by intellectuals, the appointed or self-appointed interpreters of social experience. The narrators are never absent from their narration, though, and it is a hopeless task to try to sift out their presence from their stories. It may well be that at all times there was life outside philosophy, and that such life did not share the worries of the narrators; that it did quite well without being regimented by rationally proved and philosophically approved universal standards of truth, goodness and beauty. It may well be even that much of that life was liveable, orderly and moral *because* it was *not* tinkered with, manipulated and corrupted by the self-acclaimed agents of the 'universal ought'.[19]

---

[19] It is a prominent feature of the postmodern mentality that these and similar doubts are more and more widely shared by intellectual observers. Suddenly a growing number of social scientists discover that normative regulation of daily life is often sustained through 'grass roots' initiative frequently of a heterodox ('deviationary' in official parlance) nature, and has to be protected against encroachments from above. Compare, for example, Michel de Certeau's analysis of *la perruque* (*The Practice of Everyday Life* (Berkeley: University of California Press, 1984), pp. 25ff) as the tool of defence of the self-regulated sphere of autonomy; or Hebdidge's brilliant characterization of subculture (normally the object of officially inspired 'moral panics' and detracted as a hiccup of barbarism, as a product of disintegration of order) as a phenomenon which 'forms up in the space between surveillance and the evasion of surveillance' and 'translates the fact of being under scrutiny into the pleasure of being watched. It is a hiding in the light.' Subculture,

There is hardly any doubt, however, that one form of life can fare but badly without the prop of universally binding and apodictically valid standards: the form of life of the narrators themselves (more precisely, such form of life as contains the stories those narrators were telling through most of modern history).

It was that form of life first and foremost that lost its foundation once social powers abandoned their ecumenical ambitions, and felt therefore more than anyone else threatened by the fading out of universalistic expectations. As long as modern powers clung resolutely to their intention of constructing a better, reason-guided, and thus ultimately universal order, intellectuals had little difficulty in articulating their own claim to the crucial role in the process: universality was their domain and their field of expertise. As long as the modern powers insisted on the elimination of ambivalence as the measure of social improvement, intellectuals could consider their own work – the promotion of universally valid rationality – as a major vehicle and driving force of progress. As long as the modern powers continued to decry and banish and evict the Other, the different, the ambivalent – intellectuals could rely on mighty support for their authority of passing judgement and sorting out truth from falsity, knowledge from mere opinion. Like the adolescent hero of Cocteau's *Orphée*, convinced that the sun would not rise without his guitar and serenade, the intellectuals grew convinced that the fate of morality, civilized life and social order hangs on their solution of the problem of universality: on their clinching and final proof that the human 'ought' is unambiguous, and that its non-ambiguity has unshakeable and totally reliable foundations.

This conviction translated into two complementary beliefs: that there will be no good in the world *unless* its necessity has been proven; and that proving such a necessity, if and when accomplished, will have a similar effect on the world as that imputed to the legislative acts of a ruler: it will replace chaos with order and make the opaque transparent. Husserl was

---

in Hebdidge's interpretation, is a 'declaration of independence, of otherness, of alien intent, a refusal of anonymity, of subordinate status. It is an *in*subordination. And at the same time it is also a confirmation of the fact of powerlessness, a celebration of impotence. Subcultures are both a play for attention and a refusal, once attention has been granted, to be read according to the book.' (*Hiding in the Light* (London: Routledge, 1988), p. 35.) Subculture is deliberate or semi-deliberate politics; it has its conscious or subconscious motive, programme and strategy. It often reaches its purpose: it gains attention, and then it is closely scrutinized so that its inner nature as a defence of autonomy can be gleaned. There are, however, much more massive though less vociferous and hence less visible territories of daily life that do not attract the obtrusive attention of the law-enforcing authorities and thus also the curiosity of intellectual commentators.

perhaps the last great philosopher of the modern era spurred into action by those twin beliefs. Appalled by the idea that whatever we see as truth may be founded but in beliefs, that our knowledge has merely a psychological grounding, that we might have adopted logic as a secure guide to correct thinking simply because this is how people happen on the whole to think, Husserl (like Descartes, Kant and other recognized giants of modern thought before him) made a gigantic effort to cut reason free from its worldly habitat (or was it prison?): to return it to where it belonged – a *transcendental*, out-worldly region, towering above the daily human bustle at a height at which it cannot be reached – neither glimpsed nor tarnished – from the lowly world of common daily experience. The latter could not be the domicile of reason, as it was precisely the world of the common and the ordinary and the spontaneous that was to be remade and reformed and transformed by the verdicts of reason. Only the few, capable of the formidable effort of transcendental reduction (an experience not unlike the shaman's trances, or forty days of desert meditation) can travel to those esoteric places where truth comes into view. For the time of their journey, they must forget – suspend and bracket out – the 'mere existing', so that they may become one with the transcendental subject – that thinking subject that thinks the truth because it does not think anything else, because it is free from its worldly interests and the common errors of the worldly way.

The world which Husserl left behind while embarking on his solitary expedition to the sources of certainty and truth took little note. This was a world of evil on the loose, of concentration camps and of growing stockpiles of bombs and poison gas. The most spectacular and lasting effect of absolute truth's last stand was not so much its *inconclusiveness*, stemming as some would say from the errors of design, but its utter *irrelevance* to the worldly fate of truth and goodness. The latter fate was decided far away from philosophers' desks, down in the world of daily life where struggles for political freedom raged and the limits of the state ambition to legislate social order, to define, to segregate, to organize, to constrain and to suppress were pushed forward and rolled backwards.

It seems that the more advanced is the cause of freedom at home the less demand there is for the services of explorers of distant lands where absolute truth is reputed to reside. When one's own truth seems secure and the truth of the other does not seem to be a challenge or a threat, truth can live well without sycophants assuring it of being 'the truest of them all' and the warlords determined to make sure that no one disagrees. Once the difference ceases to be a crime, it may be enjoyed at peace, and enjoyed for what it is, rather than for what it represents or what it is destined to become. Once the politicians abandon their search for empires, there is little demand for the philosophers' search for universality.[20] Empires of unconfined and unchallenged sovereignty, and the truth of unlimited and uncontested universality were the two arms with which modernity wished to remould the world according to the design of perfect order. Once the intention is no more, both arms find themselves without use.

In all probability the diversity of truths, standards of goodness and beauty does not grow once the intention is gone; neither does it become more resilient and stubborn than before; it only looks less alarming. It was, after all, the modern intention that made difference into an offence: *the* offence, the most mortal and least forgivable sin, to be precise. The pre-modern eye viewed difference with equanimity; as if it was in the pre-ordained order of things that they are and should remain different. Being unemotional, difference was also safely out of the cognitive focus. After a few centuries during which human diversity lived in hiding (a concealment enforced by the threat of exile) and it learned to be embarrassed about its stigma of iniquity, the postmodern eye (that is, the modern eye liberated from modern fears and inhibitions) views difference with zest and glee: difference is beautiful and no less good for that.

The appearance of sequence is, to be sure, itself an effect of the modern knack for neat divisions, clean breaks and pure substances. The postmodern celebration of difference and contingency has not displaced the modern lust for uniformity and certainty. Moreover, it is unlikely ever to do it; it has no capacity of doing so. Being what it is, postmodern mentality and practice cannot displace or eliminate or even marginalize anything. As it is always the case with the notoriously ambivalent (multi-final: opening more than one option, pointing to more than one line of future change) human condition, the gains of postmodernity are simultaneously its losses; what gives it its strength and attraction is also the source of its weakness and vulnerability.

---

[20] Emperor Shih Huang Ti, the hero of Borges's story, was credited with ordering the construction of the Chinese Wall *and* the burning of all the books that had been written before his time. He also boasted in his inscriptions that all things under his reign had the names that befitted them. And he decreed that his heirs should be called Second Emperor, Third Emperor, Fourth Emperor, and so on to infinity (Jorge Luis Borges, 'The Walls and the Books', in *Other Inquisitions, 1937–1952*, trans. Ruth L.C. Simms (New York: Washington Square Press, 1966), pp. 1–2.) The four decrees of Shih Huang Ti represent modern ambition at its fullest and most logically coherent. The Wall guarded the perfect kingdom against interference by other coercive pressures; the destruction of books stopped infiltration of other ideas. With the kingdom secure on both fronts, no wonder all things finally received their right and proper names, and, starting with Shih Huang Ti's reign, future history was to be only more of the same.

There is no clean break or unambiguous sequence. Postmodernity is weak on exclusion. Having declared limits off limits, it cannot but include and incorporate modernity into the very diversity that is its distinctive mark. It cannot refuse admission lest it should lose its identity. (Paradoxically, refusal would be equivalent to the ceding of the whole real estate to the rejected applicant.) It cannot but admit the rights of a legitimate resident even to such a lodger as denies its right to admit residents and the right of other residents to share its accommodation. Modern mentality is a born litigant and an old hand in lawsuits. Postmodernity cannot defend its case in court, as there is no court whose authority it would recognize. It might be forced instead to follow the Christian injunction of offering another cheek to the assailant's blows. It certainly is doomed to a long and hard life of cohabitation with its sworn enemy as a room-mate.

To the modern determination to seek or enforce consensus, postmodern mentality may only respond with its habitual tolerance of dissent. This makes the antagonists' chances unequal, with the odds heavily on the side of the resolute and strong-willed. Tolerance is too wan a defence against willfulness and lack of scruples. By itself, tolerance remains a sitting target – an easy prey for the unscrupulous. It can repulse assaults only when reforged into solidarity: into the universal recognition that difference is one universality that is not open to negotiation and that attack against the universal right to be different is the only departure from universality that none of the solidary agents, however different, may tolerate otherwise than at its own, and all the other agents', peril.

And so the transformation of the *fate* into a *destiny*, of tolerance into solidarity, is not just a matter of moral perfection, but a condition of survival. Tolerance as 'mere tolerance' is moribund; it can survive only in the form of solidarity. It just would not do to rest satisfied that the other's difference does not confine or harm my own – as some differences, of some others, are most evidently bent on constraining and damaging. Survival in the world of contingency and diversity is possible only if each difference recognizes another difference as the necessary condition of the preservation of its own. Solidarity, unlike tolerance, its weaker version, means readiness to fight; and joining the battle for the sake of the other's difference, not one's own. Tolerance is ego-centred and contemplative; solidarity is socially oriented and militant.

Like all other human conditions, postmodern tolerance and diversity has its dangers and its fears. Its survival is not guaranteed – not by God's design, universal reason, laws of history, or any other supra-human force. In this respect, of course, the postmodern condition does not differ at all from all other conditions; it differs only by knowing about it, by its knowledge of living without guarantee, of being on its own. This makes it exceedingly anxiety-prone. And this also gives it a chance.

The futures of solidarity

Postmodernity is a chance of modernity. Tolerance is a chance of postmodernity. Solidarity is the chance of tolerance. Solidarity is a third-degree chance. This does not sound reassuring for one wishing solidarity well. Solidarity cannot draw its confidence from anything remotely as solid and thereby as comforting as social structures, laws of history or the destination of nations and races from which modern projects derived their optimism, self-confidence and determination.

The bridge leading from the postmodern condition to solidarity is not built of necessities. It is not even certain whether there is such a bridge at all. Emancipated from modern hubris, the postmodern mind has less need for cruelty and humiliating the Other; it can afford Richard Rorty's 'kindness'. But kindness may be, and often is, superior, lofty and detached – frequently it feels more like a snub than sympathy. On its own, kindness would not beget solidarity – much as solidarity is not the only possible outcome (not even the most probable outcome) of the collapse of the modern romance with 'designer society'.

More than from anything else, modern designs of global perfection drew their animus from the horror of difference and impatience with otherness. And yet they also offered a chance for genuine concern with the plight of the wretched and miserable (it was this chance that attracted to the modern promise the spokesmen for the underdog). The modern conviction that society need not be as it happens to be, that it might be made better than it was, made each case of individual and group unhappiness into a challenge and a task. As long as the decent life of everybody was, by common consent, a feasible proposition, the administrators of social order felt the need to apologise for their sloth or ineptitude in bringing about a decent life for everybody.

It is not that the likes of Mayhew or Booth or Riis are not with us any more; there are in all probability more of them now than at any other time. The real difference is between the explosive effect that the revelation of human misery once had – and the equanimity with which it is received today. Today the news of human poverty and distress come as more colourful accounts among the many images of the many ways people choose or are fated (by their history, by their religion, by their culture) to live. For a mentality trained to treat society as an unfinished project for the managers to complete, poverty was an abomination; its life-expectation depended solely on the managerial resolve. For mentality repelled by global visions and wary of all prospects of societal engineering, that poverty is but an element in the infinite variety of existence. Once more, as in pre-modern times convinced of the inscrutable and timeless wisdom of divine order, one can live with daily sights of hunger, homelessness, life without future and dignity; live happily, enjoy the day and sleep quietly at night.

At the height of the modern dream of the perfect society round the corner and of the determination to turn that corner as soon as resources allowed, a tacit agreement had been reached between the managers and the managed as to the priorities to be observed on the way to global happiness. Last time, says J.K. Galbraith, such an agreement – a kind of unwritten 'social contract' (we would rather speak of a promise taken up and trusted) – came into being in Britain under Lloyd George and was agreed in the United States under Roosevelt. But, Galbraith says, 'In the 1980s this understanding was, at a minimum, put in abeyance.' That those who cannot avail themselves of the glittering prizes of rampant consumerism deserve our care and have the right to compensation is no more a matter of silent consent.

> Our poor in the US have remained poor, and the number so classified has substantially increased, as has, more markedly, the share of income going to the very rich. The conditions of life in the centres of our large cities is – the word is carefully chosen – appalling. Housing is bad and getting worse. Many of our citizens are without even the barest element of shelter, their income at near starvation levels. Schools are also bad, and young and old, sustained often by crime, contrive a temporary escape from despair with drugs.[21]

That things are bad is not news; for a great many people things used to be bad at the best of times. What is truly new is that things that are bad for some people are seldom a worry for those for whom things are good. The latter have accepted and declared that little they can do may improve the lot of the others. And they even managed to convince themselves that since social engineering has been proved rotten at the core, whatever they decide to do may only make things worse still. The promise has not just been broken. It has been withdrawn.

Kindness may be an opposite of cruelty. Both are, however, sentiments of the interested and the involved; attitudes of *concerned* people – of people who not only look but see, and who worry about what they have

[21] J.K. Galbraith, 'Assault on Ideology in the Last Decade Hit not only East but also West'. *The Guardian*, 16–17 December 1989, p. 17.

seen. Alternatives of kindness and cruelty both serve the engagement with the Other; they remain on this side of the mutual bond. Outside such an engagement, as the '*otherwise than engagement*', the otherwise than both kindness and cruelty, stands the attitude of *indifference-fed callousness*: a sort of tolerance which to its objects looks more like a life-sentence than a hope of freedom.

It is only too easy for postmodern tolerance to degenerate into the selfishness of the rich and resourceful. Such selfishness is indeed its most immediate and daily manifestation. There seems to be a direct relation between exuberant and expanding freedom of the 'competent consumer' and the remorseless shrinking of the world inhabited by the disqualified one.[22] The postmodern condition has split society into the happy seduced and unhappy oppressed halves – with postmodern mentality celebrated by the first half of the division while adding to the misery of the second. The first half may abandon itself to the carefree celebration only because it has satisfied itself that the misery of the second half is their rightful *choice*, or at least a legitimate part of the world's exhilarating diversity. For the first half, misery is the 'form of life' the second half had selected – if only through carrying on a happy-go-lucky style of existence and neglecting the duty of selection.

There is no shortage of postmodern formulae meant to make the conscience of the seduced spotless. Disciples of the Hayeks and Friedmans are around in growing numbers, ready to prove that the rich must be given ever greater prizes so that they may wish to be rich, while for the poor rich rewards are only an encouragement to wallow in poverty; and that enriching themselves ('creating material wealth') is the only service the rich may render to the poor (that is, if service is to be rendered). There are economists, political scientists, sociologists and of course politicians to reassure the rich that the poverty of the poor is their – the poor's – problem, while the resistance of the poor against poverty is the problem for the organs of law and order. There are 'photo opportunities' obligingly provided by the police to inform the public about the bottomless depravity and iniquity of the drug-infested poor. (One cannot help recalling (Goebbels's cameramen avidly recording the filthy ugliness of lice-infested ghetto Jews.) With bated breath, residents of the theft-proof, fortified homes glue themselves to their TV screens for the spectacle of brutality that is the mark of the brutalized. And there are also boffins and moral preachers to remind the shocked voyeurs that there is a 'problem' of how to prevent single mothers from breeding football hooligans, and that

[22] I have discussed this effect at greater length in *Freedom* (Milton Keynes: Open University Press, 1988) chap. 4, and of *Legislators and Interpreters*, chap. 11.

scientific studies once conducted by the expert racial hygienists may perhaps – who knows? – tell us something about its rational solution.[23]

A long and tortuous way led historically from cruelty to kindness, but there is just a small step to be taken on the return trip. The postmodern world of joyful messiness is carefully guarded at the borders by mercenaries no less cruel than those hired by the managers of the now abandoned global order. Smiling banks beam only at their present and prospective customers. The playgrounds of happy shoppers are surrounded by thick walls, electronic spies and sharp-toothed guard-dogs. Polite tolerance applies only to those allowed inside. And thus drawing the line between the inside and the outside seems to have lost nothing of its violence and genocidal potency. If anything, the potency has grown, as no missionary, proselytizing prospects salvage the outsiders from total and final condemnation. Indeed, it is not clear any more why the useless and troublesome outsiders, whose bodies no one needs and whose souls no one wants to win or convert (as they are no longer the 'reserve army of labour', nor the prospective objects of exploitation or cannon-fodder), should not be removed by force ('repatriated') if there is a place to which they can be removed, or barred from propagating if the graveyard is the only place to which they can be moved.

In *Modernity and the Holocaust* I suggested that the unprecedented condensation of cruelty which marked the twentieth-century genocides could be the result of the application of modern management and technology to the unresolved pre-modern tensions and conflicts. A similar dialectic encounter is not to be ruled out lightly under emerging postmodern circumstances. The unfinished business of modern social engineering may well erupt in a new outburst of savage misanthropy, assisted rather than impeded by the newly legalized postmodern self-centredness and indifference. The protective wall of playful unconcern that the postmodern style offers was precisely what the perpetrators of modern mass cruelties missed, and what they had to replace with custom-made artifices by stretching their cunning and ingenuity to the utmost. Since then unconcern has made tremendous advances – the other people's misery having been dissolved in the incessant flow of mildly worrying and mildly amusing (amusing *because* mildly worrying) spectacles, and become indistinguishable from other Buadrillardian simulacra; while the mental technique through which life is cut into a series of cases each to be dealt

---

23 'The word *problem*' – wrote Jorge Luis Borges – 'may be an insidious *petitio principi*. To speak of the *Jewish problem* is to postulate that the Jews are a problem; it is to predict (and recommend) persecution, plunder, shooting, beheading, rape, and the reading of Dr. Rosenberg prose.' ('Dr. Américo Castro is Alarmed', in *Other Inquisitions*, 1937–1952, p. 26.)

with separately 'as it deserves' radically removed 'the need of the other' (not to mention such abstract and by now largely discredited notions as 'the responsibility for the other') from relevant 'factors of the case'. For most pursuers of a better world, the vision of a universal paradise has been reduced to the attempts to dump the vexing aspects of life (a silo for toxic waste, an air-polluting plant, a noxious bypass or a noisy airport) in other people's backyards.

Thorough, adamant and uncompromising *privatization* of all concerns has been the main factor that has rendered postmodern society so spectacularly immune to systemic critique and radical social dissent with revolutionary potential. It is not necessarily the case that the denizens of postmodern – privatized and commodified – society enjoy the sum-total of greater happiness (one would still wish to know how to measure happiness objectively and compare it), and that they experience their worries as less serious and painful; what does truly matter is that it would not occur to them to lay the blame for such troubles they may suffer at the door of the state, and even less to expect the remedies to be handed over through that door. Postmodern society proved to be a well-nigh perfect translating machine – one that interprets any extant and prospective *social* issue as *private* concern (as if in a direct defiance of C. Wright Mills' very modern, very pre-postmodern description of, simultaneously, good democracy and good social science). It is not the 'ownership of the means of production' that has been privatized (its 'private' character, to be sure, is ever more in doubt at the age of the mergers and the multinationals). The most seminal of privatizations was that of human problems and of the responsibility for their resolution. The politics that reduced its acknowledged responsibilities to the matters of public safety and otherwise declared its retreat from the tasks of social management, effectively desocialized the ills of society and translated social injustice as individual ineptitude or neglect. Such politics is insufficiently attractive to awaken the *citizen* in a *consumer*; its stakes are not impressive enough to make it an object of the kind of anger that would be amenable to collectivization. In the postmodern society of consumers, failure rebounds in guilt and *shame*, not in political *protest*. Frustration breeds embarrassment, not dissent. Perhaps it triggers off all the familiar behavioural symptoms of Nietzsche–Scheler's *ressentiment*, but politically it disarms and gestates apathy.

The systemic consequence of the privatization of ambivalence is a dependency that does not need either coercion-supported dictatorship or ideological indoctrination; a dependency that is sustained, reproduced and reinforced by mostly DIY methods, that is embraced willingly and is not felt as dependence at all – one may even say: that is experienced as freedom and a triumph of individual autonomy. The coveted freedom of the consumer is, after all, the right to choose 'of one's own will' life-purpose and life-methodology that the supra-individual market mechanics has already defined and determined for the consumer. Consumer freedom means orientation of life towards market-approved commodities and thereby precludes one crucial freedom: freedom from the market, freedom that means anything else but the choice between standard commercial products. Above all, consumer freedom successfully deflects aspirations of human liberty from communal affairs and the management of collective life.

All possible dissent is therefore depoliticized beforehand; it is dissolved into yet more personal anxieties and concerns and thus deflected from the centres of societal power to private suppliers of consumer goods. The gap between desirable and achieved states of happiness results in the increased fascination with the allurements of the market and the appropriation of commodities; the wheels of the self-perpetuating mechanism of the consumer-oriented economy are thereby lubricated, while political and social structures emerge unscathed and intact. With the definitions and particularly the avenues and mechanisms of social mobility privatized, all potentially explosive troubles like frustrated personal ambitions, humiliating refusals of the public confirmation of self-definitions, clogged channels of advancement, even eviction from the sphere in which job-ascribed, publicly recognized meanings and identities are distributed, lead at best to a still more feverish search for market-supplied prescriptions, skills and tools of self- or image-improvement, or finish up in the disconsolate resignation of the welfare recipient – that socially confirmed paragon of personal incompetence and impotence. In neither case are the outcomes invested with political meanings. Privatized ambitions predefine frustration as an equally private matter, singularly unfit to be reforged into a collective grievance.

There is no solidarity without the tolerance for the otherness of the other. But tolerance is not solidarity's sufficient condition. Nor is solidarity tolerance's predetermined consequence. True, one cannot conceive of cruelty perpetrated *in the name* of tolerance; but there is a lot of cruelty that tolerance, through the lofty unconcern it feeds, makes *easier to commit*. Postmodernity is a site of opportunity and a site of danger; and it is both for the same set of reasons.

Socialism: modernity's last stand

Since its inception, modern socialism was and remained the counter-culture of modernity.

Like all counter-cultures, modern socialism performed a triple function in relation to the society it opposed and serviced: it exposed the deceit of representing the achieved state of society as the fulfilment of its promise; it resisted the suppression or concealment of the possibility to implement the promise better; and it pressed the society toward such better implementation of its potential. In the loyalty with which it performed this triple function lies the secret of both its glory and its misery.

Like all counter-cultures, modern socialism belonged to one historical formation with the society it opposed. That togetherness showed itself in the indispensable service socialism rendered to the dynamism and durability of modern society. By acquitting itself well of its counter-cultural role, socialism kept that society constantly on the move, articulating the problems it had to resolve to stay alive, endorsing and sustaining the attractiveness of its promise and thus securing perpetual support for its works, and in the end adding to its crisis-mangement potential and overall viability. That togetherness showed itself also in the virtually complete reliance of socialism on the programme set by modernity. Socialism's own programme was a version of the modernity project; it sharpened and radicalized the promise the whole of modern society vowed to keep. Socialism was not obliged to prove the worthiness and desirability of the modern project as such. These had already been amply demonstrated by the practice of modernity – and firmly set in public consciousness thanks to the eulogies of its official champions. Thus Marx and Engels could in clear conscience praise the admirable job performed by the capitalist administrators of modernity in melting all solids, profaning all sacraments and pushing the creative force of mankind to unheard-of limits. Lassalle could thank *Herren Kapitalisten* for doing the socialist job by clearing the site for the kind of society they only promised to build but the socialists most certainly would.

That society, the enthusiasm for which modern socialism wholeheartedly shared with modernity, was *to be built*. It was to be artificially designed and constructed, by freeing humankind from constraints of scarcity, ending human dependence on the limited gifts of nature, subordinating miserly nature to human needs – and forcing it to deliver more with the help of political will, science and technology, working in unison to magnify human *productive forces*. Socialism had no other ends but those to which the whole of modern society paid tribute, at least in public. Neither did it suggest means to those ends different from the design and management of rationally conceived social institutions already approved of and put to a daily test in the practice of modernity. What socialism did was to reconfirm the ends as worthy of pursuing, and the means as worthy of applying – by laying the blame for the 'poor showing thus far' at the door of the current, capitalist managers of the house of modernity.

The originality, uniqueness and indispensability of socialism did not consist in the invention of ends and means different from those of modernity as a whole, but in promoting the idea that like the carrying capacity of a bridge (which is measured neither by the strongest of its pillars nor by the average strength of its supports, but by the endurance of its weakest pillar), the quality of society is to be measured by the welfare of its weakest member. By socialist standards of measurement, the performance of modernity was constantly found falling short of the declared ends, and efficiency of means was found wanting. Modernity under capitalist management stood accused of underperformance and inefficiency.

The way in which socialism explained that mismanagement was kept strictly within the idiom that modern mentality conceived and understood: beneath all these failures and deceitful promises lay a spectacular ineptitude in converting nature to human uses. In proffering these charges, socialism was scathing and uncompromising. Whatever the capitalists had done to conquer nature, the socialist managers would have done or would do better. More growth, more machines, more machine operators. Capitalism was the fetter of modernity. Under capitalist management, modernity forfeited its chance to remake the world from top to bottom, to make nature pliant, malleable, obedient to human will. Private property and confined resources and the narrow vision that went with it cramped and dwarfed the unlimited potential of the tools and techniques that modernity made available. Competition gagged the reason that could speak in full voice only through global planning – only if allowed to design freely and to command without constraint. Because under capitalism private, local, not-fully-extirpated interests were allowed to interfere, more waste was produced at the end of the day than useful products. Under capitalism, modernity was inefficient, profligate and destructive. The modern style of administration could be more effective, reasonable, creative – more *productive*. More social engineering, on a grander scale, was needed to make it so.

Socialism found nothing wrong with the project of modernity. All that was wrong was the outcome of the capitalist distortion. One needs to rescue the audacity of vision and the wondrous reality-sculpting tools from the capitalist fetters so that they may show their true potential and so that everybody may enjoy the fruits. Between socialism and modernity there was no quarrel of principle. Throughout its history, socialism was modernity's most vigorous and gallant champion. It also claimed to be its only *true* champion. The more the claim was believed, the less the practical test of modernity conducted under capitalist auspices seemed conclusive. Practical defeats did not rub off on the seemliness and propriety of the project. Whatever the ugliness of its capitalist edition, modernity need not be disparaged. One could still hope for a more carefully and pleasingly edited version. The socialist critic of capitalism was modernity's most faithful and effective friend.

In the end, though, the friend proved to be the grave-digger. The alternative edition did little to correct the errors and nothing could any more protect the beauty of the project against the ugliness of its fulfilment. It did everything to make obvious what otherwise would have remained perhaps but a sinister, yet contested guess. It so happened that under socialist, not capitalist, auspices the project was pushed to its radical limits: grand designs, unlimited social engineering, huge and bulky technology, total transformation of nature. Deserts were irrigated (but they turned into salinated bogs); marshlands were dried (but they turned into deserts); massive gas-pipes criss-crossed the land to remedy the illogicality with which nature distributed its resources (but they kept exploding with the force unequalled by natural disasters of yore); millions were lifted from the 'idiocy of rural life' (but they got poisoned by the effluvia of rationally designed industry, if did not first perish on the way). Raped and crippled, nature failed to deliver the riches one hoped it would; the total scale of design only made the devastation total. Worse still, all that raping and crippling proved to be in vain. Little equality followed, still less freedom. And as for the brotherhood – it proved to be of the kind that wilts with the first breeze of liberty.[24] Socialism put modernity to its ultimate test. The failure was as ultimate as the test itself.

The cogency of the socialist message was an intellectual reflection of the entrenchment of the modern order. The persuasiveness of the socialist promise derived from the popularity of the values modernity championed and the credibility of means it supplied. For better or worse, richer or poorer, till death do them part, modern socialism wedded its fate to that of the modern project. They grew together. They triumphed together. Together they travelled to the brink of disaster.

---

[24] In the current Soviet re-evaluation of the 'communism construction project' the theme of pushing the inanities of modern world-remaking zeal to their most grotesque and horrifying extremes is harped on ceaselessly. Nikolai Skatov, one of the leading contributors to the debate, wrote recently that 'three main disasters and dangers that threaten mankind concentrated and manifested themselves in our country with exceptional force. First, Chernobyl occurred here, after all. Second, it is us who almost destroyed the most fertile black earth of the world, raped Volga (Volga!), and spat in our main wells (Baikal, Aral, Ladoga), having forgotten that, perhaps, these are the last wells from which we will drink our water. Third (or is it first?) – culture . . . Never before was culture so helpless and vulnerable, and its present tragic fate stands in the rank of global crises and catastrophes that afflict mankind as a whole.' ('Dukh vzyskuyushchij' ['The Searching Spirit'], *Pravda*, 13 November 1989, p. 4.)

The present crisis of socialism is as derivative as its past triumphs. The present crisis is not of socialism's sole making. It is the crisis of socialism as a distorted and, in the end, an ineffective form of modernity; but it is also a reflection of the crisis of the modern project as such. Socialist counter-culture outlived the culture it opposed. Through a paradox of history, it stayed for a while alone in the field defending the ramparts vacated by other troops. By the logic of historical memory, socialism went on, unthinkingly, to offer its traditional services as the counter-culture of modernity at a time when the world around questioned ever louder the values and the strategies that served as the trademark of the modern era. Like the contemporary remake of Don Quixote, it went on fighting old battles at a time when for many they had been already lost, while for the thinking minority they were not worth fighting in the first place.

Socialism's younger, hot-headed and impatient brother, communism, whole-heartedly shared in the family trust in the wonderful promises and prospects of modernity, and was awestruck by the breath-taking vistas of society doing away with historical and natural necessity, and by the idea of the ultimate subordination of nature to human needs and desires. But unlike the elder brother, it did not trust history to find the way to the millenium. Neither was it prepared to wait till history proved this mistrust wrong. Its war-cry was: 'Kingdom of Reason – now!'

Like socialism (and all other staunch believers in modern values of technological progress, transformation of nature and a society of plenty), communism was thoroughly modern in its passionate conviction that good society can only be a society carefully designed, rationally managed and thoroughly industrialized. It was in the name of those shared modern values that socialism charged the capitalist administrators of modern progress with mismangement, inefficiency and wastefulness. Communism accused socialism of failing to draw conclusions from the charges: stopping at critique, denunciations, prodding – where an instant dismissal of inept and corrupt administrators was in order.

Lenin's redefining of the socialist revolution as a *substitution for*, instead of *continuation of*, the bourgeois revolution, was the founding act of communism. According to the new creed, capitalism was a cancerous growth on the healthy body of modern progress; no more a necessary stage on the road to a society that will embody modern dreams. Capitalists could not be entrusted (as once they were by the founders of modern socialism, Marx and Engels) with even the preliminary job of site-clearing: 'melting the solids and profaning the sacred'. As a matter of fact, the site-clearing itself was neither a necessity nor a job useful enough to justify the waste of time needed for its performance. As the principles of rationally organized, good society (more factories, more machines, more control over nature) were well known and agreed upon, one could proceed directly to usher any society (and particularly a society without factories, without machines, without the capitalists eager to build them, without the workers oppressed and exploited in the process of building) into a state designed by those principles. There was no point in waiting till the good society arrived through the action of workers, fed up with the sufferings caused by the capitalist mismanagement of the progress. As one knew what the good society would be like, to delay or even slow down its construction was an unforgiveable crime. Good society could be, had to be, constructed right away, before the capitalists had a chance to mismanage and the workers to sample the outcomes of their mismanagement; or, rather, its designers should take over the management of society right away, without waiting for the consequences of mismangement to show up. Capitalism was an unnecessary deflection from the path of Reason. Communism was a straight road to its kingdom. Communism, Lenin would say, is Soviet power together with the 'electrification of the whole country': that is, modern technology and modern industry under a power conscious of its purpose in advance and leaving nothing to chance. Communism was modernity in its most determined mood and most decisive posture; modernity streamlined, purified of the last shred of the chaotic, the irrational, the spontaneous, the unpredictable.

In those now uncannily distant times the audacious communist project seemed to make a lot of sense and was taken quite seriously by friends and the foes alike. Communism promised (or threatened, depending on the eye of the beholder) to do what anyone else was doing, only faster (remember the alluring charm of convergence theories?). The real doubts appeared when the others stopped doing it, while communism went on chasing now abandoned targets; partly by inertia, but mostly because of the fact that – being communism in action – it could not do anything else.

In its practical implementation, communism was a system one-sidedly adapted to the task of mobilizing social and natural resources in the name of modernization: the nineteenth-century steam-and-iron ideal of modern plenty. It could – at least in its own conviction – compete with capitalists, but solely with the capitalist engaged in the same pursuits. What it could not do and did not brace itself for doing was to match the performance of the capitalist, market-centred society once that society abandoned its steel mills and coal mines and moved into the postmodern age (once it had passed over, in Jean Baudrillard's apt aphorism, from *metallurgy* to *semiurgy*; stuck at its metallurgical stage, Soviet communism, as if to cast out devils, spent its energy on fighting wide trousers, long hair, rock music and any other manifestations of semiurgical initiative).

This is what Gorbachev seemed to have in mind when he spoke

obsessively of the 'lost Brezhnev years': at the crucial period when the West turned its back on the steel-and-concrete dreams of the past and moved on to a softer and more light-hearted version of human happiness, the communist elite – ageing as rapidly as the project that had once kept them in power – went on drying up rivers and flooding fields. All this has been done before by the capitalist, Western modernizers – and done as mercilessly and sometimes more thoroughly. The point was, however, that the gerontocracy of the 'age of stagnation' went on doing it a bit too long . . . 'postmodern values' had already discredited such deeds in the affluent West, now resourceful and wise enough to call filth filth, and thus busy exiling its own waste to distant places and the homes of less fortunate peoples. The communist modernizing adventure shared in all the inner incongruities of modernity in general; to its general weaknesses, it added absurdities and hardships of its own making. But not in the remotest way was it geared to serve the new, postmodern expectations. The advent of the postmodern condition and postmodern mentality rubbed salt in the open wounds: not only the human objects of modernizing designs discovered their fate as misery, but they stopped comprehending the reasons in the name of which they had entered the road of misery in the first place.

The communist dictatorship over needs and monopoly over the means and procedures of needs-satisfaction makes the communist state an obvious target of individual disaffection; it cannot but collectivize individual frustrations in the same way it collectivized the vehicles of gratification. The same personal frustrations and grievances which in a market society (society that successfully privatized life responsibilities and consciences) are diffused and scattered as well as depoliticized, in a 'warden state' communist style are condensed into a system-shattering political protest. Here, the state is the agency to which complaints are addressed as naturally and matter-of-factly as have been the expectations of a better life. Unlike in the postmodern world of privatized choices, the sources of diffuse unhappiness are not themselves diffuse and cannot be kept ex-directory; they are publicly announced, conspicuous and easy to locate. Admittedly, the communist regimes excelled in stifling the flow of information and pushed to elsewhere unknown heights the art of state secrecy; and yet they proved to be much less successful than market-oriented societies in dissipating and hiding the responsibility for socially produced ills, for irrational consequences of rational decisions and for overall mismanagement of social processes. They even failed to hide the fact of hiding information and thus stood accused, as of political crimes, of the kind of 'cover-up' which market agencies of the consumer society practice daily, effortlessly and without attracting attention (less still a public outcry).

Has social engineering a future?

Social engineering lay in disgrace. Few would dare to defend its reason and moral integrity after the inglorious end to the communist experiment. Preachers of the maxims of 'Everyone for himself' and 'The state helps those who help themselves' are triumphant: did we not tell you? All the signs on earth show that once you start healing society you may well end up murdering poeple and never letting those who stay alive out of the intensive care units. Even if you stop short of such nasty things, you will still turn out more dependence than freedom, and once you reach your goal – give people resources to make their own way – they find out that making one's own way is one move the game does not allow. The odds are, then, that they will see no reason (not now, when they are resourceful again) to be thankful for your gifts.

Such and similar conclusions can boast a solid measure of historical experience to support them, and the jubilation of the free-for-all ideologists is not easy to counter: theirs seem to be the only voices heard. The days of grand social engineering projects seem to be over. And so are the times when dreams of a better society could not be dismissed offhand as either flights of fancy or declarations of subversive intent, but had to be treated seriously as a challenge to social practice and, above all, a meaningful critique of the present which the powers that be could not beat and thus had to join.

To abandon social engineering as a valid means of political practice means to discard (and, by the same token, discredit) all visions of a different society; even a sort of intellectual prohibition of the very consideration of a social model different from the extant one. The critique of inanities and injustices of present society, however obvious they may be, is disqualified by a simple reminder that remaking society by design may only make it worse than it was. Alternative ends are invalidated on the strength of the proved ineffectuality of means. Society in its present shape, it would seem, has reached the acme of stability: it has destroyed all alternatives to itself. And so we hear of the end of history, of the ultimate triumph of one social order that has conclusively proved its superiority over past competitors (a superiority even the competitors had to admit). We are told that from now on there will be no qualitative change, but only more of the same.

This is, obviously, good news for the seduced who find the extant order well geared to their desires; who can hope that their desires will be satisfied through the resources they possess or can reasonably expect to acquire; who therefore justifiably view their condition as one of freedom and would naturally conceive of any modification to the rules of the game as an undue interference and noxious constraint. This is, simultaneously, bad news for the oppressed, who find the extant rules of the game working against their well-being, threatening perhaps their very existence, and thus view their condition as constraining and in urgent need of repair. These would find it hard to believe that the present rules are impartial and give everyone an equal chance. Even less believable for them will be the assertion that the present state of the world cannot be improved upon, as this is the kind of world that can be trusted with rectifying its own ills.

Even if one agrees with Rorty that providing we take care of freedom then truth and beauty will take care of themselves, the idea that social justice will equally take care of itself is less easy to agree with. Leaving the case of justice alone means refusing assistance to those who need it, or at any rate cannot cope in its absence. It means to condone the split into the freely seduced and the oppressed, the squalor of life without prospects, the agony of feeling that 'I and others like me' have been passed by and left behind. This also means to rejoice in the collective privilege of the rich, postmodern world, and have one's mirth untainted by the wretchedness of the rest of the globe that has been kept outside the vigilantly guarded gate so that the feast inside may go on.

Social engineering has proved to be a costly ambition; the grander, the costlier. This does not mean, however, that refraining from social engineering comes free. The illusion of gain comes from a changed distribution of costs. And those who bear the costs are not those who count them. One can even say that prohibition of social engineering is itself a social engineering of sorts, once one knows (and we have such knowledge now) what consequences the 'natural' trends, if unattended and uncorrected, are likely to bring. Thus the choice is not as straightforward as the discreditation of modern designing ambitions could suggest. One thing is certain – that the choice is hardly ever politically and socially neutral. Balancing of costs and gains of, respectively, action and non-action is not just an exercise in non-partisan expertise and dry, dispassionate accountancy, but a political decision between alternatives burdened with prospectless lives and dashed hopes.

The postmodern political agenda

Nothing merely ends in history, no project is ever finished and done with. Clean borders between epochs are but projections of our relentless urge to separate the inseparable and order the flux. Modernity is still with us. It lives as the pressure of unfulfilled hopes and interests ossified in self-reproducing institutions; as the zeal of perforce belated imitators, wishing to join the feast that those who are now leaving it with distaste once proudly enjoyed; as the shape of the world modern labours have left behind – for us to inhabit; as the 'problems' those labours spawned and defined for us, as well as our historically trained, yet by now instinctive way of thinking about problems and reacting to them. This is, perhaps, what people like Habermas refer to when they speak of the 'unfinished project of modernity'.

And yet – whether or not the project keeps its remembered shape – something has surely occurred to us, to the people who undertake and finish projects. The very fact that we now speak of modernity as a *project* (a design with intentions, ends and means) testifies most convincingly to the change that happened in us. Our ancestors did not talk of the 'project' when they were busily engaged in what now looks to us like unfinished business.

Michael Phillipson gave his recently published book the title *In Modernity's Wake*. A felicitous phrase, evoking a powerful image: the ship has passed by; its passage roughened the waters, left a turbulence so that all sailors around have to rework the course of their boats – while those who fell into the water must swim hard to reach them. Once the waters quieten down again, though, we, the sailors and former passengers alike, can have a closer look at the ship that caused this all. That ship is still quite near, huge and clearly visible in all its weighty bulk, but we are now *behind* it and we do not stand any more on its deck. Thus we can see it in all its impressive shape, fore to aft, scan it, appreciate it, plot the direction it takes. We may now decide whether to follow its course. We may also better judge the wisdom of its navigation, and even protest against the captain's commands.

Living 'in the wake' means turbulence, but also wider vistas and the new wisdom they offer. In modernity's wake, its passengers become aware of serious faults in the design of the ship that brought them where they are now. They also are reconciled to the fact that it could not bring them to a more pleasant destination, and are ready to look again, with a fresh and critical eye, at the old navigatory principles.

What is truly new in our situation today is, in other words, our vantage point. While still in the close neighbourhood of the modern era, and feeling the effects of the turbulence it caused on its way, we *can* now (better still, we are *prepared* and *willing to*) take a cool and critical view of modernity in its totality, evaluate its performance, pass judgement on the solidity and congruence of its construction. This is ultimately what the idea of *postmodernity* stands for: an existence fully determined and defined by the fact of being '*post*' (coming *after*) and overwhelmed by the awareness of being in such a condition. Postmodernity does not necessarily mean the end, the discreditation of the rejection of modernity. Postmodernity is no more (but no less either) than the modern mind taking a long, attentive and sober look at itself, at its condition and its past works, not fully liking what it sees and sensing the urge to change. Postmodernity is modernity coming of age: modernity looking at itself at a distance rather than from inside, making a full inventory of its gains and losses, psychoanalysing itself, discovering the intentions it never before spelled out, finding them mutually cancelling and incongruous. Postmodernity is modernity coming to terms with its own impossibility; a self-monitoring modernity, one that consciously discards what it was once unconsciously doing.

In the process, the triple alliance of the values of liberty, equality and brotherhood that dominated the modern political battlefield did not escape scrutiny and the ensuing censure. No wonder; however hard political designers tried, they found themselves constantly in a trade-off situation, vainly struggling to reach all three at the same time. They found liberty militating against equality, equality giving short shrift to the dream of liberty, and brotherhood of doubtful virtue as long as the other two values failed to find a *modus coexistendi*. They came also to think that – given the huge and yet untapped energy of human liberty – the objectives of equality and brotherhood sold human potential too cheaply. Equality could not be easily distanced from the prospect of uniformity. Brotherhood smacked all too often of enforced unity and a demand that the ostensible siblings should sacrifice individuality in the name of a putative common cause. Not that the means fared better than the values. The conquest of nature brought more waste than human happiness. One thing in which industrial expansion succeeded most spectacularly was the multiplication of risks: more risks, bigger risks, unheard-of risks. For some time now, most 'economic growth' has been propelled by the need to defuse the risks it manufactured: risks of overpopulation, undernourishment, losing the climatically indispensable rain forests and creating socially devastating urban jungles, overheating the atmosphere, contaminating water supplies, poisoning food and air, spreading 'new and improved' diseases. More and more, the conquest of nature looked like the very illness it was alleged to cure.

And so the values began to shift. First at the bizarre, idiosyncratic margins, easy to pooh-pooh and dismiss as 'untypical' or downright loony. But then the slow movement turned into a stampede. It can be ignored no more that the new triple-value alliance gains in popularity at the expense of the old one. The new horizons that seem to inflame today human imagination and inspire human action are those of *liberty*, *diversity* and *tolerance*. These are new values that inform the postmodern *mentality*. As for postmodern *practice*, however, it does not look a whit less flawed than its predecessor.

Liberty is as truncated as before – though the parts of its body that have now been amputated are different from those that were removed in the past. In postmodern practice, liberty boils down to consumer choice. To enjoy it, one must be a consumer first. This preliminary condition leaves out millions. As throughout the modern era, in the postmodern world poverty disqualifies. Freedom in its new, market interpretation is as much a privilege as it was in its old versions. But there are new problems as well: with communal needs translated into individual acts of acquisition, the maiming of liberty cannot but affect *everybody*, rich and poor alike, exemplary or flawed consumers: there are needs that cannot be met by no matter how many personal purchases, and so anybody's freedom of choice looks severely limited. One cannot buy privately one's way out from polluted air, a broken ozone layer or a rising radiation level; one cannot buy one's way into the forest immune to acid rain or seacoast protected against toxic algae thriving on the lush nourishment of chemically processed sewage. In the few instances when buying oneself out seems plausible – like escaping dilapidated public transport in a private car, or running away from the squalor of public health into a private clinic – the choice only adds to the problem that made it necessary in the first place, adding to the misery that prompted the escape. The choice therefore becomes ineffective the moment it is taken, at best a few moments later. There are plenty of flawed, weak consumers or disqualified consumers who must yet gain that freedom that the consumer society officially recognizes; but there are also weak, uncared for, deprived aspects of *everybody's* life (including the life of the ostensibly free consumers) yet to be protected by communal effort.

Diversity thrives; and the market-place thrives with it. More precisely, only such diversity is allowed to thrive as benefits the market. As the humourless, power-greedy and jealous national state did before, the market abhors self-management and autonomy – the wilderness it cannot control. As before, autonomy has to be fought for, if diversity is to mean anything but variety of marketable life-styles – a thin varnish of changeable fashions meant to hide the uniformly market-dependent condition. What is to be fought for is above all the right to secure communal, as distinct from individual, diversity; a diversity stemming from a communally chosen and communally serviced form of life. Such diversity can struggle for recognition and its share of services, but cannot (unless proved profitable) hope to be supported, let alone guaranteed, by the cornucopia of merchandised identities. If the standards of marketability are not met, the best one can count on is the market's indifference. At worst, the hostility of the market is to be reckoned with. Communally managed collective identities may jar with the idea of individually chosen life-styles – an idea that the market must hold tight to, with the most sincere and unqualified sympathy.

If the slogan of brotherhood is translated as the practice of pastoral power, as obtrusive interference with alternative ways of life, as insistence on uniformity, as defining all difference as a sign of retardation, deviation and a 'problem' requiring 'solutions' – *tolerance* translates as 'Let's live and let others live'. Where tolerance rules, difference is no more bizarre or challenging. Difference has been, so to speak, privatized. The urge to proselytize has wilted, the crusader spirit has dissipated. The age of cultural hegemony seems to have passed: cultures are meant to be enjoyed, not fought for. In our type of society, economic and political domination may well do without hegemony; it found the way of reproducing itself under conditions of cultural variety. The new tolerance means irrelevance of cultural choice for the stability of domination. And irrelevance rebounds in *indifference*. Alternative forms of life arouse but spectator interest of the type offered by a sparkling and spicy variety show; they may even trigger less resentment (particularly if viewed at a safe distance or through the secure shield of the TV screen), but no fellow-feeling either; they belong to the outer world of theatre and entertainment, not to the inner world of the politics of life. They stand beside each other, yet do not belong together. Like the market-promoted life-styles they bear no other value than one inserted by free choice. Most certainly, their presence imposes no obligation, breeds no responsibility. As practised by market-led postmodernity, tolerance degenerates into estrangement; the growth of spectator curiosity means fading of human interest. When alien forms of life descend from the safe seclusion of the TV screens or congeal into live and self-assertive communities next door instead of confining their existence to the multi-cultural cookbooks, ethnic restaurants and fashionable trinkets, they transgress their province of meaning: the province of theatre, of entertainment, of variety show – the only one that contains the precept of tolerance, of suspension of estrangement. A sudden jump from one province of meaning to another is at all times shocking – and so forms of life previously regarded as picturesque and amusing are now experienced as a threat. They arouse anger and hostility.

In other words, market-promoted tolerance does not lead to solidarity: it *fragments*, instead of uniting. It services well communal separation and the reduction of the social bond to a surface gloss. It survives as long as it remains to be lived in the airy world of the symbolic game of representation and does not spill over into the realm of daily coexistence thanks to the expedient of territorial and functional segregation. Most importantly, such tolerance is fully compatible with the practice of social domination. It may be preached and exercised without fear because it reaffirms rather than questions the superiority and privilege of the tolerant: the other, by being different, loses the entitlement to equal treatment – indeed, inferiority of the other is fully justified by the difference. Abandonment of the converting zeal comes together with the withdrawal of the very promise of equality. With mutual links reduced to tolerance, difference means perpetual distance, non-cooperation, and hierarchy. The 'fusion of horizons' hardly steps beyond the widening range of ethnic take-aways.

This much for the values postmodernity promotes. As to the means – the rape of nature has been replaced by the concern with the preservation of natural balance; reason-induced artificiality, the warring cry of modernity is fast losing an audience, and as an object of popular cult is equally fast replaced by the wisdom of nature. Fewer people believe today in the magical capacity of economic growth and technological expansion. One thing people trust technology to deliver without fail and on a growing pace is yet more discomfort and more danger – new, less calculable, less curable risks.

Under the power-politics management, and operated by market forces, new concerns and new sensitivities are used, however, to reinforce the very processes they abhor and condemn. The clash between the social nature of risks and privatized means of their containment is the postmodern version of the old contradiction of capitalism (one between the social means of production and their private ownership) singled out by Marx as the main cause of the system's imminent downfall. In the result of this clash, risks are not reduced, let alone extinguished. They are only removed from public sight and thus made, at least for a time, safe from criticism. (Risks tend to travel over the globe in a direction opposite to that of riches; the rich countries have an awesome capacity to sell out their own poison as the poor people's meat; the only meat the poor can hope for.) Such technology-generated risks as cannot be moved are subdued with more technology – to (at least temporary) public applause. 'Nature conscious', 'ozone friendly' and 'green' petrol, aerosols, detergents or bleaches turn into big business and bring 'new and improved' profits. Ecology-conscious designers reduce the amount of carbon dioxide released by existing car engines so that more cars can be released onto more roads. (By 2015, Europe expects four times more cars than today; it is difficult to imagine a prosperous Europe without them, as one in every seven persons derives his or her livelihood from car production. It is equally difficult to imagine Europe with cars multiplying at the present speed, as the Acropolis has decayed more in the last twenty years than it did in the previous twenty-four centuries, and as Alpine forests which experts protect are fast sharing the fate of the rain forests of the upper

Amazon which experts destroy.) As before, problems are formulated as demands for new (marketable, of course) technical gadgets and stuffs; as before, those desirous to be free from discomfort and risks are reminded that such freedom 'must pay for itself' and the big bills of social catastrophe are alleged to be cleared with the small change of private shopping concerns. In the process, the global origin of problems is effectively hidden from view, and the crusade against known risks may go on producing more and more sinister – yet unknown – risks, thus undermining its own future chance of success.

This is, though, but a minor part of the deception. Another, still greater and more seminal part, is the confinement of new sensitivity in the frame of technological discourse: both the salvation and the grudgingly admitted sins are hermetically sealed in the depoliticized ('politically neutral') discourse of technology and expertise, thereby reinforcing the social framework which makes sins inevitable and salvation unattainable. What is left outside the confines of rational discourse is the very issue that stands a chance of making the discourse rational and perhaps even practically effective: the *political* issue of democratic control over technology and expertise, their purposes and their desirable limits – the issue of politics as self-management and collectively made choices.

Whatever value or means championed by postmodernity we consider, they all point (if only tacitly or by elimination) to politics, democracy, full-blown citizenship as the sole vehicles of their implementation. With politics those values and means look like a chance of a better society; without politics, abandoned fully to the care of the market, they look more like deceitful slogans at best, sources of new and yet unfathomed dangers at worst. Postmodernity is not the end of politics, as it is not an end of history. On the contrary, whatever may be attractive in the postmodern promise calls for more politics, more political engagement, more political effectivity of individual and communal action (however much the call is stifled by the hubbub of consumer bustle, and however inaudible it becomes in a world made up of shopping malls and Disneylands, where all that matters is an enjoyable piece of theatre, and thus nothing matters really much).

Thus far, the postmodern condition has brought a massive withdrawal of would-be citizenry from the traditional (or at least traditionally lauded, if not always practised) form of politics. The seduced – those who benefit or believe to benefit – call for more small change in their pockets and would not listen to the reminders of unpaid social bills. The repressed accept the majority verdict that casts them as flawed consumers and believe much as everyone else that social bills are best cleared with small change in private pockets. Their sufferings do not add up, do not cumulate; the remedy, like the ailment, appears thoroughly privatized. The illness is the dearth of shopping; the cure is shopping unlimited. The combined result is massive political indifference. Its pressure flattens the political process into the screen-deep contest of show-business personalities, with election results replicating popularity ratings. Does all this augur the end of politics?

There are signs that the postmodern era may generate political forms of its own. The way in which many an old-style, absolutist regime collapsed in recent years in parts of the world as distant from each other and apparently unconnected as Chile and Czechoslovakia, hints at such a possibility. Without any anterior theoretical articulation, rebellions that led to the collapse seemed to manifest in practice a new vision of politics and political power: a vision in which the traditional modern imagery of solid and tough 'materiality' of political domination was bafflingly yet blatantly absent.

Let us name just a few common features of such rebellions. First, they were not 'designed revolutions', planned and prepared by an organized core of conspirators with a clandestine network of alternative leadership and a blueprint for future policies. Leadership, if any surfaced in the course of the events, followed rather than anticipated the popular movement. Second, events unravelled without plan, following solely the logic of episodic succession and taking by surprise both the protesters and the targets of popular ire. Much as the battle gestated its own troops, the gradually opening possibilities generated their own strategies. Third, few if any buildings were targeted, stormed or taken, before their occupants left them or their occupancy lost political meaning; it was as if the actors did not see power as 'thing-like', residing in a specific location where it can be stored and from which it can be taken; as if instead they intuited government, rule, domination as an on-going process of communicative exchange, a series of acts rather than a set of possessions; something that can be interrupted, dismantled and later returned to and reassembled, rather than expropriated and redistributed. Fourth, the decisive blow and the ultimate cause of the collapse was not an overwhelming force of the rebels and military defeat of the rulers, but the uncompromising irony of the protesters reluctant to be manoeuvred out of their carnival-like mood of insouciant, obstreperous disrespect for the high and mighty. Single shots, when fired, met with universal outcry not just because of the suffering they caused the individual victims, but for their outlandishness, for their complete lack of resonance with the character of the event; echoes of another era, they sounded jarringly out of tune with the mood of a popular festival, celebrating the rediscovered freedom of the streets.

What the described events might have demonstrated is that even if state power does not need popular consent for its daily operation, it cannot survive an explicit refusal of such consent: means of coercion are not substitutes for consent; it is the availability of consent that makes such means effective in the first place. This could be a revelation to enlighten the era of new *postmodern* politics: armed with such new knowledge politics may turn into an entirely new kind of game, with consequences as yet exceedingly difficult to predict. This is, however, but one of the possible interpretations. The obliging speed with which the seemingly cast-iron edifices of oppressive power crumbled at the first whiff of popular refusal of meekness might have been a *local* phenomenon: a testimony to the obsoleteness of the modern state, for too long kept artificially alive by equally ageing and jaded communist regimes, and now brought into sudden relief by the practices of postmodern societies.

It is possible that what we have witnessed was the collapse of a *patronage state* – a social/political/economic formation singularly unfit for an era dominated by the postmodern values of novelty, of rapid (preferably inconsequential and episodic) change, of individual enjoyment and consumer choice. In exchange for the promise of personal provision and security, the patronage state demands surrender of the right to choose and to self-determine. The patronage state strives to be a monopolistic source of needs-satisfaction, social status and self-esteem; it transforms its subjects into clients and asks them to be grateful for what they have received today and will receive tomorrow. But for the same reason for which he feels entitled to demand gratitude, the patron cannot shake off his responsibility for the misfortune of his clients. Frustration is immediately reforged into a grievance which 'naturally' hits the patron, and his policy, as the obvious cause of suffering. Under postmodern conditions, when the exhilarating experience of ever-new needs rather than the satisfaction of the extant ones becomes the main measure of a happy life (and thus the production of new enticements turns to be the major vehicle of social integration and peaceful coexistence), the patronage state, adjusted to the task of defining and circumscribing the needs of its subjects, cannot stand competition with systems operated by the consumer market. And as it remains the only target within sight of the discontent that results, the odds are that the accumulated dissent will soon outweigh its capacity for purchasing consent and resolving conflicts. No wonder that the managers of the patronage state have apparently lost their determination to perpetuate a system geared to dictatorship over needs and the state's responsibility for their satisfaction – alongside their ability to govern.

Writing from the depth of a dissenting artist's experience, the Hungarian author Miklós Haraszti observed that in a society where the major (the only?) constraint shackling artistic freedom came from the market, 'The artist could express hatred, even towards this constraint, as long as his work was marketable . . . [but] planning, unlike the market, is not a placid sacred cow. It cannot tolerate contempt.'[25] The all-consuming ambition of the planning, designing, gardening state of modernity (one of which the communist state was a faithful disciple, even if a disciple who through his very diligence inadvertently exposed the inanity of the teaching) proved to be in the end its main drawback and fatal calamity. It kept embroiling it in potentially incapacitating crises.

The successor of the modern state places its bet on the expedient of privatizing and diffusing dissent, rather than collectivizing it and prompting it to accumulate. Having abandoned the designing ambitions, it can do with less coercion and little if any ideological mobilization. It seems to count on popular disaffection to remain scattered and to pass it by; to pass it by because it has been scattered. It may even be counting on such disaffection, as long as it stays scattered, to take care of the system's reproduction. Once declared to be a mortal danger to all social and political order, ambivalence is not an 'enemy at the gate' any more. On the contrary: like everything else, it has been made into one of the stage props in the play called postmodernity.

---

[25] Miklós Haraszti, *The Velvet Prison: Artists under State Socialism*, trans. Katalin and Stephen Landesmann with the help of Steve Wasserman (London: Penguin, 1989), pp. 80–1. Haraszti observes that the existence of censorship in state socialism is based on identity of interests between censor and censored (p. 8). Writing at the early 1980s, Haraszti added the adjective 'lasting' to the noun 'identity': a system that successfully 'absorbed the language of its victims' seemed then to Haraszti, like to virtually everybody else, destined to last forever. With the benefit of retrospective wisdom we may say that what seemed to be the strongest foundation of the system's security proved to be its undoing. Having assumed full charge of 'common interests' the communist power put its fate into the hands of its subjects; it could not survive the latter's withdrawal of consent. If in the unwritten yet binding contract between the communist rulers and the ruled one could not 'note any distinction drawn between the authorization for the domination of values and the domination of the valuable ones' (p. 26), then any protest against the type of values enforced by the rulers must immediately have turned into a protest against the principle of value-enforcement as such. All dissent turned into *systemic* crisis (whereas in a society where needs, values and dissent itself are privatized similar dissent would reinforce the market-based mechanism of systemic reproduction).

Index